D1563799

MODERNIZATION FROM THE OTHER SHORE

MODERNIZATION FROM THE OTHER SHORE

American Intellectuals and the Romance of Russian Development

DAVID C. ENGERMAN

HARVARD UNIVERSITY PRESS

Cambridge, Massachusetts

London, England · 2003

Library of Congress Cataloging-in-Publication Data

Engerman, David C., 1966–
    Modernization from the other shore : American intellectuals and
the romance of Russian development / David C. Engerman.
        p.   cm.
    Includes bibliographical references and index.
    ISBN 0-674-01151-1 (alk. paper)
        1. Soviet Union—Economic conditions—1917–1945.   2. Russia—Economic
conditions—1861–1917.   3. Soviet Union—Foreign public opinion, American.
4. Russia—Foreign public opinion, American.   5. Intellectuals—United States—Attitudes.
6. United States—Foreign economic relations—Soviet Union.   7. United States—Foreign
economic relations—Russia.   8. Soviet Union—Foreign economic relations—United States.
9. Russia—Foreign economic relations—United States.   I. Title.

HC335.E636   2003
338.947'009'034—dc22   2003056629

Contents

Author's Note

I have standardized the transliteration of Russian words to avoid the confusion of writing about *muzhiks, mujiks, moujiks,* and *moojiks* in a single book. Occasionally I have made minor corrections to quotations when the meanings have been obvious but the spellings less so. Unless otherwise indicated, all translations are my own.

MODERNIZATION FROM THE OTHER SHORE

Introduction: From the Other Shore

Between 1870 and 1940, Russia and the USSR embarked on an erratic and costly drive toward industrialization. In observing Russia's transformation, American intellectuals reformulated some of the central conceptions of their time. Rejecting the idea that peoples faced inherent limits on future growth, they developed protean conceptions of national character that celebrated industrialization as the engine of progress. America's Russia experts—diplomats, journalists, and scholars paid to interpret Russian events for American audiences—found Soviet industrialization so alluring that they championed dramatic and indeed traumatic policies of rapid modernization that destroyed the lives and livelihoods of millions in Russia and the Soviet Union. Their belief in fundamental differences between cultures, combined with the value they placed on modernization, created an enthusiasm for social transformation that ignored its human costs.

Modernization from the Other Shore shows how these new ideas of cultural difference and social change emerged and how they undergirded dramatic changes in twentieth-century intellectual life and international politics. In doing so, it draws inspiration from Alexander Herzen, the mid-nineteenth-century Russian radical. Herzen's most famous work, *From the Other Shore* (1850), contained his reflections on the revolutionary ferment of 1848, which he observed while in self-imposed exile in western Europe. Repulsed by radicals' calls that every nation must sacrifice its present for a utopian future, Herzen expressed a vision of social transformation that would benefit each generation, including the present one. At the same time, his writings expressed a determination to understand nations and peoples historically; he celebrated universal human dignity while recognizing a diverse range of national traditions.[1]

1

Herzen's vision was disregarded, on both scores, in his homeland in the century after he wrote. Soviet leaders claimed to act on the basis of universal laws of historical development, and they interpreted those laws to demand present sacrifice in the name of future benefits. Such attitudes resulted in massive destruction and dislocation in the Soviet Union, including the devastating famine of 1932–1933. That famine was a disaster, but not a natural one. In the USSR's major breadbaskets, authorities removed every morsel of food, claiming that it was needed for the defense and rapid industrialization of the country. As a result, millions of citizens, primarily in Russia's most productive agricultural regions, starved to death. American observers showed surprisingly little sympathy for those who suffered during the famine. With blithe dismissals of Russian peasants' lackadaisical work habits and inferior intelligence, many American experts blamed the shortages on Russians' innate dispositions. They saw the sacrifices, furthermore, as a necessary side-effect of Soviet modernization efforts. Russia, they declared, was "starving itself great."[2] Industrial greatness was a worthy goal, even at great human cost.

American writers, of course, would be immune from the sacrifices they called for. In Herzen's pointed language, "To sacrifice others, and to be self-sacrificing on their behalf, is too easy a virtue."[3] Who were these people of easy virtue? How could they endorse such costly plans for industrialization? What did their endorsements reveal about American ideas of modernization? How did conceptions of cultural difference shape their views of modernization? How did they envision the path to modernity?

These questions redounded around the world in the twentieth century. Under the spell of modernization, American intellectuals endorsed radical forms of social change everywhere except in the United States. They placed at the pinnacle of human achievement a society much like they imagined their own to be: industrial, urban, cosmopolitan, rational, and democratic. Backward nations, they argued, could progress toward modernity only by implementing rapid and violent changes. Modern America, however, would be exempt from such turmoil. With America's expanding global role and intellectuals' increasingly close connections to the centers of power, these ideas shaped nations all over the world. New ideas of social change and national character also shaped notions of American national identity, which itself underwent significant changes after 1870—from scientific racism and assimilationist theory before World War II to celebrations of common humanity in the 1950s and the valorization of cultural differences since the 1980s. The way Americans understood the process of social change shaped the way they envisioned their own nation. Finally, the tensions between accepting cultural differences and promoting modernization underpinned American-Soviet conflict during the Cold War. At the same time that scholars analyzed the conflict as one between two industrial powers with opposing ideologies, American diplomats construed the Cold War enemy as an inherently and irredeemably different nation. These conceptions, supported by America's global reach, made—and continue to make—the American century.

American writings on Russia and the Soviet Union were shaped by three forces, which constitute the three main themes of this book: a longstanding belief that every nation had its own unique character; a growing enthusiasm for modernization; and the appearance of new professional institutions and norms for interpreting other nations. First, American experts used national-character stereotypes to explain Russian and Soviet events. Building on centuries-old notions of Russian peculiarity, western experts enumerated traits that supposedly limited the Russians' ability to function in a modern world. Americans repeated the claims of European commentators who argued that national character emerged from geography and topography: long winters made Russians passive, and endless plains made them melancholy. Russians, in these writings, exhibited instinctual behavior, extreme passivity, and a lethargy shaken only by violence.[4] Americans argued that these characteristics—accentuating the negative—affected Russia's economic prospects. Reliance on these notions of national character crossed political boundaries; Russia's avowed enemies and ardent defenders in the United States agreed on what made Russians different.

Herzen himself illustrated the double-edged nature of such characterizations. Living in France and Italy in the 1850s, he gained new perspective on Russian character. He frequently mentioned the "Slavic genius" that set his compatriots apart from Europeans, focusing especially on Russians' soulful and communal natures. Yet he also took for granted that Russians—especially the peasants who constituted the vast majority of the population—were "improvident and indolent," better at "passive obedience" than political or economic activity.[5] Difference did not necessarily mean superiority.

Americans' notions of Russian character often contained within them the idea that Russians were Asian—"Asiatic" in the language of the day. The claim, stated as often in racial as in geographic terms, further legitimated violence in Russia. According to an oft-repeated refrain, life meant less to Asians, and therefore to Russians. Personal traits also held political implications. Asians, the argument went, could be ruled only through "Oriental despotism." Writers from Baron Charles de Montesquieu to Karl Marx depicted Asia as an unchanging—even unchangeable—morass of poverty, insularity, and despotism.[6] Whether understood as Asian or Slavic, Russians consistently faced claims that they were unready to join the modern world. Particularist views of Russia, which emphasized the nation's unique traditions and character traits, dominated American writings until the 1920s.

These particularist arguments about national character faced growing challenges in the 1920s from claims of universalism, which understood all nations and peoples as basically similar. While universalists recognized national differences, they typically claimed that modernization would erase such differences, which did not affect the fundaments of human nature. Universalism long predated the twentieth century; among its most important proponents was a contemporary foe of Herzen's, Karl Marx. Herzen and Marx differed over politics, too. Whereas Herzen feared and distrusted the revolutionary fervor of 1848, Marx did all he could to stoke it. With Friedrich Engels, Marx cheered the "specter of Communism" then "haunting Europe." To fulfill the revolution, they insisted, radicals had to obey iron-clad laws of historical development, making no exceptions for national particularity or individual privilege. According to the dictates of history, all nations would develop along a single path; the most advanced nations would thus show to backward nations the "image of their own future."[7] Americans sympathetic to Marx, as well as many who loathed his theories, increasingly invoked universalist claims.

Second, the tensions between universal progress and national difference were transformed in the early twentieth century by changing definitions of progress. By the 1920s, American experts argued that Soviet modernization, even with its staggering human and financial costs, was worthwhile. Especially excited by Soviet claims that industrialization would be rationally and centrally planned, Americans appreciated the model for its techniques as well as its goals. They also deployed their views of Russian character in the service of economic modernization. National character no longer shaped national destiny; it became instead an obstacle to be overcome on the path toward modernity.

The Bolsheviks relentlessly pursued that vision of modern industrial society. America's Russia experts, regardless of their sympathies for the Bolshevik regime, accepted or even endorsed the Bolsheviks' vision of modernity. They also recognized (and often praised) the accompanying dialectic of suffering, through which present hardship would give birth to future prosperity. They were swayed by what America's best-known Russia expert, George Frost Kennan, called "the romance of economic development." Writing about Soviet economic prospects in the summer of 1932, he called attention to Russian citizens' enthusiasm for industrialization. Those under the sway of the romance, especially youths, would "ignore all other questions in favor of economic progress," wrote Kennan.[8] Personal desires and even personal well-being were secondary to development.

Here American views were most sharply at odds with those of Herzen, who movingly proclaimed the need to value present welfare over future promise. Nature, he wrote, "never makes one generation the means for some future end"; humans should follow suit. No one should play the role of Moloch, the Biblical deity to whom children were sacrificed. As Herzen wrote in a well-known passage,

> Who is this Moloch who, as the toilers approach him, instead of rewarding them, only recedes and as a consolation to the exhausted, doomed multitudes crying "*morituri te salutant*" [we who are about to die salute you], can give back only the mocking answer that after their death all will be beautiful on earth. Do you truly wish to condemn all human beings alive to-day to the sad role of caryatids supporting a floor for others some day to dance on . . . or of wretched galley slaves, up to their knees in mud, dragging a barge filled with some mysterious treasure and with the humble words "progress in the future" inscribed on its bows?

Herzen compared the revolutionaries of his day to pagan worshippers. In the words of Isaiah Berlin, one of Herzen's most insightful interpreters, Herzen viewed "collective nouns"—like Nation or Equality or Humanity or Progress—as "merely modern versions of ancient religions which demanded human sacrifice." Even "*salus populi* [the people's welfare]" evoked for Herzen not beneficence but the "strong smell of burnt flesh, blood, inquisition, [and] torture."[9] No less than the Bolsheviks themselves, the Americans with their enthusiasm for progress and industry in Russia—and their ready acceptance of the high human costs—demonstrated the prescience of Herzen's writings.

American support for Soviet industrialization, despite its human toll, increased further with the first Five-Year Plan in 1928. Even before the widespread acknowledgment of the Great Depression in the United States—but especially afterward—the notion of a planned economy had tremendous appeal. For a generation of technocrats who came of age during the massive economic mobilization of World War I, an economy governed by technical experts like themselves seemed the only route to efficiency and social welfare.[10] As much as these experts admired Soviet planning, however, they insisted that the United States would be spared the costs of Soviet development. Soviet planning and industrialization also had wide appeal in the Soviet Union itself, even among those who opposed Bolshevik rule.[11] Admiration flowed in the other direction as well; Russians celebrated American industrial prowess even while condemning bourgeois capitalism.[12] The deepening of the Depression in the United States only increased the sense that Americans could learn from the Soviet system of economic organization. In the traumas of Soviet industrialization, many Americans found hope not just for the Soviet future but for their own. They did so while fully aware of the costs entailed, costs dramatically realized in the famine of 1932–1933.

Third, American efforts to learn from the Soviet Union gained strength from the professionalization of America's Russia expertise. Transforming institutional forms as well as intellectual content, professionalization had different impacts in diplomacy, journalism, and scholarship. Among America's Russia experts, early generations of amateur adventurers gave way to new professionals in each line of work. This change is evident in a single family tree. The most prolific Russia expert in nineteenth-century America, George Kennan, never completed high school; his first trip to Russia was to survey the route for a telegraph line. In contrast, his grand-nephew and namesake, George Frost Kennan, the twentieth-century diplomat, received training from Princeton, the Foreign Service School, and the University of Berlin before beginning his career as a Russia specialist for the Department of State. Adventurer-journalists like the elder Kennan gave way to university-trained experts and eventually to specialists in social-scientific disciplines and in diplomacy.[13] In complex ways, professionalization divided the specialists into new groupings, each of which applied its own traditions and rules to interpreting Russia and the USSR.

Although the trajectory of European ideas about Russia in places parallels and elsewhere intersects with the history of American perspectives, this book focuses on the American case. Informed American discourse about

Russia and the Soviet Union differed from the trends in western Europe. At the height of its own Victorian era, American thought maintained a stronger strain of universalism—the idea that every person or people could progress—than continental or British thought of the day. The professionalization of the social sciences in the United States came with greater pretense to scientific objectivity than did similar developments in western Europe. Finally, the lack of a significant American labor party—famously noted in the German sociologist Werner Sombart's book *Why Is There No Socialism in the United States?* (1906)—gave American ideas about the Soviet Union a different political complexion than European perspectives. These comparisons remain more implicit than explicit in the book, which describes attitudes toward Russian modernization on only one of many "other shores."[14]

American ideas about Russia's predominantly peasant population also built on indigenous Russian ones. Especially in the nineteenth century, which saw the spread of industrialization in western Europe and the rise of Romanticism, images of the peasant played an important role in arguments about Russia's present conditions and future trajectory.[15] Slavophiles, conservatives who emphasized Russia's differences from the west, celebrated the peasant commune and the autocracy as cornerstones of Russian rule and incarnations of Russian character. To them, the special qualities of Russia and its peasantry deserved conservation and protection from western materialism and industrialism. Yet admiration was at a distance. Throughout the nineteenth century, educated Russians described the sharp contrasts between themselves (collectively, *obshchestvo,* or society) and the bulk of the population (*narod,* or the people). With a combination of condescension and sympathy, intellectuals saw the *narod* as an undistinguished mass of simple people who required the help of the *obshchestvo* if they ever hoped to emerge from their noble suffering. As one member of the Populists (a group of radical heirs to the Slavophiles) put it in 1880, a Populist "does not love the *narod* only because they are unfortunate . . . He respects the *narod* as a collective whole, constituting in itself the highest level of justice and humanity in our time." Love for the *narod,* however deep and sincere, was directed not at actual individuals but at an abstraction.

Within two decades, though, such positive sentiments were drowned out by critical ones. Russian intellectuals in the last decades of the nineteenth century depicted peasants as savage, helpless, and hopeless—not to mention unresponsive to (and even ungrateful for) the *obshchestvo*'s best efforts. Russian intellectuals' experiences with the peasantry are perhaps best illustrated by the Populists' effort to bring education and enlightenment "to the people" in 1874. "The people" were so uninspired by the message of the radicals that they frequently reported them to police officials. The ensuing disenchantment with the *narod* was hardly limited to radicals, however. In Russian art, literature, and theater of the late nineteenth century, peasants were no longer repositories of rural virtue. The figurative countryside was instead populated by *kulaks*, "peasant bloodsucker[s]," and *baby*, vulgar peasant women who symbolized the moral crisis of the peasantry. Peasants previously lauded as an abstract collective fared much worse (in the minds of educated Russians) as actual individuals. Russian intellectuals' views of their rural compatriots suggest that no great geographic distances are required to turn the subjects of observation into "others." Although they lived close to the peasants, members of the Russian *obshchestvo* nevertheless remained outside the lives of those they described with such contempt. America's Russia watchers, without local knowledge, found their suspicions about the peasantry confirmed by Russian writers.

Recent scholarship on such exterior perceptions has been aided—and, more problematically, defined around—Edward Said's elegant work *Orientalism*. Said documents a range of assumptions that European scholars, writers, and artists held about the "Orient" and "Orientals." Amid his insightful readings of Flaubert and his broad generalizations about French and British policy in the Near East, Said offers a convincing criticism of European depictions of the Orient. Europeans, he writes, homogenized the Orient's inhabitants and placed them outside historical time. But Said himself pays minimal attention to the differences among depictions of the Orient, and to the ways they changed over time. Ironically enough, then, his critique of homogenization and hypostatization applies equally well to his own analysis of Orientalist discourse. Nevertheless, Said's insights about perceptions as a form of social power—and their intimate connections to imperatives of government rule—are applicable to American views of Russia.[16]

Modernization from the Other Shore invokes Herzen's metaphor of distant shores to emphasize the exteriority upon which Said built his argument. But the metaphor applied across time as well as space. The "far shore" represented not just Herzen's distance from Russia but also the safe haven he reached as the revolutionary storms of 1848 ebbed. Like Herzen's, this book is also written from a far shore—following not the flash-floods of 1848 but the decades-long storm of Soviet rule. The Soviet collapse brings both practical and intellectual changes to the study of Russia's past, and thus to those who interpret it. The opening of once-locked archives and the desire to understand the Soviet past without Cold War blinders have led to a flourishing debate. Once-secret Soviet documents have forced reconsiderations of crucial events in modern history. Russians' discussions of their country's past are all the more striking for the decrepit physical and desperate financial circumstances in which they take place.

Writing after the Cold War also offers an opportunity to reflect on American enthusiasm for the USSR in a new and less rancorous political context. To take one example: previous historians have blamed intellectuals' fascination with the Soviet Union in the 1930s on misguided leftists, or on misguided leftism in general. Yet the romance of economic development swayed American observers across the political spectrum. Partisan politics—that is, devotion or opposition to the Communist Party—cannot fully explain this important episode in American intellectual history. Impressed by grandiose Soviet plans and dismissive of backward Russians, many American intellectuals enthusiastically observed Soviet efforts at modernization. And western enthusiasms for the Soviet Union reverberated long after the Depression decade. They helped define McCarthyism and the early Cold War, as a generation of intellectuals viewed their own— and their friends'—Soviet enchantment with increasing disdain.[17]

Enthusiasm for Soviet industrialization did not require a Party card, either in the United States or in the Soviet Union. Many Russians who praised rapid modernization were not Bolsheviks. So-called bourgeois agricultural experts, engineers, and economists in Russia all found reasons to endorse Soviet goals of collectivization and industrialization. Other Russians leapt at the chance to turn their motherland into a modern great power, meaning an industrial one.[18] Western observers, too, appreciated the Bolsheviks' claims about a rationally organized society under the guidance of specialists like themselves.

Such enthusiasm also existed outside Russia. James Scott's recent synthesis, *Seeing Like a State*, suggests parallels between Soviet collectivization and other projects of what he calls "authoritarian high modernism."[19] The idea of creating a new kind of society, organized around production and easily controlled, Scott shows, found adherents around the world and all along the political spectrum. The demise of the USSR and the Cold War has already opened new inquiries into the common mindsets behind these projects, past and present.

Widespread excitement about universal progress still incorporates regional variations. Recent debates about "Asian values," for instance, reveal the persistence of a troubled relationship between universalist and particularist models of development. Since the 1980s, leaders in Malaysia and Singapore have defended their combination of industrialization and political repression with references to particular Asian values. "Each nation," one argues, "must find its own best social and political arrangements"; there are no universal theories or forms of social organization. Western critics, meanwhile, base their arguments on the notion of human rights—that is, a set of rights that applies universally, transcending culture or government.[20] The Asian values debate scrambles political alliances among Americans. Multiculturalists, generally on the left, see their claims of cultural particularism deployed by right-wing dictatorships. Meanwhile universalists, often accused of denigrating other nations and cultures, take the side of oppressed populations.

Similarly, scholars still argue about the relationship between Russian character and economic development in the post-Soviet era. The Soviet collapse, which might have brought down with it the edifice of universalist theories of human behavior, has instead unleashed a potent universalism in which all varieties of humankind are known only as *homo oeconomicus*. This is evident in recent debates about Russian economic policy. Taking great pride that they had conquered the "prejudice that 'Russia is different,'" the economists Maxim Boycko, Robert Vishny, and Andrei Shleifer celebrated their own universalism. "The Russian people," they preached in a widely read monograph, "like the rest of the people in the world, were 'economic men' who rationally responded to incentives." Russia, therefore, did not require a special form of economic organization "to compensate for its alleged cultural specificities and deficiencies."[21] These economists promoted the immediate establishment of free-market institutions, creating a capitalist Russia with a single big bang. Supremely confident that economic laws applied equally well in all times and places, they were, ironically enough, heirs to Marx's universalism.

As economic "shock therapy" created new ailments in Russia, particularist critics blamed the economists' failure to account for Russia's differences from the west. Russians, argued the longtime Russia-watcher Marshall Goldman, "have almost always seemed more comfortable in a collective or communal, as opposed to an entrepreneurial, environment." Even before the anti-capitalist slogans of the Soviet era, he continued, "the market ethic was never . . . deeply entrenched in the psyche" of Russian peasants. Particularists with a conservative bent, meanwhile, suggested that the problem was not in the economists' methods but in their very aims. Historian Richard Pipes, for instance, lists multiple reasons that Russia has never developed the key institutions of western capitalism and democracy. While explicitly rejecting a national character argument, Pipes leaves little opportunity for Russia to evolve toward the west. In making such claims, he comes all too close to condemning Russia to its own past.[22] We have yet to resolve the tensions between universal progress and national difference that Herzen observed a century and a half ago.

The questions addressed in this book parallel many of the age-old concerns that preoccupied Herzen. Chief among them is the question of difference. What do cultural differences mean? Are they innate or historical? How do they shape our understandings of human behavior and social change? Related to these are concerns about the universality of progress. How can each society find its own path of progress? Can a nation overcome its historical particularities? Should it? Finally, there is the balance between present and future. Under what conditions can individuals call for collective sacrifices in the name of future welfare? And with what consequences? Russian history provided the answers to these questions—or so American experts believed.

Ideas about the peculiarities of Russian character, belief in economic development, and the reconfiguration of international expertise all shaped American conceptions of Russia and the Soviet Union between 1870 and 1940. This book's organization underscores the pervasiveness as well as the significance of these themes. Chronological chapters emphasize the persistence of national-character stereotypes as well as the growing romance of economic development and the evolving structure of expertise. Within most chapters, biographical sections highlight the ubiquity of these beliefs, even among experts with discordant political views and divergent personal experiences.

Part I describes America's Russia experts in the late nineteenth century. Early American writings drew heavily on European ideas about Russia, which are briefly discussed in the opening chapter. The second chapter looks at the assimilation of European ideas of Russia up until the Russian famine of 1891–1892. It identifies the contrasts between the elder George Kennan and the scholar-diplomats Andrew Dickson White and Eugene Schuyler. All three focused on national character, but Kennan's writings contained important hints of universalism; he hoped that Russia might advance once the curse of autocracy was lifted. The Russian famine of 1891–1892 revealed the range of American ideas about Russia. Particularists described the famine as the inevitable result of Russian character, while others saw some hope that the Russians could develop. By the turn of the century, the first Russia experts took up posts in American universities; these academic experts are the focus of the third chapter. Harvard's Archibald Cary Coolidge and the University of Chicago's Samuel Northrop Harper incorporated the national-character stereotypes so dominant among the European writers whom they knew and read.

These new American experts took on advisory roles in the U.S. government during Russia's revolutionary era, the focus of Part II. The revolution of 1905, much of which Harper saw first-hand, prompted new interest in Russian politics and the direction of Russia's future. Chapter 4 considers the use of national-character stereotypes among American experts who agreed on little besides the instinctual nature of Russians. From conservatives like Coolidge and Ambassador George von Lengerke Meyer to liberals like Harper and his benefactor Charles Crane to a self-proclaimed group of "gentlemen socialists" inspired by William English Walling, Americans interpreted Russian events in terms of Russian character. This trend continued through the revolutions of 1917, the topic of Chapter 5. American policy-makers and the experts who advised them understood Russians as instinctive and unable to look after their own interests. The idea that Russians needed western protection became a crucial element supporting American intervention against the Bolsheviks. After the end of western intervention and the collapse of the armies arrayed against them, the Bolsheviks faced a new problem: the famine of 1921–1923. Secretary of Commerce Herbert Hoover used these understandings of Russia to justify American food relief in terms of Russian national character. Unable to speak or act for themselves, he suggested, Russians needed (by Americans' reckoning) outside assistance. At the same time, American experts saw industrialization as a solution to Russian economic woes. As Chapter 6 shows, they promoted this industrialization even at the cost of significant hardship to Russians.

As the famine receded and American aid came to an end, a new generation of professional Russia experts rose to prominence, as described in Part III. Drs. Geroid Tanquary Robinson and Robert Kerner brought new methods of historical scholarship to the study of Russia. Samuel Harper, under the influence of the latest trends in political science, reversed his decades of anti-radicalism and came to endorse Soviet policies. And social scientists like Paul Douglas and Amy Hewes began to look at the Soviet Union as a case study for understanding modern societies. These two trends—social scientists turning to Russia, and Russia experts turning to professional social sciences—are the focus of Chapter 7. The next chapter shows how the institutional groundwork of social-scientific expertise on Russia molded American social scientists' ideas about the USSR during the era of the Five-Year Plans. Stuart Chase and George Soule, inspired by the idiosyncratic economist Thorstein Veblen, celebrated Soviet planning. Calvin Bryce Hoover, building on the work of his Progressive mentor John Commons, tempered his opposition to Soviet power with admiration for its accomplishments. The educators John Dewey and George Counts drew inspiration for their own reform efforts from their studies of Soviet cultural institutions. These experts supported Soviet policies not because of any attachment to Communist doctrine, but because they saw hope for creating a new kind of modern society. Professional journalists, the subject of Chapter 9, picked up where the social scientists left off, enthusiastically reporting on the ambitious Soviet plans while acknowledging their extraordinary costs. The journalists used particularist notions—the flaws of Russian character—to explain away those costs. The final substantive chapter examines one refuge of particularism, the Foreign Service. American diplomats continued to emphasize Russians' differences from Americans, and they used these differences to explain the consequences (and especially the failures) of Soviet policies. The younger Kennan and his colleagues Charles Bohlen and Loy Henderson all employed national character in their analyses of Russia. Kennan's analyses—except, ironically, for the one that would make him famous—emphasized Russian traits over Soviet ideology. But his breakthrough piece, the so-called X-article of 1947, defined the Soviet Union primarily in ideological terms. This piece represented a new universalist paradigm for Cold War thought. By the early 1950s, particularist notions moved to the margins of academic Russia expertise—at the same time that academic thought moved toward the center of American intellectual life. And it is with these circumstances that this book concludes.

Considering questions of economic progress and cultural difference in early twenty-first century America takes on renewed importance yet brings with it new difficulties. Both universalism and particularism have significant cultural power. Economists and development officials (like Russia's shock therapists) offer startlingly similar prescriptions—usually involving more markets—to a wide variety of societies with strikingly differ-ent histories, cultural norms, and economic structures. In cultural and educational spheres, meanwhile, multiculturalists celebrate cultural differ-ence and treat universalism as unabashed ethnocentrism.

Studying the history of these ideas highlights the dangers of both par-ticularism and universalism. Valuing cultural difference as the sole social good obscures important material concerns. Cultural difference has al-ready become one of the "collective nouns" Herzen deplored, functioning as an altar at which material goals are sacrificed.[23] Yet the universalist view that all people are the same and should have the same goals is hardly more appealing. It effaces nations' dramatically different pasts and presents, erasing history with a single stroke. "We do not proclaim a new revelation," Herzen wrote in *From the Other Shore*, "we eliminate the old lie." I, too, am unable to "proclaim a new revelation," a new way of balancing a nation's past circumstances, its present conditions, and its aspirations for the fu-ture. I can only hope, to continue Herzen's words, to build a bridge "for the unknown person of the future to pass over."[24]

The rise of universalism in mid-twentieth-century American thought was one such bridge. It marked a salutary rejection of notions of cultural difference rooted in permanent factors. Universalist continua—from un-derdeveloped to developed economies, or from backward to advanced na-tions—allowed for the possibility of improvement.[25] They explicitly chal-lenged the notion that blood (race) or soil (geography) delimited and defined a nation's prospects. Celebrating industrialization as an effective means of overcoming national particularities, universalists demolished the particularist notion that a nation was destined for perennial penury. Yet universalism, whether espoused by nineteenth-century European radicals or twentieth-century American social scientists, hardly resolved the ten-sions between cultural difference and economic progress.

Industry, in the prognostications of Marx and Engels, would create a new world order in which nations were irrelevant. They envisioned that industrial capitalism would strip workers of "every trace of national char-acter."[26] The fulfillment of this universalist vision, especially under gov-ernments proclaiming their patrimony in these radical writers, involved dangerous and ultimately deadly actions. Now that the "specter of com-munism" celebrated by these revolutionaries has receded, we are in a better position to understand the all-too-present ghosts of cultural difference and modernization.

Autocratic Russia, Lethargic Russians

An Empire of Climate

Russians were different. Even before Russia became a political entity in the eighteenth century, Europeans saw those living east of the Vistula River as markedly different from themselves. As political boundaries and regimes shifted—from medieval Rus' to early modern Muscovy to the advent of imperial Russia at the turn of the eighteenth century—western commentators maintained a fairly stable stock of Russian character traits. Diplomats, traders, and adventurers joined the leading figures of the French Enlightenment in enumerating Slavic traits: conservatism, passivity, lack of hygiene, fatalism, and general backwardness.

Even as Russia itself went through major geographic and demographic expansions, these imputed traits remained constant explanations of Russian life.[1] Kievan Rus', dating back to the ninth century, covered only a small portion of what is now Russia and Ukraine but provided the ideological basis for imperial Russia, especially the close ties between the monarchy and the Orthodox Christian Church. The collapse of the Kievan state left Slavic lands under Mongol control in the thirteenth century; subjugation under the "Tatar Yoke" became a constant and ideologically charged refrain in Russian history. By the turn of the sixteenth century, the duke of Moscow had "gathered the Russian lands" into a single entity, Muscovy. Soon thereafter began the continual if irregular incorporation of lands and people—including, briefly, forts on the California coast. By the nineteenth century, the Russian Empire encompassed more than 100 million subjects as well as hundreds of distinct ethnic groups and languages, ranging from Koreans in the southeast to Poles in the northwest, from the "Little People" of the circumpolar north to Georgians and Armenians in the Caucasus and Muslims in Central Asia. Layered on top of ethnic and religious dis-

17

tinctions were those of estate (*soslovie*). All estates, from serf to nobleman, owed their position to the *tsar*, or emperor (a title taken from the Latin *caesar*). Local rule was only the extension of centralized power; all subjects owed their obedience and livelihood to the tsar.

These multifarious distinctions, however, disguise some central tendencies. According to the first All-Russian census (1897), 72 percent of Russia's inhabitants were Slavic (about 43 percent Russian, the remainder Ukrainian, Belorussian, and Polish), and 86 percent resided in rural areas. More than 75 percent of subjects were peasants. Until the emancipation of 1861, furthermore, agriculturalists were predominantly serfs owned by a very small (but not always very wealthy) nobility or by the state itself.

Conditions were difficult for a nation whose principal economic pursuit was agriculture. With only one-tenth of the land arable—and even that land had a growing season roughly half of western Europe's—Russian agriculture was by far the least productive in Europe. Population growth in the nineteenth century was as high as (if not higher than) productivity growth, making Russia's ability to provide for its subjects all the more tenuous. The circumstances of nineteenth-century Russia made it very easy to demonstrate its differences from western Europe—differences in political system, economic organization, freedom of expression, and overall wealth. Yet the terms Europeans used to describe nineteenth-century Russia differed little from those used to describe Rus' or Muscovy.

Among the most important themes in European accounts of Russia was tyranny. The idea of despotic Russia was a resilient one, surviving changes in individual rulers as well as dynasties and even governments. Most commentators saw Russia's differences as permanent, even inherent; they attributed traits to a combination of topography and climate. Russia's great plains and long winters forged Russian character. Russians were not unusual in this regard, however; European observers traced all nations' attributes to physical setting.

Europeans generated the ideas about Russia that nineteenth-century Americans read, cited, and eventually adapted. Most of the European writings described here implied a particularist perspective: Russians were inherently different from Europeans. Yet in America, this view was not as popular as was the list of character traits themselves. American experts in the nineteenth century detached characterizations from causes. The Americanization of European notions of difference took place amid contradiction and confusion, as U.S. experts invoked timeless traits specified by

European writers while leaving open the possibility that those traits might be overcome. Repeating European claims about the geographic origins of Russian character, some American writers went on to argue that national character might shift under a new government or, eventually, in a new economic system. While stable European views of national character contrasted with mercurial American ones, they also established the intellectual boundaries within which most western discussions of Russian character took place.

Early modern ethnographers believed that the despotic character of Russian rulers was intimately linked to the character of the Russians themselves. Sigismund von Herberstein, a sixteenth-century diplomat from Vienna, provided the language for future debates when he contemplated whether Russians' character necessitated a despotic state, or whether a despotic state itself had altered the Russians' character. His book *Notes upon Russia* (1517–1549), the most frequently cited (and plagiarized) account of Russia in the early modern era, opted for the former: "The people," he wrote, "enjoy slavery more than freedom."[2] A century later Adam Olearius, another central European diplomat, paraphrased Aristotle to make a similar claim: Russians were "comfortable in slavery." So passive were the Russians, he wrote, that they had to be "driven to work" using "cudgels and whips."[3] Despotism and poverty, then, were the lot of the Russians.

As western European culture grew increasingly self-confident and self-aware in the early modern era, ideas about Russia played an important albeit indirect role. Crucial components of European identity grew out of encounters with societies and peoples to the east. As Larry Wolff argues suggestively, many of the governing concepts of the Enlightenment—civilized society, civilization, and perhaps even Europe itself—emerged out of the intellectual encounter with the inhabitants of Europe's easternmost lands. The conceptions of civilization, when applied to Russia, most often centered on the efforts of Tsar Peter I (1682–1725). Peter the Great embarked on an ambitious effort to Europeanize Russia. He built the city of Sankt-Peterburg (given a Germanic name) as a "window on Europe"; he traveled across western Europe, learning military and economic techniques; and he introduced new laws to force the Russian nobility to appear and act more European. Western European thinkers adored Peter with a touch of narcissism, as he sought to make his subjects more like themselves.

Even Baron Charles de Montesquieu, who considered Peter's actions "instances of tyranny," nevertheless had great appreciation for the changes. In *The Spirit of the Laws* (1748), Montesquieu argued that the previous customs of Russia had themselves been foreign imports. These manners, which Peter had considered brutish, were the residue of previous—that is, Tatar—conquest. In Europeanizing Russia, Peter was bringing Russians back to their own natural manners and customs. What made these customs natural? Here Montesquieu employed a climatological theory of national character and brought it into wider use. "The empire of climate," he wrote, is "the most powerful of all empires." It shaped each nation's traditions, which in turn shaped national character and ultimately structures of government. Climate influenced a people's initiative and independence. Russia was firmly within Europe, according to Montesquieu, so Peter's reforms merely gave "the manners and customs of Europe to a European nation." But others would employ Montesquieu's argument about climate to reach the opposite conclusion, namely, that Russia was not within Europe and that Russians were irredeemably different from Europeans.[4]

Not all *philosophes* were so enthralled by Peter or his subjects. One of the central works of the French Enlightenment, Jean-Jacques Rousseau's book *Social Contract* (1762), for instance, used Russia as a foil for descriptions of western European political systems. Eschewing climate, Rousseau claimed that forms of government could be directly derived from national character. A "wise lawgiver," he wrote, "considers first whether the people for whom he designs them are fit to endure them." Peter the Great's efforts at modernization were, Rousseau argued, ill-adapted for Russians themselves; Peter wished to "civilize" the Russians "when it was necessary only to discipline them." Any efforts to turn "ungovernable" Russians into citizens rather than subjects denied their essential character.[5]

If Russians were not European or civilized, what were they? Throughout the early modern and modern eras, ideas about Russia overlaid ideas about Asia and the Orient. Aided by a vague cartography that placed the boundary between Europe and Asia somewhere between the Volga and Ob" rivers, most European geographers agreed that Russia straddled the two continents. (Only in the nineteenth century did the notion that the Ural Mountains separated Europe from Asia become a consensus.)[6] Geographic divisions grounded notions of cultural difference. Thus character traits ascribed to Russians overlapped considerably with the traits applied to Asians. The complex of categories including Oriental and Asiatic (the word Asian appeared only rarely until late in the twentieth century), uncivilized, and non-European all intersected to define Russians as recognizably different from peoples to their west. The Russian Empire, in short, emerged only in the context of its alterity, or otherness, vis-à-vis western European societies and peoples.

As the Russian Empire expanded eastward and southward, incorporating Caucasians and Central Asians, the geographic categories muddled even further. As an imperial power, Russia undertook the Europeanization of Asia. Yet in other contexts the imperial nation—certainly its past and often its present—was itself Asian. But these fluid conceptual categories typically left few European or American observers bothered by either ambiguity or contradiction.

Although Russia's differences from Europe were usually cast in negative terms, the rise of romantic nationalism in the early nineteenth century offered a competing perspective. Romantics believed that each people had its own spirit or national genius, expressed in cultural, political, and social forms. As Romantics began to trade in national traits, the Russians offered what the historian Martin Malia called "soul for export." Russia's gifts of spiritualism, psychological depth, and collectivism were visible in everything from social organization to culture. Popular within Russia as Slavophilism, praise of Russia's distinctiveness echoed across Europe. Those interested in art, music, painting, and dance found in these creative forms expressions of the Russian genius.[7]

While European writers and ethnographers celebrated the differences between themselves and the Russians, interstate politics proceeded on an entirely different plane. Focusing far less on national character than other observers did, the royalty of Europe welcomed the Russian tsars as full members of its international system in the eighteenth and nineteenth centuries.[8] Russia was excluded from European civilization but was nevertheless part of the European political system. Derided as barbarian and Asiatic by intellectuals, Russia nevertheless gave rise to exotic cultural endeavors admired all over Europe. Although Russia was celebrated as a participant in Europe's civilizing mission, its own membership in the club of civilized nations was itself in doubt.

The dichotomies between politics and culture, civilized and uncivilized, were frequently mapped onto Russian society itself. Both native and foreign commentators described Russian society as a thin European crust of elites, looking toward if not resident in the imperial capital of St. Petersburg. The rest of society they identified, often in derogatory and despairing terms, as a mass of barbaric peasants. The idea that Russia straddled Asia and Europe, furthermore, could take two forms. A geographic model drew the dividing line between Asia and Europe somewhere on Russian soil, whereas a sociological one emphasized that Russians themselves could be divided into a small civilized elite amid a sea of Asiatic peasants. Regardless of the axis of difference, though, few commentators asserted that Russia was wholly European.

The categories evolved little as the Enlightenment and the French Revolution heralded the start of the modern era—indeed, less than Russia itself had changed. As Tsar Nicholas I ascended to the throne in 1825, the basic terms for understanding Russia—uncivilized, backward, despotic, and Asiatic, yet spiritual and collective—had clearly recognizable precursors dating back three hundred years. Expanding commercial, political, and cultural ties between Russia and the rest of Europe, and increasingly the United States, created new demand for outsiders to explain Russia. The new generation of Russia observers in Europe undertook their studies using conceptual categories passed down through the centuries.

One of the most elegant of these new accounts came from a French nobleman, the Marquis Astolphe de Custine, who traveled through Russia in 1839. Like his contemporary and fellow countryman Alexis de Tocqueville, Custine aimed for political theory more than travelogue. He wanted to visit the gendarme of Europe, as Russia was then known, in search of arguments against representative government. He returned a liberal constitutionalist—with an intense distaste for Russian institutions and Russian people. Like von Herberstein three centuries earlier, Custine concluded that Russia's despotism was well-deserved: "Other nations have tolerated oppression; the Russian nation has loved it; she still loves it." Russians were not made by despotism; they made it. And that despotism revolted him sufficiently to upend his political beliefs. While unremittingly negative about his experience in Russia—upon crossing the border en route back to France, he proclaimed, "I am free!"—Custine nevertheless described Russians using both negative and positive glosses on the same image. Russians were "superstitious" and "lazy" but at the same "poetical" and "musical."[9] Russian character, in short, expressed itself both in its reprehensible political system and in its exotic arts.

The other well-known western account of Russia from mid-century, by a German nobleman, focused less on governance and culture and more on economic issues. This report, like Custine's, charted Russia's differences from Europe. Baron August von Haxthausen devoted much of his travelogue on Russia to rural life and rural institutions, especially the *mir*, or commune. As the most distinctive aspect of Russian agriculture in the nineteenth century, the peasant commune was a common focus for students of Russia. To the growing Slavophile movement, which celebrated Russia's uniqueness and its distance from European social structures, the commune represented Russia's special contribution to world civilization. The *mir* operated through collective enterprise rather than competition. It revealed the intimate connection between the peasants and the land, and it was free of the individualism, secularism, and anonymity of the increasingly urban life in western Europe. As the Slavophile Konstantin Aksakov put it, "a commune is a union of people who have renounced their egotism, their individuality, and who express their common accord . . . [It is] a triumph of the human spirit."[10] Critics of Russian economic backwardness also focused on the commune, analyzing many of the same attributes. Collective decision-making, these critics argued, undermined individual responsibility and incentive while also making the commune rigid and conservative. For westernizers within and outside of Russia, the commune was also a symbol of Russia's uniqueness—though with a negative valence attached.

Haxthausen's view of the *mir* shared much with that of his Slavophile interlocutors. Like the Slavophiles, the German traveler recognized and even celebrated the web of mutual obligations that defined communal life. But Haxthausen was no shill for the Slavophiles. In describing the commune as a flexible and responsive institution, he also predicted that communal principles would eventually yield to private interest and competition. Haxthausen offered an analysis of the *mir* that put Slavophile assumptions to westernizing ends. He shared with the Slavophiles the claim that the *mir* expressed "the fundamental character of the Slavonic race." The *mir* represented everything that was unique about the Slavic peasantry, most notably communal instincts and an intimate connection with the land. But he also proclaimed the commune an economic failure; it did "not possess the condition for making progress in agriculture." The *mir*, furthermore, revealed some of the most problematic aspects of Russian character, traits such as laziness and conservatism. Although Haxthausen's views evolved in later years, it was his earlier ideas, published in his travelogue, that shaped others' understandings of Russia.[11] That book canonized the communal principle as a central element not just in Russian life but also in Russian character. Alexander Herzen borrowed freely from Haxthausen in his descriptions of the peasants, even noting with embarrassment that it took a German to "discover . . . the Russia of the peasantry."[12]

Discovering Russian peasant institutions was hardly the straightforward task that Herzen implied. The intense debates over the meanings of the *mir*—as a sign of Russia's uniqueness or a source of its economic problems—hardly contributed to a careful understanding of the peasant commune's history and variation. Its past was (and is) shrouded in mystery. The Slavophiles took this uncertainty as evidence of the *mir*'s organic evolution rather than as an indication of its uneven and variegated development amid the competing pressures of tax collection, serf ownership, and agricultural production. The historian Geroid Tanquary Robinson's definition suggested the commune's multiple functions and interpretations; he called the mir "a tax-apportioning and tax-responsible organization with certain functions of land-control which are by no means clearly defined by the records of the time, but had either grown out of, or would eventually develop into, that wide community of interest in the land which—at least in later times—was so characteristic of Russian peasant life." The *mir*, then, was an instrument for the communal control of land. Frequent land repartitions, through which holdings would be redistributed and equalized among the commune's families, suggested a strong belief in equality, at least as the Slavophiles saw it. Yet the commune's crucial role in tax collection is evidenced by the spread of the repartitional commune after the creation of the Soul Tax in 1724. Serf owners, responsible for collecting taxes on each of their bondsmen, had a fiscal interest in ensuring that each serf could afford to pay the tax.[13] Whether a creature of the Russian soul or of the Russian Soul Tax, however, the commune played an important role in any discussions of Russia's future.

Karl Marx read his countryman's analysis of the peasant commune with great interest and even greater disdain. Writing to Friedrich Engels in 1858, Marx mocked Haxthausen's gullibility in accepting the scripted communalism promoted by Russian authorities. Behind the Potemkin communes, Marx suggested, sat decrepit structures eaten away by capitalism's advance. He insisted that capitalist development would inevitably lead to socialism. According to his theory, the peasant commune's sole contribution to progress was to disappear under the pressure of rural capitalism. All nations would proceed along the same trajectory. Capitalism would render meaningless distinctions between nations and peoples, leaving only two classes facing off against each other: the proletariat and the bourgeoisie. The idea that a nation could find a detour on this path of history was anathema to Marx. Only Asia, which stood outside historical progress, could avoid the inexorable movement toward socialism. Thus Herzen's and Haxthausen's claims that the Russian *mir* might be the kernel of Russian socialism—that is, it might help Russia bypass capitalism—challenged not just Marx's understanding of Russia but his understanding of history as well.

Marx reconsidered this view of Russia later in his career. After the dramatic collapse of the Paris Commune in 1871 made European revolution seem less likely, Marx turned eastward, where his works were widely read and hotly contested. Both he and Engels learned Russian and immersed themselves in economic reports and political polemics about the Russian countryside. Even these diehard universalists came to the tentative and ill-expressed conclusion that Herzen's paeans to the Russian commune may have been right after all. In letters, prefaces, and ephemera—but never in a sustained work—Marx claimed that the *mir* might in fact be the seed of a socialist order in Russia, "the finest chance ever offered by history to a nation . . . [to avoid] all the fatal vicissitudes of the capitalist regime." Marx's thought evolved from universalism in mid-century to particularism in his later years. Marx eventually reconciled himself to Herzen's heirs, the Russian Populists, and also, in an indirect and unacknowledged way, to the German writer he once mocked.[14] Yet Marx's new views on Russia were not widely known outside a small circle of revolutionaries.

Haxthausen's work became required reading for westerners interested in Russia, especially for those uninterested in revolution. His description of the communal principle appeared frequently in western European and eventually American writings on Russia. Haxthausen's book also influenced perhaps the most important English-language work on Russia in the nineteenth century, Donald MacKenzie Wallace's economically entitled book *Russia*. Originally published in 1877, Wallace offered direct acknowledgment of Haxthausen's work. Like his German predecessor, Wallace emphasized the economic limitations of communal agriculture. As a practical Englishman, he saw the commune primarily in terms of its social and political functions rather than its spiritual contributions. Wallace did not ignore Russian character, however. He suggested both positive and negative traits that made Russians unique. They were "singularly free from rancor and the spirit of revenge," possessing "a patient endurance that would do honor to a martyr" as well as a "dogged passive resistance." But he also cited the Russians' "poor work habits [and] minimal exertions" as well as their "incorrigible laziness." Wallace put this last point into geographic perspective: to visitors arriving in Russia from points east, he speculated, Russians would appear energetic enough, while those coming from the west would see them as indolent. The work ethic, it seemed, descended on a gradient from west to east. Wallace laid the blame for Russia's economic woes not on the commune, as Haxthausen had, but on these character traits, and especially on improvidence.[15]

Just after Wallace's *Russia* came another major European book whose impact on America's Russia experts was even greater: the French historian Alfred Rambaud's work *History of Russia from the Earliest Times to 1877*. Rambaud was far more concerned with historical issues than were many previous writers on Russia. But his scholarship also served a contemporary political purpose: to promote an alliance between Russia and France. Rambaud defended his interest in a diplomatic alliance with an ethnographic argument emphasizing similarities between the French and the Russians. Rambaud blamed the "Mongol hordes" for imposing despotism, arguing that the Russian state was out of line with the desires of the Russian people. His book is striking for both its historical detail and its relative lack of attention to national character. And yet claims about Russia's uniqueness and distance from Europe nevertheless creep into his argument. His description of the peasant commune, for instance, borrows from the Slavophile notion that the *mir* represents a "primordial" element of Russian society. In this sense, Rambaud's task paralleled Montesquieu's: using geography and climate—the topic of Rambaud's first chapters—to establish Russia's position within Europe.[16]

Rambaud's fellow countryman Anatole Leroy-Beaulieu used the same approach in his history *The Empire of the Tsars and the Russians* (1881), albeit for opposite political goals. Leroy-Beaulieu's principal aim was to explain Russia's vast cultural distance from France in the hopes of maintaining significant political distance between the two powers. But he shared with Rambaud a common structure, opening his work with a lengthy discussion of the effects of climate and geography on Russian life. Leroy-Beaulieu provided detailed and damning analyses of national character, harping on Russians' inconsistent work habits, patience, submissiveness, and lack of individuality. He saved his sharpest words for fatalism, which he deemed the greatest failing in Russian character. Leroy-Beaulieu found the roots of all these traits in the land: Russians' resignation and submissiveness, he explained, resulted from their constant struggles against nature. The lack of originality and individual distinctions, similarly, could be traced to the terrain's long stretches of level plains and general lack of geographic features.[17]

Leroy-Beaulieu's argument was not highly original. His logic and language shared much with Montesquieu and his "empire of climate"—though Leroy-Beaulieu's aim was to separate Russia from France while Montesquieu sought rapprochement. As Leroy-Beaulieu's history became a key reference for European and American Russia experts, his catalog of character traits and his explanation of their causes similarly became common currency for most, if not all, Russia observers.

From von Herberstein in 1549 to Leroy-Beaulieu in 1877, these writers assessed Russia's political and economic potential in terms of national character. Emphasizing traits like laziness and fatalism, they explained Russia's backwardness in terms of its inhabitants' nature. Rooting Russian character in climate and geography, the European tradition offered few opportunities for improvement. Backwardness was not just a relative condition but an essential and permanent one.

2

Endurance without Limit

American observers developed a more fluid definition of Russian character than did Anatole Leroy-Beaulieu and Alfred Rambaud. Even though their arguments were at odds with each other, both Frenchmen fixed Russia's traits—passivity, lethargy, and fatalism—in the country's land and climate. In contrast, the most widely read nineteenth-century American writer on Russia, George Kennan, inventoried a similar set of Russian character traits while leaving open the possibility of individual transformation. Borrowing freely from the language and logic of domestic reform debates over the status of the poor and disenfranchised, American Russia-watchers applied the same kind of character arguments as European scholars. Kennan's American contemporaries, the diplomats Eugene Schuyler, Andrew Dickson White, and Charles Emory Smith, as well as the authors William Dudley Foulke and Isabel Hapgood, sounded more like the French historians—but even they offered the Russians some chance of improvement, however remote. The American authors imported definitions of Russian character while modifying arguments about its origin. They typically asserted that Russian character, though deep-rooted, could in the right political circumstances change for the better. The tsarist autocracy, in the mind of these Americans, was to blame for Russian character and the economic circumstances it created. During the famine of 1891–1892, American observers and relief officials blamed both the peasantry and the tsarist regime. Given the peasants' putative inability to care for themselves, these analysts placed the ultimate responsibility for peasant conditions on the autocracy. Only a small cadre of Marxist authors, residing in New York but participating in a trans-Atlantic debate among Russian radicals, took the universalist stance that Russia in the 1890s was on its way to modernity.

Westerners frequently attacked Russian despotism, and with reason. The power of the autocrat and the ubiquity of state controls earned Russia the nickname "gendarme of Europe." In the words of the Fundamental Laws of 1832, all laws and statutes "emanate from the Autocratic Power." The autocracy of nineteenth-century Russia severely limited cultural and especially political freedoms, operating with few checks on its power aside from its own incompetence. (Amid the constitutional struggles of 1905, one critic, referring to Tsar Nicholas II, said that Russia did not need a constitution to limit the monarchy; it already had a limited monarch. Although Nicholas's predecessors were more effective than he, the autocracy was hardly an efficient governing machine.) Laws against opposition sent thousands into Siberian exile and many more to western Europe. No representative institutions, even consultative ones, provided a power base that might compete with the imperial court. The tsarist bureaucracy also controlled economic activities, limiting the spread of factories, owning large numbers of serfs, and regulating (or monopolizing) trade in key commodities.[1] Whether or not it expressed the nature of Russian character, Russian rule was indeed strict.

Rather than claiming, as did Leroy-Beaulieu and his predecessor Marquis de Custine, that Russian character made Russian despotism, writers in Victorian America suggested that Russian character was a product of its despotism. Politics made character, not vice versa. This difference in perspective makes the surface similarities with the French authors all the more striking. Those employing a Victorian argument about improvement relied on a familiar list of character traits and frequently cited European authorities. Yet they also asserted that Russian character could eventually be overcome.

The tension between difference and the possibility of improvement appeared, *mutatis mutandis,* in important elements of Victorian thought in America. It encompassed the central tenets of Victorianism: a sense of optimism, a faith in individual improvement, an appreciation for the benefits of an ordered society, and a belief that character was defined by the ability to overcome nature and natural urges. While holding on to notions of cultural hierarchy rooted in personal virtue, American Victorians left open the possibility (in principle anyway) that individual people and perhaps even entire peoples could improve. But principle and practice did not always coincide. Peoples who might theoretically improve were rarely afforded equal status. According to the historian Daniel Walker Howe, this tension—between the prospect of change and the rigidity of hierarchies—became "one of the most tragic contradictions within American Victorian culture."[2]

These tensions in American thought defined the contours of American views of Europe as well as national self-definition. The possibility of improvement was more prominent in American than in British Victorianism, and far more prevalent than anywhere in continental Europe.[3] An immutable character, such as that proposed by Rambaud and Leroy-Beaulieu, offered scant support for Americans hoping to alter politics in Russia and contribute to an economic transformation there. The idea that Russia's despotism—and not Russians' nature—created that nation's economic problems, furthermore, served to confirm America's identity as a prosperous, progressive, and democratic nation. National achievements resulted not only from material conditions but from the struggle to succeed. Thus even those Americans most vociferously asserting the particularities of Russian character also suggested that Russians might overcome that past, becoming more democratic, more progressive, more civilized—and perhaps, more American.

Debates about Russian character took place, by default, in general-interest magazines, lecture series, and books. The lack of any institutional framework for Russian studies in the United States contrasted sharply with the sophisticated infrastructure for Slavic studies in Paris. Even German and English universities, which lacked such formal organizations, had more scholars devoted to Slavic and Russian studies than America did.[4] The first widely read American works on Russia came from an adventurous and amateurish sort, not from scholars and journalists, as in Europe. Although some of the amateur experts referred to the work of European scholars, American interpretations were on the whole more impressionistic and less systematic than their European counterparts.

The lack of institutional structures and academic practices is visible in the writings of George Kennan, an adventurer turned journalist. Kennan began his career far from a university, as a telegraph operator in small-town Ohio. Seeking exotic experiences, he joined a Siberian expedition charged with mapping out a possible telegraph line. This project, begun in 1865, would have connected western Europe and the United States by crossing all of Russia, going across the Bering Strait, into Alaska and Canada, and then across to New York. It was rendered irrelevant by the completion, in 1866, of the first trans-Atlantic cable, which provided a far shorter route.[5] Kennan sought to redeem this otherwise fruitless trip by

writing an account of it. The result, *Tent Life in Siberia* (1870), incorporated Kennan's understanding of individual character as well as his reliance
on ethnographic stereotyping of seemingly exotic groups. His use of the
concept of character, so important to the Victorian world view, focused on
an individual's intelligence, rationality, education, bravery, manliness, and
above all self-control. Kennan rated Siberian natives not only on material
conditions and social organization but especially on individual character.
The southern Kamchatkans, for instance, could be described only "by neg-
atives. They are not independent, self-reliant . . . [nor] avaricious or dis-
honest." In contrast, the isolated Koraks scored much better on Kennan's
test: thanks to their "temperate, chaste, and manly habits," the Koraks "remained better men, morally, physically and intellectually."[6] While far from
civilized, even members of exotic and backward groups could, in Kennan's
estimation, exhibit the highest traits of individual bearing.

Kennan defined national character by expanding upon his evaluation of
individual character. As one friend observed, "Character is the sharp test
he puts to himself and other men, and on that standpoint alone he finds
common ground with those about him."[7] In this way, some members
within a national or ethnic group might be people of character while others are not. Kennan broke with the European tradition that derived individual traits from group membership—a Russian was lazy by virtue of
being Russian. Instead, Kennan defined a nation by how much character its
citizens had. This inversion shaped not just his ethnographies of native Siberians but also his views of Russians and Americans. He sought to associate only with men and women of character, regardless of their nationality.

With a determination to improve his own condition, Kennan began a
series of lecture tours shortly after returning from Siberia in 1868. He returned to Russia in 1870, searching for adventure as well as additional lecture material. He found plenty of both in the Caucasus Mountains, which
had only recently been incorporated into the Russian Empire. His writings
about the mountains' inhabitants took a distinctly anthropological bent, as
he described in some detail the "interesting racial types" of that region. He
continued to distinguish between individual character and collective levels
of civilization. Thus the mountain-dwellers of the eastern Caucasus, who
were "hospitable, brave, [and] generous" and had "a deep vein of poetic
feeling," were nevertheless "semi-barbarous." The distinction between individual traits and level of civilization remained strong in Kennan's writings as he broadened his travels through the Russian Empire.[8]

His audience at home also broadened in the 1870s, as his lectures took him farther and farther from his Ohio birthplace. He began writing for national magazines. He tried to stake out a position as America's premier Russia expert, both by intensifying his own efforts and by diminishing those of potential competitors. Frustrated by his inability to get his own translations published, for instance, Kennan mercilessly attacked one of Eugene Schuyler's. Reviewing Schuyler's edition of a Leo Tolstoy novel, Kennan accused the translator of promulgating "perfectly barbarous" prose that was "worse than useless." Kennan's assault had an ulterior motive, as he admitted to his father: "if I can't get any of my own translations published, at least I can cut up those fellows who do."[9]

The victim of Kennan's self-serving assault, Eugene Schuyler, had taken a different path to studying Russia. A scion of one of New York's original Dutch families, Schuyler enjoyed a privileged childhood that culminated in his matriculation at Yale University at age fifteen. Despite being immature and unpopular (or perhaps because of that condition), Schuyler excelled academically. He stayed in New Haven after graduation, completing an advanced degree in the field of philosophy and psychology, most likely in modern philology, in 1861. His was one of the very first Ph.D. degrees granted on American soil.[10] Schuyler was first attracted to Russia during the Civil War, when he visited a Russian warship harbored in New York. He parlayed this interest and his family connections into a consular posting in Moscow, where he moved in 1867. Schuyler quickly fell in with the Imperial Russian Geographical Society and was enrolled as an honorary member.[11]

Schuyler soon began publishing articles on Russia and Russians in general-interest magazines. One of his first articles, on the Russian peasantry, borrowed from the full inventory of stereotypes about Russian character. Like Baron August von Haxthausen, Schuyler emphasized the stark differences between Russian peasants and western Europeans. Schuyler's characterizations, like Haxthausen's, shared a sensibility with Slavophile commentary on rural Russia, though they drew different implications about Russia's differences from the west. While Slavophiles lauded the stability, spirituality, and collectivism of Russian peasants, Schuyler and others looked at the same traits and derided rural Russians as tradition-bound, fatalistic, and dependent. He emphasized their "conservatism and adherence to traditions," their moods (which ran the gamut from plaintive to depressed), and their deficiencies in organization and independence. The Russian peasant was "a singular compound of laziness . . . [and] carelessness." Peasants lacked most of the capacities necessary to be successful:

they had "no sense whatever of the value of time" and were "singularly improvident." As for intellectual skills, Schuyler had dismally low expectations. He conceded that the peasant "is by no means as stupid as he is often called." Schuyler emphasized the "he"; he believed peasant women were, without exception, "densely stupid." All in all, he concluded, Russian peasants exhibited the symptoms of "primitive" people in their lack of morals, in their "shiftlessness," and in their work habits. Russia's only hope for prosperity was somehow imbuing its peasants with self-reliance, though this would be a difficult task.[12] Like the authors of earlier European accounts, he emphasized inborn traits and connected them directly to Russia's economic failings.

The same traits that Schuyler ascribed to Russian peasants also fit (in his estimation) Central Asians within the Russian Empire. Schuyler traveled through Russian Central Asia in 1873, most likely at the invitation of a member of the Imperial Russian Geographical Society.[13] His descriptions of Central Asia reveal the extent to which he had internalized the Geographical Society's civilizing mission. Schuyler insisted that the "interests of civilization demand[ed] order" in Central Asia; order, in turn, demanded Russian imperial rule. Although he did not shy away from criticism of the Russian administrative practices in the region—indeed, he created a minor international incident after his confidential criticisms appeared in print—Schuyler had no objection to the Russians' overall aims. A strong Russian presence in Central Asia, Schuyler reported to the secretary of state, was "beneficial . . . not only to the [region's] inhabitants but to the world." A diminished presence, in contrast, would soon leave Central Asians living in "anarchy" or "despotism."[14]

Schuyler's positive assessment of Russian activities in Central Asia relied on his low opinion of Central Asians. The Kirghiz, for instance, demonstrated a "simplicity of life" that made them "far more children of nature than most other Asiatics . . . [with] all the faults and virtues of children." Yet even this was an upward revision of Schuyler's first impressions (after an 1869 trip): "the Kirghiz have all of the vices and few of the virtues of savages." Schuyler spent more time on vices than virtues, emphasizing the hedonism, dishonesty, dirtiness, and depravity of the Kirghiz and their neighbors. In his opinion these flaws justified Russian rule in the region. So long as Central Asians valued power over reason, Schuyler claimed, the Russian military campaigns should continue—for the good of Central Asia and the rest of the world.[15]

Schuyler also applied his approval of Russia's imperial mission retroactively to the Europeanizing mission of Tsar Peter the Great. Like the *philo-sophes* writing shortly after Peter's death in 1725, nineteenth-century writers still used Petrine reforms to locate Russia's position on the ranks of civilized nations. St. Petersburg, by then a bustling imperial capital and not just an ambitious settlement built on swampland, reflected what Russia had learned from western Europe, as well as Russia's hoped-for status as a European power. In nineteenth-century Russia, Peter became a symbol of Russia's entry into Europe, the subject of Slavophiles' demonization and westernizers' unstinting praise. Among Peter's most devoted nineteenth-century biographers was a friend of Schuyler's, Aleksandr Brückner, who had planned to commemorate the bicentennial of Peter's birth (in 1872) with a major new historical work celebrating Peter's role in the Europeanization of Russia. It was most likely Brückner who persuaded Schuyler to write a biography of Peter.[16]

Schuyler's work on Peter the Great first appeared in the widely read magazine *Scribner's Monthly* and shortly thereafter appeared in book form.[17] Most of the articles kept their focus sharply on Peter himself: his personality, his education, his travels (especially to Europe), and his family. These sketches were framed by an overall interpretation emphasizing Peter's success in single-handedly bringing Russia out of Asia and into Europe. Like Brückner, Schuyler emphasized pre-Petrine Russia's "oriental" qualities, seeing them in everything from tax laws and diplomatic practice to real estate ownership and relations between the sexes. Even foreign policy reflected Russia's Asian tendencies. Before Peter, Russia stood as "virtually an Oriental power; its envoys understood the feelings and ways of Orientals," thus facilitating smooth relations with the Turks. Schuyler contrasted Russians to the small foreign colony in Moscow, which distinguished itself with a "higher culture." Predictably, Schuyler attached great importance to Peter's 1697 tour of western Europe: it marked "the division between the old Russia . . . and the new."[18] Peter, in Schuyler's framework, strove to turn an Asian nation into a modern European one.

Schuyler's biography of Peter, the first serious historical analysis of Russia undertaken by an American, earned the respect of most reviewers. A posthumously published collection of his essays garnered the praise of James B. Angell, a historian and president of the University of Michigan. In the *American Historical Review*, the organ of a newly professionalizing historical discipline, Angell wrote that Schuyler's works "justly entitled him to a place in this magazine."[19] Whatever his claims to primacy and expertise,

Schuyler could make few claims to originality. His arguments deviated little from those of the major Russian historians of the era, especially Brückner's. The central insight of Schuyler's biography—that European-ization was a centuries-long process of raising inferior cultures to European standards—came mostly from the secondary works upon which he relied. Like Brückner, Schuyler made an explicit connection between Peter's Europeanizing mission in the eighteenth century and later tsars' civilizing mission in Central Asia.

Schuyler's application of the basic narrative of civilization, as reflected in his writing on both Petrine Russia and more recent imperialism, furthermore, had a class inflection. His harsh portrayal of Russian peasants suggested that they too remained uncivilized. Yet while he saw the civilizing and Europeanizing mission at work in eighteenth-century Russia and nineteenth-century Central Asia, Schuyler saw fewer possibilities for Russian peasants to overcome their barbaric state. He traced all three phenomena—Peter's Europeanization of the elites, Russian imperial expansion, and the sorry state of the peasantry—back to the eighteenth century and Peter's "premature" efforts to bring Russia into Europe. By jumping the gun, Peter had forced the Russian tsars to focus on external expansion over internal development.[20]

Schuyler and Kennan held similar views of Russia, in spite of the latter's personal and petty dislike for the former. Like Kennan, Schuyler emphasized stratification within Russian society. Both authors, furthermore, ascribed national character to different social groups within Russia. Finally, they agreed about the dearth of Russia experts in the United States.[21] But their differences were also significant. Whereas Schuyler attributed Russians' defects to national character traits, Kennan saw these as individual, personal failings. And whereas Kennan described Central Asians as exemplars of martial spirit and vaunted individual character, Schuyler saw only primitive tribes.

Kennan's focus on individual character over national character is also evident in his writings about the Siberian exile system. His first book, *Tent Life in Siberia*, did not even mention the exile system.[22] Although he would later become famous for his broadside against exile, Kennan in the 1880s offered a spirited defense of the Russian penal system. He devoted most of an 1882 address to his own exploits in the Russian east; the workings of penal colonies received less attention. When he did describe the exile system, it was primarily to diminish its victims. Prisoners in Siberia received

Kennan's contempt rather than his sympathy; he described the criminals as "vulgar" and the political prisoners as "wide-eyed nihilists." Those sent to Siberia, in short, lacked the most essential aspects of character—as always, Kennan's key measure of personal worth. Those foreign reformers who criticized Siberian exile, Kennan concluded, exaggerated its cruelty and overestimated the personal quality of its inmates.[23] Still, Kennan hoped to return to Russia in order to establish definitively the conditions of exiles in Siberia. In a pitch to a newspaper editor, he made the case using the idiom of science. Given all the stories about exile to Siberia—"romantic" as well as "tragic" ones—Americans needed "real definite knowledge" about the circumstances there. Kennan's key issues involved the mix of political prisoners and common criminals, which soon came to define his perspective on the whole exile system.[24]

Although the newspaper editor declined Kennan's proposal, *Century* magazine agreed to sponsor Kennan's return to Russia. In 1884, Kennan visited Moscow and St. Petersburg in order to prepare for a lengthier trip through Siberia the following year. His articles began to appear in 1887, running monthly for two years. They later appeared as a book, *Siberia and the Exile System,* in 1891. The Siberia series combined narratives of personal conversion and scientific discovery. Kennan admitted the prejudices he brought to his travels: "all my prepossessions were favorable to the Russian Government." He started out deeply critical of the political prisoners, whom he had assumed to be "unreasonable and wrong-headed fanatics of the anarchist type with which we in the United States had become so familiar." But his first-hand study of the exile system exploded these assumptions. His views had been "changed by an overwhelming mass of evidence."[25]

Kennan's observations convinced him, first and foremost, that the revolutionaries whom he had disparaged were in fact men and women of character. They were not the "more or less incomprehensible 'cranks'" he had expected, but "bright, intelligent, well-informed men and women, with warm affections, quick sympathies, generous impulses, and high standards of honor and duty"—all ingredients of the good character so central to Kennan's world view. The so-called nihilists were in fact well-educated, familiar with the works of Shakespeare, Mill, and Spencer, and up-to-date on contemporary American affairs. One political exile might even "have been taken for a young professor, or a post-graduate student, in the Johns Hopkins University." He proudly recounted meeting political prisoners in

Tomsk, accompanied by an official from the Ministry of the Interior. That official served not as a chaperon but as a full participant in the meeting, which was based "upon the common footing of personal character." As he wrote from Tomsk to his *Century* editor, "One sees at once that they [the political prisoners] are educated, reasonable self-controlled gentlemen, not different in any essential respect from one's self."[26] Politics mattered less to Kennan than character.

Kennan's newfound enthusiasm for political prisoners in Siberia led him to criticize the exile system, especially its treatment of different types of prisoners. In previous writings, Kennan had lumped revolutionaries together with criminals as collectively unworthy. After his trip to Siberia in the 1880s, though, he went to great pains to establish the differences between them. Like the active political reformers of his era, Kennan insisted on the scientific classification of criminals. With this classification came specialization and hierarchy. Just as American reformers criticized their own penal system for treating all felons identically, Kennan railed against the Siberian exile system for forcing men and women of good character to associate with common criminals. This mixing was not just a hardship for the politicos; it violated the social order. Kennan's biographer Frederick Travis makes this point well: Kennan "*never* expressed sympathy for the plight of the 'common' criminal exiles; in fact some of his sympathy for the political prisoners derived from the fact that they had to endure contact with the common criminals."[27] His views of the exile system, then, were profoundly shaped by the social hierarchies that he framed in terms of individual character. His conception of cultural difference more broadly was similarly defined by personal character. Compared with other expert writings (even those from his own era), Kennan's descriptions of Russia were deeply imbued with Victorian sentiments: rooted in a strong sense of social hierarchy, yet offering hopes for improvement; more concerned with individuals than with peoples. Kennan's view of Russia differed from both earlier and later analyses. Prior European accounts had little room for improvement, while subsequent American ones focused primarily on national rather than individual character. Kennan's ideas thus represent a transitional moment in the emergence of a particularly American perspective on Russia and Russians.

Not all American ideas about Russia were as distinctively American as Kennan's. Schuyler, after all, echoed the writings of his Russian interlocutors. And William Dudley Foulke, the author of another prominent book about Russia, sounded suspiciously like the French historian Leroy-Beaulieu. In comparison with his friend Kennan, Foulke incorporated more fully the notion of an essentially Russian nature into his views of Russia's present circumstances and future prospects. After an early career as a reformer (working for civil service reform and woman's suffrage, among other causes), Foulke rather mysteriously turned to the study of Russia. "I became greatly interested," he coyly recalled, "in the history of Russia, especially in the events showing the encroachments of that empire" upon its neighbors.[28] Not able to speak Russian, Foulke relied heavily on French books about Russia.[29] The organization of his first and only book on Russia, *Slav or Saxon* (1887), follows those of Leroy-Beaulieu and Rambaud, opening with a detailed description of Russia's land and climate. Citing Leroy-Beaulieu directly, Foulke wrote that Russia's broad open spaces militated against "originality and individuality." Weather also played a role: the "long winters of torpor and inactivity" alternated with short summers of frantic work. This left Russians prone to "excesses of liberalism and conservatism, of veneration and cynicism, of hope and despondency, of intelligence and ignorance."[30]

These traits contained significant political implications, according to Foulke. Russians' lack of individuality conduced to a centralized government, making people "much more easily subjected to the control of a single will." And the lack of originality or distinctiveness worked in the same way: "the people became a unit like the land, their occupations are the same, their thoughts, their aspirations." Even the halting reforms of mid-century Russia could be explained by character traits. The Russians' tendency to extremes dictated both "the boldness of their projects of reform [and] their timidity in execution." In sum, national character shaped political structure: "a peculiar fitness for this form of government seems . . . to be ingrained in the Russian people." Foulke's pessimism was tempered by the claim that this submissive Russian character, so well suited to despotism, was not natural to the Russians but had been imposed upon them. National character, in this formulation, was ingrained but not innate.[31]

Russia's tendency to despotism, Foulke averred, had arrived from the east. Like the French historians whose work he had studied, he identified many Russian characteristics as Asian in origin.[32] The Asiatic elements had entered Russian character and Russian life while Slavs were under the so-called Tartar Yoke—when they were ruled by Mongol Khans, from the thirteenth to the sixteenth centuries. These elements had "retarded" Russia's growth and delayed its "civilization."[33] The category of Asia played many roles in Foulke's writings. In a travelogue on Russia, Foulke bemoaned his confusion about the "inscrutable thoughts, motives and methods of the vast population of the Orient." Throughout that book, he located Russia in Asia. Everything from the Moscow skyline to the clothing of St. Petersburg drivers was "oriental." The Asian elements both predated and outlasted Peter. Foulke, like Schuyler, saw Peter's modernization plans as a violent effort to "drag [Russia] . . . into the current of European life." The tsar's failure meant that Asia represented not just Russia's past but also parts of its present.[34]

Russian character and Asian heritage, Foulke fulminated, had created a barbaric state that was now threatening benign British rule in Asia. The contest between Slav and Saxon—which Foulke used as the very title of his book—was thus a battle between "the last great despotism on earth" and the civilized powers. Here Foulke quickly adopted the heated language of political debate, referring to Russia's expansionism as "the growth of everything we detest." Russian ideas, he continued feverishly, were "so outlandish, so semi-barbarous in every way . . . that we do not see how they can be forced down the throat of humanity."[35] Russia's domestic despotism and international aspirations endangered not just the United States but civilization itself.

The historian and cultural critic Brooks Adams, writing fifteen years after Foulke, concurred with this argument. Adams blamed Russia's "Asiatic heritage" for its expansion. But free of Foulke's alarmism, the historian saw one bright spot in this heritage: while it explained Russia's tendency toward territorial aggrandizement, it also doomed those same efforts to failure. Here he cited flaws in Russian character to explain the failed policies. Although he admitted that Russians possessed "patience and tenacity of life," they remained "ignorant and uninventive, indolent and improvident." Like Foulke and the French historians of the era, Adams attributed the Russian character, which he derided as "defective," to Russia's topography and climate.[36] Adams and Foulke had both explained Russia's undesirable expansion in the late nineteenth century as a result of both Russian national character and Asian governmental tendencies. To Adams, this national character defined Russia's future as well as its present.

Compared with Adams, Foulke saw Russian character as more fluid and therefore more dangerous. In his opinion, it shaped not only Russia's internal despotism and external expansion but also its economic circumstances.

Contrasting Slav and Saxon, Foulke stressed not just political conditions—despotism versus democracy—but also economic performance.[37] In the concluding chapter of his book, Foulke juxtaposed the "great . . . advance of human progress in those communities [promoting] voluntary co-operation and free industrial activity" and the retardation in countries dominated by "the stern methods of military subjugation." The form of government, in short, determined a nation's economic prospects. Given Foulke's arguments that despotism was firmly implanted in the Russian terrain (albeit originally an import from points east) and fertilized by the traits of Russian national character, Foulke implied that national character limited economic achievement. By providing for the success of autocracy, national character thus dictated the economic circumstances of Russia.

Foulke was too deeply imbued with a Victorian sense of universal progress to make this claim unambiguously. He offered a plan for Russia's future that contained both political and economic components: "The hope of coming times lies in the overthrow of the centralized despotism, in the establishment of civil liberty in Russia, and in the substitution of industrial methods for its present military system."[38] Russia might evolve into a state with civilized economic and political systems. Yet here Foulke's optimism for the future of Russia came up against his original explanations for Russian despotism and backwardness in the first place. If despotism was the result of Russian national character, and national character was in turn the result of topography and climate, under what circumstances (other than continental shift or global warming) could a new form of government emerge? And if this despotism hindered Russian economic progress, what chances were there for material progress? Material advance, he wrote, would require a change in Russian national character. He believed that national character could be shaped by outside forces; given that it had become congenial to despotism under the Khans, it could, in principle anyway, be made congenial to democracy.

Slav or Saxon received a positive, if muted, response from American Russia-watchers. George Kennan wrote to Foulke enthusiastically about the book, as did the Russian émigré revolutionary Sergei Kravchinskii (writing under his pseudonym, Stepniak). Both appreciated Foulke's summation of Russian history, and Kravchinskii singled out for praise Foulke's chapter on the "Russian climatic and geographic and natural conditions in connection with the national character." An anonymous reviewer in the *North American Review* agreed with Foulke's criticisms of Russian politics, questioning only his optimism: could the Russians really become free?[39] Foulke's book and the responses to it suggest the confusion of American ideas about Russia. Russian character determined the economic and political life of the nation. And while geography and meteorology created and defined character, that character was not immutable.

Whereas Foulke (like Leroy-Beaulieu) used national character to sound a tocsin about Russia, other Americans used character to encourage closer ties between the two countries; in doing so, they repeated Rambaud's argument. The translator Isabel Hapgood, one of Victorian America's most prolific Russophiles, used Russian character to make her case. In numerous articles, in lectures on the Chautauqua circuit, and in a steady stream of translations and correspondence, Hapgood offered energetic support for Russia's writers and government in the 1880s and 1890s.[40] Her indefatigable efforts to bring Russian literature to Americans came to fruition in the late 1880s, as her championing of Leo Tolstoy led to a surge of American interest. Harmony was short-lived, however; she soon broke with Tolstoy over artistic differences.[41]

Hapgood's rift with Tolstoy did not end her enthusiasm for Russian culture. She still promoted to American audiences what she saw as typically Russian cultural expressions—literature (even Tolstoy's), epic songs (*byliny*), and music. Hapgood used each of these genres to illustrate Russia's distinctive traditions. In celebrating Tolstoy, for instance, she highlighted his differences from westernizers like the novelist Ivan Turgenev.[42] A strong believer in Russia's unique artistic contributions—based on its differences from American and European cultures—Hapgood enumerated many traits that could be found in all Russians. Even while distancing herself from simplifications of Russians' "'complicated' national character," she concluded that they possessed a "naturally simple, sympathetic disposition . . . tinged with a friendly warmth whose influence is felt as soon as one crosses the frontier." Even after asserting her wariness about such generalizations, Hapgood offered her own: Russians are "as a nation, too long-suffering and lenient in certain directions . . . allow[ing] too much personal independence in certain things." Her book *Russian Rambles* is sprinkled with similar assessments of Russian character derived from a set of familiar character traits: Russians have a "native . . . courtesy," are famous for their endurance, and "possess a natural dignity which prevents their asserting themselves in an unpleasant manner except in rare cases."[43] While putting a positive gloss on these traits, Hapgood's catalog was strikingly similar to those of Russia's harshest critics. What critics termed passivity, she called dignity. Russian peasants, she suggested, exaggerated these aspects of Russian character.

Presumably echoing the paternalistic conceptions of her Russian noble interlocutors, Hapgood emphasized peasants' unreliable and irrepressibly hedonistic behavior. A retroactive apologist for serfdom, she observed in the 1890s—three decades after emancipation—that peasants "retained a soft spot in their hearts for the comforts and irresponsibility of the good old days of serfdom."[44] Her argument thus echoed that of apologists for American slavery. White writers from Northern and Southern states nostalgically proclaimed slavery the ideal social organization for blacks. Slaves had developed (in the words of one journalist) "mutual family interests and kind personal feelings" toward their owners and masters, without whom they became "lazy" and "improvident."[45] Hapgood applied this condescending view of Russian rural-dwellers to the major Russian news story in America in the 1890s, the famine of 1891–1892.

As the American "Tolstoy craze" waned in the early 1890s, new events propelled Russia into American magazines and newspapers. Reports of failed harvests and widespread starvation in Russia attracted significant attention in the American press. Russia's agricultural circumstances had always been highly vulnerable to poor weather; one economic historian estimated that famine occurred every six to seven years throughout recorded Russian history.[46] Scholars have traced this precariousness to a variety of circumstances and policies. Technological and organizational innovations that improved western European agriculture rarely made their way to rural Russia. Government policy also played a major role. As a trio of successive finance ministers—Nicholas Bunge (1883–1887), Ivan Vyshnegradskii (1887–1892), and Sergei Witte (1892–1903)—undertook a state-sponsored industrialization drive, they relied increasingly on revenues from Russia's largest sector, agriculture. Exports were especially important, as these finance ministers sought to accumulate sufficient reserves to go on the gold standard. Grain was the most readily available export.[47] Russian economists and economic officials of the era clearly recognized the trade-offs. When confronted with the news that a potential harvest shortfall might reduce gold reserves, Vyshnegradskii summarized his policy succinctly, if harshly: "We will not eat enough, but we will export!"[48]

The government's export drive, in conjunction with generally low agricultural productivity, left much of Russia vulnerable to food crises. Contingent factors—poor weather and an ill-timed cholera epidemic—made the crisis of 1891–1892 even worse. The Central Producer Region, home to some thirty million Russians in and around the Volga Valley, experienced especially severe problems. The harvest of 1891 was roughly half its normal level, with some provinces seeing declines of up to 75 percent.[49] In spite of such dramatic numbers, the tsarist government was slow to establish a relief agency.

Only in November 1891, months after initial warnings, did the government establish the Special Committee for the Aid of the Needy Regions Suffering from Poor Harvests. With Crown Prince Nicholas (the future Tsar Nicholas II) at the helm, this committee provided food loans to as many as 11 million peasants each month. It also coordinated relief and sanitation activities in the countryside, aimed both at feeding the population and at slowing the spread of cholera. Nevertheless, as many as 400,000 Russians died from starvation and cholera that year.[50]

Although the Special Committee did not solicit foreign assistance, it soon received many offers of aid from American groups. Relief organizations in Minnesota, Wisconsin, and Pennsylvania had sprouted up even before the Russian committee. By mid-winter these groups, joined by the American Red Cross, undertook fundraising campaigns. A national group, the Russian Famine Relief Committee, convened many American notables, including the American minister to St. Petersburg, fifteen senators, and twenty-two governors.[51] The famine thus brought a new type of commentator into American discussions about Russia: the relief official. Many of these officials adopted the character-based analyses of Russian life that other experts had employed.

In terms that paralleled those of Haxthausen, Donald MacKenzie Wallace, and other European analysts of rural Russia, American diplomats and relief workers frequently connected the famine to Russian traits like laziness and endurance. This logic resonated with that of American urban reformers. In the words of one historian, these reformers blamed poverty on the "moral deficiencies and character flaws of the poor."[52] Two American representatives in St. Petersburg, Charles Emory Smith (1890–1892) and Andrew Dickson White (1892–1894), implied that the famine's causes and consequences were rooted in peasant deficiencies. White, the first president of both Cornell University (1868) and the American Historical Association (1884), had begun his distinguished career by writing about Russia. After graduating from college in 1853, he and a friend (Daniel Coit

Gilman, later the founding president of Johns Hopkins University) worked together in the American legation in St. Petersburg. Resident in the Russian capital in the 1850s, White quickly came to dislike his hosts. In his private letters he railed against the imperial regime: "There is no government so thoroughly barbarous . . . unless it will be found in early Asiatic monarchies."[53] Even though he, like American reformers, was willing to blame the poor for their condition, he saw Russia as a special case.

White's stay in Russia barely preceded the Great Reforms, the major transformations in Russian political and economic life undertaken by the tsar-liberator Alexander II.[54] After the 1855 defeat in the Crimean War, official Russia undertook a thorough examination of social and political institutions. By the late 1850s, the question of serfdom received special attention. As Russian elites contemplated reform of this institution, the last vestige of feudalism in a major European power, questions of Russia's future came to the fore. The emancipation of the serfs in 1861 promised great changes in Russian society. But these promises were not fulfilled. Rural-dwellers shed the status of serfs but nevertheless struggled under massive debts in the form of redemption payments designed to reimburse the landlords for the loss of their property. They offered anything but redemption for the former serfs, who faced severely restricted economic opportunities. The emancipation edicts, furthermore, vested the peasant commune with control over land and labor.

White used the occasion of emancipation to return to Russia, if not literally then at least intellectually. He wrote an article for *Atlantic Monthly* in 1862 describing the end of serfdom and the fate of the peasantry. White emphasized the role of great men in his analysis, as he had while living in St. Petersburg. In his estimation, Peter the Great "transformed Russia from a petty Asiatic horde to a great European power." Alexander II represented the "glory of Russia" in its nineteenth-century incarnation. But White also wrote about the peasants themselves, describing how the end of serfdom shaped their futures. He characterized the peasants as stubborn, curious, reverent of both divine and terrestrial powers, and "naturally kind." These traits, White implied, did not preclude a democracy but necessitated what he called a "patriarchal democratic system," one in which social betters would look after the peasants' best interests. The patriarchal aspects of this system, White hoped, could allow the former serfs to convert their "cunning and cheatery" into behavior more appropriate in a market economy.[55] The key to Russia's future lay in its peasantry and their behavior.

White and other American observers carried these assessments of the Russian peasantry into their analyses of the famine of 1891–1892. They used a variety of peasant traits to explain the causes and consequences of the famine. Observers often cited peasants' lack of self-control. White's predecessor Charles Emory Smith, for instance, called peasants "thriftless and improvident," insisting that such behavior had led them into their present plight.[56] The lack of control manifested itself most visibly and frequently, Americans suggested, in front of a bottle. Excessive drinking became a symbol for irresponsibility; as one British relief worker put it, rural Russia consisted of "King Vodka and his retainers."[57] A prominent relief worker from Philadelphia admitted that the drought played some role but nevertheless insisted that drinking remained "one of the real underlying causes of destitution" in Russian villages.[58] William Edgar, who spearheaded the Minnesota relief efforts, went further, blaming the bulk of Russia's economic problems on peasants' improvidence and predilection for vodka.[59] George Kennan also blamed peasants' woes on drink, but pointed his finger at the Russian government, whose reliance on profits from its alcohol monopoly, he wrote, led it to promote drinking. Ready access to alcohol provided too much temptation for innately intemperate peasants. Thus peasant drunkenness, to Kennan, was another problem created by the corrupt and regressive autocracy.[60]

White and others also blamed peasant fatalism for the famine's spread. This trait was so ingrained that it even endangered peasants' lives, White argued. Ranking Russian peasants as "little, if any, above Asiatic barbarism," he concluded that their fatalism led to apathy about hygiene, which in turn left them susceptible to diseases like cholera.[61] The newspaper editor Murat Halstead, writing in *The Cosmopolitan*, largely agreed. His article cited a poor work ethic as the primary cause of Russia's economic troubles. Halstead blamed peasants for their own sufferings, but—perhaps because he doubted the peasants' ability to take responsibility for their own welfare—he saw government policy as the root cause. What Halstead called the peasants' "fatal submissiveness" had been cultivated by the government.[62] Similarly, merchant-turned-relief-official Francis Reeves blamed the peasants' problems on their resort to "the outer darkness of a blind fatalism." Like Halstead and Kennan, Reeves did not place ultimate blame for such behavior on the peasants, but instead accused the Russian Orthodox Church of enforcing this stoicism.[63] Reeves thus took a trait that Hapgood had praised—Russian spirituality—and reframed it in negative terms. But Reeves, like Halstead and especially Kennan, also used these traits to make a political point. Peasant characteristics may have led to the famine, but ruling authorities, the interlinked church and state, bore the ultimate responsibility.

The famine also offered many American observers proof of a trait they had long associated with the Russians, the ability to withstand great hardship. Hapgood mentioned this in her praise of Russian character, as did more critical writers. William Edgar, for instance, wrote how the sufferings of the "patient Russian peasant in his unparalleled misery" touched the hearts of Midwestern farmers and millers. It was this outpouring of feeling that led to his own efforts on behalf of Russian famine relief.[64] Kravchinskii wrote on the eve of the famine that the peasants' best hope lay in overcoming the "dumb patience" that had hitherto defined them.[65] The British Russophile W. T. Stead, writing in the American edition of his London-based *Review of Reviews,* offered a similar explanation with more exaggerated language; the peasants were "most long-suffering, inured to hardship and accustomed to privations, stolidity and passivity."[66] Stead's American counterpart in promoting a positive image of Russia, Isabel Hapgood, similarly extolled Russian peasant heartiness.[67] But it was the diplomat Charles Emory Smith who made the most of this trait, suggesting that Russians' unique talent for suffering would help them return to eventual normalcy:

> Worn and emaciated with long struggle, stripped of their material, the peasants face the requirements of a new harvest year under a load which would crush almost any other people. But their patience and endurance are without limit, and whatever their destiny, they accept it with a grim stoicism.[68]

Peasants' passivity (even under difficult conditions) both explained their problems and provided hope for a solution.

Finally, American relief workers often maligned the peasants' intellectual abilities. Even the generally sympathetic William Edgar admitted that peasants' "brains do not appear to be very active." Elsewhere he called Russian agriculturalists "steeped in superstition and quite beyond the reach of reason." He even compared peasant women to cows in their blank and thoughtless expressions.[69] Clara Barton, the head of the American Red Cross, similarly derided the peasants' ignorance and superstition, calling them "blind to the light of civilization."[70]

The ostensible traits of Russian peasants made them susceptible not just to extreme poverty and even famine but also to plunder at the hands of Jews in the Russian countryside. Discussions of Russia in the 1880s and 1890s frequently revolved around Jews, in large part because of the prodigious numbers of Russian Jews emigrating to western Europe and especially the United States following the pogroms of 1881. The peasants' limited intellect, poor work habits, and ingenuousness left them prey, the argument went, to speculators and usurers in the villages, including both *kulaks* (rich peasants) and Shylocks. According to one author, the peasants' fatalism and "guileless" attitude could not match the Jews' "concentrated avarice, craftiness, rascality and financial ability."[71] Such views were also held by American diplomats in St. Petersburg, many of whom warned that direct famine relief would benefit not the benighted peasants but only their Jewish exploiters.[72] At one level, these statements represent the era's anti-Semitism. But at another, they demonstrate how national-character assessments—of both Jews and Russians—shaped perceptions of and policies toward Russia.

Some American observers implied that peasants' best protection against Jews came from their former masters and present landlords. Edgar shared Hapgood's nostalgia for Russian serfdom. Like the literary impresario, Edgar argued that "the peasant is apparently much worse off [in 1893] than he was before the emancipation," especially if one set aside "the question of personal liberty." He even saw advantages in the famine crisis: it was a "blessing in disguise" because it brought "the peasant and his ancient ruler back into their old relations." Edgar based this nostalgic claim not only on peasants' inability to look after their own affairs but also on their fierce loyalty to their landlords and especially to the tsar. The peasants had no desire for liberty, Edgar wrote, but were happy as serfs working for their owners. Like American slaves, Russian peasants could prosper only under the tutelage of a noble landlord who could assume responsibility for their development. A review in the fledgling journal *Annals of the American Academy of Political and Social Science* expressed a similar idea: Russian peasants' loyalty, dependence, and lack of interest in liberty combined to leave the peasant eager to return to dependence on their landlords.[73] Whether or not the authors made explicit reference to the circumstances of recently freed slaves in the American South, the power of a similar false nostalgia is evident throughout American writings on Russia in this era.

Whereas many American observers blamed the peasants' stupidity, fatalism, endurance, and dependence for their poor conditions, others saw the organization of the peasant economy as the principal problem. Assessments of economic institutions, particularly the *mir*, or commune, were closely connected to assessments of character. As a writer in *The Chautauquan* commented, the *mir* was the best expression of the "most essentially national instincts of the Russian character": a sense of "primitive equality," of mutual dependence, and of patriarchal organization, not to mention the traits of loyalty and lethargy.[74] Yet, Edgar and others noted, the *mir* was at the same time responsible for Russia's antiquated and unproductive agricultural system. Thus national character, manifest in the *mir*, was a leading factor in Russia's economic troubles. Articles in *Annals* and *Forum*—both excerpted in the widely read *Review of Reviews*—criticized the "despotism of the *mir*," which crushed any opportunities for individual enrichment. Only through "individual ambition," Edgar argued, could Russia plug "the great hollow void [that is, agriculture] in the very heart of the Empire."[75] While favoring an individualistic turn in the Russian economy, many American observers saw few prospects for such a change. Edgar echoed Haxthausen in claiming that as unproductive and backward as it was, the communal system fit the character of the peasantry.

Some American observers underscored their particularism by arguing that Russia lay outside the boundaries of Europe. The diplomat Charles Emory Smith wondered in print: "Is it possible that a single drought has produced a famine of this sweeping character? . . . Is it possible that such utter destitution, which reads more like ancient or remote oriental visitations, can come within the range of the modern European system?"[76] The famine was proof that Russia belonged to a different place; such devastation could never happen in a truly European country. George Kennan offered an answer to Smith's question: "There is probably no other country in Europe where, after the failure of the crops for a single year, the peasantry would be reduced in less than two months to living on roots, bran and weeds."[77]

If Russia was not in Europe, where did it belong? Many writers followed up on Smith's suggestion of "oriental visitations" to suggest that the famine proved that Russia was indeed an Asian nation. Observers compared Russia to India, in part because of the colony's size but also because of its frequent famines (including 1866, 1877, and 1891).[78] One article in *The Nation* even viewed the Indian situation as more favorable than the Russian one because of the effectiveness of new British famine-prevention efforts.[79] The fact of the famine only confirmed that Russia's position was closer to

Asia than to Europe. To particularists the Russian crisis was the result of Russian national character.

To other observers, though, the famine was proof not that Russia was outside of Europe but that Russia's present was Europe's past. Neatly inverting Marx's claim that the industrialized nations offered a backward country "the image of its own future," these observers suggested that the current Russian crisis had been a frequent occurrence in Europe—but only in Europe's past. The relief official William Edgar, for instance, described his writing about the Russian famine as "a grim, gaunt fairy tale, of years long past, of conditions which advancing civilization have [sic] made impossible." *Review of Reviews* also implied that famines were an anachronism in the modern world; the Russian famine, its editorial declared, "gives us a glimpse of what men suffered in other centuries."[80] Russia was on the same path of progress as the rest of Europe, but lagged far behind. Russia was different, this argument implied, but not inherently so.

American observers of the late nineteenth century certainly did not welcome Russia into the circle of modern nations and used the language of European commentators to promote exclusion. Yet they offered different, even contradictory explanations for Russia's exclusion. To Foulke, White, and Smith, Russia's differences were innate, rendering its inhabitants inferior in intellect and industry. Others, including Halstead, Reeves, and most notably Kennan, blamed these same traits on Russians' autocracy or orthodoxy, not their nationality. To this latter group, the famine demonstrated not that Russia's problems were inherent but that Russians could—at some distant date—achieve European levels of industry and material standards if they could only throw off their oppressors.

Not all American participants in debates over Russia fell in line with these two positions. Two Russian immigrants, Isaac Hourwich and Vladimir Simkhovitch, offered a more radical universalist argument that Russia was at that moment becoming a modern industrial nation. The immigrants' claims, rooted in Marx's ideas, set American discussions of Russia in sharp relief. Rejecting national-character stereotypes entirely, they instead portrayed the *mir* as the primary source of the peasants' oppression. While they agreed with native-born Americans' assessments of the commune, they placed higher hopes on its dissolution. Their hopes were rooted in the belief that the *mir* was a mechanism for political and economic exploitation, not a repository of Russia's spiritual values. Although the two immigrants both lived in New York in the 1890s, their ideas were more intimately tied to Russian discussions of the rural question than to American ones. Their attacks on Populism were similarly part of a Russian argument. While both the United States and Russia saw debates over Populism, the ideas and meanings of the movement differed substantially in the two countries. Russian Populism began as an elite movement "to the people," whereas American Populists had a distinctly anti-elitist tinge. Russian Populists, in spite of their battles with Marxists, were more firmly rooted in Marxian debates than were their American counterparts. Political context also mattered: American Populists rose and fell in electoral politics, while Russian Populists faced the threat of constant harassment and arrest from tsarist police.[81]

Simkhovitch and especially Hourwich were engaged in the heated Marxist-Populist debates of the late nineteenth century, which took place among intellectuals in the Siberian villages housing exiles, in underground *kruzhki* (reading circles) across Russia, and in the communities of Russian revolutionary exiles scattered throughout western Europe. Most participants agreed that the ultimate goal for Russia was communism, but they differed sharply on how to achieve that goal. The dispute hinged on the role of the peasant commune. While Populists celebrated the *mir*'s primitive communalism as the germ of a communist Russia, the Marxists saw the commune as a relic of feudalism and an impediment to historical progress. One of the most significant—and heftiest—Marxist contributions was by Vladimir Lenin, *The Development of Capitalism in Russia* (1899), which insisted that expanding market relations were on the verge of destroying the commune, ushering Russia closer to capitalism, and therefore communism.

Lenin, prone to composing withering criticisms of other authors, had high praise for Hourwich. He noted Hourwich's "splendid" work and "marvel[led]" at his statistical skills. Hourwich had written only the second American dissertation on a Russian topic, but that hardly accounts for Lenin's kudos. In his dissertation Hourwich argued that the peasant commune was collapsing under the pressures of economic inequality and the spread of a cash economy.[82] That his argument paralleled Lenin's should come as no surprise. Hourwich had long been active in Russian radical circles; his sister, in fact, had helped translate *Das Kapital* into Russian. His own activities led not only to his exile in Siberia (during which he met George Kennan) but also to his eventual flight from Russia. He settled in New York, where he edited a weekly Russian-language newspaper, *Progress*, and enrolled at Columbia.[83] Hourwich's argument was precisely that of Friedrich Engels, who had written that the famine "in the end must serve the cause of human progress," though Hourwich felt the need to declare his "independence of judgement" in reaching the same conclusions as Engels.[84] Both blamed the famine not on the peasants but on the general conditions of the Russian economy, on "the backwardness of Russian agriculture." Both Hourwich and Engels, furthermore, saw the famine as a landmark event for Russia, signaling the emergence of a new social system: capitalism.[85] In this sense good news came with (in fact came *from*) the bad: the famine would help separate workers from the land and would turn peasants into workers. By spurring progress toward capitalism, the famine had brought communism that much closer.[86]

Hourwich's analysis closely paralleled that of another émigré to the United States, similarly inclined toward Marx's vision of progress. Vladimir Simkhovitch completed his dissertation at the University of Halle (Germany), where he met his future wife, Mary Kingsbury. When she returned to the United States in 1898 to run the Greenwich House settlement, he soon followed, eventually landing an appointment as professor of economic history at Columbia University.[87] A longtime student of Marxism, Simkhovitch drew many of his key concepts from the Marxist tradition; he later wrote a monograph on varieties of Marxism.[88] Following these concepts, Simkhovitch associated the Russian *mir* with what he called Russia's "dwarf-economy" (*Zwergwirtschaft*). The commune, he wrote, impoverished not just its own members but the national economy as a whole. Simkhovitch targeted two common views of the *mir:* that it was the natural and authentic realization of essential Russianness, and that it provided a possible path to freedom. He dismissed as a "fable" the claim that the *mir* was organic (*ursprünglich*); it was simply an artificial creation to improve tax collection. Nor was the *mir* uniquely Russian; it was instead a form of social organization that appeared (or had appeared) in all nations.[89] If the *mir*'s past was a myth, so was the notion that it could provide for Russia's future. Although Populists invested the *mir* with their hopes for a communist Russia that would provide for peasants' freedom, Simkhovitch doubted the feasibility of this perspective. The Populists were instead fighting for the "preservation of a system under which an existence worthy of the dignity of man is completely impossible."[90] The key to Russia's future was the elimination of the *mir*. To the extent that the famine could speed that process, even a catastrophe of that magnitude could be beneficial. Recognizing the "sufferings of the present generation of peasants and artisans," Simkhovitch looked steadfastly toward a brighter future: "painful as this period is, it must soon pass away."[91]

Simkhovitch and his friend and fellow Marxist Isaac Hourwich agreed on most issues about the *mir:* it was not a manifestation of the Slavic spirit; it oppressed its members and hindered economic growth; and its decline, signaled by the famine of 1891–1892, was both imminent and beneficial.[92] Framing their analyses in terms of economic structures rather than personality types, Simkhovitch and Hourwich believed that the commune represented Russia's past but not its essence. Russia, to them, was not a mythical and mystical land, remote from Europe. Its development was simply one more chapter in the universal narrative of progress, slightly later than but no different from earlier chapters set in Britain, France, Germany, and the United States. Yet these ideas had little currency in an American context. Hourwich and Simkhovitch interacted more with each other, and with socialist colleagues abroad, than with other observers in the United States. Their writings on the famine and its aftermath stand in sharp contrast to American writings.

This contrast between émigré Marxists and native-born Americans is visible in the ways in which various authors in the United States distanced Russia from themselves. The divergent descriptions reveal the extent as well as the essence of the divide between Hourwich and Simkhovitch's universalism and the others' particularism. Universalists agreed with particularists that Russia was not like the United States or western Europe, but used different language and different logic to make the case. Universalists saw Russia as backward or underdeveloped. Like other backward nations, it would eventually reach a higher stage of history, capitalism. Russia had yet to show the signs of civilized society, Hourwich concluded, but it nevertheless would march slowly on the path of historical progress.[93] Events like famine were unfortunate necessities en route to progress. Russia's ultimate fate was no different from that of any other nation.

Most American writers, in contrast to these universalists, emphasized Russia's differences from Europe and used the country's particularities to explain its predicament. They vested distinctive institutions, like the *mir,* with mythical origins, considering them manifestations of the Russian spirit. Russian character, in turn, was rooted, quite literally, in the soil. Echoing if not quite imitating European writers of the day, American observers emphasized Russian character and traced it to the Russian land and

Russian climate. Russia's political institutions, its economy, and its people owed their distinctiveness to the most specific features of geography and meteorology. Unlike the French historians whom they often drew upon, American authors like George Kennan and William Dudley Foulke could imagine Russian development and Russian progress. Yet their arguments along these lines were at times vague and inconsistent; indeed, Kennan and Foulke devoted more time to cataloguing differences than to theorizing about convergence. Their free appropriation of American analogies— about freedpeople, felons, and farmers—suggests both the implicit universalism and the amateur reformism of their work. Yet at the root of their arguments, or in the knot of their intertwined explanations, was the idea that Russia could someday overcome its natural limits as well as the shackles of autocracy. This belief contained a kernel of universalism but nevertheless differed from the full-fledged universalism of Hourwich and Simkhovitch. The immigrants' ideas, imported from Russia via Siberia and Germany but ultimately traceable back to Marx, had little influence on mainstream Russia experts in the United States. As American experts sought to explain Russian events—and as Russia itself hurtled toward revolution— they found answers in national history, national character, and national uniqueness.

3

Studying Our Nearest
Oriental Neighbor

The establishment of American research universities and the elaboration of social-scientific disciplines within them brought new attention to Russia in the decade following the famine. An earlier group of self-defined intellectuals, members of the American Social Science Association, had demonstrated no interest whatsoever in Russia. That group's organ, the *Journal of Social Science,* published only one article on Russia in its four decades— and that was a letter by a Russian that appeared in the journal's inaugural year, 1869.[1] But the 1890s saw some changes. America's oldest university, Harvard, hired the nation's first scholar who devoted significant attention to the study of Russia. Archibald Cary Coolidge contributed not only intellectual but also financial resources to the study of Russia in the United States. Because his interest in Russia emerged from his training in the history of international relations, Coolidge all but ignored internal Russian developments. And the University of Chicago hired its first Russia specialists soon after opening its doors in 1892. In contrast to Coolidge, Chicago's Samuel Northrop Harper studied Russia out of his hopes for political liberalization there. The two experts also applied their energies differently: Coolidge's work as scholar, advisor, and impresario earned him the title of the father of Russian studies in the United States.[2] By this measure, Harper might be termed the field's bachelor uncle; though he devoted more time to Russia than Coolidge did, Harper left no progeny or legacy.

The familial resemblance between Coolidge and Harper can be traced back to the writings of the French historians Anatole Leroy-Beaulieu and Alfred Rambaud, with whom both Americans had direct contact. The establishment of Russia as a legitimate field for academic study solidified the role these two French historians would play in American thought. Although the professionalization of history proceeded slowly in its early years, its principal aims all tended toward the ideas propounded by Leroy-Beaulieu and Rambaud. Professional historians wrote primarily for other scholars, applied broad theories rather than relying on personal observation, and explicitly addressed the works of previous scholars.[3] In seeking to meet these professional goals, Coolidge and Harper paid close attention to geography and climate as well as to the persistence of character traits in their explanations of the Russian past and explications of present-day Russia.

The initial push for university-based studies of Russia emerged, surprisingly, not from within the academy but in a broader public debate. Isabel Hapgood, looking for ways to keep American attentions on Russia after the famine crisis waned in 1892, started things off. In a letter to *The Nation*, she outlined the need for a professorship in Russian and the criteria on which it should be established: it would be based ideally in either Boston or Chicago (that is, it would be at either Harvard or the University of Chicago) and would require near-fluent language skills. Insisting that the job "demands a speaking and writing knowledge of Russian such as no American man possesses," Hapgood called for the position to be filled by a scholar from St. Petersburg or Kiev.[4] The letter generated two responses. The first, from fellow translator Nathan Haskell Dole, took note of the unlikelihood that such a professor would be "overrun with pupils," but insisted that the position be held by someone also proficient in English. More unusual was a letter from a teacher in Kansas City, L. S. Wiener ("A Russian"), promoting the idea that non-Russian foreigners might also be suitable.[5] In her reply, Hapgood intimated that she actually meant her claim that "no American man" was up to the job to be gender-specific. She readily (perhaps too readily) dismissed any personal aims while also mentioning her "somewhat unusual talents" in Russian.[6] And there the matter rested, at least for a few years.

In the meantime, Archibald Cary Coolidge found the professorial position he would hold for more than three decades. Coolidge began his Slavic career hesitantly and perhaps even accidentally. Born into the highest ranks of Boston Brahmins, he could claim direct ancestors as illustrious as Thomas Jefferson and Pocahontas. His financial comfort assured by a trust fund, Coolidge followed the family tradition by matriculating at Harvard College. He graduated *summa cum laude* in 1887 with a degree in history. Like most historians interested in advanced study, Coolidge set out for

Berlin and Paris; he attended Leroy-Beaulieu's lectures on Russian history and life.[7] After two years of classes in Paris, he relocated to the University of Freiburg and undertook research in American constitutional history. While vacationing in Scandinavia, he took a side trip to St. Petersburg, where, by chance, he was hired by the American legation's secretary, George Wurts. This led to an eight-month stopover there, during which Coolidge gained some language proficiency. His immersion in the life of the Russian capital provided an excellent internship in both European diplomacy and Russian traditions. He faithfully learned Russian customs around drinking both tea and vodka, calling the latter a "pretty feeble liquor."[8] Yet Coolidge became restless with this life of serious travels and less-than-serious studies. Although he did not wish to "travel for the fun of it indefinitely," to return home without a degree would be a "confession of failure." By 1892, unable to settle into a permanent diplomatic posting and tired of travel, Coolidge finished his dissertation on the American Constitution. That work explored the philosophical antecedents to the Constitution, especially those emanating from overseas.[9]

Back in Boston, Coolidge attained a Harvard position in a manner suiting a gentleman of his wealth and standing: family connections. In 1893, Harvard's President Charles W. Eliot summoned the chair of the history department and inquired about finding a place for Coolidge. The chair obliged and Coolidge soon became a fixture in the department. His Russian expertise had been progressing, but only slowly. While he had hoped to become an expert, Coolidge conceded that Isabel Hapgood knew "twenty times as much about Russia" as he did.[10] Overcoming his initial deficit, he began teaching his own course at Harvard, on the history of northern and eastern Europe, in 1894. With the zeal of the newly converted, Coolidge soon thereafter wrote a manifesto encouraging others to teach such a course. That manifesto, published in the fledgling journal *American Historical Review,* called for the further historical study of northern Europe, by which Coolidge meant Scandinavia, the Baltic States, Poland, and Russia. He emphasized how the study of that area would further scholarly pursuits in history. Historical research on northern Europe would, in particular, advance knowledge about the "influence of physical geography on character and history"—a topic well explored by Rambaud and Leroy-Beaulieu. Indeed, Coolidge's lecture notes from undergraduate classes make frequent reference to these historians.[11] Coolidge also applied some of the tenets of the German "nation-study" approach. Russian history, he declared, required thorough instruction in literature, social customs, and especially language.[12] He soon began to redress Harvard's lack of instructors in these ancillary fields.

Coolidge's interest in expanding Harvard's offerings in Slavic Europe coincided with a renewed public call for university programs in Russian language. The translator Nathan Haskell Dole brought up this issue again in 1894. In Harvard's alumni magazine, he called upon the university to create a chair devoted to the study of Russia, which he called "our nearest Oriental neighbor." He justified the position on the grounds of national and intellectual need: he hoped for an increase in the limited trade relations while also noting the importance of Slavic for studies in comparative philology.[13] Dole's exhortation and Coolidge's interest turned into Leo Wiener's good fortune. Having left the Midwest shortly after his *Nation* letter, Wiener was working at the Boston Public Library while his sponsor Francis Childs investigated the possibility of a Harvard appointment. Coolidge desired Wiener's appointment so much that he not only arranged for a position in the Division of Modern Languages but also paid Wiener's salary for many years.[14] The Russian-born Wiener was an idiosyncratic Slavicist who spoke upward of forty languages. A prodigious worker, he translated twenty-four volumes of Tolstoy's writings into English in two years; other works included a two-volume *Anthology of Russian Literature*. Until his disillusionment with Bolshevik Russia, Wiener actively translated and taught Russian language at Harvard. He even published a book that catalogued Russian traits: fatalism, improvidence, sexual immorality, and habitual drunkenness. Following on the works of George Kennan and Andrew Dickson White, Wiener spread the blame for these traits between geography and politics.[15] After 1917, he immersed himself in an improbable combination of Gothic literature, Scandinavian languages, and Yiddish.[16] Once he secured Wiener's appointment in 1894, Coolidge returned to his teaching, research, and academic entrepreneurship.

What Alexander Pushkin once wrote of Mikhail Lomonosov—"he founded our first university. Better put, he *was* our first university"— applied with only slight exaggeration to Coolidge's role in promoting American scholarship. Aside from his own scattered writings in the history of international relations, Coolidge was a renowned undergraduate teacher, a hardworking graduate advisor, a powerhouse within the history department, a major supporter of intercollegiate athletics, and College Librarian. His financial contributions may even have exceeded these intellectual and organizational ones. He paid the salary of Wiener but also of the historian Frederick Jackson Turner. He also purchased numerous collections for the library. Outside of Cambridge, Coolidge advised the State Department, helped organize two (stillborn) Russian-studies programs, participated in the Institute of Politics in Williamstown, Massachusetts, and served as the founding editor of *Foreign Affairs*.[17] Calling Coolidge a Russia expert, then, seems too limited.

While Coolidge brought Russian studies into the academy, through both scholarship and sponsorship, he also steered the field initially toward Russia's international rather than its internal history. As his brother recalled, Coolidge's interests tended toward "the affairs of nations rather than of men" (and perhaps of women—Coolidge's contacts with women seem minimal after his fiancée scuttled their engagement when he was twenty-nine).[18] Coolidge's two books dealt with international relations among European states. His approach was, in large part, a reflection of the historical profession in that era, which defined historical study almost exclusively in terms of international diplomacy or institutional histories of church or state.[19]

Coolidge's scholarly work on "the affairs of nations" centered around the operations of the European state system. His lecture series on the Triple Alliance (between Germany, Austro-Hungary, and Italy), for instance, focused exclusively on the machinations of emperors and foreign ministers.[20] Another set of collected lectures, published as *The United States as a World Power,* occasionally touched on Russia's relationship to Europe as well as the United States. "Was Russia European?" Coolidge asked rhetorically. His answer defined Europe and Asia in terms of geography as well as character; close examination revealed that even European Russia (that is, west of the Urals) had "many Asiatic elements." Coolidge's writings, especially when referring to domestic aspects of Russian life, bore the imprint of his education in France and Germany. They relied heavily on explanations of Russian character, alternately attributed to biology (the Slavic race) and environment (Russian climate and terrain). His reference points for these views were explicitly European: he contrasted the "serious work" of European scholars on Russia with the "ignorant nonsense" so widely circulated in the United States.[21] (The Harvard historian made a positive impression on Leroy-Beaulieu when they met in 1904, while the French scholar was on an American tour.)[22] Although far better trained than predecessors like Eugene Schuyler and William Dudley Foulke, Coolidge nevertheless incorporated many of the same arguments—in large part because they all read the same sources.

Coolidge defined national traits geographically and connected them to national destiny. A chapter comparing the United States and Russia, for instance, mentioned parallel traits as well as contrasts—most notably the "Slav autocracy."[23] Coolidge offered more clues into his cognitive geography of Europe in unpublished writings. At the time of his death in 1927, he had three book-length manuscripts in various states of completion. In one of these, "The Expansion of Russia," Coolidge traced Russia's relation to its European as well as its Asian neighbors. Russia's entry into Europe came not through internal political or economic development but only through intermarriage with western European royals. Even without making any contributions to "the general advancement of the world," Russia had become an equal member of the European political system.[24]

Russia's transformation into a European nation awaited Peter the Great. Coolidge, like Schuyler, attributed to Peter the full metamorphosis of Russia's government from a "loose Asiatic despotism" into a "modern autocratic and bureaucratic state." The autocrat did not succeed, however, in transforming the entire population. The result was two nations within Russian borders: a "European, polished and occasionally corrupt upper class on the one hand [and] a great mass, on the other, still plunged in ignorance where they have remained for centuries."[25] This dualism, Coolidge suggested in letters written during his Russian travels, existed in his own day; Russia remained a mix of European and Asian. Even St. Petersburg, the home of Peter's transformation, exhibited its share of "eastern flavor."[26] Like Kennan and Schuyler, Coolidge applied character traits—coded as geographic categories—to express social stratification in Russia.

Coolidge also defended Russian imperialism in terms similar to Schuyler's. In published and unpublished writings on Russia's expansion, he steadfastly defended Russia's colonial mission against those, like William Dudley Foulke, who viewed Russia as inherently expansionist. Coolidge argued that Russia's territorial aggrandizement was not the result of either a messianic vision or a genetic predisposition; it was instead the path of "least resistance and most profit." Coolidge's assessment of Russian policies in Central Asia shared with Eugene Schuyler's the idea that military campaigns would be the only way to establish order there. One manuscript made a blanket claim: "No civilized modern state submits in the long run to the neighborhood of a jumble of barbarous principalities and tribes, unable and often unwilling to maintain order within their own boundaries or to prevent depredations beyond them." Like the British rule over India, Coolidge argued, the process of Russian expansion was a natural and ultimately a progressive one.[27] Again, this echoed Schuyler's argument, though Coolidge was more interested in international relations than in the prospect of social transformation.

Although Coolidge wrote little about Russia's social structure, its intellectual and cultural history, or its inhabitants, his writings do occasionally give some glimpses into his underlying view of Russian national character. These writings on sociological topics emphasize national character far more than his diplomatic writings do. Building on the major historians of Russia, Coolidge's manuscript on Russian expansion elaborated a detailed argument on the impact of the geography and climate on Russian character and history. The difficult climate, Coolidge argued, led to a "vigorous [and] hardy population" able to adjust to the innumerable hardships of life on the barren steppe. At the same time, he mentioned the "moral as well as the physical drawbacks of such a climate." The combination of enforced idleness during long winters and frenetic activity during the short summers created a peasantry more devoted to intoxication than to production. This cycle created a "spasmodic character" in Russia, not just in economic pursuits but in all of Russian life. The long winters, additionally, contributed to what Coolidge called a national melancholy.

Climate affected not just national mood but national politics. Given the cultural conditions in Russia, Coolidge noted on the first page of this bulky manuscript, "there are many advantages in a highly centralized organization, which guides and raises, as well as restrains[,] the masses." Autocracy, however repugnant to the "Anglo-Saxon," had its place in Russia. This manuscript thus went a long way toward fulfilling one part of the research agenda outlined in his *American Historical Review* article; it explored the relationship between geography, climate, and history.[28]

In other writings, however, Coolidge emphasized biological over environmental determinants of national character. In distinguishing between Russians and Ukrainians (or Great and Little Russians, in the terminology of the day), Coolidge emphasized racial mixtures. Both groups contained Slavic blood and therefore exhibited Slavic characteristics. The Russians had mixed with the Finns, which gave them "endurance . . . patience and common sense," while the Ukrainians had inherited their "impulsive . . . lighthearted . . . [and] artistic" nature from admixture with the Turks. Elsewhere, Coolidge described the political implications of physical anthropology, arguing that national borders demarcated different races. He also invoked the same logic in reverse. The Pan-Slavic movement was doomed to failure, Coolidge wrote, because the wide variation in Slavs' head shape suggested different races that would be unable to unite under a common ideological banner.[29]

In spite of this emphasis on character traits when describing Russian and Slavic society, Coolidge took quite a different position when considering Russian diplomacy. He insisted on multiple occasions that "in spite of differences in history, ideals and ways of looking at things, [Russians] are a good deal like the rest of us. In most respects neither particularly better nor worse than others."[30] Russian character affected neither the form of expansion (which shared much with the British) nor Russians' behavior in international politics. In the world of diplomacy, it seemed, there were only deracinated diplomats and statesmen. Coolidge envisioned diplomacy as the province of elites unfettered by attachments, predispositions, or any factor other than rational calculus of national interest. This realist view—placing power above precept, objectivity above morality, and national interest over individual desire—was a dominant mode of understanding international relations in the twentieth century.[31] Coolidge's realism survived his close contacts with all-too-human diplomats. Many of his undergraduate students rose to senior positions in the Departments of State and Commerce.[32] Indeed, Coolidge had so many friends and students in high diplomatic positions that his role as a formal and informal advisor to the State Department—he visited so often that the doorman knew him by name—was perhaps inevitable.[33]

Coolidge also was the leading figure in American academic studies of Russia. At least four of his students went on to teach in Harvard's history department (plus one in its government department), while the Russian history programs at the Universities of Illinois, Missouri, and California were founded by other Coolidge students.[34] Coolidge's central role at the crossroads of power and knowledge made him one of the founders (and leading funders) of Russian studies in the United States. In his ideas about Russian character, however, Coolidge could lay few claims to novelty. He continued to frame his analyses of Russia, especially its domestic affairs, in terms similar to those of nineteenth-century American amateurs and French historians. Only diplomats, he implied, stood outside and above the character traits of those whom they represented. Whereas Kennan al-

lowed that individuals of character might overcome their natural dispositions, Coolidge narrowed this group only to those serving in international
politics. In his teaching and other writings, though, Coolidge codified and
brought into the ivory tower extant ideas about a homogeneous Russian
character as well as the connections between Asia and political underdevel-
opment. His career suggests how earlier American and European ideas
about Russia entered academic discourse in the twentieth-century.

Like Harvard, the University of Chicago sought to provide instruction
on Russian topics in the 1890s. In 1893 the university hired Isaac Hourwich, the Marxist immigrant who had earned his Ph.D. at Columbia. Originally appointed instructor in statistics, Hourwich soon expanded his
responsibilities to include Russian literature. Yet by 1895, Hourwich was
no longer employed at Chicago. He may have been caught in a turf battle
between the departments of political economy and sociology, both of
which wanted control over the appointment in statistics. Or perhaps, as
one historian claimed, Hourwich was fired for supporting the Populist upsurge in the Midwest in the mid-1890s; such a move would have been fully
consistent with a university administration that buckled to sponsors' political strictures in at least one other case in that era, involving the economist
Edward Bemis. It is tempting to contemplate the possibility that Hourwich
had been engaged in fierce debate against Populists in Russia only to be
forced from his job in Chicago for supporting American Populists. But the
evidence about his dismissal is incomplete.[35]

Slavic studies at Chicago received both encouragement and funding
from Charles Crane, a wealthy Chicago-area philanthropist with a strong
interest in Russia. Ever since his first trip to St. Petersburg in 1884 while
working in the family's plumbing-fixtures business, Crane had been captivated by what he called "the genius of the Russian people." He identified
that genius with Russian Orthodoxy and folk tales.[36] Quitting work, ostensibly for health reasons, Crane roamed the world with frequent stop-offs to
St. Petersburg and Moscow. During one of those visits he met Coolidge,
then still with the American legation, and soon thereafter began to sponsor
Russia-related activities in the United States.[37] Crane's first gifts for Russian
studies in the United States supported the translation and publication of
Anatole Leroy-Beaulieu's book *L'Empire des tsars et les Russes;* the American version appeared in 1893. Crane may also have helped pay Wiener's
salary at Harvard.[38]

Crane's longest-lasting eleemosynary relationships, though, were not in

Massachusetts (where his family owned a summer estate) but nearer to his home in Chicago. He had long been interested in establishing a Russian studies center at an American university. His reasons had as much to do with his love of Russia and Russians as his distaste for Russian Jews. For too long, Crane complained, the tsar and his subjects had received bad American press because of the dominant role Jews and other non-Russians played in explaining Russia to American audiences. Hosting William Rainey Harper in St. Petersburg in 1900, Crane broached the topic with the luminaries he met there, including the education minister Konstantin Pobedonostsev and the writer Leo Tolstoy. Crane found a particularly positive reception when he informed Tsar Nicholas II of his support for a chair in Slavic studies at the University of Chicago, to be filled by visiting scholars—"not by some Pole or Jew or German but by a distinguished Slav."[39] The first visitor, the liberal historian Pavel Miliukov, arrived in Chicago in 1903. Tomas Masaryk, the first president of independent Czechoslovakia, and the legal scholar Maksim Kovalevskii soon followed.[40] Slavic studies found both a beachhead and a sponsor in Chicago.

Crane did not stop with the establishment of a visiting lectureship. He soon expressed to the university president his desire to support a scholar interested in Russian affairs. Traveling with Harpers *pere et fils* in France, Crane soon became convinced that the president's son Samuel was his man. While later admitting that "Uel" Harper was "not brilliant," Crane appreciated the younger Harper's conversational skills and his desire to learn through experience rather than books.[41] Samuel himself, meanwhile, was in his senior year at his father's university (1901–1902) and had no clear direction about post-college careers. Crane introduced Harper to Paul Boyer, a distinguished French scholar of Russia who thereafter took the young man under his wing.[42] His father clinched the deal by announcing that Samuel should become the "first authority in the United States on things Russian."[43] The son agreed, though not out of personal ambition. There seemed to be little going on in Russia, Samuel Harper reasoned in 1902, so Russian studies would be a path to "easy expertise."[44] With this inauspicious prediction, Harper undertook the study of Russian language and culture at the École Spéciale des Langues Orientales Vivantes in Paris. His program there mixed intensive language study with courses in geography and history. The works of Rambaud and especially Leroy-Beaulieu featured prominently in the syllabi.[45] After two years in Paris, Harper returned home.

Harper's life at the University of Chicago was shaped in large part by his benefactor's desires. Crane had stipulated that Harper was to spend half of each year outside the United States.[46] While this proviso must have appealed to the peripatetic Crane, Harper was more troubled. As early as 1903, he expressed a concern about visiting "this interesting but savage nationality [toward] whose study I am directing myself."[47] The terms of appointment—which initially placed Harper in the Extension School rather than in the more prestigious College—apparently sparked some resentment by other faculty members.[48] Harper's terms of employment meant that he could remain in his position in spite of such jealousies. Harper was content to teach in the Extension School and in fact often tried to dissuade potential students of Russian language by calling it a field of study suitable only for "freaks" and "nuts."[49] He did not work to establish an academic empire like Coolidge's, but instead cultivated his own small garden.

After his first plunge into Russia in 1903, Harper traveled there frequently, making a number of important contacts with American diplomats, intellectuals, and other visiting scholars. Waiting in the halls of a government office, for instance, Harper met Bernard Pares, the founder of Slavic studies in Britain. They remained close for four decades, through two revolutions in Russia and both of their tergiversations about Russia. Their relationship was solidified after Pares invited Harper to his Russian studies program at the University of Liverpool, where Harper helped edit the *Russian Review* and taught courses between 1911 and 1913.[50]

By that time, Harper had already undertaken further training in political science. He had petitioned Crane in 1909 that graduate work at Columbia would add significantly to his ability to understand and explain Russian events. After a few years of research in Russia and teaching Russian language in Chicago, he felt that graduate study in politics would broaden his teaching to include not just philology but also contemporary affairs. Appointed a graduate fellow in Columbia's political science department in 1909–1910, Harper studied with some of the most important social scientists of the era, including the insurgent historians Charles Beard and James Harvey Robinson as well as the economist E. R. A. Seligman; the Marxist economic historian Vladimir Simkhovitch was also on the faculty. Out of the classroom, Harper fell in with groups of American reformers like Arthur Bullard and Sinclair Lewis; he also met some of the Russian radicals living in New York. When these contacts were combined with his family's and benefactor's connections, Harper found a wide social network, stretching from the squalid dens of Russian Marxism to Greenwich Village cafes of American socialism to the luxurious estates of the Rockefeller family.[51] He made quite an impression on Charles Beard, who offered as much commentary on his profession as on his student when he wrote that Harper "uses his brain far more than most people who devote themselves to scholarly pursuits."[52]

Harper's writings on Russian politics combined his early study in France with the techniques he learned at Columbia. Not surprisingly, he invoked national character to enumerate obstacles to the development of Russian democracy. The cultural and political circumstances of the peasantry, Harper believed, were serious impediments to Russian democracy. He relied on a familiar set of stereotypes: peasants were "happy-go-lucky," free from responsibility, deeply conservative, and casual (if not downright lazy) in their work habits.[53]

These broad stereotypes about peasant life entered into Harper's discussions of Russian behavior more generally. He identified four traits that shaped Russian character and politics. First, Harper emphasized above all the highly charged emotional currents in Russian character. Rarely succumbing to reasoned argument, he wrote, Russians experienced deeply felt emotions, often in "great outbursts of moral energy." Second, Harper criticized Russian work habits as spasmodic alternations of arousal and discouragement. The latter often dominated, leaving Russians paralyzed by apathy and lethargy. Russian discouragement led to Harper's third trait—pessimism—which had a similarly enervating effect on Russian life. Finally, Harper identified Russians' lack of "backbone" as a political and not just a physiological issue.[54]

Although mentions of these traits were typically scattered through Harper's writings, they are consistent with the broad outlines of his argument about Russian political development. One 1910 lecture makes explicit many of these connections. The basic theme of the lecture reveals the extent to which he incorporated national character into his perspective of Russian life. Harper began by calling attention to Russia's young and therefore shallow culture, which meant that "the people have remained nearer to nature and thus more under her sway"—an especially important consideration given Russia's extreme climate. It should not be a surprise, Harper continued, that so many qualities of Russian character could be attributed to physical environment. The pattern of long lulls followed by bouts of intense activity applied equally well to Russian weather and Russian political life. Pessimism similarly grew out of the Russians' relation to the land around them: the "melancholy Russian soul," Harper wrote, grew out of the "flat and monotonous" Russian plains. Political apathy, by the same token, emerged from the sense of powerlessness brought forth by the sheer size of the country. These arguments, familiar from Leroy-Beaulieu, suggest how American interpretations of Russian politics relied implicitly on assessments of Russian character as derived from geography and climate.[55]

Like Coolidge, Harper brought the geographic emphasis of Leroy-Beaulieu to bear in analyzing contemporary Russia. Building on their Parisian studies, both Americans connected geography to national character and then to current events. The arrival of new Russia experts in American universities provided an institutional home for these particularist notions. Both Harper and Coolidge had plenty of opportunities to apply these ideas about Russian character to Russian politics.

Harper's 1902 prediction that Russia would remain quiet went wrong the following year, when the Kishenev pogrom joined a growing swell of rural protest. By 1905, as Russia's war effort against Japan sputtered and collapsed, the conflicts made their way into the cities. Harper observed first-hand the turmoil of a Russian nation in the throes of war and revolution. Like other Americans, whether enthralled or disgusted by the revolutionary activities in Russia, he borrowed from the familiar stock of ostensible Russian character traits in explaining the political convulsions of Russia's first decades in the twentieth century.

Revolutionary Russia, Instinctual Russians

4

Little above the Brute

Samuel Harper, true to Charles Crane's wishes to employ a scholar engaged with Russian events, was in the Russian capital, St. Petersburg, in early 1905. On Sunday, January 22, Harper was observing a peaceful demonstration of workers led by Father Georgii Gapon. Many workers carried images of Tsar Nicholas II to his principal residence, the Winter Palace. Calling on the tsar—who was not in the palace that day—to improve their working conditions, the protesters were met instead with gunfire. Hundreds of the autocrat's loyal subjects were killed. With them died not just their pleas for a better life but also hopes for a peaceful transformation of Russia. Harper immediately went to the American Embassy in St. Petersburg, where he debriefed embassy staff and the ambassador himself.[1]

Bloody Sunday was the culmination of increasing waves of unrest in Russia. The protests started in the countryside, as rural Russia convulsed with peasant riots and pogroms after 1902, and spread to the cities as the impact of Russia's war with Japan led to a deterioration of the home front. The Russo-Japanese War opened with a surprise attack on Russian naval forces at Port Arthur in February 1904. From this initial defeat, the Russian war effort went primarily downhill, quickly developing into dual international and domestic fiascos for the tsar's government.[2] Worsening work conditions provoked strikes, especially in the political and industrial capital of St. Petersburg. University students demanded educational and political changes, leading to frequent closures of universities. Peasant disturbances spread through rural Russia, encouraged by groups of Socialist-Revolutionaries, rurally oriented radicals who stood on one extreme of Russian revolutionary politics. The Social Democrats, including the Bolshevik faction, adhered more closely to Marx's vision of proletarian revolution. All the while, revolutionary groups accelerated their campaign of assassinations, killing two successive ministers of the interior and members of the tsar's family.

The battles expanded dramatically in the wake of Bloody Sunday. The sponsor of that protest, the Assembly of Russian Workingmen, was hardly suffused with radicals. Indeed, the organization had been founded as a police union, a government tool to channel labor unrest in a suitably loyal and non-violent direction. Protests accelerated through the spring and summer, drawing from all segments of the populace. Professionals and peasants joined workers and radical intellectuals in complaints about difficult economic straits and constrained political life. Rural unrest focused on economic issues, little improved since the famine of 1891. A growing Peasant Union called for "land and liberty." Hundreds of spontaneous local protests met these goals by seizing nobles' land. Sailors entered the fray in June, protesting their abysmal conditions—provoked by reports of maggots in their soup—by mutinying on the battleship *Potemkin*. In 1905 the Treaty of Portsmouth (New Hampshire), which won President Theodore Roosevelt a Nobel Peace Prize, brought an end to Russia's external battle against Japan, though the country's internal ones only intensified. Mutinies and strikes continued into the fall. Government efforts to calm the protests, including the promise of an elected Duma (parliament), did not satisfy protestors, who noted that the Duma's powers were only advisory and not legislative.

In the hopes of averting a general strike in St. Petersburg in October 1905, the tsar issued a Manifesto and began making fundamental political and economic changes. Stutter-stepping toward economic reform in 1905 and 1906, the tsar's government lowered interest rates and—most radically—abolished the redemption payments that had weighed down rural Russians since the emancipation. By 1907, new laws created obligations for individual peasants (rather than the commune), striking a death blow to the *mir* as an administrative unit. The October Manifesto decreed that the Duma would have more than simply consultative powers. The Fundamental Laws, issued in May 1906 on the eve of the first Duma, fleshed out the framework of what would have been a constitutional monarchy; yet they also set severe limits on Duma activity. What some elements within the government gave, others took away: the first two Dumas managed to sit in session for a few months before they demanded what the tsar rather sensitively considered unreasonable concessions. The imperial cabinet prorogued the first and second Dumas and further restricted the franchise to ensure that subsequent parliaments would be more reliable, or at least more pliable. Russia's so-called constitutional experiment, then, raised expectations without yielding significant results.

These expectations were felt primarily but not exclusively within Russia itself. American Russia-watchers, regardless of their political proclivities, used the Russian situation to prove their points. To conservatives like Isabel Hapgood, Teddy Roosevelt, and Ambassador George von Lengerke Meyer, Russian events demonstrated that the "barbaric and unruly" common people in Russia needed stricter discipline.[3] Liberals like Crane, Harper, and their friend Pavel Miliukov saw in the protests Russia's long-awaited opportunity to join the ranks of European democracies.[4] And American-based radicals, immigrant and native-born alike, grew excited about the possibility of a revolution that would transform Russia's despotism into a socialist state. Socialist writers like William English Walling quickly lit out for Russia in the hopes of listening to—and spreading—"Russia's message." Walling also hosted radical luminaries like the author Maxim Gorky on their trips to the United States.[5]

In spite of their political differences, though, most American observers shared a common stock of images about Russia and its population, especially the peasantry. All of them, whether they advocated more discipline or more freedom for the Russian people, saw the peasants as an elemental force motivated by instinct over ideas. The peasants thus required organization if not downright domestication in order to fulfill the divergent political hopes of American observers. For all the dramatic changes in Russia, then, American observers applied a familiar set of tools to interpret them. Irrespective of political position, America's Russia experts continued to view events in terms of national character. This is not to say that they shared the same allegiances or held the same hopes. But it does reveal the extent to which assessments of national character suffused writings about Russia and its inhabitants.

Conservatives and defenders of the tsarist regime were perhaps the most extreme in their depictions of Russia's political problems. They saw a peasantry unworthy of democracy and unable to defend its own interests. The chief villains, of course, were radicals. Hapgood blamed them for the turmoil, calling them "reckless degenerates . . . actuated merely by insane ambition." They were "impelling" the workers to undertake self-destructive protests. She contrasted the radicals with Russian peasants, who displayed innocence and a deep-seated love of the soil. (The connection between radicalism and rootlessness often took an anti-Semitic cast, especially but not exclusively among American conservatives.) Peasants not only loved the soil but were shaped by it. Topography and climate created their "combination of spasmodic energy and aversion to activity." These wild swings of mood and activity, Hapgood proposed, were responsible for the current crisis. Ordinary Russians, "swept off their feet" by both "real wrongs" and "mistaken" ideas, had no sense of reason or logic.[6] Only through proper guidance and control, Hapgood concluded, could Russia regain personal and political stability. She believed the tsar had people capable of providing such leadership. For instance, she endorsed Sergei Witte, recently appointed to a ceremonial post on the Council of Ministers, as a man so competent and ambitious that he seemed "almost American."[7] Alfred Rambaud's contribution to American letters made much the same point, though in the context of a full-fledged condemnation of parliamentary democracy. Like American conservatives, Rambaud argued that the masses were incapable of self-government.[8] Those wary of mass democracy in their own countries expressed heightened fears of democracy in Russia.

Andrew Dickson White, long since retired from diplomatic service, took a different tack, focusing on peasants' submissiveness. He described the military and political implications of the Russian passivity he had noted earlier, calling the peasants serving in the army "dumb driven cattle . . . often devoted but always ignorant."[9] White extended this bovine metaphor to the political realm in a bold but mistaken prediction: "The peasantry is little above the brute. It would be just as reasonable to expect wild cattle on the plains to revolt against the cowboys as to expect the Russian peasants to revolt against the aristocracy." When describing those ordinary Russians who did protest their circumstances, White resembled Hapgood, writing that they were ill-equipped for democracy. Their blind devotion to the tsar, exhibited during the Bloody Sunday protest, illustrated their low "mental caliber."[10] The bulk of the Russian population remained "in ignorance of all that it is desirable for men who should take part in self-government [to know]." With sufficient education and discipline, democracy may yet arrive in Russia, though that unlikely event would nevertheless require a "long and stormy period" of transition.[11]

The American ambassador in St. Petersburg, George von Lengerke Meyer, in spite of his personal dislike for White, agreed with his predecessor's assessment of Russia.[12] A college acquaintance and lifelong neighbor of Coolidge, Meyer also shared the Harvard historian's Boston patrician roots. After local leadership posts in the 1890s, Meyer's scope expanded; he served as the speaker of the Massachusetts House of Representatives and ambassador to Italy before moving to Russia in 1905; later posts included postmaster general and secretary of the navy.[13] Meyer described the Russian peasantry with condescension and more than a little venom. From his first arrival in St. Petersburg, he wove ideas of immaturity and barbarism into his descriptions of Russians. He understood the uprisings of 1905–1906 in such terms, explaining that Russians could never initiate a true revolution: "They were not built that way. They get warmed up, then come several days of fete, and after the effects of vodka has [sic] worked off, their energy is quieted down."[14] The peasants, he concluded in the summer of 1906, "having become aroused and dissatisfied[,] are acting like animals and without any judgement or reason."[15] Although Meyer blamed inherent character for these violent expressions of revolutionary sentiment, he did not consider Russians responsible for their own actions. The ultimate blame, he wrote, rested with state bureaucrats, who "imagined that they could continue to govern 100,000,000 peasants by keeping them uneducated and living almost like animals." Similarly, he saw the Russo-Japanese War as a morality play about governments as well as people: "Education, good government, and freedom are always victorious over ignorance, misrule and despotism."[16] And in the Russo-Japanese War, Russia was clearly on the side of despotism.

George Kennan derived a slightly different moral from the war. Emphasizing government responsibility for character flaws, Kennan expressed the hope that Russians would throw off the autocracy and fulfill the promise inherent in their character. His renewed interest in Russia came after a forced sabbatical. The Russian government had banned Kennan after his incendiary writings and lectures on the Siberian exile system—which apparently led Mark Twain to declare, "If dynamite is the only remedy for such conditions [in exile], then thank God for dynamite!"[17] Kennan chose instead to visit and write about Korea, Japan, and Cuba. In his travel writings, he typically reduced cultures to a handful of stereotypes before proceeding to a "long list of vices or defects." He roundly insulted each of those types for their lack of ability, self-control, manliness, or all of the above.[18] As his travels widened, his intellectual baggage about character showed a few nicks and scuffs but generally remained intact. Character continued to be Kennan's key measure.

With the outbreak of the Russo-Japanese War, Kennan had the chance to bring these concerns about individual and national character back to the topic that had launched his career. As he had in his Siberian exposé, Kennan wanted to showcase the failings of the Russian Empire. In making the case against Russia, though, he revealed more than his political views; he also offered a thorough definition of the two reigning concepts in his view of the world and its peoples. His war correspondence framed the war as a battle between "civilized" Japan and "semi-barbarous and medieval" Russia, neatly reversing the typical association between Asian nations and barbarism—and closely paralleling Meyer's private writings. In an article called "Which Is the Civilized Power?" Kennan specified seven criteria for civilization in making the claim, leading off with "mental and moral culture." He then listed a number of broad criteria such as religious tolerance and respect for law, before returning once again to a concern for issues of character such as "individual and national development in the personal virtues that may be described as the characteristics of a gentleman (modesty, morality, humanity, and fairness)." The article reads like an indictment of Russia's government and people; on each of the seven criteria, Kennan found Russia wanting.[19] During and after the Russo-Japanese War, he compared the Japanese favorably with eastern Europeans, particularly those who emigrated to the United States. He complained to President Roosevelt that "we admit the lowest, most ignorant and most degraded classes from eastern and southeastern Europe . . . but we propose to bar out . . . people who are sober, industrious, orderly, clean, moral and well-educated [that is, the Japanese]. It's so irrational as to be grotesque." Kennan's barometer of civilization leaned heavily toward individual actions and individual character. The behavior of individuals determined a nation's level of civilization.[20]

Kennan was quick to criticize many aspects of Russian character along the same lines as he did Cuban or Korean character. Russian peasants, he wrote, were "rude and coarse," obsequious and unclean. Kennan's extraordinarily thorough clipping files brim with materials on Russian character, thus revealing his reliance on previous interpretations, including those of scholars like Leroy-Beaulieu. He dutifully recorded evidence of Russians' passivity, submissiveness, capacity for suffering, penchant for association (to the point of "bordering strongly on communism," as he noted in 1901), and superstition. As Eugene Schuyler had done in the 1870s, Kennan argued the notion that the treatment of women was one yardstick of civilization; he suggested that "the lot of Slavic women grows better as the Slav is further from Eastern barbarism and nearer to Western civilization."[21] But he differed from some conservatives in that he often wielded these character flaws against the Russian government. Declaring himself—in spite of these criticisms—a "friend of the Russian people," Kennan blamed Russians' collective failings on the country's rulers.[22] He also noted the extent to which these failings constrained national life.

Liberals like Samuel Harper went further than Kennan in blaming the Russian state. Present in St. Petersburg for the explosions of 1905, Harper devoted much of his energy, at least while in Russia, to learning about the struggles for democracy among liberal intellectuals like Miliukov. On Bloody Sunday and many other occasions, Harper functioned as a casual informant for the embassy, keeping its staff up-to-date while declining invitations to become a secretary there. This informal and unofficial role would become his niche.[23]

A steady stream of informative articles issued from Harper's pen in the years following the turmoil of 1905. Tending more toward description than analysis, Harper's articles detailed the nuances of Russian electoral law, Duma composition, and political intrigue. With his unshakable belief in Russia's bright future, Harper managed to interpret any event, no matter how reactionary, as advantageous to the cause of Russian liberalism. For example, when the first Duma (1906) met its demise after only ten weeks, Harper excitedly observed the brief and unsuccessful protest that followed the Duma's dissolution. Even in its failure Harper found cause for hope: the liberals must eventually prevail.[24]

The second Duma, convened in March 1907, met a similar fate; after only three months in session, the tsar dissolved it. In an article for *The World To-Day*, Harper catalogued the new restrictions imposed—disenfranchised workers and new limits on Duma debates, for instance—before predicting (accurately) the growing impatience of the autocracy. Yet even here he found much to celebrate, most notably the emergence of the Constitutional Democracy (Kadet) Party, the rapid rise of which outshone the fall of the Duma itself.[25] New restrictions on the franchise instituted in the wake of the second Duma's collapse left little room for optimism; perhaps for this reason Harper chose to write about it in an exegetical rather than an analytical mode.[26] With a version of dialectical reasoning, Harper was even able to maintain his good cheer through the increasingly reactionary policies of 1907 and 1908. These policies, he wrote, would amplify the sense that more fundamental change was necessary.[27] Harper remained sanguine by invoking the germ theory of democracy so influential in nineteenth-century American political science, claiming that "Russia possesses . . . the living germ of all political evolution." While most American scholars writing in this vein traced American democracy to the Germanic Mark, formed in the misty Teutonic forests, Harper suggested a Slavic variant of this argument.[28]

Harper was rarely so explicit about the basis of his high hopes for Russia—perhaps because the reeds for hope were themselves so slender. Unlike White and other conservatives, he argued that some innate Russian qualities could allow democracy to flourish. But he also differed from Russian liberals like Miliukov. Whereas the Russian intellectual made the case for democracy in universal terms, Harper stuck to his particularist guns: Russia's democracy would emerge from its own unique characteristics.

Harper's optimism also differed from that of his political allies. Whereas Miliukov believed that rational efforts to establish political liberalism would eventually prevail, Harper based his hopes for Russian democracy in his assessments of national character. Long believing that Russians were ruled by emotion and impulse rather than by reason, Harper had faith in Russians' instinct for democracy. His hopes for liberal democracy in Russia were fueled by the peasants' desire, expressed only as "semi-conscious ideas," for a new political order.[29] Liberal visions for a new Russia, then, rested on the stirrings of instinct rather than on deliberate action. Even if incapable of reasoned and conscious action, the liberals' peasants were instinctually drawn toward democracy. Unlike conservatives, who saw Russia's peasants as the greatest obstacles to Russian progress, liberals placed their hopes in them.

Many American radicals, like their liberal counterparts, placed the peasants at the center of Russia's future. Three self-described "gentlemen-socialists," William English Walling, Arthur Bullard, and Ernest Poole, observed first-hand the crucial events of the abortive revolution. They also provided much of the on-the-spot coverage in American magazines.[30] This group of well-off and well-bred radicals varied in their reporting styles but had the same basic message of hope about the future of the Russian Empire, which they all placed in the hands of the peasantry. They were unabashedly partisan and amateur in their approach to Russia, relying on first-hand experience rather than on careful study. The revolution of 1905 had sparked the trio's interest in Russia.

Like the Slavophiles sixty years earlier and the Socialist-Revolutionaries of that era, these American socialists invested the peasant with the principal role in defining Russia's political and economic future. Similarly, they wanted Russia to take advantage of its backwardness by finding a path to developed socialism that did not run through industrial capitalism. These views, while by no means dominant among American literati, nevertheless constituted an important element of informed opinion in the years leading up to World War I.

Walling's reformist impulses began when he was a student at the University of Chicago, perhaps urged on by his iconoclastic advisor, Thorstein Veblen. Upon finishing college at a youthful nineteen, Walling undertook post-graduate studies at his alma mater before enrolling at Harvard Law School. In 1901, at the age of twenty-four, Walling moved to University Settlement in New York City, a gathering place for Progressive reformers as well as Greenwich Village radicals. His initial interest in Russia grew out of his work with Russian immigrants, primarily Jews, in and around University House. Inspired by the intensifying protests after Bloody Sunday, Walling left for St. Petersburg with Arthur Bullard. The pair spent most of the next two years traveling through Russia interviewing revolutionaries (including Vladimir Lenin and Leon Trotsky), peasants, workers, and intellectuals. Walling boasted to his parents that "there is no single man to whom all Russia is so open"; he was especially proud of his contacts with revolutionaries, who, he said, tell him "what they tell no one else."[31] He also held the unhappy distinction of being one of the few American-born Russia experts to experience Russian prisons first-hand: he and his Russian-born wife, Anna Strunsky Walling, were arrested in 1907 on charges of "suspected revolutionary activity."[32]

Walling published a series of articles on these experiences, initially in *The Independent* and then as a 1908 book, *Russia's Message*. These writings revealed what one historian has rightly termed an "almost mystical" devotion to the Russian peasantry.[33] Walling portrayed the Russian peasantry as, quite literally, the redemption of Russia. Especially excited by the *mir*, he proclaimed that the communal organization would soon give birth to a new Russian society—one founded on the elements of social unity and political and economic democracy that (to Walling) defined the *mir*. His initial enthusiasm was based not on peasant interest but on peasant instinct. Communal principles, he wrote, were "part of the peasant's very soul." Walling also celebrated peasants' pacifism, which he considered a direct outgrowth of passivity and not a thought-out stance against war. Whether rooted in psyche or spirit, peasant communalism was certainly not rooted in intellect.[34]

As excited as he was about peasant instinct, Walling was even more hopeful about peasant innocence. He struck out directly against prevailing interpretations of peasant backwardness, laziness, and ignorance. *Russia's Message* contained a chapter entitled "The Russian People: Their True Character," which claimed that socialism was in tune with the "psychology of the people." He devoted another chapter to cataloguing other writers' unduly negative views of the peasantry. Walling focused his attack on Leroy-Beaulieu for claiming that Russian character was fully formed and undesirable. In contrast, Walling insisted that the Russians had not yet formed their own character, but were still susceptible to outside influences: "The real character of the peasant has remained a mystery until to-day. He constitutes the greatest unknown element of the white race . . . If his nature is undeveloped it is in the same proportion unfixed and unspoiled—in other words, the nature of the generic man."[35] Walling hoped to mold Russia's unfinished humanity into a future ideal. What others saw as Russia's main curse—backwardness—was to Walling its chief blessing. Unlike the developed nations stuck "in the framework of material and political conditions fixed by some long-dead generation," Russia was "comparatively free." As a result, the country could pursue its own forms of social and political organization. These forms included neither the commercial system that Witte sought to impose on Russia nor the legislative system then under vigorous debate; capitalism and parliamentary democracy were not authentically Russian.[36]

Most reviewers of *Russia's Message* disagreed sharply with Walling's hopeful view of the Russian peasantry. One reviewer accused Walling of a "disregard of historical facts," while a second insisted that his views be taken with "several handfuls of salt." The reviewer for *The Nation*, in contrast, accepted Walling's view of the peasantry, calling it "the virgin material for the rebuilding of . . . Russia."[37] Different American views of the Russian future revolved around different roles for the Russian peasants. But how different were American evaluations of the peasants themselves?

Despite angry assertions to the contrary, Walling's assessments of Russia shared much with those of Leroy-Beaulieu. He too underscored Russians' passivity and fatalism. What others called lethargy, Walling termed "passive revolt." And like those he criticized, Walling accepted the idea of peasant inertia, concurring with Leroy-Beaulieu about Russian fatalism and endurance. True, Walling and Leroy-Beaulieu traced Russian character back to different roots. Echoing the optimism of authors like Kennan, Walling insisted that such traits were the "temporary results of oppression," the consequences of impositions by an "alien Government." Leroy-Beaulieu instead attributed the "barbarism" of Russian behavior to innate traits.[38] Unwilling to specify a single source of this occupying force, Walling described the Russian monarchy as a "half-Asiatic, half-German institution." Given that Russian barbarism had been imported (either from east or west), then democracy could emerge once the foreigners had been expelled. Optimists and pessimists shared diagnoses of the Russian peasants.

A few years after he returned from Russia, Walling's adoration of the peasantry began to waver. He grew gradually more frustrated with peasant passivity. He was increasingly influenced by Marxian thought, joining the Socialist Party of America in 1910 and discussing Russia with Isaac Hourwich. Walling's optimism waned in proportion to his pro-peasant sentiments. By 1912, his frustration had reshaped his view of Russian political life:

> the general strike of 1905 in Russia . . . might have attained far greater and more lasting results if the peasants had been sufficiently aroused and intelligent to destroy the bridges and tracks, and it is not doubted that a Socialist agricultural population consisting largely of laborers would do this in such a crisis.

Hence Walling, like so many other socialists, came to doubt the ability of the peasantry to act in a suitably revolutionary manner. Only laborers, he argued, could have saved the revolutionary movement.[39] Whether excited about revolution or discouraged, Walling based his ideas of Russia on the peasantry.

Walling's "fire and zeal" for Russia affected those near him. He "turned all of us into revolutionists," one friend recalled. His traveling companion Arthur Bullard was a perfect example. Coming from a less prosperous but equally pedigreed family, Bullard—whose family arrived in North America in 1639—shared more than an itinerary with Walling. Like his fellow traveler, Bullard believed that the peasantry would create a new Russia. Lacking Walling's mysticism, Bullard nevertheless viewed the peasants with a hopeful condescension. Through their own experiences—they cared little for abstraction—peasants had derived their own socialist sensibility. Their

knowledge of democracy, of a concrete, local, and social variety, was inborn and had little to do with formal political or economic theories.[40] His
faith in the peasants, then, inhered in their instincts rather than in their capacities for rational action.

Walling's ideas also reverberated in the writings of the novelist Ernest
Poole. Poole, who later won the first Pulitzer Prize for fiction, mastered the
role of journalistic amanuensis in his Russian correspondence. Working as
a Progressive journalist in Chicago and New York, he went from one left-
wing cause to another, writing about strikes, settlement houses (where he
met Walling), and similar topics. After the death of his mother, Poole later
recalled, he "desperately wanted something new to work for . . . I found it
in Russia." Poole lit out for St. Petersburg soon after Bloody Sunday. Once
there, he posed as a shoe salesman and sent out his articles surrounded by
reports on the shoe business in order to evade censorship. Thus began
what Poole called his "glamorous adventure into a Russia wild, strange and
deep."[41]

Perhaps because he found Russia so unfamiliar, Poole wrote most of his
dispatches in the form of first-person narratives by the people he met—
typically uninterrupted by analysis or even context from the author. He interviewed university students, workers, peasants, and soldiers as well as
Jews and other national minorities. In thirteen of his fourteen stories,
Poole wrote a total of perhaps a dozen sentences in his own voice; in only
one story do his own words outnumber those in quotation marks.[42] Revolutionaries especially impressed Poole. He recalled fondly the "hardy
tribesmen" he met among the Caucasian revolutionaries and the slow-
burning anger of reluctant revolutionaries who joined the movement only
after watching friends and family suffer at the hands of the police. The idea
of revolution so captivated Poole that he began to see its proponents everywhere; at least two captions for photos of Russian children alluded to
"revolutionists in embryo."[43]

While Poole felt deeply the romance of revolution, he was also swayed
by the adoration of the peasant that so affected Walling. One episode in his
autobiography suggests this mood while also encapsulating the gentlemen-
socialists' approach to Russia. Traveling through rural Russia, Poole found
himself in an argument with his translator over the nature of the Russian
peasant. The translator insisted that peasants exhibited practical and even
"shrewd" behavior. Poole, however, invested them with a more mystical
meaning: "They were deeper than that [practicality], these Russians, mys-

terious as the Far East."[44] That Poole used a translator, first off, underscores the limits of his linguistic capabilities. At the same time, though, his extensive travels through the countryside suggest the breadth of his experiences in Russia. Most significantly, Poole, like Bullard and Walling, saw the Russian peasants not merely as agriculturalists but as Christlike symbols of redemption: they would deliver Russia from its current woes through their simple kindness and good instincts. Their sufferings would ennoble rather than embitter them.

The pro-peasant views of these American socialists are all the more striking when contrasted with those of Russian-born socialists like Isaac Hourwich and Vladimir Simkhovitch, who sharply criticized peasant capabilities. Hourwich's engagement with the events of 1905 was not just a distant analytical one; cheered by the signs of political liberalization in early 1905, Hourwich returned to Minsk and ran for a seat in the first Duma. Although he was victorious in the election, infighting between two left-wing parties deprived him of a seat; he soon returned to the United States and took up work as a government statistician in Washington.[45] His writings on the revolution, like those on the famine, emphasized the political struggles against the increasingly repressive autocracy. Yet Hourwich expressed frustration about the inconsistency of peasant protests, which he blamed on the illiteracy and "limited intelligence" of Russia's rural inhabitants.[46] Vladimir Simkhovitch agreed. He called attention to the "ignorance of the peasantry" as the "cornerstone and foundation" of the Russian predicament. The events of 1905, he later wrote, were possible only because— for the first time—"the peasants are beginning to think."[47] Simkhovitch's other writings in the first years of the century suggest that his earlier agnosticism about national character had faded. He based one article on the concept of Russian "Byzantinism," explaining that Russia's eastern encounters made the country different from other Slavic nations, not just in its history but also in its composition. Russians, he wrote in 1905, "are lazier, more fatalistic, more obedient to authority, more good-natured, more recklessly brave [and] more inconsistent" than other Slavs.[48] Simkhovitch's new emphasis on peculiarly Russian traits indicates that he had abandoned, or at least moderated, his hope that Russia would proceed along the same historical path as other nations.

Behind the émigré Marxists' skepticism stood a Russian peasant familiar not only to those conservatives holding deeply anti-Russian and anti-peasant views, but also to those sharing the mystical enthusiasm of American

socialists. Walling understood peasant passivity as calmness and paci-
ficism—at least early in his career. And he saw peasant irrationality as an
instinct that would lead Russia to be true to itself and its character.
Agreeing with Leroy-Beaulieu about the flaws of Russians' behavior,
Walling and his compatriots drew precisely the opposite conclusions. One
major difference came in arguments about origins: the optimists hoped
that overturning Russian autocracy would allow Russian nature to bloom
at both an individual and a state level. Other analysts, in contrast, saw the
Russian government as the fulfillment of the Russian character.

This widespread agreement over the nature of peasant behavior cut
across not just political but also professional lines. As American expert
opinion on Russia began its migration into academic institutions in the
1890s, notions of Russian character followed. Academic interest in Russia
was still minimal even after the turmoil of 1905. Coolidge's 1895 plea for
further study had seemingly fallen on deaf ears. America's Russia scholars
produced little of substance. Simkhovitch's handful of articles topped the
list, while Harper and Coolidge published one journal article each. Only
the *Annals of the American Academy of Political and Social Science* made
any significant note of Russia, and few of its articles were authored by
Americans. A set of collected essays on Russia assembled on the eve of
1905 included only one American-born author among its five—and his
contribution described Slavic immigrants in the United States.[49] Given the
paucity of publications by Russia scholars, many accepted amateurs like
Walling into the community of experts. Harper, for instance, frequently
recommended Walling's book *Russia's Message* to those interested in learning more about Russia.[50]

Even while inching into the ivory tower, America's Russia experts did
not shed earlier conceptions of Russia's differences from Europe and the
United States. Both Harper and Coolidge, in their writings on domestic
circumstances, relied on Russian national character to explain Russia's political backwardness. Although socialists like Walling held more positive
views of the peasants, they too shared notions of peasant fatalism and endurance. At the same time, contacts between scholars and diplomats increased. Harper received multiple invitations to join the embassy staff in
St. Petersburg. Coolidge's connections revolved around the rarified resi-
dences of fellow Boston Brahmins like Ambassador Meyer.

Such personal connections would soon be supplemented and eventually
supplanted by new institutional and professional contacts. During World

War I, both Harper and Coolidge took on government responsibilities, facilitated by the flexibility of their academic positions and their universities' desires to contribute to the war effort. Journalists covering Russia also served in government positions during the war, but primarily in information services. Regardless of their path to government service, American experts carried with them long-standing notions of Russian character.

5

Sheep without a Shepherd

Reflecting in 1918 on the tumultuous events in Russia, the philanthropist Charles Crane told President Wilson that knowledge about old Russia no longer sufficed to explain recent events. "Any understanding of the previous state," he wrote, "gives little help in interpreting the present."[1] The previous year, after all, had seen two new Russias proclaimed. A liberal Provisional Government replaced the war-weakened autocracy in February; that government, in turn, was deposed when the Bolsheviks declared Soviet power eight months later. And from there, events descended from dramatic to chaotic. In January 1918, Bolsheviks summarily dissolved the duly elected Constituent Assembly, whereupon numerous anti-Bolshevik armies gathered steam. The revolution rapidly devolved into a multifront war, with the Bolsheviks in control of central Russia but under attack from all sides: Admiral Kolchak and others from the east, Generals Wrangel and Denikin as well as General Kaledin's Don Cossaks from the west, and a multinational Allied force from the north. Those who did not join an army nevertheless contributed to the turmoil of 1917, as assassinations, land seizures, and banditry were endemic. The American government supported many of these armies, providing food, arms, funds, and occasionally even soldiers; the British and French governments funded a similar array of anti-Bolshevik forces.[2]

Contrary to Crane's advice, America's experts relied on a familiar set of ideas about Russian national character as they sought to understand the bedlam of revolutionary Russia. Foremost among these ideas was the notion that Russians were instinctual rather than rational. In the heady days of spring 1917, belief in Russians' instinct for democracy offered a ready explanation for the quick end of Romanov rule. Later, in the summer and fall, less savory aspects of Russian character—irrationality, emotionalism, and lack of intelligence—provided explanations for the rising tide of radicalism. American officials repeated experts' ideas, using the language and logic of national character in developing America's Russia policy. Russians were incapable of looking after their own interests, policy-makers and experts agreed, and thus required benevolent intervention on their behalf. As in earlier periods, however, experts exempted a small elite from these generalizations; invocations of Russian mobs and masses further underscored the irrationality of ordinary Russians. They also offered a partial exception for Siberia, the residents of which were described as better suited for self-rule than other Russians.

Yet if the content of American expert knowledge of Russia did not shift dramatically during the Russian revolutions and ensuing Civil War (1917–1920), its form and application did. To an unprecedented degree, the views of Russia experts circulated among diplomatic posts, in the upper echelons of the State Department, and even in the White House. Never before was Russia expertise so highly valued in Washington, as policy-makers solicited the opinions of Samuel Harper, Archibald Cary Coolidge, William English Walling, and others. The close contacts between experts and diplomats meant that this shared intellectual framework operated at a tangible interface between knowledge and power—over briefings, meals, and drinks in Washington, New York, Petrograd, Moscow, and elsewhere.

The professional contacts were significantly bolstered by personal connections, most of which found their way back, at some point, to Charles Crane. President Wilson often turned to him for advice on Russia, and even tried to appoint him ambassador to St. Petersburg.[3] Richard Crane, the philanthropist's son, served as the private secretary to Secretary of State Robert Lansing. The elder Crane, furthermore, encouraged Samuel Harper's interventions into policy debates, helping the scholar overcome some of his reluctance. As George Frost Kennan astutely observed, Harper was caught between a fear of being excluded from policy debates and a fear of being "wholly included."[4] But his writings on Russia circulated widely at all levels of government service: from Wilson and Lansing to friends and contacts in Russia like Ambassador David Francis and the commercial attaché W. Chapin Huntington. President Wilson supplemented Crane's ample contacts by staying in touch with former students, including the writer Ernest Poole and the sociologist Edward Alsworth Ross. Arthur Bullard and William English Walling, similarly, established their conduit to Wilson through a key advisor, Colonel Edward House.[5]

Whereas these experts' ideas circulated at the top of government, others' analyses foundered at lower levels. The Inquiry, a group of scholars assembled to gather material and make recommendations about the eventual peace settlement, provided many scholars with applied research experience—none of which had any impact on Russian policy. Harvard's Archibald Cary Coolidge headed the Inquiry's Eastern European Division and invited many of his current and former students to join him. Coolidge's staff included Vladimir Simkhovitch as well as young Americanists like Samuel Eliot Morison and R. B. Dixon. The group was as distinguished for its later scholarly achievements as for its lack of specific knowledge about the topics assigned. Safely isolated from major policy debates on Russia, the Inquiry scholars undertook their work with great seriousness if not great effect.[6]

Almost all these experts expressed their enthusiasm for the end of the Romanov dynasty in 1917, for reasons related to both the prosecution of the war and the prospects for Russia. Hopeful that a new government would improve Russia's weak military performance, President Wilson and his advisors lauded the Provisional Government's proclamations that the new Russia would continue to fight against Germany. Democratic Russia, they believed, would be more progressive and more effective than its predecessor. Autocratic Russia came to an ignominious end in February 1917, when Tsar Nicholas II could not quell the rising protests in Petrograd (as St. Petersburg had been renamed during the war). Rural areas provided little support; whether influenced by Socialist-Revolutionary agitators or acting independently, peasants showed more interest in seizing land than in sustaining government. American observers rejoiced that one of the last remaining monarchies had left the stage, replaced by liberals professing the highest ideals of democracy. The journalist George Kennan, personally acquainted with many in the new government, praised the revolution as an "unmixed blessing." Even the stiff President Wilson, a political scientist, joked that the Provisional Government (initially led by Prince G. E. L'vov, a lawyer and social reformer) had to be good—its leader, after all, was a professor.[7]

In celebrating the Provisional Government, American experts and policy-makers continued to rely on notions of Russian instinct. They quickly shifted from bemoaning Russians' despotic instincts to celebrating their democratic instincts. Untroubled by contradictions, American observers attributed Russian politics to innate dispositions rather than to conscious aspirations, thus reinforcing the claim that Russians were incapable of rational thought. This allowed them to adapt to dramatically changed political circumstances as the Provisional Government teetered and collapsed.

Samuel Harper, for instance, had maintained his hopes in liberal Russia even during the post-1905 era of reaction by investing all hopes for Russia's future in the democratic instincts of its people.[8] After the tsar's abdication, Harper activated his political networks to encourage President Wilson's support of the new Russian government. Wilson's well-known war address to Congress in April 1917 pleased Harper on this score. As if borrowing Harper's phrasing, the president celebrated democracy as a "natural instinct" of the Russians, one that had survived the imposition of a foreign autocracy. Both Wilson and Harper hoped that this newly liberated democratic spirit would bolster the war effort against German autocracy. In his war address Wilson welcomed "the great generous [Russian people], in all their naive majesty and might," to the war effort. From the first American involvement in the European war, then, Wilson declared an alliance with the Russians based as much on condescension as on shared interests.[9]

Wilson's desire to support a new Russia—and his hope that it would not withdraw from the anti-German alliance—led him to send a blue-ribbon commission there soon after America's entry into the war. The membership of the mission provides an excellent indication of the White House's perceptions of American interests in a liberal Russia. Elihu Root, the distinguished Wall Street lawyer and former secretary of state, quickly emerged as the consensus favorite for chairman. The presidential advisor Colonel House proposed a mission consisting of a Jew, a businessman, a labor leader, and an educator. William English Walling and Arthur Bullard were proposed when a socialist was added to the wish list. The muckraker Charles Edward Russell eventually got the nod after Walling declined. Charles Crane accepted an invitation to join the mission, and then set about arranging Harper's appointment as well. After Lansing challenged the jejune scholar's suitability for such an august panel, Harper accompanied the group in an unofficial capacity. George Kennan was considered but ultimately deemed unfit to travel at the age of seventy-two. The Root Mission brought together generations of American Russia observers, with a wide range of specialties and knowledge.[10]

President Wilson sent word to the new Russian premier, Prince L'vov, that the Root Mission would arrive in Russia in June 1917 to show solidarity and to study the possibilities of American aid for Russia. Upon its arrival, the mission met up with its translator, Frank Golder, a student of Coolidge's who had been conducting research in Russia when the war broke out. The mission's work began with a set of unreflective platitudes befitting an official function. Root outlined the elements of Russian national character that would make Russia a welcome addition to the ranks of democratic nations. Some of these characteristics (kindliness and "noble idealism," for example) corresponded well with other commentators' views of Russia, while others (like self-control and courage) seldom appeared in American expert writings on Russia—or for that matter in Root's other writings. The mission's chairman closed with an extended quotation from Wilson's war address, including the references to Russian's democratic instincts.[11]

Root's private correspondence, however, revealed a different perspective on Russia. "Please say to the president," reported the elder statesman, writing candidly to Secretary of State Lansing, "that we have found here an infant class in the art of being free containing 170 million people and they need to be supplied with kindergarten material; they are sincere, kindly, good people, but confused and dazed." Root and the members of his mission lobbied the White House to pay for such "kindergarten materials" in the form of education and information programs in Russia.[12] As the Root Mission concluded its work, its members spoke of the chance for democracy in terms of Russian national character. Russians had, in the words of Chairman Root, the "solid, admirable traits" that would "pull the nation through the present crisis." Root pointed to the Russian capacity for self-government at the local level to argue that there was a basis for building democracy. But this process, the mission believed, would require both economic aid and education.[13]

The mission's official report, summarized in an hour-long meeting with the president in August 1917, similarly placed its hopes for Russia in the population's innate character and instincts for democracy. Mission members agreed that "the Russian people have the qualities of character" to restore domestic order and continue the war effort. Any problems along the way—and there had been escalating protests over that summer—were, the report underlined, "not the result of weakness or fault in the Russian people," but side-effects of the war. For proof of these claims, mission members pointed again to Russian successes with small-scale self-government: the *mir*. Using this logic, American experts declared local democracy the kernel of a future Russian political system.[14]

The socialist Russell maintained his faith in Russia's democratic future in spite of worsening conditions. On the very day of the Bolshevik takeover in October 1917, he wrote to Wilson about Russians' "feeling for democracy." Wilson thanked Russell profusely for so aptly expressing the president's ideas; the president also forwarded a copy to the director of American propaganda operations, asking him to "read and inwardly digest" Russell's letter because it hits "very near the heart of the subject."[15] Russian democracy was a feeling, not an idea.

In spite of their generally optimistic public pronouncements after their return, the high hopes of Root and most of his fellow missionaries proved evanescent. By the time the mission dissolved, Crane and Harper both worried that Russian democracy was on the ropes. Even with their enthusiasm for political change, they understood that a new Russian government would not immediately and completely remake Russian character. So as their optimism turned to pessimism, Crane and Harper resorted once again to character traits—this time negative ones like the tendency to "pass the buck." As Harper put it in early 1918, Russian politics were defined not by reason but by "human instinct and profound emotion." Russian character could, the two suggested, explain Russia's failings.[16]

Perhaps Stanley Washburn, the journalist serving as the mission's secretary, best expressed the double-edged depiction of Russian character. He wrote that the Russians were "gentle, kindhearted and docile, with the best of instincts, but slow of comprehension."[17] While enumerating the good qualities of the Russians, Washburn also implied that they operated on the basis of impulse rather than intellect. Along with the other members of the mission, Washburn had high hopes for Russians' democratic instincts while also criticizing the average person's limited intellect and ambition. As events in Russia diverged from Americans' optimistic prognostications, experts still emphasized instincts, albeit less endearing ones.

Through spring and summer 1917, the Provisional Government's hold on power grew tenuous, thanks in part to the emergence of an alternative power center, the Soviet of Soldiers' and Workers' Deputies.[18] Prime Minister L'vov ceded his position to Aleksandr Kerenskii, a left-wing lawyer. The Soviet, with its insistence on "Peace, Land, and Bread," attracted followers in the ranks of the army, industrial plants, and peasant villages, causing frequent trouble for the Provisional Government. Shortly after the tsar's abdication, the Soviet issued Order Number One, calling for the democratization of the armed forces. Lenin returned to Petrograd in April 1917, adding new energy to a growing radical movement; a May Day rally showed the strength of radical parties. Springtime protests culminated in the July Days, when striking workers took the initiative, only to be reined in by the Petrograd Soviet. The names of the factions disguised the composition of the Soviet through 1917: the Bolshevik (or majority) faction of the Social Democrats was outnumbered by the Menshevik (or minority) faction. In other soviets, especially rural ones, the Socialist Revolutionary Party dominated.

Peasants, even those who had initially cheered the Provisional Government, began presenting more radical demands. In many localities, they claimed the land they had worked, expelling or killing the landlord if necessary. The Bolshevik slogans appealed to many peasants: peace would bring back sons serving in the army, and land redistribution would provide peasants with what they considered rightly theirs. As popular dissatisfaction with Kerenskii's government grew, the Bolshevik faction soon maneuvered its way into control, then engineered a takeover of the government. The Bolsheviks declared Soviet power on October 25, 1917 (November 7 in the west); with typical modesty, they called it the Great October Socialist Revolution. The Bolsheviks escalated their parliamentary and extra-parliamentary efforts to rule an increasingly divided nation, expelling non-Bolshevik elements from the Soviet while engaging in armed battles against various White Russian armies.

Many Americans—but few experts—warmly greeted the Bolshevik takeover. John Reed's dramatic dispatches from Petrograd electrified Greenwich Village denizens inclined toward social or political revolution. Dedicated radicals in the Socialist Party of America, meanwhile, vied with one another for the approval of the Bolsheviks.[19] But radical Americans' response to Bolshevism is a fascinating chapter of another story.

Great confusion about the Bolsheviks reigned among American observers, supporters and detractors alike. Experts often did not distinguish between Bolsheviks and Soviets, and perhaps for this reason they resorted to creative if inaccurate translations of Bolshevik as "whole-hogger" or "maximalist"—a description of political agenda rather than putative electoral strength.[20] Other experts made a misleading claim that the Soviet system was an outgrowth of the *mir*. Among other problems with this argument was the fact that peasant communes had been under legal threat after the rural reforms of 1906–1911. Named for the prime minister of the time, the Stolypin reforms sought to unshackle the individual peasant from communal obligations. Although the *mir* persisted in many cases, the reforms underscored its history as a creature of government, not a terrestrial incarnation of the Russian soul. The most prominent propagator of this myth was Raymond Robins, a Chicago-based reformer serving with the Red Cross in Russia (while also acting as a back channel between the U.S. government and the Bolsheviks).[21] The theorized connection between *mir* and soviet suggested that socialism emerged organically from Russian institutions. In spite of the Bolsheviks' own claims to universal applicability, then, American experts saw Bolshevism as peculiarly Russian.

The Bolshevik takeover, welcomed by no academic or government experts, created both strategic and interpretive problems. Senior diplomats and military planners feared that a Russian withdrawal from hostilities would materially help the German war effort. By freeing up the Entente's eastern front, it would prolong the war and increase American and Allied casualties. Such a shift seemed likely; even before taking power, Bolshevik leaders called for a separate peace with Germany. America's Russia experts searched for mechanisms to keep Russia in the war. At the same time, the Bolshevik takeover forced experts to revise their views of Russia itself; only months earlier, they had declared the Provisional Government the fulfillment of Russians' democratic instincts, and welcomed it to the democracies' battle against monarchy. Yet by autumn they had a very different regime to explain. Fortunately, the notion of instincts was flexible. Claiming that Russians' actions were based on impulse rather than on rational thought, American experts adjusted their explanations. Even the most optimistic proclamations of the Root Mission, for instance, described the lack of intelligence and maturity among Russians. Stupidity, gullibility, and impulsiveness were now cited to explain the Bolshevik takeover and ensuing violence. For instance, Harper wrote to the assistant secretary of state that radicalism had long existed in Russia both as a "theory and as a trait of character." He still maintained his optimism that Russians could return to the path toward liberal democracy as soon as they began "sobering up."[22]

Harper's invocation of sobriety—and the general lack of it in Russia—was a common refrain in American analyses of Russian events. As wartime limits on alcohol sales in the United States gave rise to the Prohibition amendment, references to drunkenness took on extra significance. Prohibitionists often made their case on the basis of the faulty character of working men, especially immigrants.[23] Even in the hopeful days surrounding the tsar's abdication, American commentators feared that the workers' intoxication from radical theories might endanger liberal democracy in Russia. Frank Golder, the Root Mission's translator, presciently expressed this concern less than two weeks into the Provisional Government's brief rule.[24] But the language of excess gained more currency after the Bolshevik takeover. By summer 1918, Ambassador Francis endorsed American intervention in Russia by declaring that "the Russian people have been in a dream or a drunk and are now beginning to awaken or sober up." Francis called for American guidance and assistance to reestablish a (non-Bolshevik) government in Russia.[25] An erstwhile advisor to the State Department offered a slightly different but equally optimistic view months after the Bolshevik takeover: Russians were hung over from their "socialist debauch" and ready (though unable) to establish a popular government.[26] One American diplomat combined these two arguments to make a sales pitch: "I do know that the country is becoming nauseated after its debauch; that any who can give them Bromo Seltzer will be welcome; and that we have a better brand of Bromo Seltzer than anyone else."[27] In other words, hungover Russians, not to mention inebriated ones, were hardly in a position to take care of themselves.

American policy-makers and experts also used racial comparisons to diminish the Russians' ability to manage their own interests. Observing unrest elsewhere in the world, they frequently implied that Russians were as fit for democracy as Jamaican blacks, Mexicans, or Filipinos—that is to say, not fit at all. George Kennan and Charles Crane, for instance, both made such claims. By making comparisons to ostensibly inferior racial groups, they demonstrated the great distance American experts saw between themselves and the Russian population.[28]

Arthur Bullard, then working for the Committee on Public Information (CPI), combined such racial arguments with other anti-peasant views in an important memorandum to Colonel House. Bullard's January 1918 memo opened with a double-barreled criticism of Russia: he compared Russia to Jamaica and the Philippines and complained that Russians could not muster a leadership class to compare with whites in either colony. Repeating common depictions of the Russians, Bullard argued that strong evidence had convinced him that they "were unusually dense." The socialist-turned-patriotic-propagandist also employed the notion that the Russian peasantry operated according to theories of mass behavior. Bullard concluded that the peasantry was a "misunderstood and misunderstanding mass" who suffered through miserable conditions and as a result had become impatient and undisciplined. One of the most worrisome aspects of the Russian situation, Bullard claimed, was that this mass of peasants, who would not respond to reasoned argument, had taken up arms. In such heated circumstances the peasants "might be overwhelmed in blood [or] whipped and tamed into sullen hate," but they could not be dealt with rationally.[29] Written precisely as Bolsheviks were dissolving the duly elected Constituent Assembly, conducting peace negotiations with Germany, and stepping up the "Red Terror," Bullard's memo remains one of the most significant policy statements on Russia that year. His views of the Russian peasants, like his views of Russian politics, had shifted dramatically since his celebration of the peasant in 1905. Whether rhapsodizing about peasants' wishes for democracy or warning about peasants' mass actions, Bullard maintained his belief that instincts, not ideas, actuated Russia's rural inhabitants.[30]

The themes of Bullard's memo, if not the same policy prescriptions, appeared regularly in the writings of other American experts. Like the Bolsheviks, American experts often invoked the concept of the masses. But unlike the Bolsheviks, who sought salvation in the masses, Americans used the term pejoratively. Kennan, one of the most conservative Russia experts at this time, had long relied on "the mass" as one of his fundamental categories of social analysis. He used it to decry disorder in Russia as well as in the United States, expressing the fear that the American labor movement was trying to institute mass rule. To Kennan, the Russian masses distinguished themselves especially by their intellectual obtuseness. Stupidity left the peasants in a precarious position, gullible enough to accept the Bolsheviks' ideas even though they amounted only to the "crazy plans of unbalanced brains."[31] Kennan's sentiments resonated with Secretary of State Lansing, who had similar misgivings about ordinary people. Lansing followed Kennan's advice about the mass of Russians, peppering his sharply critical analyses of the Bolsheviks with references to mobs and masses. The diplomat's December 1917 memorandum to the president described Bolshevism as an outgrowth of the Russian masses: the dictatorship, Lansing fumed, consisted of little more than "idealism and ignorance supported by weapons." The secretary of state feared that the Bolsheviks' "mob violence" would leave "the ignorant and incapable mass of humanity" dominant in Russia. He expressed his anxiety even more strongly to the president in a memo written in early January 1918. Like Kennan, Lansing fulminated that the efforts of the workers, whom he called "mentally deficient," would lead to the "enforcement of the will of the ignorant [that is, the proletariat], indifferent to all save their own pleasures." Kennan and Lansing feared the mob because it exhibited no self-control or intelligence and was prone to violence. The Bolsheviks' mobilization of the masses could lead, in short, to a violent overthrow of the social order.[32]

Discussions of revolutionary Russia among American experts also incorporated the idea that the country's lower classes were "elemental." The notion that they were driven by obscure and unchangeable natural forces meant that they could not respond to appeals to reason or intellect. Edward Alsworth Ross, for instance, often suggested that the peasants could not be stopped or even steered by any rational force. As one of American sociology's founding fathers, Ross was drawn to Russia by his interest in two related phenomena: social control and racial difference. Ross's influential book *Social Control* outlined the structures (from religion to education to law) that kept societies from splitting apart in moments of dramatic change. Ross's theories covered northern European stock, with its supposed individualistic and rational orientation. But how would other racial groups react to dramatic change? Ross embarked on the study of Russia with some skepticism; his writings about Slavic immigrants to the United States mentioned their "soft and yielding" nature, their melancholy, and their fatalism. Yet Russia in 1917 would provide, in Ross's words, "the richest experience possible to a sociologist" since the French Revolution.[33] After unsuccessfully seeking to join the Root Mission as an observer, Ross embarked for Russia in summer 1917 under Crane's sponsorship.

Many of Ross's reports on Russia appeared in print, and Crane forwarded others to President Wilson, one of Ross's former professors.[34] In these reports, mostly sympathetic to the Bolsheviks, Ross described the peasantry as itself a natural force: he compared peasant protests to the "flow of molten lava," making up a "majestic and appalling social phenomenon, as elemental . . . as a tidal wave."[35] Samuel Harper used similar language to explain the increasingly anarchic circumstances of 1918. Russian conditions, he wrote, were the "outburst of elemental forces" that overwhelmed all actors, including the Bolsheviks.[36] Ernest Poole, who was earlier sympathetic to the Russian peasants, combined his notion of peasant mysticism with an invocation of their elemental nature. His 1919 book, *"The Dark People,"* sought to reveal the "deep, surging forces" in the countryside.[37] Even those most hopeful about the Russian peasants or the Bolsheviks employed the logic used by some of the new regime's fiercest American critics.

The best illustration of the relationship between negative characterizations of the Russians and Russia policy is found in a memorandum by W. Chapin Huntington, the commercial attaché in Petrograd and a long-time friend of Samuel Harper's. His detailed report of November 1918 received wide circulation in both public and private circles, ending up on President Wilson's desk and eventually making its way into the press. It contains a compendium of almost every criticism levied against Russian national character. Russian peasants, Huntington wrote, represented "human nature in all its nakedness," unrefined and uncontrolled. His version of Russian character was a familiar one: he catalogued the Russians' passivity, inertia, and indecision while also acknowledging their well-developed sense of forgiveness. These traits made Russia into a "country of tragedies," replete with "isolation," "vastness," and "mediocrity." Like most American observers, Huntington recognized a Russian elite not susceptible to this criticism. But the other nine-tenths of the population, he insisted, were "amorphous . . . like sheep without a shepherd." The fundamental problem, in sum, was that "there are simply too few brains per square mile" over Russia's great expanses. Huntington then turned to the question of American policy, concluding (like Harper) that Russia's recovery required not just economic but also military assistance.[38] The message was clear: given the chaotic circumstances and the weaknesses of Russian character, American aid was essential. Enthusiastic about the report, Harper gave a copy to an equally impressed Charles Crane, who in turn sent it to President Wilson's private secretary. Assistant Secretary of State William Phillips, who also received the report, shared their general assessment of the memorandum's utility. Material from this dispatch also appeared in both the *Annals of the American Academy of Political and Social Science* and *Scribner's*.[39]

As Huntington summarized, the combination of Russian characteristics led many American experts to the conclusion that Russians would be unable to help themselves. Whether lazy, drunk, stupid, irrational, or some combination thereof, Russians remained simply incapable of acting responsibly in their own interests. Harper reached this conclusion, for instance, in a detailed report for the State Department on inheritances from tsarist Russia that would challenge the new regime. He pointed especially to the "low educational level" of the peasants, concluding that it made them "all the more ready to embrace the most extreme destructive behavior." His pessimistic report, dated March 1918, also described the failure of the peasants to reach a "state of culture requisite for constructive work."

Andrew Dickson White weighed in with the claim that the Russian peasantry's potent mixture of "fanaticism with . . . other uncivilized qualities"
made it "very unsettled in nature."[40] The American diplomats Charles
Moser (Harbin) and J. Butler Wright (Petrograd) echoed these claims.
Russians' inability to help themselves is a "national defect," wrote Moser.
Wright told Secretary of State Lansing that the Americans could not "expect any initiative from within."[41] Using stereotypes about Russian character, then, American experts and diplomats understood post-revolutionary
conditions in terms of a nation unable to help itself.

If American experts saw Russian peasants as "sheep without a shepherd," they also feared that lupine Bolsheviks would take charge of the
flock. Contrasting peasant innocence with Bolshevik deceit, they worried
that peasants would follow radical wolves to their own slaughter. Samuel
Harper, for instance, contrasted Bolshevik "cynicism and dishonesty" with
the naiveté of the "simple, direct peasant" who could not understand why
anyone would lie. Thus could he explain the spread of radicalism as the result of manipulation of the "ignorant masses."[42] Secretary of State Lansing
expressed similar concerns in the weeks after the Bolshevik takeover, as did
Maddin Summers, the American consul in Moscow. The Bolsheviks, wrote
Summers, appealed to the "instincts and appetites" of the uneducated
peasants and workers in Russia.[43]

William English Walling made similar claims in a more bilious manner.
He raged at the Bolshevik determination to secure "leadership of the ignorant by any and all means." Such determined efforts, wrote Walling, could
only be the mark of a "peculiar and abnormal type of persons." The hopes
he had placed in the peasants in the 1908 edition of *Russia's Message* gave
way in the 1917 reissue to hopes in Russian intellectuals. Anti-Semitic insinuations, based on categories of inborn traits, abounded in descriptions
of the Bolsheviks. Walling's remarks about abnormality were followed by
his thinly veiled references to undesirable Jewish qualities among Bolshevik leaders ("members of a non-Slavic race . . . [with a] German dialect as
their mother tongue").[44] Harper, too, used naive Russians as a foil for "brutally logical but fanatical Jews" who ran the Bolshevik Party. And Crane,
whose anti-Semitism was not paired with any particular sympathy for the
Russian peasants, similarly tarred Bolshevism by associating it with Jews.[45]

The context of World War I, furthermore, shaped American views of
Russia and its revolutions. This context proved especially dangerous for
dissenters, many of whom faced prosecution under the Espionage and Se-

dition Acts. Immigrants were especially vulnerable and often faced depor-
tation for questioning foreign policy during and even after the European
war. In the famous *Abrams* case of 1918—in which Justice Oliver Wendell
Holmes, Jr., coined the phrase "clear and present danger"—four Russian-
born anarchists were sent back to Russia for opposing American intervention in the Russian Civil War.[46] Within policy circles, though, there was little such dissent.

Harper, like others involved in American policy debates, had long been
concerned about the impact of Russia's domestic battles on its war effort.
From his first writings about Russia in 1917, Harper fretted about German
support for Russian radicals. Although he was primarily concerned about
this issue from the perspective of the European war, his frequent accusa-
tions of German perfidy also reflected his doubts that Russians could arrive at radical political positions on their own. In one of the least successful
applications of Russian expertise in government service, Harper authenti-
cated a set of forged documents allegedly proving German aid to the
Bolsheviks. Russians were incapable of revolution without help from others.[47] Harper was not alone in his concern about Germany's role in Russian
political life. Like Harper, Walling feared that the spread of radicalism to
the Entente powers, while providing short-term benefits for the prosecution of the war, would ultimately be counter-productive. The contagion
of revolution, once headed westward, might not stop in Central Europe,
Walling worried. His important memorandum on this topic, lauded by
Wilson and Lansing alike, called radicalism a "despotism of ignorance."[48]
Given that radicals deviously played on ignorance, Russians were especially
susceptible to their wiles.

The combination of Bolshevik ruthlessness and Russian helplessness led
American policy-makers to contemplate intervention to protect the Russian population. Consistent with Wilsonian idealism, as well as with America's military goals, intervention was understood and defended as a move
to protect the Russians' own interests. Even if Russians themselves opposed
any such involvement, American officials still construed their actions as
benevolent. This claim was neither, as realists would later suggest, a cover
for the cold calculations of national interest nor, as idealists might wish,
part of Wilson's beneficent plan for global democracy. Intervention in the
Russians' interest, like the related concept of trusteeship, was instead a policy oriented (as policy-makers saw it) toward protecting helpless people
from a ruthless adversary. Thus Harper called for action against the Bol-

sheviks while railing against the use of "that ugly and malodorous word, intervention"; American actions, in his view, could more accurately be described as "active economic and military assistance."[49]

Although Harper made these lexical points in summer 1918, he was attentive to the potential need for American involvement even before the Bolshevik takeover. As early as July 1917, Harper worried about the radical activities of Russian workers. He wrote to Richard Crane warning that "it may be necessary to shed a little blood" in order to "pinch the workmen and bring them completely back to their senses."[50] Most Americans were more subtle about the possibility of violence but nevertheless called for Russia to be ruled with an iron fist. Secretary of State Lansing reached a similar conclusion only a month after the ascension of the Bolsheviks. He prodded President Wilson to move quickly, arguing that lengthy Bolshevik rule would impede the reestablishment of order. The military situation was of special concern; if Russia withdrew from the war against Germany, he argued, the conflict would be prolonged by two years or more. Russia's only hope, Lansing concluded, lay in "a military dictatorship backed by loyal, disciplined troops." He even had his dictator in mind: the Don Cossack ataman General A. P. Kaledin. Calling the general a "man of ponderous determination . . . radiat[ing] force and mastery," Lansing hoped to use him as a nucleus around which an anti-Bolshevik coalition could form.[51]

Ambassador Francis agreed with the secretary's diagnosis but reached a slightly different conclusion. Yes, the Russians were incapable of ruling themselves and therefore required a strong man to maintain order and keep up Russia's war effort. But, Francis argued, the Bolsheviks might themselves be the best strong men available. He reconciled himself to the Bolsheviks' cruelty by suggesting that violence was unavoidable in a society that did not value human life. Approvingly quoting a British commentator, Francis agreed that Russians "will obey strength . . . and nothing else."[52] Arthur Bullard made a similar claim at roughly the same time: only the Bolsheviks, he wrote with grudging admiration, "had the men of sufficient daring to cut all the Gordian knots, to meet the real issues frankly, daringly, unscrupulously."[53] While opposed to the Bolsheviks, these American observers were impressed with them.

The idea of military intervention attracted many other American observers and policy-makers. By spring 1919, as Kolchak's anti-Bolshevik campaign briefly rallied, Walling joined the chorus calling for toughness against the Bolsheviks. In the *New York Times,* Walling paternalistically insisted that firmness with the Russians—even to the point of withholding food relief from a starving population—would be for their own good.[54] The Bolsheviks, having "organized Russian ignorance" against the allies, deserved an aggressive military response. The retired historian White similarly emphasized the need for discipline: "Russia's only salvation," he wrote in the Cornell alumni magazine, "lies with . . . a strong man with the army behind him."[55] The commercial attaché Huntington, reporting to the State Department from Irkutsk, went so far as to describe public opinion there—by which he meant elite opinion—as "a universal longing for order and an equally universal conviction that it cannot come from within."[56] Most significantly, President Wilson expressed, on more than one occasion, the idea that Americans should act for the Russians' own good, as the Russians themselves were unable to do so. In a May 1918 meeting with a British intelligence officer, Wilson complained about the Russian problem. As his interlocutor reported, "[The president] remarked that he would go so far as intervening against the wishes of the Russian people—knowing that it was eventually for their good—providing he thought the scheme had any practical chance of success."

Practicality, not principle, was the obstacle to intervention. Unable to find an acceptable plan, Wilson continued to oppose military action through spring 1918. Yet his own thinking shifted in the early summer of that year. Wilson drafted a carefully worded aide-mémoire to Allied leaders justifying intervention. Dispensing with some of the usual arguments for military action—he doubted that it would help the war against Germany, or that it would bring stability to the Russian confusion—Wilson wrote that intervention "is in the interest of what the Russian people themselves desire." With the lexical precision of a former professor, Wilson declared that the military activities he proposed were not "what the Russian people themselves desire," but only "*in the interest*" of what they desire. And President Wilson, not the Russians themselves, would define those interests.[57]

Wilson's aide-mémoire specified that Americans would concentrate their military and economic efforts on Siberia, whence, Wilson hoped, a "commission of merchants, agricultural experts, labour advisers, Red Cross representatives, and agents of the YMCA" would soon be sent. Many Americans in business and government saw Siberia (which Americans typically defined to include all Russian territory east of the Urals) as Russia's land of opportunity. Siberia might function as the hearth of Russian democracy and a bountiful land of economic plenty.[58]

Americans' Siberian dreams were as deeply rooted in character assessments as were the claims for intervention. Siberians, simply put, were not

Russians. Projecting images of the American West onto Russia's east, American commentators saw Siberians as a hardy, independent stock much like the American pioneers. And while Frederick Jackson Turner (a student of Wilson's) argued that American identity was made in the crucible of the frontier experience, these Siberophiles typically understood the differences between Siberians and Russians as biological. The journalist George Kennan, long after his treks across Russia, frequently invoked the unique character of the *sibiriak* (Siberian) in his public and private writings. One May 1918 article in *Outlook,* for example, carefully distinguished between conditions in European Russia and Siberia—and also between American policy options for the two regions. Russia's western sections, including Moscow and Petrograd, "must be left to work out her own salvation or her own complete destruction," Kennan conceded. Americans could do little there because of the lack of organized anti-Bolshevik forces. But in the east, Kennan cheered, circumstances differed. Siberians had long been a "bolder and more independent people" than the *muzhiki* (peasants) of European Russia. Kennan hoped that Siberians could use American help to establish an independent government, which could then work its way westward, eventually toppling the Bolsheviks. "Little, if anything, can be done to help European Russia," Kennan claimed, "but in Siberia we might do much."[59]

Kennan sent this article, along with a letter elaborating on his argument, to Secretary Lansing, who offered his endorsement before forwarding it to President Wilson. The letter highlighted the chaos in western Russia and called—even more explicitly than his article had—for an American expeditionary force in support of Ataman G. M. Semenov in Siberia. If the general's forces reached Lake Baikal, Kennan predicted, it would inspire the Siberian population to take up arms (to be conveniently provided by the U.S. Army) against the Bolsheviks. The journalist bolstered his policy proposal with a statement about his expertise in "Siberian character." Months later, Kennan sent a more detailed set of suggestions to Lansing about a Siberian expedition. Wilson again endorsed these plans while expressing his disappointment that Kennan's age precluded his taking an active role in American programs in eastern Russia.[60]

Less experienced Americans shared Kennan's interpretation of Siberian exceptionalism. In a 1918 memo solicited by the president, the sociologist Ross evaluated America's policy options in Russia, commenting on the potency of the soviets as institutions (strong), on the Bolsheviks' odds (uncertain), and on the peasantry's need for economic relief (desperate).

Ross closed the report with an optimistic look at Siberia, where the inhabitants were "more intelligent and aggressive than the Russians." Russians who emigrated eastward, Ross implied, were free of the stupidity and passivity plaguing other Russians. His deep-seated belief in the centrality of biology in explaining human behavior—he included three pages of anthropometric data in his own autobiography—made these claims all the more striking. The Siberians were a breed apart.[61] Similarly, the historian Coolidge had plenty of opportunities to teach his students, many of whom served in government, about his belief in Siberians' heightened individualism compared with that of western Russians; the combination of physical and personal attributes, Coolidge wrote, made Siberians a "strong but unlovely type." One of Coolidge's charges on the Inquiry, the historian R. B. Dixon, repeated this canard in his analysis of Siberian populations.[62] Diplomats with Siberian experience also shared this view. The "self-reliant" character of western Siberians, one widely circulated report concluded, ensured the Bolsheviks' ultimate failure in the region.[63] The ubiquitous Charles Crane weighed in with a similar claim. In a letter to Wilson, he recalled the "old tradition that Russia will someday be saved by Siberia." Wilson must have been relieved to read these words only days after authorizing American intervention there.[64] Not just the decision to intervene but the form and place of intervention were shaped by Americans' views of Russian character.

With the decision to intervene, American expert opinion about Russia—and Russian national character—had seemingly reversed course. Caught up in liberal enthusiasm after the end of tsarism in March 1917, Russia-watchers lavished praise on the new Provisional Government; they represented it as the fulfillment of Russians' democratic instincts. But as soon as that new regime was threatened, American optimism quickly dissipated. After October 1917, American experts and policy-makers, by and large, continued to express their arguments in terms of Russian character traits. Russians, they wrote, were prone to extremism and emotionalism and were incapable of rationally understanding their circumstances. Given this situation, experts concluded, the solution was to intervene on the Russians' behalf.

This reversal of opinion gives rise to a temptation to see national character as a screen hiding American national interest. Yet this reasoning misses the fundamental continuity underlying all the assessments of Russian national character in Russia's revolutionary years. In moments of highest exultation as well as deepest despair over Russian events, American experts and policy-makers assumed that Russian politics were fundamentally irrational. Whether they emphasized Russians' democratic instincts or those impulses that made them susceptible to radicalism, Americans implied that Russians were driven by instincts and impulses rather than by ideas and ideologies.

This widespread consensus about Russia—shared across political and occupational lines—reached the highest levels of policy-making. World War I and especially the intervention in Russia ended the relative isolation of America's Russia expertise from circles of power. The small group of university-based Russia experts took important advisory roles; policy-makers sought out their opinions, and their writings were in constant circulation at the highest levels of government. Under the terms of his employment, as dictated by Charles Crane, Harper became a fixture in Washington policy circles. His responsibilities did not end with the reports he wrote for Ambassador Francis, Secretary of State Lansing, and President Wilson; he also worked behind the scenes with the Root Mission and other inquiries. Indeed, Harper even became an official member of the State Department's Russia Division, an appointment he had been "praying for."[65] Coolidge and Harper had been slated to meet to evaluate a set of documents claiming that the Germans aided Lenin, though the Harvard historian did not participate. Instead, Coolidge established the Inquiry's section on eastern Europe, employing a coterie of present and former graduate students. By spring 1918, Coolidge had left this project behind to embark on a trip to Russia for the State Department. Visiting Murmansk and Archangel, he sent reports on economic and political conditions to the War Trade Board as well as to Lansing and his senior staff.[66] Charles Crane, the philanthropist and roving Russophile, kept Harper, Coolidge, and Ross engaged in policy advising, funneling their memoranda to senior diplomats and policy-makers. Through independent connections, Walling and his fellow gentlemen-socialists also contributed to the mix.

This official role for Russia experts would fade, along with so many other wartime exigencies, at the end of the conflict. Yet the contacts established during this period of intense discussion were maintained in the decades to come. As the United States scaled up its engagement in Russian affairs, America's Russia experts founded their own networks, closely tied to policy concerns. The experience of cooperation during the Russian Civil War also carried over to American relief policy during the Soviet famine of 1921–1923.

6

Feeding the Mute Millions
of Muzhiks

The defeat of the last anti-Bolshevik armies in late 1920 did not mean the end of American activities in Soviet Russia, nor did it ensure the stability of the young Bolshevik regime. By 1921, the Soviet Union faced another famine and American authorities contemplated not armed intervention but food relief. Leading the relief efforts was Herbert Hoover, who first achieved public prominence for his role as wartime "food tsar." The energetic engineer continued at the helm of the American Relief Administration (ARA) while also serving as secretary of commerce (and, as the joke went, "undersecretary of everything else").[1] In spite of his longstanding opposition to Bolshevism—which he considered the outcome of the "violence of a mass of ignorant humanity"—Hoover organized a major aid program in Soviet Russia, the largest before Lend-Lease during World War II. Between 1921 and 1923, hundreds of Americans worked with thousands of Russians to provide millions of meals. The ARA organized the shipment of 750,000 tons of supplies—for which it paid more than $60 million—in barely eighteen months.[2] This program was a far cry from William English Walling's 1919 plans to conquer the Bolsheviks by withholding food, a proposal with which Hoover had largely concurred.[3]

The shift in tactics was not accompanied by a change in ideas. Hoover and his staff maintained the attitude of paternalism and condescension so visible during debates over military intervention. They repeated the notion that Russians were unable to defend their own interests. One scholar, for instance, called for "moral trusteeship" over Russia, a theme also struck in various newspaper opinion pieces.[4] And from the previous episode of famine relief a generation earlier, Hoover and his staff incorporated the notion that Russia's national character explained its economic woes. Yet the famine of 1921–1923 also saw new uses for familiar ideas about Russian traits. Character explained economic tribulations, but it also suggested a solution to Russian backwardness. Some observers within the ARA began to balance present sufferings against future possibilities, often favoring the latter. They saw national character as an obstacle to be overcome, not as a permanent limit on Russia's potential. In the 1890s only Marxists like Isaac Hourwich had taken this view. But in the aftermath of World War I many Russia experts with little knowledge of Marx and even less enthusiasm for the Bolsheviks suggested that character did not preclude Russian economic development. Herbert Hoover, in contrast, was emphatically opposed to this line of thinking.

Competing visions of Russia's future shaped discussions of ARA strategy. Those interested in overcoming Russia's backwardness hoped that American aid would contribute to the economic reconstruction and eventual industrialization of Russia. Hoover, on the contrary, insisted that the sole aim of ARA activities was emergency relief for the amelioration of famine conditions. The conflict between relief and reconstruction affected every aspect of the ARA effort. Soviet leaders, interested in rapid industrialization, considered American aid stingy and unhelpful; many ARA middle-rank officials sympathized with this view. To Hoover, however, the Bolsheviks' priorities supplied further proof (as if any were needed) of their perfidy. Both sides of this debate employed similar understandings of national character, but they differed in their views of how Russian particularities affected Russian modernization. The American debate over Russia, ironically enough, began to emphasize the nation's economic possibilities at a moment of dire weakness.

The looming food shortages of winter 1921 were only the most severe indication of widespread Soviet economic crisis. Seven years of war—World War I followed by the Civil War—had disrupted all aspects of Russian economic life. Even without war, the agricultural sector was hardly sturdy. Since the major famine of 1891–1892, smaller food crises had occurred in 1897, 1901, 1906, 1911, and 1914.[5] Plagued by low productivity, scattered transportation networks, and a history of discriminatory government policies, rural Russia faced constant threats. Official policies created more problems when the Bolsheviks took power. Reared in the orthodox Marxist tradition, which saw peasants as the outmoded vestiges of a precapitalist order, Lenin and leading Bolsheviks had little political use for the peasantry. Political opportunists like Lenin, however, quickly reconfigured

(or ignored) Marxist precepts in an effort to recruit peasants to the Bolshevik cause. Bolshevik tactics, not surprisingly, focused more on what the
peasants could offer the centralizing state (namely, food) than vice versa.
Hence shortly after taking power, Soviet leaders instituted a policy they
came to call War Communism, in which they claimed control over all
aspects of economic life, including all food products. In response, rural
Russians reduced their sowing area or hid crops, further shrinking food
supply. Soviet plans for the food—primarily to feed favored groups like
soldiers and urban workers—left little for those growing it. Indeed, by late
1920, urban food consumption levels actually outstripped those in food-
producing regions.[6] Even Petrograd sailors, once staunch supporters of Soviet rule, rebelled against political and economic conditions. A group at
the Kronstadt naval base in the Gulf of Finland declared their opposition
to Bolshevik rule and War Communism in a mutiny in early 1921. The rebellion was brutally suppressed.[7]

Indications of a poor harvest joined news of political unrest in spring
1921, leaving Soviet leaders to consider a broad range of responses. Declaring the period of War Communism over, the Politburo inaugurated the
New Economic Policy (NEP) that March. Rather than controlling all aspects of the economy, as it had sought to do under War Communism,
the Russian government under NEP controlled only the "commanding
heights"—major industrial and financial concerns. Smaller enterprises, especially in the agricultural sector, could participate in a relatively open
market. The failure of total grain requisitions led to the creation of markets for agricultural and other goods. The economic reins remained loos-
ened for much of the decade.[8]

Other Politburo directives dealt strictly with the food shortages at hand.
Lenin proposed using the army to address the looming crisis. By conscript-
ing as many as one million men from the afflicted regions, he hoped to reduce the size of the needy population by providing the draftees with a
more reliable source of food: Red Army rations. More important, an expanded army could help increase grain collection by increasing compulsion.[9]

Politburo members also looked abroad for solutions. They authorized
the importation of grain using scarce foreign-currency reserves.[10] They
also began the search for foreign aid. Responding to a proposal from the
writer Maxim Gorky, the Politburo created an all-star relief committee,
which included a number of non-Party cultural luminaries, such as the

economist Aleksandr Chaianov and the theater director Konstantin Stani-slavskii. The committee immediately appealed "to all honest European and American people" for aid. But once this task was accomplished, the Polit-buro dissolved the committee as part of a new round of attacks on disloyal intellectuals.[11]

Herbert Hoover responded immediately to the appeal of this short-lived committee. His reply to Gorky highlighted the "purely voluntary and un-official" nature of the ARA—a disingenuous description given Hoover's cabinet post and the fact that the ARA derived more than 40 percent of its post-1921 revenue from government sources.[12] Why would Hoover sup-port famine relief to Russia? Certainly not out of political sympathies. American agricultural markets may have weighed on his mind; farmers burned corn because of low prices in the post-war agricultural depression. Throughout the famine-relief program, Hoover insisted on supplying only American grains; he rebuffed numerous efforts to use ARA funds for the purchase of European or Russian grain. This strict policy apparently had the desired effect, as ARA purchases did help increase the price of Ameri-can corn.[13]

Negotiations between the ARA and "Soviet authorities" (Hoover refused to call them a government) began in the Baltic city of Riga in August 1921. The talks moved slowly because of Soviet concerns about potential politi-cal abuse by the ARA. These anxieties were heightened by the ill-timed boasts of one wartime ARA staffer who took credit for toppling the short-lived Soviet regime in Budapest in 1919. Before the negotiations began, a Soviet diplomat wrote to Lev Kamenev, the Politburo member soon ap-pointed to head relief efforts, that an agreement with the ARA would "open the door to all sorts of intrigues and efforts to disorganize our re-gime." Georgii Chicherin, the People's Commissar for Foreign Affairs, also feared that pro-Bolshevik westerners would change their minds once they observed Russia's chaos first-hand.[14] The Riga Agreement was eventually hammered out, and food relief began shortly thereafter. The ARA would provide relief supplies and pay for its own staff, while the Soviet govern-ment would cover local transportation costs as well as the salaries of the ARA's Russian employees. But earlier worries were hardly forgotten; no sooner was the pact inked than the Politburo established a special commis-sion for surveillance of the foreign aid workers. The first ARA employees included many veterans, further raising Soviet hackles. Lenin wrote, "we must track [them] with all our powers . . . The war must be cruel and *un-*

yielding."[15] From the start, Soviet distrust shaped policies toward American relief.

While Soviet officials busied themselves with their surveillance apparatus, American officials endeavored to expand their knowledge of Russian circumstances using less secretive techniques. Hoover appointed Colonel William Haskell, whose previous relief experience had been in Armenia and Turkey, as director of the ARA Russian Unit. Hoover especially praised Haskell's knowledge of the "Eastern European mind." Harvard's Archibald Cary Coolidge, "hankering for a little more experience in government" after his Inquiry service ended, became Haskell's advisor and chief liaison with local authorities.[16]

In addition to appointing senior officers, Hoover dispatched James P. Goodrich, formerly the governor of Indiana, to evaluate conditions in Russia. After consultations with ARA experts, the governor quickly confirmed early reports on the urgency of the situation, exhorting Hoover to provide seed grains as well as food. Goodrich carefully studied the question of concealed supply, likely at the behest of the ARA economist Lincoln Hutchinson. On the basis of his belief in Russian peasants' "semi-oriental nature," Goodrich felt that they were indeed hiding grain.[17] He did not use such appellations only in passing; Goodrich believed that most peasant customs—like the Russian peasants themselves—were of Asian origin. Thus he blamed the famine on peasants' "oriental fatalism" and the low value they placed on human life.[18] National character explained much about the famine's origins.

Other ARA advisors expressed similar sentiments about Russians, emphasizing their poverty, lethargy, and passivity. The ARA historian Harold Fisher (whose official history noted the "oriental" traits of uncleanliness and tardiness in Russia) mentioned that the Latvian Aleksandr Eiduk, the first Soviet representative to the ARA, was appreciated by the Americans because he "moved with a celerity not characteristically Russian." Fisher furthermore identified the peasants' "stolidity" in the face of death as revealing a character trait; Russian peasants, he concluded, died as impassively as they had lived.[19]

Like the group advocating American intervention during the Russian Civil War, famine officials in the early 1920s drew political conclusions from Russians' supposed passivity. Colonel Haskell, for instance, insisted that the Russians would accept whatever government ruled them. Hoover carried this further, arguing that the Russians could not take care of themselves but had to rely on the kindness of strangers. The former Treasury official Oscar Crosby made the most alliterative version of this claim: who will take responsibility, he asked in a learned journal, for the "mute millions of muzhiks?"[20] Given the chaotic circumstances, as well as Russians' unshakable passivity, many American experts argued that the Bolsheviks were (as Goodrich told Soviet diplomats) the only people capable of ruling Russia at the time.[21] But this grudging willingness to work with the Bolsheviks did not dissipate American-Soviet tensions.

As western relief workers streamed into Russia in fall 1921, Hoover soon departed from the strategy he employed in his European work. His earlier efforts had begun with the phase of "acute need," during which all resources were marshaled to provide food for those in danger of starvation. After that need had been met, the "Reconstruction" stage began. Hoover's wartime strategy improved upon prior American approaches, which had typically focused only on immediate relief for the starving.[22] In Soviet Russia, though, Hoover broke with his wartime practice by limiting ARA work to the initial, "acute need," phase—thus rejecting long-term goals.

Hoover ran up against Soviet strategies that placed relief as secondary to reconstruction. As one American official recorded the sentiments of Kamenev in early fall 1921,

> the problem preoccupying the Soviet government was not the incidental one of feeding any number of children for them to die [soon thereafter] . . . under famine conditions similar to those now existing. Mere relief, as such, does not interest them [members of the Politburo]; they are concerned with securing some sort of real aid to produce more of what they need.[23]

Kamenev acted on these priorities as head of a new government organ, the All-Russian Commission for Aid to the Starving (known by its Russian acronym, Pomgol). In addition to sponsoring a network of kitchens and aid points across the afflicted regions, Pomgol also worked with foreign relief groups. The agency coordinated and supervised large western groups like the ARA and the International Red Cross Mission, small sectarian groups aiding their Russian coreligionists, and various workers' aid missions. From the start, Soviet officials looked toward long-term economic prospects. A report by a leading economic organ, for instance, outlined the goals of anti-famine measures as, first, "the restoration of agriculture and the liquidation of the consequences of the poor harvest," and second, "the creation of industries."[24] Even in the midst of crisis, Soviet officials were thinking of long-term economic goals.

These priorities affected Soviet relations with western organizations. As the Soviet representative Eiduk told one reporter, "Let us not forget . . . that however productive the work of the ARA might be, it copes with only a small part of our gigantic task."[25] The International Red Cross Mission, led by the Norwegian explorer Fridtjof Nansen, took on assignments more closely aligned with Pomgol's goals, stressing what it termed "constructive relief." As early as August 1921, a Soviet representative in London warned Chicherin of the differences among the major western relief agencies: "Hoover's aims include the immediate relief of individuals," the diplomat wrote, while Nansen planned a range of activities aimed at economic regeneration.[26]

Some of the smaller American organizations working under ARA auspices took on reconstructive tasks. Three groups in particular showed a strong inclination toward reconstruction: American Mennonite Relief, the [Jewish] Joint Distribution Committee (JDC), and the American Friends Service Committee (AFSC). The Mennonites signed an agreement with Soviet Russia to provide mechanical equipment on the premise that "it is desirable not only to relieve those suffering but also to remove the causes of famine conditions." The JDC undertook both emergency food relief and reconstruction work—even after the ARA pointedly warned its officers that "reconstruction is not part of the ARA program . . . [W]e are most definite in our stand that the ARA shall not in any way be tied up with any reconstruction operations."[27] Any disputes between the ARA and American organizations with different plans, however, were soon overshadowed by ARA conflicts with Soviet relief organizations, which had even more quickly and resolutely turned toward economic reconstruction.

The ARA's relationship with Soviet authorities hardly improved beyond the tense negotiations in Riga. Minor conflicts, sparked by Soviet suspicions as well as American impatience, occupied a great deal of time and energy. For instance, Soviet secret police searched the ARA offices so frequently that the Americans eventually placed their papers neatly on desktops to minimize disarray. The ARA filing system itself revealed other sorts of tensions; the file on "relief difficulties" contained the notation, "see also rascality, dishonesty, etc."[28] More important, perhaps, was the perennial ARA dissatisfaction with Russian transportation. The Russian railroads, facing shortages of fuel, locomotives, and rolling stock, frequently delayed or lost food shipments. Pilferage of grain—hardly a surprise given the general conditions in Russia—further reduced ARA shipments.[29] The Soviet representative Eiduk compounded these problems with his hostile attitude. Coolidge, who dealt with Eiduk more regularly than did any other ARA official, blamed continual problems not on individual Russians but on Russian character as a whole. Such conflicts were "inevitable" thanks to the "slackness, irresponsibility, habits of prevarication and other faults inherent in the Russian character." Elsewhere Coolidge amplified these concerns, explaining that Russian "defects" such as "stupidity, ignorance, inefficiency and above all meddlesomeness" further hindered his work with the Soviets. His boss, Haskell, made similar statements. Coolidge's personal encounters with Soviet diplomats led him to recant his earlier views that diplomats stood above the character of their nations.[30]

But programmatic differences—relief versus reconstruction—and not just qualities of national character lay at the root of Soviet-American problems. State Department officials came to this conclusion after observing four months of ARA work; one diplomat reported that "the Soviets are always pushing the [ARA] to undertake activities for which it is not organized." Kamenev put the matter directly to Coolidge in a February 1922 interview. Recognizing the transportation problems that hampered the relief effort, he asked for American aid to improve the railways. Once rebuffed, he groused that ARA proscriptions against such aid would slow any progress in famine relief. Meanwhile in London, a senior Soviet trade official approached the ARA office there about arranging American credits for the purchase of agricultural machinery, but was quickly rebuffed by Hoover.[31]

The expansion of the scale (though not the scope) of ARA activities, far from alleviating American-Soviet tensions, only exacerbated them. In late December 1921, Hoover announced that the ARA had obtained twenty million dollars in funding from various U.S. government wartime surpluses. In public venues, Soviet leaders reacted coolly to the news; behind the scenes, they scaled up surveillance efforts.[32] The increase in food shipments further taxed already overstretched Soviet transportation resources. Friction over this issue reached crisis proportions in spring 1922, as ARA officials piled up complaints about shipping delays. Using Soviet surveillance for his own purposes, Haskell wrote a sternly worded cable to Hoover, intentionally ignoring the usual security procedures. In it, Haskell complained about the failures of Soviet transportation and suggested that Hoover immediately cease food shipments unless and until Soviet authorities could get the trains moving. The trick worked, as Kamenev and Eiduk promptly appeared in Haskell's office, full of promises of improvement. The Politburo also asked Feliks Dzerzhinskii, the head of the secret police, to oversee work with ARA. His direct threats, the Politburo hoped, would "establish order" in the transportation sector.[33]

At precisely the time that Haskell sent his open telegram, Hoover confided to his assistant that he expected American aid to end by that September. Early estimates indicated that the 1922 harvest was sufficient to feed the population, thus ending the acute crisis. Yet Walter Brown, the director of the ARA's London office, expressed his concern over the politics of leaving an area still stricken with hardship if not famine. Closing down operations in Russia, Brown wrote, would provide fodder for "radicals and counter-revolutionists, the 'I-told-you-so' press and politicians in the USA."[34] A group of senior ARA officials, writing separately, agreed with Brown about the risk of adverse publicity.[35] Attacks on the ARA lent credence to these warnings. Paxton Hibben, a supporter of Soviet Russia with plenty of relief experience, sent Hoover a copy of a speech he had given to the Foreign Policy Association. In that speech, Hibben called for "really constructive relief"; the ARA's current plan of "the relief of a very few people . . . would inevitably lead to the death of a great many and possibly to another famine." Hibben called on the ARA to provide not just seed grain but also agricultural implements and other essential machinery. Hoover's response was quick. He politely but firmly rejected the proposal and then initiated surveillance of Hibben. Reports from J. Edgar Hoover at the Bureau of Investigation and military intelligence sources detailed Hibben's activities with a combination of sycophancy ("The Secretary should surely consider himself flattered to be hissed at" by the likes of Hibben) and paranoia (Hibben "is an extreme radical and is considered dangerous"). Brown and his colleagues thus had reason to worry about publicity.[36]

Herbert Hoover and his advisors negotiated the treacherous shoals of public opinion by working out a new relief strategy for late 1922 and beyond. The ARA, according to this new plan, would focus on feeding children, especially the homeless ones (*bezprizornye*) congregating in major urban areas. Yet ARA changes were far less drastic than those planned by the Soviet leadership.

Apparently without knowledge of the impending shift in ARA strategies, Soviet officials made some changes of their own. Declaring in fall 1922 that the moment of crisis had passed, the Politburo dissolved its famine-relief committee, Pomgol, and created the Committee to Struggle against the Consequences of Famine (Posledgol). The new committee took over some residual Pomgol responsibilities but turned especially toward longer-term projects. Posledgol would engage in food relief only for homeless children and a small number of ill or disabled adults. Its principal goal was to reconstruct the economy by repairing the transportation network, rebuilding dilapidated or destroyed machinery, and creating new industries throughout the afflicted region. In announcing the changes, Russian President M. I. Kalinin stressed the broader scope of relief efforts; reconstruction of agriculture and industry became the highest priority. And rather than focusing exclusively on food relief for the rural population, as Pomgol had done, Posledgol would work to improve all branches of the economy. In emphasizing its new mission, one official contrasted Posledgol with tsarist anti-famine efforts in 1891. In the bad old days, he wrote, "as soon as acute forms of famine were liquidated, no sort of truly preventative measures to prevent famine, or to eliminate its causes, were undertaken." The article promoted industry as the key to avoiding future famines.[37]

Soviet officials knew that the switch from emergency relief under Pomgol to economic reconstruction under Posledgol came with high costs. They might end up sacrificing the lives of those in the famine region in the name of a brighter economic future, fulfilling Alexander Herzen's nightmare of turning the present generation into "caryatids holding up the floor for the next generation to dance on." But Soviet leaders deemed such sacrifices necessary for the survival of the regime and the progress of Russia. President Kalinin, the symbol of Bolshevik concerns for the peasantry, had the unenviable task of explaining to starving citizens their new role as, essentially, caryatids. By one report, Kalinin exhorted a group of starving peasants who feared imminent death: "You must not think of the present merely. I ask you to think of the future."[38] And indeed, the Soviet leadership seemed more focused on the future than on the present.

The change in attitude—from present to future, from relief to reconstruction—had immediate and direct implications for ARA work. These became clear when Karl Lander, Eiduk's replacement, delivered a memorandum to Haskell about an impending policy change. After reiterating the new goals of Posledgol—"regenerating the ruined industries [and] raising the productivity of our agriculture"—Lander's memo announced the change. During the period of acute famine, he wrote, Soviet authorities had gratefully accepted help in any form and from any source. But now that the emergency had passed, paying even the small Soviet share for ARA activities seemed excessive; it would divert funds from Posledgol's long-term aims. Thus, Lander reported, Soviet officials would no longer contribute to ARA-operated kitchens. Haskell's sharp and prompt reply insisted that Lander's letter amounted to an annulment of the Riga Agreement. Unless the letter was withdrawn, Haskell threatened, the ARA would close up shop immediately. After some tense negotiations, Lander retracted the letter, explaining that he did not intend to renege on the basic agreement.[39] He nevertheless continued to lobby for a shift in ARA policy. One letter to Haskell, for instance, solicited ARA help in "extending productive relief . . . as the most rational kind of relief."[40] And productive relief, as the Soviet leadership defined it, focused on promoting industry. One way to do this was to export grain to Europe in exchange for foreign currency to purchase industrial equipment.

The most public dispute over relief policy involved Soviet grain exports. This conflict coincided with the creation of Posledgol. From the ARA's perspective, the disagreement began when a Soviet economic official predicted in an *Izvestiia* article that Soviet Russia would need to start exporting grain to western Europe. Rumors of grain exports reached the ARA's offices in the United States throughout the summer and early fall. When first questioned about these reports, Kamenev offered a series of evasive and misleading answers. For instance, he explained to Haskell that the vagaries of the train system required Russia to export from southern ports at the same time that it imported into northern ports. Yet on at least one occasion, Soviet ships apparently loaded grain for export alongside American ones unloading relief supplies for Soviet Russia.[41]

By November the Politburo had removed any confusion about the exports, which it called "urgently necessary and of profound interest" to the government. It also charged a high economic official, A. I. Tsiurupa, with oversight of the export operations.[42] Maxim Litvinov, the deputy commissar for foreign affairs, preferred a direct and unapologetic discussion of exports to Kamenev's evasiveness: "The export of grain from Russia is a fact which is impossible and pointless to hide," he wrote to his colleagues. Litvinov enumerated justifications for the exports, most notably that foreign currency was needed to import machinery.[43]

ARA leaders and other American observers offered a clear understanding of what was at stake. Haskell, for instance, offered his qualified approval of the exports. He agreed with Soviet officials that Russia could obtain the tools of reconstruction only from abroad, and that it could pay for those tools only with grain. "I know it sounds absurd," confessed the ARA's Moscow chief, "but there is something in their argument."[44] But Haskell's boss, Hoover, sternly protested the "inhumanity" of a policy of "exporting food from starving people" in order to provide for "the economic improvement of the survivors."[45] Hoover thus rejected the very trade-off that Kalinin had awkwardly defended to needy peasants. It took four lines of twenty-four-point type for one loquacious headline writer to express his dismay:

> What's the Game of the Russian Reds—Win the World by Force of Arms, or Intrigue and Crafty Tactics? Bolsheviks, Playing Both Ends against the Middle by Crying "Good Lord, Good Devil," Are Backed by an Army of 800,000—US Sends $20,000,000 to Starving Russians, and Soviets Export 38,000 Tons of Grain![46]

Soviet newspapers, in contrast, offered more sober and supportive accounts of the exports. One article assailed western commentators' inability to understand the need for grain sales. Even the least educated Soviet peasants, it insisted, understood that grain exports were in their own interests; any hope for economic reconstruction required the foreign currency that exports would yield.[47]

Similarly, Soviet officials expressed their concern that ARA leaders (especially Hoover) had mistaken views of the paths to progress. They focused their ire on the ARA's ban on reconstructive work. As early as October 1922, Ol'ga Kameneva, the head of Posledgol's foreign department, blamed the ARA's "bourgeois" character for its limited vision. Hoover's agency was interested merely in "saving the lives of the starving," Kameneva seethed, while workers' organizations "kept [in mind] the task of productive aid." "By the time of the transition to the second—reconstructive—phase," she continued, "[the ARA] had completely disappeared."[48] Conceding that it "has accomplished a great deal of relief for the starving," she complained that "constructive work occupies a more distant place" in ARA priorities. Kameneva went on to praise those western organizations (somehow seen as less bourgeois), such as the Quakers' AFSC and the Jewish JDC, which had undertaken small-scale reconstruction projects. As one newspaper report noted, "saving the starving from death . . . [is] only a half-measure." Representative Lander took a somewhat more detached view than his boss. Reflecting on the transition from relief to reconstruction, he noted that "the Posledgol stage of work brought us a mass of difficulties and complexities [in our dealings] with foreign organizations."[49] Posledgol, in sum, magnified disputes between reconstruction efforts and American relief—disputes already evident, in a less venomous form, during Pomgol's existence.

ARA officials, still focusing their anger on exports rather than on the broader Posledgol strategy, came to a similar conclusion. One internal report acknowledged that the Soviet government "was no longer primarily interested in famine relief. It is interested in economic rehabilitation." This change of direction explained the deterioration of ARA relations with the Soviet authorities: "we mistake for ill-will," the report hypothesized, "what is merely comparative indifference" to feeding programs like the ARA's.[50] Soviet leaders, who had long expressed their interest in economic reconstruction, turned to grain exports in the midst of famine in order to further their goals. Their willingness to risk the ire of American authorities—their largest source of emergency aid—suggests just how highly they valued reconstruction.

Perhaps the most striking instance of the Soviets' stress on reconstruction involved not the export of grain but the import of expertise. In one ill-advised moment, Lenin asked Hoover to serve as an economic advisor in Russia. The Comintern leader Karl Radek explained to Frank Golder the reasoning. He and a few other leading Bolsheviks held that Hoover, "being an organizer, was interested in construction and not destruction." Colonel Haskell actively promoted the chance to bring his chief to Moscow. Although the impetus for the invitation came from his man in Moscow, Hoover never dignified it with a response.[51]

Although Hoover rejected an advisory position with the Soviets, many on his staff expressed their desire to assist in Soviet reconstruction. As the export controversy broke, the economist Lincoln Hutchinson wrote Hoover a detailed memorandum criticizing the ARA approach. Hutchinson had first grown interested in Russia after seeing George Kennan lecture. He spent the 1910s shuttling between various posts in Washington, D.C. (serving with the War Industries Board, the Inquiry, and eventually in Hoover's Department of Commerce), and a faculty position at the University of California.[52] Appointed a special investigator for the ARA, Hutchinson undertook a series of scouting missions to evaluate economic conditions and the process of relief all across Russia. On the basis of these observations, Hutchinson sent Hoover a detailed evaluation of ARA activities in August

1922. He accused the organization of having "as a governing factor . . . a desire to punish and humiliate the gang of ruffians who hold power in Russia today." Hutchinson implored the ARA to take as its "clear-cut, single-minded purpose to do everything possible—even to the making of sacrifices [*sic*]—to get Russia started on the road to economic recovery."

Hutchinson's policy recommendations rested primarily on his analysis of Bolshevik policy and post-war economic conditions. These recommendations were hardly the result of pro-Soviet sentiments: he called the Politburo "a mélange of visionaries, cut-throats, assassins, thieves, and riff-raff so unspeakably rotten that any decent man shrinks from the thought of having any dealings with them." But constructive economic aid from the United States, he argued, could hasten the arrival of a new regime in Moscow. Reconstruction alone could produce the "gradual elimination . . . of the present personnel of the government, and their replacement by efficient men of affairs." Hutchinson's colleagues Harold Fisher and Cyril Quinn (Haskell's deputy in Moscow) endorsed such a policy of constructive engagement.[53]

After returning to California in 1923, Hutchinson revisited his earlier prognostications, elaborating on his logic. Upon first arriving in Russia, he recalled, he had hoped to find a way to "punish the unspeakable scoundrels" in power there. He quickly saw, though, that any solution in Russia required economic restoration, which in turn required American support. Two factors led Hutchinson to change his mind. First, harking back to his days in export promotion, he wanted to ensure that America would have a role in any future Russian market. And second, following on the source of his original inspiration for Russian studies, Kennan, Hutchinson believed that the character of the Russians would limit their ability to recover on their own. Picking up on one of Kennan's frequent themes, he doubted that a "sluggish" and "fatalistic" people like the Russians could change their own circumstances without external support.[54] Only with appropriate guidance (which Hutchinson himself sought to provide) could Russia make economic progress. Hutchinson's beliefs about national character, then, supported his view that American economic aid was essential for Russia.

Hutchinson's traveling companion in Russia, the historian Frank Golder, held similar views about Russia, Russians, and Bolsheviks. Golder shared Hutchinson's distaste for the Bolsheviks as well as the hope that economic reconstruction would be a key weapon against them. At the time of his stint with the ARA, Golder was, debatably, America's best-qualified expert on Russia. Trained by Archibald Cary Coolidge, Golder had worked extensively in Russian archives and had assisted important official initiatives related to Russia, from the Inquiry to the Root Mission. After the war, he briefly returned to his teaching appointment at Washington State College before joining the Hoover Library at Stanford, where he served until his ARA appointment.

Earlier than most observers, Golder promoted economic reconstruction as an essential aspect of ARA policy. Shortly after the announcement of Posledgol, he echoed Lander's call for a rational strategy: "in view of our claim that we are a relief organization run on scientific lines, we ought to look ahead in our relief and instead of carrying the peasants along for the minute alone, do something for the reconstruction of the country." He then sent Hoover's chief Washington aide, the future governor and secretary of state Christian Herter, a letter paralleling Hutchinson's. Distancing himself from the present leadership, Golder argued that recognition would further the American goal of ending Bolshevik rule. Although Golder did not (as he put it), "love the Bolos," he believed that only through political engagement and economic reconstruction could Hoover bring about the results they both desired in Russia: the overthrow of the Bolshevik regime and the return of Russia to the international commercial system. Hoover and the Russia desk officer at the State Department both reported their interest in, but not their conversion to, Golder's argument.[55]

Golder's vague duties with the ARA also allowed him to take on semi-official diplomatic reporting. His weekly letters to Herter received wide circulation among senior ARA staff as well as foreign service officers, earning Golder praise as "one of the most valuable sources" on Russia.[56] Golder's reports covered a variety of events, from insider briefings with Soviet officials and scholars to updates on ARA work. One recurrent theme in the letters is his general disparagement of rural Russians. Golder worried that Asian populations—which included, by his definition, inhabitants of the Volga Valley—had let their instincts take control. Bolshevik rule intensified these unpleasant circumstances, revealing the "wild instincts among the half-civilized" Russians. Under such conditions it had become all but impossible to find civilization in Russia; everyone from Kalmuks to Cossacks took "the mind back to Atilla and to the Middle Ages." Although the famine exacerbated the return of repressed instincts in Russia, Golder had identified such aspects of Russian life years earlier; one of his Inquiry reports drew attention to the "idiotic stare [and] animal look" he thought peculiarly Russian. His sentiments were apparently ill-disguised. He reported that Russian peasants frequently asked him: "What does the world think of Soviet Russia? Does it think the Russians are a lot of wild men? . . . What does the world think of us? Does it think we are crazy or a lot of wild savages? . . . Do Americans believe that the Bolsheviks are a lot of barbarians?"[57] Savage or not, Russian peasants clearly understood how relief workers perceived them.

Golder's Russian travels left him disheartened about Russia in particular, and about economic and cultural progress in general. By the time famine relief got under way, Golder was already "discouraged at the slow rate of progress." He began to sour on the country he had been studying for a decade: "My experience in Russia has made me suspicious of everyone who talks Russian." Nonetheless, Golder did not want to isolate the country from the rest of the world. To the contrary, his disillusioned view of Russian life—with "animal instincts" running rampant and the "fatalistic" population unable to look after its own interests—brought him to encourage American efforts at Soviet reconstruction. Only a rebuilt economy, Golder argued, would end the population's "state of savagery"—while also necessitating the end of the Bolshevik regime.[58] Economic growth, in short, could redeem Russia.

Hutchinson and Golder were not the only American aid officials who expressed a growing interest in assisting Soviet economic reconstruction. Governor Goodrich, roving through Russia again in early 1922, made a similar case. American policy, he complained to Hoover, "is only delaying the economic and political development of the country." Seeing economic stability as an enemy of Communism, Goodrich argued that American aid, by reviving the economy, could help curtail Soviet power. The best way to "moderate and eventually replace" Communist rule, then, was "to lend a hand in Russia's rebuilding."[59] His support for economic aid, like Hutchinson's and Golder's, had little to do with sympathies for the Soviet government.

Other support for reconstruction came from the National Information Bureau (NIB), an organization that monitored American philanthropies. NIB sent a commission to Russia in late 1922 to investigate conditions there, under the informal guidance of the lawyer Allen Wardwell, who had served with the Red Cross in Petrograd in 1917. This commission praised ARA efforts but also urged Hoover to endorse the food exports as "offer[ing] hope of real relief" in the long term. Before releasing its recommendations, the NIB commission presented its findings in a tense meeting with ARA officials. Hoover challenged the criticisms, petulantly suggesting that the NIB could begin their own relief efforts if they did not like his. He would have nothing to do with Russia beyond ameliorative relief.[60] The final NIB report, published in early 1923, painted a bleak picture of Russia's "demoralized economic life," cataloguing war-related destruction and disorganization, poor weather, and Bolshevik policies. Most controversially, the NIB report also offered an endorsement of Soviet economic policy: "To the extent that peasants who were kept alive last year through American aid are left to die in 1923, America's effort is inadequate. Emergency aid and the restoration of agriculture are both necessary." The NIB publicly offered qualified approval of the grain exports, so long as they "contributed to the rebuilding of peasant farms." Not surprisingly, Hoover's staff in Washington, which had already rebuffed ARA advisors making the same arguments, reacted strongly against this external criticism.[61] Hoover in particular was determined to defend his policy of relief without reconstruction.

The policy attracted even more criticism after a news leak in spring 1923. That March, Hoover's office asked William Haskell to send a telegram, designed for public release, summarizing the present economic situation in Russia. An optimistic assessment of Russian conditions could then be followed by the announcement that the ARA would cease its operations later that year. His secret plan to bring Hoover to Russia disregarded, Haskell used this opportunity to promote Russian reconstruction to the American public. In addition to the solicited telegram, Haskell sent to Washington a detailed letter expressing his pessimism that Americans could contribute to the Russian economy solely with emergency aid. Instead, Haskell called for major public and private efforts to "bring about the reconstruction of Russia." Like the other ARA officers promoting reconstruction, he disavowed any political sympathies for the Bolsheviks. But without an influx of foreign capital, he warned, "I know that one hundred million people are never going to be dragged out of the mud."[62]

In the telegram itself, Haskell suggested that government relief measures, combined with those of foreign aid organizations, would see Russia through until the next harvest. But, he added, "what Russia needs now is money or credit against which it can purchase necessities to rehabilitate agriculture, transportation, [and] vital industries." On these grounds, he defended the Soviet decision to export grain; "upbuilding without foreign financial help," he concluded, "is slow and ineffective." Haskell ended the telegram with the hope that individual Americans would remit aid to the Soviet economy. Conceding that "reconstruction lies outside the province of the ARA," he sought to "give the public the correct situation so that any assistance can hereafter be directed to proper purposes." The Washington office, however, disapproved of Haskell's conclusion and rewrote the telegram without giving any indication of its emendation. The press release containing Haskell's (edited) telegram concluded with the non-sequitur "Economic reconstruction is outside the province of the ARA which is purely an emergency charitable organization for the amelioration of famine conditions."[63] Haskell's message of American reconstructive aid was thus squelched by ARA headquarters.

A sympathetic observer—most likely Alexander Gumberg, a Russian-born American who devoted his whole career to American-Soviet *rapprochement*—somehow obtained copies of both the original telegram and the press release. Raymond Robins, a Progressive whose enchantment with the Bolsheviks dated back to his service with the Red Cross in Petrograd during the revolution, may have also been involved in the leak. Robins's friendship with Lincoln Hutchinson provided him with inside information about the ARA, including Hutchinson's critical memorandum to Hoover. Robins, furthermore, frequently was a mentor and sponsor of Gumberg's as well as the NIB's Allen Wardwell. Whatever the source, sharply critical reports of the in-house editing job appeared in both *Izvestiia* and the left-wing weekly *The Nation* only days after Haskell sent his telegram. *Nation* editors accused Hoover of "stabbing Russia." Working with ARA insiders, Robins and Gumberg apparently sought to sway public opinion toward helping Soviet Russia undertake economic reconstruction.[64]

Hutchinson and his fellow traveler Golder thus joined Haskell and Goodrich in making the case for reconstructive aid in Russia. They agreed with the Soviet leadership that reconstruction and eventually industrialization were the key to Russia's future. But Soviet officials differed sharply with these Americans about which door to the future would be unlocked. To the former, not surprisingly, a strong economy would consolidate the Bolsheviks' hold on power, whereas the Americans saw an opportunity to reconstruct Russia out of Bolshevism.

But what about Herbert Hoover, the director of the ARA? In many ways Hoover shared his critics' enthusiasm for economic development—with one notable caveat. Hoover recognized the importance of broader economic aid but (overruling his staff) did not want to provide such aid to the Bolsheviks. In his reply to Gorky's request in August 1921, Hoover acknowledged the need for "the rehabilitation of transportation, of agriculture, [and] of industry," but insisted that they demanded "measures beyond the reach of charity." As the ARA began to wind up its relief efforts, Hoover reiterated the need for reconstruction: "What Russia needs is economic reconstruction, the re-creation of productivity," he wrote in one widely distributed letter.[65] But any such efforts, Hoover insisted, must await the demise of Bolshevik rule; as he put it delicately in a memorandum to the secretary of state, reconstruction could take place only "when the proper moment arrives." Unlike many of his critics (Hibben, Robins, and Wardwell, among others) or some of his organization's own experts (Haskell, Hutchinson, Goodrich, and Golder), Hoover insisted that Russia's economic prospects depended on its political fortunes. Rejecting any significant support for the Bolsheviks, he offered only emergency aid. Yet even this food aid, he later conceded, had "helped the Soviet regime set up in business."[66]

Indeed, as the ARA workers wrapped up their work in spring 1923, Soviet Russia was much stronger than when they had entered eighteen months earlier. Food supplies, while not plentiful, had stabilized. As a stroke-weakened Lenin held onto the reins of power, many Politburo leaders turned to the internal struggles that would dominate Soviet politics in the 1920s. Although the ARA's departure significantly shrank the western presence in the USSR, a welter of other organizations continued with reconstructive work on a small scale. The Nansen mission, awarded the Nobel Peace Prize in 1922, signed new agreements with Soviet officials, establishing research stations designed to aid the regeneration of Russian agriculture.[67] The JDC expanded its programs in the early 1920s, starting with a $1.5 million grant for the mechanization of agriculture in its service area. The JDC efforts eventually blossomed into "Agro-Joint," which created Jewish agricultural settlements in Crimea.[68] Finally, the Quakers' AFSC took on additional tasks of agricultural regeneration, work that garnered Hoover's praise: "The upbuilding of Russia requires assistance particularly in agricultural reconstruction."[69] All these activities found a place in NEP-era Russia, which had abandoned total government control of the economy in favor of market forces, albeit constrained ones, in limited sectors of the economy. The relative openness of the Soviet economy encouraged certain foreign activities like relief programs, national resource concessions, and production and licensing agreements.[70] But these activities were small compared with the ARA's relief program.

The efforts of the ARA, the Nansen mission, and smaller relief agencies did not prevent as many as five million people from dying of starvation or related diseases between 1921 and 1923.[71] This toll hardly marked the end of starvation in the Russian countryside; portions of the afflicted regions again faced famine as early as 1924, and major famines in 1932–1933 and 1946 brought additional devastation to rural Russia. But between 1921 and 1923, American aid played a significant role in reducing the suffering of Russia's rural population for the duration of its relief efforts there. Hoover's goal of alleviating starvation thus met with success.

For Soviet leaders, ARA relief was insufficient. They held to the broader goal of quickly rebuilding the economy so they could then turn to the task of industrialization. As Kamenev, the chief of famine-relief efforts, put it in a Politburo debate as relief wound down: "The Party must work, systematically and persistently, to speed . . . the reconstruction of industry and especially heavy industry, not stopping at any sacrifice and having no mercy for any other power."[72] Few Americans involved in the famine relief subscribed wholly to this view. But many American experts working on famine relief, or closely connected to Russia policy, endorsed aspects of Kamenev's exhortation. These experts, especially ARA investigators like Lincoln Hutchinson and Frank Golder, saw economic reconstruction as a goal of equal if not greater importance than emergency relief. They came to this conclusion not out of appreciation for Marxist doctrine—and certainly not out of enthusiasm for the Bolsheviks—but because they saw economic development as a dire need for Russia. Interpretations of Russian national character contributed to the sense that Russians needed help from without. For this group of experts, economic reconstruction stood apart from politics. In contrast, Herbert Hoover insisted that politics took precedence, that the American government should isolate Russia, which he called "an economic vacuum," until the Bolsheviks were swept from power.[73]

The tensions between economic and political understandings of Russia would persist into the 1920s, as a new cohort of experts sought to explain the rise of the Soviet Union and its implications. Lincoln Hutchinson, reflecting on the USSR's first decade of existence, acknowledged the "disaster [brought to] hordes of individuals" but also praised the "general level of prosperity of the masses." This view would grow more popular among American experts later in the 1920s. Frank Golder, for one, remained optimistic about the Russian future: "the peasants and workmen will multiply rapidly," he predicted, "and the . . . earth will yield abundant riches." What, then, should Americans do about Russia? By 1924, Golder had retreated from the bustling world of politics and aid work into a sedate library carrel. Calling for a new generation of experts to devote themselves to the study of Russia, he placed his hopes in intellectual engagement with the country. Experts with the "necessary training, the open mind, [and] the big vision," Golder believed, could find new solutions to the Russian problem.[74] It is those experts, and their solutions, that marked a new American approach to Russia.

Modernizing Russia, Backward Russians

CHAPTER

7

New Society, New Scholars

With the accession of the Bolsheviks to power, American commentary on Russia expanded both in quantity and in range of opinion. The new regime in Russia attracted levels of revulsion and admiration that far surpassed Americans' commitments for or against tsarist Russia. The end of European hostilities in November 1918 soon brought the war home to the United States. In 1919 major strikes, racial violence, and ambitious (if grossly unfulfilled) dreams of revolution reverberated across the United States. The overwhelming forces arrayed against radical change painted every challenger to the status quo as a Bolshevik. The full resources of state power fought radicalism, particularly that connected (however loosely) with Bolshevism, easily overpowering individuals with revolutionary sentiments. Attorney General A. Mitchell Palmer spearheaded attacks on "Bolshevists" and immigrants, usually equating one with the other.[1] Even after the ebb of the anti-Red tide in 1920, substantial segments of published American opinion remained harshly opposed to Bolshevism in Russia and the United States. At the same time, though, the Bolshevik revolution inspired radicals new and old. For example Isaac Hourwich, like many others, maintained his Marxism, helping translate *Das Kapital* into Yiddish, but rejected Bolshevism. This caused some family tensions; his son Nicholas helped lead left-wingers out of the Socialist Party of America and into a Leninist Communist Party. This initial split was a harbinger of the factional politics to dominate American radicalism for decades.[2] Greenwich Village bohemians celebrated revolutionary culture while the longtime socialist leader Eugene Debs boasted that he was Bolshevik "from the crown of my head to the soles of my feet."[3]

The heightened attentions to Russia in post–World War I America also affected America's Russia expertise, albeit in unexpected ways. Like Frank Golder, who retreated from the noisy political sphere to the quiet recesses of a library, Russia experts sought refuge in scholarly ideals and scholarly idylls. To protect themselves from claims of partisanship in this moment of heightened political fear, scholars of Russia invoked the key concepts of social science in the 1920s—objectivity, science, and usefulness.[4] The field of Russian studies became more professional by cross-fertilization with the social sciences and by expanding into new institutions.

Scholars and observers with a strong interest in Russia moved closer to the mainstream of the social sciences in the 1920s. The sociologist Jerome Davis and the political scientist Samuel Harper—both of whom had written about Russia before the Bolshevik takeover in 1917—drew directly from the main currents of their respective disciplines in their analyses of Russia. A complementary trend brought American social scientists to the study of Russian affairs. Social scientists, especially those with a reformist bent, examined the emerging Soviet Union for the lessons it might provide to the United States. Paul Douglas (University of Chicago) and Amy Hewes (Mount Holyoke College) both examined the Soviet Union as a case study in their social-scientific work—a direction that many others followed in the late 1920s and early 1930s.

New institutions evolved to accommodate the expanded interest in Russian and Soviet affairs. More and more Russia experts found positions within American universities, many of which planned centers devoted to the study of Russia. The proliferating foreign-affairs think tanks in the 1920s housed other specialists like the Russian immigrants Vera Micheles Dean and Leo Pasvolsky. New networks of scholars helped pull together this broad range of Russia experts; Robert Kerner and Geroid Tanquary Robinson (along with Golder) sought to create the appurtenances of a scholarly discipline, including a journal and a professional association.

The field's new institutional and intellectual directions shaped the study of Russia. At times, the transformations were direct and obvious, as in the case of Harper, who completely rethought his attitude toward the Bolsheviks as a result of his immersion in political science. Kerner quickly jettisoned the ethnic cheerleading of his early work in favor of a more rigorous scholarly approach. Robinson similarly abandoned his Village bohemianism as his training in Russian studies continued. The transforming effects of structural change emerge most clearly from close biographical studies.

For Samuel Harper, long devoted to Russian liberalism, the Bolshevik takeover in October 1917 was nothing less than betrayal. As a prominent advisor in diplomatic circles during and after Russia's revolutionary up-heavals, he energetically promoted American military and material sup-port for anti-Bolshevik forces. He soon received an appointment to the State Department, where he served as the sole member of the Russian Di-vision's Chicago office. After that appointment expired and he returned to full-time work at the University of Chicago, Harper continued his opposi-tion to the Bolsheviks. A series of articles from 1924 maintained the same critical stance that he had employed in promoting intervention in policy circles. One article, entitled "The Communist Dictatorship," outlined Bol-shevik efforts to dominate all aspects of central and local administration. He identified "impulses of recovery" scattered across Soviet Russia, but be-lieved that they existed despite—not because of—the Soviets. Harper still opposed American diplomatic recognition of Soviet Russia for fear that it would strengthen the "Bolshevik microbe." The pathogen was becoming "less virulent" as the Russian "economic organism" regained its strength.[5] Harper credited the New Economic Policy with healing Russia's economic wounds. The policy's benefits also spread to the United States; by attract-ing the attention of western businesses, NEP legitimized interest in Soviet Russia.[6]

Hoping to return to Russia—and perhaps dissatisfied with his marginal position at the University of Chicago—Harper weighed and then declined a job offer from a firm doing business in Russia; it would have been tempt-ing, he told a friend, to "'cash in' on my Russian 'investment.'"[7] But Harper quickly assented to a second opportunity to travel to Russia, as part of a comparative study of "civic training." He leaped at this offer to return to Russia while at the same time strengthening intellectual affiliations in his own institution.[8] His ticket to Russia was a project called "Studies in the Making of Citizens." It was the brainchild of Charles Merriam, a promi-nent member of Chicago's department of political science and a leader of his discipline. Through the project, Merriam hoped to learn more about the "methods used to indoctrinate children with a love of the state." His in-terest in this subject grew out of a ubiquitous concern of 1920s political scientists: the impact of popular sentiments—particularly irrational ones —on society and politics.

Popularized in Walter Lippmann's incisive and pessimistic studies of public opinion, concerns over mass irrationality spurred the behaviorist turn in political science. Merriam and his cohort sought to shift their discipline from the study of political ideas and political systems to the study of political behaviors. They did so with a skepticism of participatory democracy and some distrust of the electorate—a skepticism honed, in Merriam's case, by his own loss to a local political boss in a city election. Merriam's civic training project examined these issues while also addressing some of the key questions of early behaviorism: How susceptible was the population to anti-statist demagoguery? What means of indoctrination or propaganda—not yet dirty words—could the state use to assure popular allegiance? Merriam envisioned a broad collaborative project covering education in Fascist Italy and Soviet Russia as well as civic education in multiethnic societies like Great Britain and Switzerland. The project even included a study of initiation rituals in ancient and medieval military societies.[9] Harper, not surprisingly, was assigned the volume on Bolshevik Russia. This marked a departure from his earlier work on parliamentary politics, a departure directly traceable to his exposure to mainstream political scientists and their concerns.

Harper arrived in Moscow in summer 1926, where he hosted Merriam. Both were impressed with the scope of Soviet education efforts, broadly defined. Harper noted that the legacies of pre-revolutionary Russia hindered Soviet progress; those legacies, in turn, had a great deal to do with national character. Creating Soviet citizens would be all the harder, Harper concluded in his monograph based on the 1926 trip, because "the lack of patriotism has been a trait attributed to many Russians." But the problems created by Russian national character extended beyond this defect. The Soviets' desire to extinguish peasant apathy faced an uphill battle, Harper wrote, because this "apathy developed under the conditions and habits of the Russian past." Only with "the driving force of enthusiasm" did Soviet leaders have any hope of creating a productive and loyal citizenry. Campaigns for education and production thus needed to overcome deeply rooted stubbornness and apathy.[10]

The comprehensiveness and zeal of Soviet efforts to foster popular allegiance impressed Harper and Merriam. By seeking to eradicate most previous forms of loyalty—national, regional, religious, and ethnic—the Soviet education effort faced added challenges, Merriam concluded. New states like Fascist Italy could build on prior nationalism, whereas the Soviet Union had to start from scratch. No wonder Merriam considered the USSR "the world's most interesting and suggestive experiment in civic

education, rich in materials for the students of civic processes." But his excitement about Soviet education did not extend to left-wing politics in
general. Merriam aligned himself with the National Civic Federation, a
Progressive-era organization for "industrial peace" that had swung to the
right in the aftermath of World War I. Formed in 1905 to promote "better
understanding" between labor and capital, the federation by the 1920s had
become a staunch opponent of the Soviet Union as well as American labor
unions in general.[11]

Unlike Merriam, Harper reconsidered his opposition to the USSR as he
studied it from the perspective of civic education. In newspaper articles
written upon his return, Harper offered the highest praise for Soviet efforts
to "raise" the peasantry through education. Thanks to these efforts, Harper
continued, a "new type of peasant" populated the Soviet countryside. Neither ignorant nor cowed, like their predecessors, these new peasants were
"articulate, discontented and hopeful" about the future. Harper's writings
on this phenomenon were either condescending or tone-deaf: he elaborated little on the content of the peasants' criticisms of the government but
nevertheless credited the government with the rural population's newfound ability to articulate complaints.[12]

Harper's praise of the Soviet government soon extended beyond the
educative functions he aimed to study. Changes in rural Russia impressed
Harper greatly. Led into the countryside by the American journalist
Maurice Hindus (himself born in rural Belorussia), he was struck by the
persistence of "extreme backwardness" in the villages. But he also found
plenty of evidence of the "quickening of economic life." Harper credited
Bolshevik institutions like the Red Army for contributing to Russia's modernization. Returning soldiers, he noticed, brought to their home villages
not only new ideas but new consumer goods; thanks to these soldiers, for
instance, soccer had supplanted intervillage brawls as "the main sport of
rural Russia."[13]

Harper furthermore connected civic training to economic policy, praising the new system for turning the Russian peasant into a "citizen in production." Collective agriculture, he argued, also helped produce the newly
articulate peasants. Present in Moscow as high-level debates raged over
economic policy, Harper sided with those Bolshevik leaders pushing for
rapid transformations. He approved of the new Soviet goal of "reconstruction" rather than merely "restoration" of industry, concluding that the
state's new goal must be "the industrialization of Russia." Harper also en-

dorsed more intensive efforts to meet this goal given that the "economic possibilities of the New Economic Policy . . . have been exhausted."[14] Only through industrialization, he added, could the Soviets complete the cultural transformation of the peasantry. This view was a far cry from his earlier opposition to the Bolsheviks. As a direct result of his engagement with social scientists, then, he now saw the Bolsheviks' mission as social and political transformation. Having learned new analytical instruments of political science from Merriam, Harper was now playing a different tune.

Harper's State Department colleagues, accustomed to the more familiar score of anti-Bolshevism, found his new ideas discordant. One diplomat responded to Harper's articles by invoking the specter of a pro-Soviet clergyman: the "articles sounded more like Sherwood Eddy than you," he wrote to Harper. The letter concluded with a combination of personal affection and professional dissent:

> What in the world has happened to you? Have you joined those who have fallen under the spell of the Bolsheviks? A few months in Russia have done funny things to a good many people, but your shift, from a conspicuous defender of our Russian policy to one of the most effective Bolshevik propagandists in America today, beats me. Are we really all wrong down here [in the State Department]?[15]

Although Harper maintained his friendships with the State Department's Russia specialists—at least until personal contretemps in the mid-1930s—his ideas about Russia diverged even further from theirs. As he expanded his investigations from parliamentary politics to education and from there to economics, Harper began to see Soviet rule in a positive light. These new topics, the result of engagement with contemporary scholarly concerns, offered him a new perspective from which to observe the Soviet Union, a perspective not available to the State Department personnel whose principal focus was political.

Harper was unusual in the thoroughness and speed of his transformation from anti- to pro-Bolshevik as a result of reading in the social sciences. Nevertheless, other American observers also found their ideas altered when expressed in the social-scientific language of the day. Like Harper, the sociologist Jerome Davis began his involvement with Russia before the revolution and with no direct commitment to scholarly analysis. Davis, the son of missionaries, was literally born into the Social Gospel movement and was animated by its goal of improving the life of the poor.

After graduating from Oberlin, he studied social welfare at Columbia University. Offered the chance to work with Russian prisoners of war in 1917, Davis traveled to Moscow, Petrograd, and Turkestan for the YMCA.[16] Although he was at first "bitterly" opposed to the Bolsheviks, he soon changed his mind. While they "merit a good deal of criticism," he wrote in 1919, the American government should nevertheless recognize the Bolsheviks as rulers. He offered two arguments for recognition: first, if given a choice between Bolshevism and a return to tsarism, most Americans would wish for the former; and second, the Bolsheviks, though deeply flawed, represented the Russian people with all their imperfections.[17] Davis elaborated on both these themes over the next few years. He continued to support diplomatic recognition in the hopes that it would moderate the Bolsheviks.[18] And he continued to inventory energetically the flaws of Russian national character. The Russians' "very childlike" nature, Davis argued in 1920, explained the Bolshevik success. Given the population's immaturity, Russia needed a strong leader, the "iron will" that the Provisional Government head Aleksandr Kerenskii lacked.[19] Like many American advisors during the Russian Civil War, Davis emphasized the inability of the Russians to look after their own interests.

After observing three years of revolutionary change, Davis returned to Columbia with an increasingly academic focus. He switched advisors from the social welfare advocate Edward Devine to Franklin Giddings, the dynamo behind a resolutely empirical sociology, though both scholars left their mark on Davis's writings. Davis's early articles maintained Devine's social reform tone. As part of a study funded by the Inter-Church World Movement, for instance, Davis examined the lives of Slavic immigrants in the United States. He concluded with a call for better wages and working conditions in American factories. The ominous subtitle of one work, "Bolsheviks or Brothers?" described a choice that, Davis argued, lay in American hands: if American employers persisted in their poor treatment of immigrants, the newcomers would certainly become Bolsheviks. These immigrants had been "isolated from the best of America" and thus had little reason to assimilate to or support their new home country.[20] The book had a hopeful tone that Slavs in America would indeed become brothers and not Bolsheviks.

By the time his book on immigrants appeared, however, Davis had begun to favor the language of academic sociology over that of social reform. This was in large part a reflection of Giddings's influence on the young scholar.[21] Giddings, in part rebelling against his own religious upbringing, had turned to Herbert Spencer's theories for both political and intellectual inspiration. Giddings wanted the new field of sociology to emulate the natural sciences wherever possible; "we need men . . . who will get busy with the adding machine and the logarithms," he wrote in 1909. The center of Giddings's empirical work was his theory of "consciousness of kind." Humans, Giddings wrote, were innately attracted to others who were similar to themselves. Applications of this theory would explain human behavior much better than the purely economic, political, or religious factors studied by related disciplines.[22] Enthusiastic about Giddings's ideas, Davis quickly integrated them into his own writings, often using the concepts to buttress positions he already held. Thus Davis's "sociological interpretation of the Russian Revolution" cited Giddings's notion of "likemindedness" in order to defend his previous claim that the Bolsheviks were representative of the Russian population.[23]

Yet Davis seemed to apply such scientism inconsistently. His doctoral dissertation revealed little of Giddings's imprint, following instead the social reform tradition of his earlier work. For example, in a move hardly scientific in his advisor's terms, Davis set about cataloguing the Russian national character, using this impressive list to explain the potential for a less antagonistic relationship between American employers and Russian immigrants:

1. predominance of feeling over will
2. does not perceive inconsistencies
3. horror of any kind of rule or compulsion
4. little forethought; yields to the pleasure of the moment
5. feels that passion excuses everything
6. dislike of any kind of law
7. intellectual curiosity
8. places soul or personality above all else
9. believes in humility
10. willing to endure a good deal
11. patient and stolid
12. sociable[24]

This list demonstrated to Davis both the blessings and the curses of Russians. On the one hand, their indifference to danger and their endurance made them attractive employees in factories; their thrift and humility helped them survive poor conditions. On the other hand, traits like impulsiveness and lack of discipline presented obstacles for industrial work in the United States or Russia.[25] Davis's investigations represent a midpoint in the process of professionalization; he combined social-scientific analysis with the sort of impressionistic work that had characterized earlier writings on Russia and Russians.

This combination of amateur and professional approaches also appears in Davis's discussion of Soviet affairs. As he had done in his analysis of the revolution, Davis connected Russian events, including the rise of Bolshevism, to Russian character. Yet he also lauded the Bolsheviks for attempting to overcome the weaknesses of the Russians. He praised Bolshevik economic policy, for instance, because it had "jolted [the Russians] out of centuries-old habits." Similarly, he explained Soviet political centralism as a necessary result of Russians' lack of education and inexperience with democracy.[26]

Throughout the 1920s, Davis continued the struggle for Russian-American *rapprochement* in diplomatic circles as well as in American factories. Leaving his post at Dartmouth College to take the Gilbert Stark Chair in Practical Philanthropy at Yale's Divinity School, Davis continued to employ Giddings's language of scientism. His contributions to two books, one in the late 1920s and the other in the early 1930s, were dry factual explications of the party-state apparatus.[27] Other articles used Russia to address sociological issues of the day: a comparative study of children's views of occupational prestige (American schoolchildren ranked bankers and professors at the top of their lists, while Russians listed peasants and aviators) and a study concluding that Bolshevik leaders had been radicalized by their reading and their teachers.[28] Davis adapted the language of scientism to his long-running campaign for American diplomatic recognition of the USSR. A 1926 article, for instance, invoked Giddings's call for the empirical study of human society before concluding that recognition was in the best interests of science.[29] Although he was later dismissed from Yale for his condemnation of capitalism, Davis's writings in the 1920s illustrate the close match between the language of positivist social science and pro-Soviet sentiment.

By the late 1920s, Harper and Davis shared a new social-scientific vocabulary as well as pro-Soviet sentiments. Ironically, both had learned their scientism from their staunchly conservative mentors, Merriam and Giddings, yet had drawn from their teaching reasons to endorse aspects of Soviet policy. The contrast between these Russia scholars and their mentors demonstrates that social-scientific approaches to the Soviet Union were not inherently disposed toward a single view of Soviet events. These episodes also show that professional social science and pro-Soviet sentiment were hardly mutually exclusive—and indeed, that the two ideas, so often held in explicit contrast, could be mutually supportive.

Other scholars whose training and initial interests were in economics also found social-scientific approaches conducive to the study of the Soviet Union. The labor economist Paul Douglas at the University of Chicago, for instance, followed his disciplinary interests to the study of the Soviet Union. Best known for deriving the Cobb-Douglas function, which remains a key measure in the field, Douglas also joined forces with the institutional economists of the 1920s, including his Columbia classmate Rexford Guy Tugwell. These economists insisted that economic processes must be analyzed in the context of social and political institutions rather than as isolated operations in an idealized free market. Tellingly, Douglas's contribution to the institutionalist manifesto of the early 1920s, edited by Tugwell, proclaimed the importance of non-economic forces like altruism on economic behavior.[30] Douglas's interest in Russia emerged out of his commitment to institutionalism as well as to labor politics. His first trip to Russia, for example, was as part of an expert commission accompanying a trade-union delegation in 1927. Upon his return, Douglas sang the praises of Soviet trade unions on two counts. First, he argued, unions helped promote higher productivity by improving worker morale and ensuring adequate training and compensation. Second, he lauded unions' concern for "worker psychology." Paralleling his colleague Harper's argument that collective farms served an educative function, Douglas argued the same for factory-based trade unions. Douglas, who had by then begun his path-breaking study of real wages in the United States, also praised Soviet compensation practices.[31] Reformist impulses, combined with the institutionalist drift of academic economics, produced Douglas's sympathy for the labor policies of the Soviet Union. Focusing on ostensibly parallel institutions in the United States and the Soviet Union, Douglas portrayed the USSR as a high point of Progressive policy.

Upon returning from Moscow, Douglas reported to Harper that trade unions would soon eclipse the Communist Party as a power center in the Soviet Union. Enthusiastic about this possibility, Douglas proposed a multidisciplinary study of Soviet economic and political life. Although he hoped to include an impressive range of western scholars (mostly American), his project soon stalled. Soviet officials balked at opening their nation to such thorough study, fearing the consequences of a negative report. As the deputy commissar for foreign affairs Maxim Litvinov warned the Politburo in a memorandum: "We have not received a single ruble's credit from America on the basis of a professor's information, although these professors' negative opinions may influence businesspeople." Even Douglas's enthusiasm for the Soviet Union as Progressivism incarnate failed to sway the Politburo, which ultimately rejected his proposal.[32]

After the project's collapse, Douglas persisted in teasing out the economic implications of Soviet economic policy. At a meeting of academic economists, for instance, he detailed the process of price formation in the USSR. His contribution to a 1929 collection co-edited by the perennial Socialist presidential candidate Norman Thomas enumerated a dozen or so lessons from both American and Soviet economic policy in the 1920s. Citing wartime Germany as well as Soviet Russia, Douglas insisted that economic change must necessarily be shaped by human intervention—a view that before long would gain currency well outside left-wing circles.[33] Douglas soon shifted from promoting economic policy to enacting it. He helped establish the League of Independent Political Action, a group determined to pull electoral politics to the left. And he soon found himself awash in New Deal causes, advising on federal and state legislation for pensions, social security, and unemployment.[34] His writings about the Soviet Union shrank as he delved into New Deal policies and then (as his colleague Charles Merriam had) into electoral politics. Douglas's career culminated in his election in 1948 to the U.S. Senate, where he was among its most liberal members.

Like Douglas, the sociologist Amy Hewes grew interested in the Soviet Union primarily as a result of her studies of working conditions and labor policies. Trained in sociology at the University of Chicago, Hewes published widely in economics journals. In her articles on Soviet topics, she examined the trade union movement as well as social-welfare provisions in factories. Both topics received close attention from American social scientists in the 1920s: economists, sociologists, and Progressive reformers looked to unions as one effective means of ensuring that workers benefited from productivity growth in the American economy. Hewes examined the legal, economic, and political status of Soviet trade unions in order to make broad theoretical conclusions. She outlined an "economic interpretation of history," by which economic institutions—like unions—came into being to meet specific economic needs. The demise of capitalist labor relations in Russia, she argued, spelled the end of the unions' usefulness— yet Soviet trade unions showed no sign of disappearing. Her article on the topic was as much an argument about the need for unions under capitalism as it was a call for their reconfiguration under Communism.[35] Similarly, Hewes addressed employer-based insurance programs (including workers' compensation, life insurance, and medical insurance), many of which American reformers tried in the early 1920s to import from Europe. She wanted Soviet Russia's regulations—which she called "one of the most comprehensive systems of social insurance in existence today"—to become part of these discussions.[36] Hewes's writings on Soviet labor relations, then, were situated at the nexus of Progressive reform and social science; she used the Soviet Union as one more case upon which to base new American programs and historical interpretations.

For Douglas and Hewes, disciplinary training created and shaped an initial interest in Soviet Russia. Both conducted research on the Soviet Union as a case study for broader trends—economic institutions for Douglas, social welfare for Hewes, and labor unions for both. This case-study approach implied a degree of political and economic commonality across nations, which in turn led Douglas and Hewes toward positive impressions of Soviet economic practices. Although their trajectories (from social science to the study of the USSR) were the opposite of Harper's and Davis's, Douglas and Hewes both illustrate the increasing connections between social science and studies of the Soviet Union. In all these cases, the drift toward professionalization left room for—indeed, facilitated—the espousal of pro-Soviet views. All four scholars, after all, derived and defended their positive appraisals of the Soviet Union with social-scientific concepts.

Russia experts working outside the social-scientific disciplines of the 1920s were also affected by the professionalizing trends of the day. This was especially true among historians, who, like the social scientists, underscored the scholarly and non-partisan nature of their own work. At the same time, historians were especially active in promoting Russian studies as a discipline of its own. They dreamed of permanent, all-encompassing networks of Russia scholars in the United States, even if they created only small and evanescent ones. However impermanent, these networks included not just university-based scholars but also American government officials with responsibility for policy toward the USSR. These professional contacts through formal networks slowly began to replace the personal connections that had defined the relationships between earlier generations of scholars and diplomats.

The immediate impetus for establishing a national network of Slavicists in the United States came, curiously, from abroad. During a semester-long visit to the University of California in 1924, the British Russianist Bernard Pares encouraged Harvard's Archibald Cary Coolidge to establish a "Standing Conference of Slavonic Studies." Such an organization, Pares suggested, would provide "a collective authority" for its members. It would also make Pares's work easier by promoting contacts with *Slavonic Review,* the journal he had founded three years earlier. Edited at Pares's office at the University of London, the journal (later renamed *Slavonic and East European Review*) had from the start invited American authors.[37]

While still in the United States in May 1924, Pares proposed that American Slavicists gather as a group at the upcoming American Historical Association (AHA) meetings. That luncheon event, organized primarily by Robert Kerner, a historian at the University of Missouri, attracted a handful of foreign scholars as well as representatives from thirty American universities. Robert Kelley (a former Coolidge student) and Richard Crane also attended from the State Department, along with diplomats representing many eastern European countries in Washington. The luncheon featured a talk by Pares's London colleague R. W. Seton-Watson entitled "The Future of Slavonic Studies." Seton-Watson called for a program of "regional studies" uniting the study of language, literature, history, and economics. The group established a Joint Publication Committee, chaired by Harper, which explored the feasibility of creating an independent journal. The committee ultimately voted to work with Pares's *Slavonic Review,* at which point it added three American contributing editors: Kerner, Harper, and Robert Lord, a Harvard Polonist.[38]

Kerner spoke briefly at the AHA luncheon he organized, noting enthusiastically the increased interest in Slavonic studies. Although he had started studying central Europe for personal reasons—his parents had emigrated from Czechoslovakia—Kerner quickly learned the skills of a professional historian. Educated at the University of Chicago before starting his graduate work with Coolidge, Kerner conducted research in Europe for a dissertation on eighteenth-century Bohemia. Through his connections to Coolidge, he joined the Inquiry; while there, Kerner promoted Czechoslovak independence so energetically that coworkers accused him of unprofessional activities. After leaving government service, he continued his advocacy for Czechoslovak causes. He celebrated the rise of independent Czechoslovakia while confidently asserting that it was in no danger of succumbing to Bolshevism.[39] By the mid-1920s, though, Kerner took a broader vision of the role of his expertise. In his comments at the AHA luncheon, he proclaimed that expert knowledge of the Slavic world was essential to America's future. The Slavs formed "the largest white group in the world" and were a subject of special interest on the verge of the drastic immigration reforms of 1920 and 1924. Slavic nations had also become "a vital factor in world politics and economics."[40] Both points fit well with Kerner's principal concerns at that early stage of his career.

Kerner's comments on the racial characteristics of Slavs were consistent with his abiding interest in racial science. Through the early 1920s, Kerner read widely and deeply in racial theory, including popularizers like Lothrop Stoddard (himself a Coolidge student) and Madison Grant. Stoddard and Grant, in a series of popular polemics, placed the world's population on a rigid racial hierarchy, topped by the Nordics. Other Europeans, whom Grant termed Mediterraneans and Alpines, were vastly inferior to the Nordics; non-Europeans, according to Stoddard, rated lower yet. These authors based their claims of Nordic superiority on skull capacity and cephalic index, which measured skull shape.[41] Kerner seemed to identify closely with the writings of Grant and Stoddard.[42] But he soon turned away from what he called "racial metaphysics" and toward an emphasis on historical factors. In a 1924 speech, "The Importance of Eastern European History," Kerner opened by noting the prevalence of the "Alpine type" across the region. Authors like Grant and Stoddard, he suggested, might view the "relative backwardness of the peoples of Eastern Europe . . . as the product of alleged racial characteristics." He instead insisted on the importance of environmental and historical factors over biological ones: backwardness could not be traced to the "inferiority of races, or to put it another way, stupidity of peoples." The region's conditions, he asserted, were "the result of historical forces and habitat."[43] This phrasing closely paralleled that of Franz Boas, the anthropologist who led the assault on Grant's racial hierarchies and argued for environmental (not racial) origins of cultural difference. Boas's influential book *The Mind of Primitive Man* (1911) asserted that "historical events appear to have been much more potent in leading races to civilization than their [racial] faculty."[44] Trumpeting the importance of history and the limited role of race allowed Kerner to defend both his own heritage (derided by Grant) and the prerogatives of his discipline. But his anti-racialism had its limits. The study of history should expand, he argued, but only to incorporate the examination of a wider range of whites.

Kerner's claim about the importance of Slavic studies to world politics offered an opportunity to apply academic expertise to policy, a perennial interest of his. Kerner first sought political involvement during World War I, when he volunteered to serve on the staff of the Root Mission in 1917. After that effort failed, he worked on the Inquiry with his advisor Coolidge, at which time he took his case for Czechoslovak independence directly to President Wilson. It is also possible that his early desire to work for the government grew out of his wish to avoid conscription.[45] In any case, his interest in government service never waned.[46] By the early 1920s, Kerner had broadened his horizons, researching and writing on a variety of Slavic topics, from the southern Slavs (soon to unite as Yugoslavia) to the Russian Revolution—usually with an eye to the contemporary implications of his historical work. For instance, Kerner insisted that studies of Soviet Russia should be at the center of social-scientific research; scholars could use unique material for the investigation of contemporary society— including the links between race, culture, and economics.[47] He thus offered an endorsement of just the sort of work that Samuel Harper, Jerome Davis, Paul Douglas, and Amy Hewes were undertaking.

By the mid-1920s Kerner had followed his own advice about policy relevance, shifting his research focus eastward to Russia. Although at least one student questioned his linguistic capabilities in this new field, few could question his commitment to Russian studies.[48] In 1925 he presented a scholarly paper on Soviet Russia, in which he analyzed changes in agricultural organization, which he saw as the key to Russia's recent tumult. Kerner blamed the revolution of 1917 on a "vast elemental agrarian movement," an upsurge of peasants' "instinct for private property."[49] He explored similar themes in an essay on Leo Tolstoy, further illustrating that abandoning biological notions of behavior need not lead to the demise of national-character stereotypes. Kerner lauded the novelist's "penetrating" knowledge of the Russian peasantry, defined by its fatalism and its "unconscious, elemental swarm" nature. He defended this characterization of the peasantry with reference to its "vast elemental movements" during the revolutions of 1905 and 1917. By 1931, Kerner had begun work on the topic that would engage him for the remainder of his career: Russia's eastward expansion. This work culminated in a short book *(The Urge to the Sea)* that explained most of Russian history in terms of an unstoppable, even innate, drive to the Pacific.[50] Focusing on an area long ignored by scholars—and important to foreign policy—Kerner's newfound research topic allowed him to combine his desire to contribute to policy debates with his desire to create a distinctive school of historical analysis.

Even with his shifting scholarly interests, Kerner never abandoned his earlier commitment to developing professional Slavic studies. From his very first publication, he emphasized the importance of scientific study of the Slavic world, complete with a suitable scholarly infrastructure of library holdings and a journal. As a professor and administrator, Kerner placed a high priority on scholarly research for both teacher training and empirical discovery. Comparing scholars to "pioneers of knowledge," for instance, Kerner called in 1926 for an expansion of graduate programs in Russian studies.[51] The prerogatives of professional Slavic studies shaped his research agenda. Studying Russia and particularly Russian expansion gave him purchase to a political role unavailable to a central European specialist.

By the time of Kerner's "pioneer" manifesto in 1926, the historian Geroid Tanquary Robinson was already toiling on the frontiers of knowledge, working in Russian archives. Robinson's early career demonstrates another way in which a commitment to the professional study of Russia led to the shedding of earlier attachments and ideas. Whereas Kerner came to Russian studies via eighteenth-century Bohemia, Robinson arrived by way of a more recent bohemia: Greenwich Village of the 1910s. Fresh from European service during the war, Robinson soon found himself among the group clustered around *The Dial*. His attraction to radical thought predated his arrival in New York, though; he had written a passable interpretation of Marxism as a high school senior in 1913.[52]

The Dial brought together many of Greenwich Village's (and indeed America's) finest thinkers. Its staff included John Dewey, Robert Morss Lovett, and Thorstein Veblen; it published articles by Franz Boas and Lewis Mumford, among others. In addition to helping edit the magazine, Robinson wrote articles on a variety of domestic and international topics. Reacting to the yearlong domestic labor strife in 1919, he envisioned a form of labor organization and economic control that could prevent unrest by providing workers with a louder voice in and larger share of the economy than was currently the case. No rabble-rouser, Robinson criticized the strikers as exemplifying American "national dumbness" and the workers' materialism. But he hardly stood on the side of the status quo; he called for a major but gradual reorganization of society led by labor unions. As industries came under the control of unions, Robinson proposed, broader social change would become possible. Education would imbue students with a stronger sense of reason, so that they would be guided by rationality rather than by instinct. Robinson called for the reformation of the basic units of society "based on general developed intelligence."[53] He also wrote about Russia, though these articles did not appear in *The Dial*. Even so, Robinson's Russia pieces reveal his immersion in the Pragmatism and politics of *The Dial* staff. He looked forward to seeing socialism in operation so its efficiency could be adequately tested. He opposed intervention in Russia in 1919 on the grounds that Bolshevism would "destroy itself" in due time. Watching the self-destruction of Bolshevism would allow the world to "profit from the experiment in socialization."[54] Robinson's arguments, here and elsewhere, tracked closely with those of his fellow staff member John Dewey, who similarly sought to promote the rational reorganization of society.[55] They also resonated with the ideas of Thorstein Veblen, whose criticisms of the separation of ownership and management appeared alongside Robinson's.[56] Robinson and Dewey remained personal as well as intellectual comrades, vacationing together for decades after leaving *The Dial*.[57]

As Robinson parted with *The Dial* in early 1920, his interests slowly migrated toward Russia. As an associate editor of the anarchist A. J. Nock's new magazine, *The Freeman,* Robinson continued to write about labor and ethnic relations. He contributed to the widely read volume *Civilization in the United States* (1922), which one historian has termed a "*Dial* collective effort."[58] While working on *The Freeman*, Robinson also published his first articles on Russia. An early article explored the implications of erasing the distinction between economic and political systems into "a country permanently organized, politically and industrially, for production." The Bolsheviks, then, had allowed for a "large-scale experiment" in social organization. The experiment's ultimate measure of success, Robinson concluded, would be Russia's ability to build its industrial sector. In any case, from Russia's experiment he expected to learn about labor organization (like Hewes and Douglas, he followed union activities closely), about political institutions, and ultimately about social structure.[59] These views placed Robinson squarely in the mainstream of Greenwich Village political thought at the time.

While working for *The Freeman*, Robinson commuted to Columbia University, where he completed his BA (delayed by his war service) and began graduate study in Russian history. He continued to commute, intellectually speaking, between the Village and the university through the early 1920s. He wrote for the Village's little magazines as well as for academic journals. Robinson offered a broad interpretive framework for the study of Russian history in the 1922 volume of *Political Science Quarterly*. Reviewing a number of recent works on Bolshevism, he noted that public interest in Soviet Russia's future had impeded analysis of its past. He called for a more historical perspective on Russian events, demanding that the "Communist experiment" be understood "primarily [as] a Russian problem of the past." The Soviet present, he argued, owed much to Russian heritage and traditions. Robinson also called for a "decentralization" of Russian history. The Russian Revolution was not simply political, he claimed, but could be analyzed as four "distinct revolutions": agrarian, industrial, commercial, and political. In each realm the revolution began with a destructive phase before turning to a constructive one. Robinson focused particularly on the agrarian and industrial revolutions. In the former case, he identified "the communism of the village"—which he carefully distinguished from Bolshevik Communism—as a dominant force in rural life. Perhaps in the future, Robinson hoped, this rural communism might become "the constructive principle of the agrarian revolution." The industrial revolution, in contrast, had no clear direction for its constructive phase. Although destruction of the old urban industrial order came rapidly, it had no obvious path of "natural reconstruction." What urban Russia needed, therefore, was "an industrial dictatorship which would prevent the whole fabric of urban society from going to pieces." Robinson distinguished between this form of dictatorship, organized through local-level soviets, and Bolsheviks' "political dictatorship" over an entire nation.[60]

As Robinson made the transition from Village intellectual to academic expert, his work increasingly echoed the New History then regnant at Columbia. As James Harvey Robinson (no relation) adumbrated in his 1912 manifesto, New Historians looked beyond high politics to everyday life, borrowing freely from the other social sciences to do so. The New Historians also placed a special emphasis on recent history and sought to apply historical knowledge in the interests of "human betterment." James Harvey Robinson's influence at Columbia long outlasted his 1919 departure, as his students and admirers dominated the department for decades. Geroid

Robinson's advisor, Carlton J. H. Hayes, was a student and close friend of the elder Robinson; most of the young Russianist's other advisors were also in the New History camp. The two Robinsons, furthermore, may have been in direct contact through mutual friends at *The Dial;* both wrote for the magazine.[61]

Geroid Robinson enthusiastically embraced the New Historians' high professional standards. Here he expressed increasing concern about the state of America's Russia expertise. Popular interest in Russian affairs, Robinson cautioned the Slavicists assembled at the 1924 AHA meeting, could be detrimental to historical scholarship. By subordinating the past to the present, those interested in contemporary Russian affairs were more likely to produce "journalism than sound professional scholarship." The proper role of the scholar was to study the relationship between past and present—and not to prophesy about the future.[62] Robinson was rejecting his post-war journalistic work.

As Geroid Robinson sought to apply the precepts of New History to the study of the Russian past, he gravitated toward a study of the agrarian revolution. This subject may well have resonated with personal experience—he long maintained nostalgic recollections of his early childhood on a Virginia estate, run much like the patriarchal plantation of Southern mythology.[63] Yet Robinson challenged many of the clichés about patriarchal agriculture. First, he rejected claims of peasant passivity. Mocking observers who believed that "the Russian *muzhik* has been for centuries almost as inert as the soil he tills," Robinson insisted that they had ignored life in rural Russia. He then went on to recount three centuries' worth of peasant revolts.[64] In 1925 Robinson left for Russia, courtesy of a fellowship from the fledgling Social Science Research Council (SSRC), in order to study rural Russia before the Bolsheviks. After some initial stonewalling—he was told the archives were "in no condition to be seen"—he gained access, most likely by telling Soviet officials that he was studying the politically correct topic of peasant revolutionaries.[65] After almost two years in Russia, Robinson returned to New York to take up a teaching post at Columbia and write up his results.

The fruit of Robinson's labors, *Rural Russia under the Old Regime* (1932), remains a landmark work of Russian history. One historian recently complained that it was so comprehensive that it closed off the study of the Russian peasantry for two generations.[66] True to his earlier manifesto, Robinson devoted little space to St. Petersburg politics, instead charting peasant politics from the rise of serfdom to the revolution of 1917. With gusto and sarcasm, he unabashedly took the perspective of peasants in their struggles against landlords and owners. He wryly commented, for instance, on the source of aristocratic prosperity: "the peasant millions were hardly likely to forget the 'Golden Age of the Russian Nobility' [in the late eighteenth century]—but they would perhaps remember it by some other name." The emancipation of the serfs in 1861 offered rural-dwellers limited political freedom, he wrote, but at the same time created new economic burdens. Released from labor obligations to their erstwhile owners, freed serfs were now forced to grow cash crops in order to make redemption payments. Yet the income from these crops barely covered peasants' ever-increasing expenditures, leading to the crisis of the 1890s—which Robinson described in his famous chapter "The Hungry Village." The shift toward a cash economy increased economic differentiation in the country-side, eroding communal structures but providing no discernable improvements in productivity. Robinson's portrayal of rural Russia closely accords with Marxist views about the rise of capitalism there, especially Lenin's book *Development of Capitalism in Russia* (1899). But Robinson's history is hardly a knock-off of Lenin's, exhibiting much more concern with the immediate plight of the peasantry than did the latter. Robinson explicitly challenged Soviet views of rural Russia, especially the obsessive criticisms of *kulaks,* the rich peasants condemned as capitalist exploiters. Robinson noted: "Some of the peasants were 'capitalists,' to be sure, in that they were employers of labor, but even among these 'capitalists' nearly all were laborers too, in that they still knew the jerk of an unruly plow handle and the drag of a sackful of grain between the shoulders." *Rural Russia* concluded on the eve of the Bolshevik revolution, setting up its projected sequel with a teaser: in 1917, Robinson wrote, "the great scene [of peasant revolt], so often rehearsed in part, would be played out this time to the finish."[67] Peasants, he insisted, were the true motive force of Russian history.

Robinson's promised sequel never appeared. Overwhelmed by teaching and administrative duties as he rose through the academic ranks in the 1930s, Robinson returned to Russia for research only in the purge-plagued year 1937. Perhaps distracted by other duties, he had only the vaguest idea of his research plans for that trip. But his own interests were ultimately moot. By the late 1930s, access to materials—particularly anything that might cast doubt on the Soviet commemorations of 1917—was hard to come by.[68] So Robinson turned to other pursuits, contributing to the con-

tinuing professionalization of the field through committee service, graduate advising, and his small seminar on Russian studies at Columbia.[69]
There is little in his interwar experiences to presage his post-war achievements as one of the founders of modern Sovietology. Yet his writings of the
interwar era suggest another aspect of the professionalization of Soviet
studies.

Having come to Soviet studies out of the same reformist milieu that inspired Paul Douglas and Amy Hewes, Robinson soon turned to the concerns of academic Slavic studies. Like the New Historians who trained him,
he argued for the separation of punditry from professionalism, for high
standards of historical research, and for an examination of social as well as
political events. Although this trajectory differed from that of Kerner, who
started in Slavic history because of his ethnic heritage, both Robinson and
Kerner soon internalized the standards of professional academic history: a
reliance on documentary research, a limited public profile, and close contacts with the discipline's mainstream as well as fellow regional specialists.
Only with the rising Cold War would Kerner, Robinson, and a younger
generation have the impetus and the resources to fulfill this vision of Russian studies. But their earlier writings provide their own testimony to the
power of professionalization in the American academy after World War I.
Moreover, their efforts to bring together the growing number of Russia experts also laid the groundwork for Sovietology's Cold War incarnation.

America's Russianist community expanded during the 1920s in both
size and scope. Whereas pre–World War I experts typically worked independently—many had no formal institutional affiliation—new institutions of the post-war decade made room for Russia experts. The first foreign-affairs think tanks emerged in this period and often included on their
staffs specialists in Russian affairs. Primarily based in Washington, these
new institutions sought to influence policy-makers with serious studies of
current events. They typically asserted their impartiality, though each had
its own leanings: the reports of the Institute of Economics (later part of the
Brookings Institution) reflected the liberal economists who established it;
New York's Foreign Policy Association belied the internationalist orientation of its founders, who had lobbied in support of the League of Nations.[70]

Although these organizations worked at the crossroads of the academic
and policy worlds, their researchers were not necessarily rooted in either
one. The think tanks' personnel criteria, less stringent than universities',

brought a new sort of expert into the Russia debate: a well-educated student of international affairs without a Ph.D. Russian émigrés, with their linguistic abilities, had a special advantage in competing for think-tank posts. Their writings shared a great deal with those of other Russia experts in America, especially in their reliance on both national-character stereotypes and an enthusiasm for economic development. And even without the professional credentials, they often participated in—indeed helped organize—workshops and presentations that brought Russia experts together.

Leo Pasvolsky's career reflects the transition from journalist to think-tank specialist. Paslovsky arrived in the United States from Russia as a child. His father, according to one friend, was a leftist journalist of "mildly revolutionary character" who rightly feared political reaction after the abortive revolution of 1905. Upon graduation from the City College of New York, Pasvolsky took up his father's career, editing the anti-tsarist *Russian Review* as well as a Russian newspaper while (allegedly) debating Leon Trotsky during the latter's brief sojourn in Brooklyn.[71] He also wrote a pamphlet celebrating his native land's economic potential: "Russia is not a land of wild unsettled deserts, over which wild animals roam in freedom," he plaintively began. Russia, Pasvolsky proclaimed to an American audience, could develop along European lines, but only if its immature industrial sector could attract foreign capital: "The spark of foreign capital will set [her latent industrial possibilities] into flame and will release all this colossal energy to mould a new Russia."[72] Pasvolsky joined his fellow liberal émigrés in welcoming the fall of the tsar in March 1917; the new Provisional Government, he argued, boosted Russia's development prospects.

Not surprisingly, Pasvolsky's enthusiasm for the Provisional Government quickly mutated into anti-Bolshevism. Distressed about what he called the Bolshevik "mutiny," Pasvolsky criticized radical Russian groups and the workers and peasants they purported to represent. He railed against "Her Majesty the Crowd," which now ruled "in the ruins of the Russian soul." While not usually prone to such spiritual interpretations of Russian affairs, Pasvolsky did use "Mother Russia" as a touchstone in lambasting the Bolsheviks. Having lived too long in western Europe, he wrote, the Bolshevik leaders had become deracinated cosmopolitans: "For them Russia, as Russia, does not exist. For them the world exists, and Russia is only a part of it." Pasvolsky also promoted American intervention against the Bolsheviks, even serving as translator of the Sisson Documents, the forged papers that supposedly proved Bolshevik-German complicity.[73]

In spite of his faith in the Russian nation, however, Pasvolsky held a rather dim view of the majority of its inhabitants. Like many proponents of American intervention, he doubted the ability of peasants to discipline themselves. Unlike the earlier Slavophiles who praised the peasant as the embodiment of the Russian soul, Pasvolsky argued that the intelligentsia "reflect[ed Russia's] national soul" while the peasants remained engaged only in "primitive forms of seeking."[74] He thus lauded the wartime prohibition of alcohol sales as the principal means of introducing rationality into Russian life. Even with this ban on spirits, though, Pasvolsky described the revolution and Civil War in terms of mass debauchery followed by a hangover. Russia had seen "all the ties that hold civilized life together broken asunder in the orgy of destruction, the orgy itself soon over and the masses awakening from their frenzy merely to find themselves already in the grip of an iron discipline imposed by the determined group which alone had not lost its head during the orgy."[75] Pasvolsky placed little faith in workers or peasants, blaming them for many of the disruptions of revolutionary Russia. Workers' lack of vigor lay at the root of all Russia's production and transportation problems, he told one senior diplomat; the millions of agriculturalists were even less active. The Bolshevik Party, meanwhile, owed its strength in the countryside to demobilized soldiers who returned with "Bolshevik ideas . . . but very little desire to work." Although Pasvolsky aimed most of his criticisms of Russians at the lower orders, he did on occasion bemoan Russian national traits like idealism and lack of thoroughness—both of which darkened the prospects for economic and political development of the kind enjoyed by western Europeans.[76] To the extent that Russia's prospects rested on its workers or peasants, the future looked bleak indeed.

Pasvolsky hoped that Russia's two greatest impediments—its national character and its government—could be overcome by economic development. Like Frank Golder, Lincoln Hutchinson, and William Haskell of the ARA, Pasvolsky hoped to reconstruct Russia out of Bolshevism. Russia's dire economic and political ailments could be remedied, he argued, "by means of rapid and energetic development." Such "economic strides" could produce political progress—that is, the overthrow of the Bolsheviks. Unlike the ARA officers and of course the Bolsheviks themselves, Pasvolsky believed that the longest economic strides could be achieved if Russia's immediate economic future looked like its past. Exporting grains, minerals, and other raw materials would integrate Russia into the world economy and allow for eventual improvement. In spite of his fierce opposition to the Bolsheviks, Pasvolsky called for a balanced analysis of the Russian economy, free from the "storm of invective" that clouded American discussions of Russian politics. He drew a clear line between economic and political systems and devoted himself to the study of the former.[77]

Pasvolsky's most thorough analysis of the Russian economy came in a 1924 book co-authored with the director of the Institute of Economics, Harold G. Moulton. Starting from the position that Russia needed foreign (and especially American) capital, the book argued that Soviet Russia had to pay the wartime debts of the tsarist and Provisional governments. To pay these debts, Russia required foreign currency, which could, in turn, come only from the export of agricultural products and other raw materials. Although Lincoln Hutchinson criticized the book for claiming that the new Russia must be "merely a sort of replica of the old," Pasvolsky's long-term goals were much the same as Hutchinson's: to put Russia on the same path to industrialization that western European nations had followed. The two economists differed, however, on how best to find that path. Hutchinson hoped that rapid economic change would yield political benefits. Pasvolsky, by contrast, insisted that the first step was political change (what he called "the return of political sanity"); he also called for a long-term outlook.[78] Pasvolsky brought this attitude toward reconstruction into his later work in Washington. As the chief economic advisor to the secretary of state during World War II, he was present at the creation of the post-war economic order. His ideas for Russian economic development in the 1920s—currency stability, exports of primary materials, and full payment of foreign debts as prerequisites for aid—all reappeared as hallmarks of these post-war institutions.[79] By then, Pasvolsky had little hope that economic aid could undermine Soviet rule. But in the 1920s, his vision of Russia, in terms of both national character and economic development, placed him squarely in the center of American debates about the USSR.

Vera Micheles Dean, much like Pasvolsky, parlayed her Russian heritage into a think-tank position. She, too, focused on the importance of economic development in Russia. Dean's family moved to the United States in 1917 because her father, a Jewish businessman, feared the Bolsheviks' impact on the family fortunes. Dean attended Radcliffe College and Yale University before joining the research staff of the Foreign Policy Association (FPA), a group founded in 1921 out of the remnants of a group lobbying for American membership in the League of Nations. By the time Dean joined the FPA in 1928, the organization had shifted gears toward non-partisan research and publications. Her importance as a Russia expert rested on both her own writings and her position as a node in the networks of American scholars. As an FPA staff member, she organized numerous public meetings and events that convened American diplomats, scholars, and journalists with knowledge about Russia.[80] The professionalization of Russia expertise did not automatically bar those, like Dean, without formal credentials. Having quickly insinuated herself into expert networks, she shared their views about national character and economic development.

Dean, following earlier generations of experts, emphasized inconstancy, "Byzantine subservience," and political passivity as reasons for Russia's current economic and political crises. Given these traits, Dean argued, any form of governance based on popular participation would be "hopeless." The "peasant masses," she wrote, could not act independently—but at least they knew enough to "crave leadership." Bolshevik rule, though hardly democratic, was thus suited to the Russian character.[81]

What went for politics also went for economics; Russian character shaped Soviet developments in both spheres. Russian laborers, Dean wrote, lacked the discipline of their western counterparts, thus complicating industrialization efforts in the Soviet Union. Yet their "remarkable physical endurance" and long experience of sacrifice might allow Soviet-style development to succeed. The Soviet authorities sought to trade Russians' sacrifices for "future benefits which will eventually accrue to the state"—in other words, to extract from the populace the resources to fund state-led industrialization. Dean believed that such sacrifices could be easily obtained in Russia in the early 1930s since the masses shared the Bolsheviks' desire for advancement: "Side by side with sincere concern for the improvement of living conditions, care of mother and child, a new humanitarian spirit, one finds readiness to sacrifice human lives without hesitation to the achievement of plans dictated from above."[82] Dean balanced the imperatives of economic development with the problems of political repression, but demonstrated her clear preference for the former. Liberty and individual rights had never played any part in Russian life, she argued, and thus Russians would not feel their continued absence. They would instead be empowered by the manufactured goods produced by Soviet industries.[83] The Soviets might need to enact "repressive measures" to build these industries, Dean argued elsewhere, but they would have no compunctions in doing so; they were willing to either "break or transform" the peasant as need be.[84] Most Americans, she believed, held similar views. In comparing American support for Fascist Italy with that for Bolshevik Russia in 1931, Dean assured readers that the Soviets garnered greater American sympathies "for the attempt of the Communists to modernize Russia's economic life."[85] Modernization justified any sacrifices necessary to achieve it.

Dean's claim, while hardly an accurate depiction of American public opinion writ large, offered an apt summary of the thinking of America's Russia experts in the 1920s. These experts found a new appreciation of Soviet goals as a direct result, in many cases, of the increasing professionalization of Russian expertise. Institutional form shaped intellectual content. Social-scientific reformers like Paul Douglas and Amy Hewes applied their vision to the study of Soviet social welfare and labor policies. Jerome Davis's experiences in Russia convinced him of the value of scientific sociology. Samuel Harper's case was the most dramatic; a long-time foe of the Bolsheviks, Harper reversed his opinion after exploring one of the major concerns of post-war political science, the question of civic education.

The new institutional landscape remade American studies of Russia. In the academy, a loose network of Russia scholars established its authority on the basis of its members' professional training. Experts used this authority as an entree into policy discussions, both public and private. Thus Geroid Robinson and Robert Kerner rejected their initial approaches to Slavic history in the name of professional standards. Vera Dean and Leo Pasvolsky, working in newly established think tanks, strove for balance in their analyses of Russian affairs. Collectively, these authors offered more reasons to support Soviet rule than to challenge it. Many, like Pasvolsky, Harper, and Davis, minimized their discussion of the Bolsheviks' overall political goals in the interests of objectivity; their aim of evenhandedness did not affect arguments based on national character. Others, like Dean, argued that political repression was well-suited to the Russian character. Both claims—about national character and about the need to endure hardships *en route* to economic modernity—would appear even more frequently as the Soviet Union reeled under the elevated ambitions of its first Five-Year Plan.

8

The Romance of
Economic Development

By 1928 the New Economic Policy had come under attack on both economic and political fronts. NEP's markets for agricultural and some manufactured goods had led to material improvements over War Communism, but they hardly solved the USSR's economic problems. Food production expanded substantially in the mid-1920s, but relative prices between the agricultural and manufacturing sectors were constantly out-of-kilter, leading to a series of so-called scissors crises. Meanwhile, industrial production neared pre-war levels.[1]

The prospects of slow and steady economic growth—and even that was hardly guaranteed—soon became a political issue. Joseph Stalin's tactical maneuvers through the 1920s turned economic policy into political intrigue. The rising Bolshevik leader eliminated rival after rival by frequently shifting alliances, ostensibly linked to economic policy. By the end of the decade, Stalin had dispatched his most formidable rival, Leon Trotsky, into exile while simultaneously adapting Trotsky's vision of rapid industrialization under state control.[2] The inauguration of the first Five-Year Plan in 1928 marked the end of NEP and the start of a new era in Russian history.

Five-Year Plans would construct a new Soviet society both economically and culturally. As Stalin exhorted in 1929, backward Russia would yield to the modern, industrial Soviet Union:

> We are advancing full steam ahead along the path of industrialization—to socialism, leaving behind the age-old "Russian" backwardness.
>
> We are becoming a country of metal, a country of automobiles, a country of tractors.
>
> And when we have put the USSR on an automobile, and the muzhik

153

on a tractor, let the worthy capitalists, who boast so much of their "civilization," try to overtake us! We shall yet see which countries may then be "classified" as backward and which as advanced.[3]

These ambitions for economic growth shaped—indeed, misshaped—Soviet life for the next decade and beyond.

To achieve rapid growth, Stalin called for central planning. One central agency, Gosplan, would in theory coordinate all economic activity. The agency's proponents argued that only such coordination could produce an acceptable rate of economic growth. Central planning, not coincidentally, also improved mechanisms of state control over economic processes. The threshold for acceptable growth was high; Stalin demanded that the Soviet Union reach in one decade a level of industrialization that had taken other nations five times as long to achieve.[4]

These bold, even grandiose, expectations soon became planning goals. The first Five-Year Plan created new cities on windswept plains, remote from population centers but convenient to natural resources. Collectivization violently remapped a countryside once dotted with peasant villages into a more easily controlled grid of huge collective farms.[5]

These grand plans came with high costs, evident even in the delusionally optimistic official statistics. Soviet citizens, except for a few select favorites of the Communist Party, faced shortages of food, clothing, and shelter—indeed, shortages of everything but lines. Living standards, hardly luxurious to begin with, fell precipitously as people struggled to find even the most basic goods. Housing ranged from ripped tents on the Siberian steppes to decrepit and cramped apartments shared with strangers. These were the conditions suffered by compliant citizens. Those whom the regime defined, often arbitrarily, as saboteurs, *kulaks,* or bourgeois remnants faced arrest, forcible resettlement, loss of property, limited access to essential goods, or even execution. Thousands became *lishentsy,* "former persons" with no political or economic rights.[6] The burdens of the Five-Year Plans were as great as the goals.

Soviet leaders also promoted a new cultural superstructure to accompany the new economic base. Their plans for moral and intellectual landscapes were as dramatic as their hopes for the physical one. Education programs sought to create "new Soviet men." New and restricted approaches to scholarship claimed to demonstrate the inevitability of communism. New, and even more tightly restricted, forms of literature and art celebrated the achievements of the Bolshevik Revolution. Those who strayed from the Party line on intellectual expression faced dire consequences.[7] The punishments became even more severe in the mid-1930s, as the prison camp system continued its malignant growth across Soviet territory.

Soviet officials used a trio of institutions to promote their grand goals to foreigners while concealing the costs. Prominent foreigners, irrespective of political affiliation, were ushered through the Soviet Union by VOKS, the All-Union Society for Cultural Connections with Foreign Countries. Soviet authorities both courted and controlled foreign journalists through the Press Office of the People's Commissariat for Foreign Affairs. Those unlucky visitors not qualifying for these services were left at the mercy of Intourist, which from its founding in 1928 earned the enmity of tourists and Soviet officials alike. All three organizations, furthermore, preferred a positive impression to an accurate one. They sharply limited access to both flaws and critics of the Soviet Union; censorship was common, and Party cheerleading constant and shrill.[8]

Western intellectuals and radicals nevertheless flocked to these Soviet tours, making them a rite of passage in some circles. One historian estimates that approximately five thousand westerners visited the USSR each year in this era, many of them intellectuals who maintained their enthusiasm for the USSR in spite of what they saw first-hand.[9] The notion of a society organized around modernization, such as the Soviet Union purported to be, had great appeal for these intellectuals. The Soviet aim of simultaneously constructing economic and cultural modernity through conscious planning, they hoped, would save the USSR from the consequences of an accidental and haphazard modernization left to market forces—consequences recently thrust upon the United States.

American intellectuals looked to the Soviet Union for solutions to what they saw as the problems of modern America—or, more broadly, the problems of modernity itself. Even amid the glitter of the Roaring Twenties, many social scientists focused on the nation's failings. A common thread in their criticisms was the notion that America's remarkable economic progress had outstripped its cultural and social advance. The theory of "cultural lag," so prominent in the 1920s, served as a metaphor for this aspect of interwar social thought. While the progenitor of the term, the sociologist William F. Ogburn, despaired that purposeful human action to reduce this lag was "futile," a generation of activist thinkers disagreed.[10] The iconoclastic economist Thorstein Veblen blamed atavistic modes of production and consumption for distorting the modern economy. He also envisioned new economic arrangements to solve industrial problems. The labor economist John R. Commons praised workers who adjusted to the behemoth industrial organizations by joining unions and fighting for their economic interests rather than slowing industrial progress by fighting for control over the labor process. And the prolific (even ever-present) philosopher John Dewey sought to bring up-to-date outmoded ideas like rugged individualism as well as outmoded institutions like schools. Veblen, Commons, and Dewey all sought to reshape their society through conscious human design, bringing America's cultural and social arrangements in line with its dynamic economic system.

Soviet plans thus attracted a variety of American thinkers with contrasting areas of interest. The economists Stuart Chase and George Soule—like their intellectual inspiration, Thorstein Veblen—enthusiastically endorsed Soviet economic organization, especially its planning apparatus. The economist Calvin Bryce Hoover, trained by John Commons and his student Selig Perlman, applied the lessons of institutional economics. And the educator George Counts, like his mentor John Dewey, appreciated the Soviet attempts to apply Deweyan principles of Progressive education. All agreed that the results of the so-called Soviet experiment could and should benefit American social scientists, and by extension, American society. As they studied Soviet society, their concerns about modern industrial society in general and the United States in particular were never remote. How could an increasingly complex economy be managed? What role would the laborer have in the massive industrial enterprises? What would it take to make agriculture—and agriculturalists—modern? How could a citizenry be educated for the modern world?

Progressive reformers, economists, and growing numbers of business leaders explored coordination and planning as means to meet the challenges of the modern industrial era. Conservatives like Secretary of Commerce Herbert Hoover preached "associationalism" while liberals envisioned powerful central mechanisms for economic decision-making.[11] The Soviet Union thus provided lessons for the reorganization of the American economy and society. To take one gauge: the landmark *Encyclopedia of the Social Sciences*, the main compendium of American social-scientific knowledge in the 1930s, referred to the USSR in dozens of articles on topics as diverse as agriculture, industrial hygiene, literacy, and vocational education.

Awareness of the Plans' tremendous costs did not diminish the determination of these intellectuals to apply lessons from the Soviet Union to American society. On their trips to Russia or in their readings about Soviet events, they made their own calculations of Plan-related hardships. They certainly did not wish to replicate in the United States the shortages and repression faced by Soviet citizens. Instead, they insisted that America could learn universal lessons about modernity from the Soviet Union without suffering the same costs. They blamed the high costs in the USSR on Russian national character, which they all saw as poor material for building a modern society. Peculiarly Russian traits, as much as Soviet economic policy, were responsible for the Plan's hardships. Ubiquitous claims about Russian indolence and endurance, often expressed in an Orientalist idiom, explained to these observers why Soviet modernization came at such a high price—but one that would be discounted in the United States.

George Frost Kennan's phrase "romance of economic development" applied well to these American experts. Writing in the summer of 1932 about the USSR's economic prospects, Kennan fixed on one aspect of Soviet life that might overcome the manifest failings of the Plans: the excitement that the Plan's aims had generated among Soviet citizens, especially youths. Russians would endure great sacrifices in the name of economic progress.[12] Foreign observers, meanwhile, were willing to countenance—though not themselves suffer—such hardships in the name of progress. True to Alexander Herzen's *bon mot*—"[t]o sacrifice others . . . is too easy a virtue"— many American experts expressed a readiness to sacrifice Russians to the goals of Soviet planning.[13]

Enthusiasm for the Soviet Union also revealed another aspect of American thought in the interwar years: a hypersensitivity to the failings of democratic politics. For a variety of reasons, experts set aside their concerns about Soviet political goals. Technocrats like Douglas and Chase (and, in a slightly different form, Hoover) saw economic achievements as more important than political participation. Pragmatists like Dewey and Counts focused more on the Progressive means of Soviet education than on its ultimate political ends. Even Dewey, the era's most vigorous and dedicated theorist of democracy, offered explanations for Soviet repression. Once again, invocations of national character played a role: Russia's ostensibly Asian qualities further supported these experts' denigration of democratic politics. Notions of Asia, redolent with despotism, certainly did not suggest an embrace of democracy. Although American intellectuals disagreed on whether repression was an inevitable part of the modernizing process, they did agree that, owing to national peculiarities, Russian modernization would not be democratic. These intellectuals attributed the costs of Soviet modernization to its Russian context while celebrating its benefits as universal.

Previous generations of scholars have explained Americans' romance with Soviet economic development in terms of partisan politics, psychopathology, or pure polemic. Enthusiasts for the Soviet Union, in these reckonings, were diehard Marxists, alienated intellectuals, or simply fools —perhaps all three. Turning their backs on capitalism after the Great Crash in 1929, the argument went, such intellectuals looked with desperation to the Soviet Union. They worshipped central planning for its ostensible rationality and efficiency, ignoring the massive social and economic problems it created. But this interpretation, with its powerful simplicity, reduces an important chapter in American intellectual history to caricature.[14]

Every particular of that received wisdom is ripe for challenge. Some of the greatest American minds of the 1920s praised aspects of Soviet life. They did so not because they were alienated from American society but because they were active participants in heated public debates about the future of their country.[15] Nor was their support for the Soviet Union linked to an endorsement of communism or Stalinism. To their own detriment, most of these intellectuals had not read enough Marx or Lenin to support the Soviet Union on doctrinal grounds. They turned their attentions to the USSR, furthermore, before the stock market plummeted in October 1929—and well before the general agreement that the crash had resulted in a major depression.[16] Finally, and most distressingly, these intellectuals recognized the hardships faced by Soviet citizens but endorsed Soviet policies nonetheless. Whatever allowed their support for the Five-Year Plans, it was not ignorance of the costs.

Soviet officials often invoked military metaphors in their defense of centralized planning and control. They promoted the first Five-Year Plan as part of a war against Russian backwardness, replete with descriptions of battles on the "grain front" and "storming fortresses."[17] These metaphors implied obedience and sacrifice, not dispute and democracy; they emphasized control and rationality, not the free market of goods or, for that matter, ideas. As such, they appealed to America's Russia experts, who added their own arsenal of war metaphors.

Analogies to war reflected well on Soviet economic organization, especially among a group of intellectuals who endorsed the U.S. government's economic controls during World War I. Thorstein Veblen, whose biting and idiosyncratic writings condemned modern capitalism for its focus on making money rather than on making things, became the intellectual godfather of this group. To Veblen and his protégés, wartime regulatory agencies offered an unprecedented opportunity to rid American capitalism of the wastefulness caused by seeking profit rather than production. The war convinced Veblen that "commercial expediency" did not provide acceptable means for organizing an economy. Instead, modern economies required a "general staff" with an intimate knowledge of the production process. At stake, he warned, was "the material welfare of the civilized peoples," threatened by the dominance of commercial interests.[18] Veblen himself joined this general staff in 1918, serving with the United States Food Administration (USFA). During his tenure he sought to put his technocratic principles into practice. Observing first-hand the partisan politics and chaotic labor arrangements in North Dakota agriculture, Veblen called for a "scheme of registration" through which the USFA would create a "collective labor force" and then allocate laborers as it saw fit to various farms and agencies. His plan, never implemented, called for the regimentation of labor in the name of efficiency.[19]

As the American war economy demobilized, Veblen grew increasingly excited about Russian economic planning. Working on the editorial staff of *The Dial*, the Greenwich Village biweekly, he associated frequently with the magazine's "editorial soviet." Greeting the Bolsheviks with great enthusiasm, he and his colleagues closely followed the progress of the Russian Civil War, a map of which was updated daily by his fellow editor Geroid Tanquary Robinson. Veblen found much to like in revolutionary Russia. By wresting control of industry away from owners who were more concerned with their own profits than with production, the Bolsheviks would improve efficiency and ultimately the material welfare of the population as a whole. Veblen championed such changes for his own country. Together with John Dewey and Helen Marot, he organized the *Dial*'s section on post-war reconstruction. These essays called for the United States to follow Russia, abolishing absentee ownership by bringing major industries under public control.[20]

Veblen's interest in plotting a new means of industrial control emerged out of his encounters with Marx—in this case not Karl, but Guido Marx, a longtime friend who taught mechanical engineering at Stanford University. With some fanfare, Marx in 1920 announced a seminar series on "the social function of engineers." Attended by only a few curiosity-seekers, the seminar provided Veblen with the material for an article entitled "Practicable Soviet of Technicians." Veblen envisioned a soviet consisting solely of engineers and technicians who would manage all aspects of economic life. Business owners, Veblen argued, represented only narrow commercial interests; technicians, by contrast, "might be said to represent the community at large."[21] His formulations of technical control over all economic activity brought together many of his criticisms of the American economy: his fierce opposition to the pecuniary operations of business; his harsh criticism of the irrationality of consumer decisions (brilliantly satirized in *The Theory of the Leisure Class*); and his veneration of the technician. As Daniel Bell later quipped, this work represented a "'short course' in the Veblenian system."[22]

The small "soviet" that grew out of Veblen's seminar, while hoping to organize all of American society, could barely keep itself together. A loosely organized Technical Alliance was the only surviving remnant of the 1920 seminar—and that hardly ran like a well-oiled machine.[23] Even without an organizational center, Veblen's ideas attracted a small but dedicated group of like-minded individuals, many of whom (like Veblen himself) served in the expanded regulatory state during World War I. Among the most prominent was the engineer-turned-economist Stuart Chase. Chase trained at MIT before transferring into Harvard's famous class of 1910 (which included Walter Lippmann, T. S. Eliot, and John Reed). After graduation, he spent four years with the Federal Trade Commission, eventually facing dismissal for his continued advocacy of stronger regulation.[24]

Chase, like Veblen, promoted strong state intervention guided by experts such as himself. He saw this intervention as the key to increased efficiency, higher standards of living, and lasting social peace. Chase happily subordinated political participation to material well-being, all in the name of science and progress. As with Jerome Davis, Chase's wartime experience led him to reject an emphasis on what he later demeaned as "moralistic" reformism in favor of a scientific approach. (Chase was so devoted to reform that his honeymoon in western New York was spent not appreciating the view in Niagara Falls but studying unemployment in Rochester.)[25] Chase followed Veblen—whom he called "one of my idols as a young man"—in arguing that human behavior could be effectively molded by government authority, so long as that authority was guided by the right sort of engineers.[26] Through the early 1920s, Chase helped run the Labor Bureau, which sought to spread the gospels of empiricism and efficiency among moralistic and disorganized Americans. His book *Tragedy of Waste* (1925) documented the wastefulness of capitalist enterprise through duplication of effort, inefficiencies in distribution, and underemployment. The answer, Chase exhorted in his mentor's terms, was to create an "Industrial General Staff" to organize production, reduce waste, and increase well-being.[27]

Chase's interest in expert control of the economy brought him to the Soviet Union in 1927, where he led a contingent of specialists attached to a labor delegation. Chase immediately took to many aspects of Soviet economic policy, especially the planning agency Gosplan. He quickly dismissed any concerns about political ideology: "economic realities," not "mazes of doctrinaire theory," were his principal interest. Chase gave Soviet central planning—still in its more limited NEP phase—the edge over capitalism: "on paper the socialistic system has the best of it. It is clean cut, straightforward and logical." American capitalism, in contrast, was "industrial anarchy."[28]

True to his scientific creed, Chase needed to gather more data on Soviet planning. Only the passage of time would reveal whether Gosplan—already a "courageous and unprecedented experiment"—would become a shining economic example or "just another memorandum for the waste basket of history."[29] Although he recognized the sharp political differences between Soviet and American political systems, Chase focused entirely on economics. Democracy itself seemed of little use unless it proved superior economically. He had one criterion for both American and Soviet policy: Would planning eliminate waste and raise the standard of living? After returning from Russia, he kept his optimistic view of Soviet planning. He compared Gosplan to America's wartime agencies, especially the War Industries Board ("God rest its soul"), and excitedly described its authority over all economic activity in the Soviet Union. Chase located Gosplan "at the border-line of the capacity of the human intellect." In his view, the Soviet system provided an economic model for the United States, rendering any political differences irrelevant.[30]

Chase's celebrations of engineers and economic planners preceded the Crash. Just as the stock market plummeted that October, Chase perspicaciously completed a long essay called "Prosperity: Fact or Myth?" Offered the opportunity to amend the piece before its publication that December,

Chase bravely stuck to his original text. He argued that stronger government control—citing the War Industries Board and Gosplan as examples—was essential for the continuation of American economic growth. Long-term prosperity, Chase concluded (echoing Veblen), awaited the "liberation of the engineer."[31]

Chase's interest in central planning, already strong, deepened along with the Depression. As the financial crisis became an economic one in 1929 and 1930, Chase returned to this theme. Invited by the editors of *The Nation* to inaugurate their series called "If I Were Dictator," Chase took the title quite literally. He called for a National Planning Board staffed by technocratic Progressives like himself, Douglas, and their colleagues Rexford Guy Tugwell, Wesley Claire Mitchell, and George Soule. Chase's fantasy Board would issue edicts (called "ukases," from the Russian) for many programs that in fact became hallmarks of the New Deal: public works, old-age pensions, and regulation of the agricultural sector.[32] When the literary critic and fellow traveler Edmund Wilson accused him of libeling Russia, Chase rebutted that he indeed supported "the Russian dictatorship" and offered "repeated . . . hints at the advantages of economic dictatorship in this country."[33] Nor did Chase limit this message to American periodicals; his editorial in *Pravda* lauded the first Five-Year Plan for demonstrating the effectiveness of "benevolent (*blagodetel'naia*) dictatorship."[34]

Combining Soviet and wartime analogies, Chase called for a ten-year plan in the United States to be administered by a "Peace Industries Board." As with NEP institutions in Russia, Chase's proposed Board would control the commanding heights of American industry while leaving small-scale production within the private sector. The article also revealed Chase's nostalgia for wartime planning. He chided the Russians for claiming that they had invented economic planning, when in fact his beloved War Industries Board had initiated the planning era. Irrespective of its origins, though, Chase viewed central planning as an economic necessity that transcended political ideology.[35]

Numerous technocratic Progressives—many of whom appeared on Chase's economic dream team—echoed Chase's call for economic planning. The economist Paul Douglas, for instance, called Gosplan "an invaluable administrative device." Like Chase and Veblen, Douglas endorsed an "economic general staff" to set prices and production levels.[36] His fellow technocrats typically insisted that economic planning was a technical issue that lay beyond the reach of any political ideology.

Chase's Labor Bureau colleague George Soule also looked to revolutionary Russia for insights into economic planning—insights he hoped to apply in the United States. Soule spent the 1910s at the unofficial organ of technocratic progressivism, *The New Republic,* as well as at the Technical Alliance.[37] By 1922, he had joined the newly established National Bureau of Economic Research (NBER), which aimed to inject impartial economic analysis into policy debates. Like Chase, he spent the rest of the 1920s promoting economic analysis for both labor and management. Though a longtime planning enthusiast, Soule did not warm to the Soviet case as quickly as Chase, turning to the subject only at the very end of the 1920s. Like his colleague, Soule emphasized fact-finding and the need for human control over economic activity. Unperturbed by political ideology, Soule argued that Soviet planning had little to do with Marx, but was instead a manifestation of Soviet interest in "constructing a great industrial civilization . . . by an exercise of national will." Soule expressed some concern about political methods yet ultimately framed the issue in economic terms. Worried about the spread of "political dictatorship," he shared Chase's reliance on economic criteria: by whatever means, the Soviet Union had surpassed all other nations (past or present) in attaining high rates of economic growth. He called for the sort of dispassionate and apolitical analysis that the NBER promised: "From a cool distance which permits a large perspective," he concluded, "we can perhaps make better use of the Russian experience." Stressing economic growth over political participation, Soule initially lauded the Soviet Union's efforts to bring an unruly economy— and a population "Asiatic in tradition and steeped in superstition"—under the control of planners.[38]

Soule's book *The Coming American Revolution* (1934) extended his earlier arguments, calling for a revolution in planning in the United States. But Soule's revolution shared little with the violent upheavals foreseen by Karl Marx or celebrated in the rhetoric of Soviet propagandists. The American revolution would be gradual, rational, and led by economic experts like himself. Downplaying the chaos of Russia's political changes, Soule instead directed his attention to the role of experts; the Bolshevik takeover provided a "prime example of the important part played by intellectuals in the development of social forces."[39] The technocrats' revolution, then, would be a bloodless redistribution of power toward themselves. The inspiration for this revolution was deeply American, but the lessons came from Russia.

After visiting the Soviet Union in 1936, Soule reconsidered the balance between planning and democracy but continued to praise Soviet policies. He attributed Russia's successes to "socialist planning and control." The planning apparatus, Soule continued, not only provided more goods for individuals but also managed to account for non-material welfare in the form of insurance and education. He gave the Soviet Union a clean bill of political health, suggesting a national-character argument when he claimed that Russians in no way "felt any lack of freedom."[40] He viewed political freedom as valuable but worth sacrificing for economic welfare, in Russia as well as in the United States. Thus, he wrote in 1939, the "survival value" of democracy would be all the greater if "we do a good job in organizing our economic life."[41]

Whereas Soule sought to balance democracy against prosperity, Chase was willing to leave politics out of the equation entirely. Political participation mattered little to Chase, who instead emphasized economic organization and output. He often used Russian history and culture, which he saw as barren ground for the growth of democratic institutions, to justify the lack of political freedoms in the USSR. He expressed this argument in terms of national character, enumerating the traits that made Russians ill-equipped for industrial society. Russians were a "naive and simple people," he wrote, prone to bouts of gloominess. More significant for economists, though, was the Russians' lack of discipline. Lazy and inconsistent, they still abided by the "ancient working habits of the east."[42] "The primary thing for the visitor to realize," Chase lectured an audience at the Foreign Policy Association shortly after his 1927 trip, "is that Russia is in the East."[43] Overcoming Russian lethargy would require more than just central planning; it would take a great deal of pressure from the state. Chase argued that Russian workers required a "method of persuasion" different from that of their American counterparts, who responded to the "God of money." That method, he made clear elsewhere, had less to do with firing and more to do with the firing squad.[44] In Chase's view, Soviet modernization had to struggle to overcome Russian nature—violently, if necessary.

These troublesome traits, Chase hinted, were especially prominent among the peasantry. He portrayed the peasants as living a timeless and primitive existence, unchanged since the days of their distant forebears. They faced years of famine in which they "starved by the hundreds of thousands" and enjoyed occasional good years in which they "ate a little less black bread [that is, more white bread], danced in the villages . . . and

ran [up] the birth rate." Even the 1917 revolutions were only a brief inter-
ruption in this "everlasting rhythm." But Soviet leaders intended to change
the beat of time, ruthlessly if necessary, and Chase tapped his feet in approval.

Chase was far from alone in viewing Russians as foreigners in the modern world. Many observers noted the peasants' lack of time-consciousness
and inattention to detail. Others emphasized their lack of alertness, which
could make factory work dangerous for them. "To weave them into the industrial fabric," as the economist Karl Scholz put it, would require a sturdy
loom able to handle troublesome snags.[45] Chase expressed little sympathy
for the obstacles to creating an industrial society whole-cloth out of an agricultural one, going so far as to endorse violence: "I am not seriously
alarmed by the sufferings of the creditor class, the troubles which the
church is bound to encounter, the restrictions on certain kinds of freedom
which must result, nor even by the bloodshed of the transition period. A
better economic order is worth a little bloodshed."

The costs of modernization were well worth paying, but Chase hoped
that the United States would never see the bill. As Herzen had feared,
Chase not-so-courageously endorsed the sacrifice of others. Harsh measures that were appropriate in a "handicraft society" like Russia, he wrote,
had no place in an advanced country like the United States. The prospect
of instituting Soviet-style planning in a "highly mechanized society" indeed "blanches the heart."[46] Yet he still wanted American officials and
economists to learn from Soviet efforts at economic control. His book on
the New Deal—which brought the term into popular usage—invited a
"minority of intelligent Americans" to promote strong economic control.[47]
To do so required "above all" scientific knowledge, to be gleaned from detailed studies of labor, production, and distribution. Armed with the scientific method, Chase exhorted, the American economy could become more
efficient, more productive, and ultimately more prosperous. This required
deeper knowledge of Russia, and so he went on another study trip to Russia in 1932, this time with long-time experts Samuel Harper and Geroid
Robinson. Chase was also involved in the stillborn Economic Institute for
the Study of Economic Conditions, Methods, and Problems in the USA
and the USSR.[48] Learning about Russian economic policy prompted his
further interest in promoting economic and political change in the United
States: "Why should the Russians," he wondered, "have all the fun of remaking the world?"[49]

Chase and Soule were hardly the only Americans to dream about re-making the world along Soviet lines. American discussions of planning typically included invocations of the Soviet example. Soule, for instance, led a forum at the Foreign Policy Association on the topic of planning, with the Moscow-based journalist Louis Fischer describing Soviet policies. The American Academy of Political and Social Science likewise convened an expert group to discuss the past, present, and future of planning. The historian and social critic Charles Beard proposed a "single national authority" to take charge of America's "five-year plans." Beard's board, unlike Chase's, acknowledged the benefits of democracy; his "Standard-of-Living Authority" was to publish its proposal so that opponents could counter with one of their own. Rexford Guy Tugwell, the Columbia University economist (and a leading figure in President Roosevelt's Brain Trust) who accompanied Chase and Douglas to Moscow in 1927, co-wrote an economics textbook that concluded with chapters on Soviet planning and the prospects for planning in the United States.[50]

After the New Deal, Chase himself continued to publish numerous popular books and articles on economic affairs. But in fall 1978, writing to his old friend Tugwell, Chase thought not of these books or of his more recent activities but of their 1927 trip to Russia. Together with the Columbia historian J. Bartlett Brebner, Chase reminisced, they had formed the "Three Musketeers in Moscow," working as gallant knights under a flag of social engineering that never came to be.[51] Their technocratic vision of a planned society remained unrealized in either the Soviet Union or the United States, yet it attracted wide interest during the boom of the 1920s as well as the bust of the 1930s. Building especially on the writings of Thorstein Veblen, technocrats like Chase, Tugwell, Douglas, and Soule sought to exert tight control over all aspects of the economy. While they ultimately hoped to see this vision fulfilled in the United States, they saw the special urgency for economic planning in the Soviet Union, with its unreliable population, despotic traditions, and backward economy. Modernization would not be bloodless but was nevertheless essential. Russian national character would complicate, not ease, the process—but this hardly constituted a reason to abandon the goal of rapid industrialization. Others would carry this argument even further.

Although Chase and Soule combined admiration for Soviet economics with an appreciation of Soviet politics, these positions were not necessarily linked. The economist Calvin Bryce Hoover expressed consistently anti-

Soviet sentiments while celebrating Soviet planning. Hoover, moreover, began from an entirely different political and intellectual milieu than did Chase and Soule. Trained in the economics department at the University of Wisconsin in the early 1920s, Bryce Hoover (no relation to either J. Edgar or Herbert) imbibed that department's Progressive spirit, especially as articulated by the Christian socialist Richard Ely. Hoover's principal influences at Wisconsin, aside from Ely, were the labor economist John R. Commons, whose writings on labor and industrial capitalism defined one branch of Progressive economics, and Commons's student-cum-colleague Selig Perlman. By the time Hoover turned to the study of the Soviet Union in the late 1920s, he bore the strong imprint of his Wisconsin training, in terms of approach (the collection of documentary material), topic (economic institutions), and conclusions (Soviet industrialization was costly but essential).

Commons, also a student of Ely's, had maintained close ties to organizations like the American Association for Labor Legislation and the National Civic Federation (before its anti-union phase). Commons's academic work also focused on labor issues; his famous article on American shoemakers (1909) argued that labor unions emerged to retard the erosion of wages, which itself was an inevitable response to market pressures.[52] A lifetime supporter of the American Federation of Labor (AFL), Commons shared its focus on the economic rather than the political functions of unions. Workers, Commons wrote in 1921, should not seek to manage the businesses they worked in—they were "incompetent" for this task in any case—nor should they hope for radical changes in politics or society. Their principal aims were job security and higher wages.[53] Commons was a critical but loyal supporter of capitalist economies, promoting a "reasonable capitalism."[54]

Hoover worked more closely with Commons's protégé Selig Perlman than he had with Commons and Ely. He credited Perlman with preparing him for his later studies on the Soviet Union.[55] Perlman's own path to Wisconsin had been an unusual one. A Russian Jew raised in the Pale of Settlement, Perlman discovered Marx's writings after reading Georgii Plekhanov, the father of Russian Marxism. Plekhanov, who would become a Menshevik opposed to Lenin's determination to make immediate revolution, held that the arrival of communism required first the growth of capitalism. But it was Perlman's ethnicity, more than his politics, that led to his departure from Russia in 1905; strict quotas on Jews in higher education prevented Perlman's matriculation in a Russian medical school. He went to study medicine in Italy, where he was eventually introduced to William English Walling. Walling arranged for Perlman's emigration to the United States, and later for his studies at the University of Wisconsin.[56]

At Wisconsin, Perlman began working with Commons, writing about immigrant labor movements in the United States. His own views of the labor movement closely paralleled Commons's: workers wanted job security and high wages, not the political transformation that intellectuals imagined. Whereas Commons based his argument on the functioning of competitive capitalism, Perlman focused more on comparative psychology. The goals of "organic labor," as he called it, differed from those of intellectuals who believed that "labor must espouse the 'new social order.'" Such a desire "appears too remote" to the workers, Perlman wrote, minimizing their appreciation of such "higher freedoms."[57] By disposition, workers cared more about economics than politics.

Perlman's interest in the relationship between individuals' psychological make-up and their economic position is especially evident in his descriptions of the Russian peasantry. True to his Russian political education—Plekhanov, after all, had called the peasants "barbarian-tillers of the soil"—Perlman held Russia's rural-dwellers in low regard. Russian peasants, he argued, were marked by "mental sluggishness" as well as hopelessly naive political views.[58] Shaped by the *mir*, Perlman continued, they chafed at any government beyond the local. What he called "apolitism" ran "like a red thread through the pages of Russian history." Peasants resisted progress, which would in any case have to come from without. Such tremendous transformations, Perlman argued, could not take place peacefully. He saw "no occasion for shocked surprise at the bloody methods" of the Bolsheviks in 1917, nor would he condemn the violence of Stalin's economic plans. Later, when reflecting on Stalin's economic policy, Perlman praised the Bolsheviks for building "a new civilization in Russia." The method may have been barbaric from a western perspective, but at least "it was constructive." This new civilization had remade Russian character, eliminating early defects like sloth, inactivity, and passivity.[59]

Perlman's views of historical progress, the peasantry, and revolution in general were well within the Marxist tradition. His student Hoover incorporated aspects of Perlman's Marxism but assimilated them into a different political framework. Although his parents subscribed to the left-wing weekly *Appeal to Reason*, Bryce Hoover lacked Perlman's doctrinaire socialist credentials. The two writers nevertheless shared similar views of Russian workers and peasants, views that emerged when Hoover turned to the study of Russia in the late 1920s.

Before embarking on his Russian travels, Hoover studied and taught macroeconomics and finance. He left Madison in 1923 to spend two years as an instructor at the University of Minnesota, then under the leadership of the business-cycle economist Alvin Hansen. Hoover's early research picked up on Hansen's interest: he studied financial policy at the Federal Reserve Bank of New York.[60] In 1925, he joined the economics department at the newly reconstituted Duke University, where he remained for the next four decades. Once at Duke, Hoover turned to Russia, at last following up on an interest sparked by Perlman. He won a research grant from the Social Science Research Council to study Soviet monetary policy. Hoover relocated his family to Berlin while he went on to Moscow, where he dove into research with a vigor no doubt enhanced by his coffee obsession. Although he had begun to study Russian at Duke, he still relied heavily on translators for his research.[61]

By the time Hoover arrived in Moscow, he had expanded the scope of his research into a broad survey of Soviet economic organization. He published some of his initial findings in the British *Economic Journal* before he left Moscow. These articles paid close attention to the high costs of Soviet policy, the low standards of living, the constant threat of famine, and the forcible demise of peasant agriculture. Hoover weighed these costs against numerous achievements: an "impressive" savings rate, rapid expansion of industrial production and employment, and, ultimately (in terms similar to Perlman's), the construction of "an entirely different civilization." John Maynard Keynes praised the articles as the best analyses of Soviet events to reach the west.[62]

Returning to the United States in 1931, Hoover quickly published his lengthy manuscript, eventually entitled *Economic Life in Soviet Russia*. The book was generally well-received, winning accolades from academics (for its plodding thoroughness) and journalists (in spite of that attribute). The erstwhile Moscow correspondent Eugene Lyons later singled out *Economic Life* as one of the best and most balanced books on Soviet Russia. Throughout the book, Hoover measured the present costs of Soviet policy against the promised benefits. The costs were many: political dictatorship ("never before have the mind and spirit of man been so robbed of freedom and dignity"), disorganization in the name of economic planning, and above all drastically reduced living standards—even "actual famine condi-tions."[63] Yet Hoover never claimed that the process of economic develop-ment would be easy.

As he gained expertise and experience in Soviet affairs, he made increas-ingly explicit comments about the price of progress. At an economists' roundtable in 1931, Hoover called Russia "a land in which force and fear reign supreme," citing a lack of personal freedom, secret police activity, and a virtual war in the countryside. But, Hoover continued, "this impressive record of fear, force and terror cannot obscure the degree of economic suc-cess which has been achieved." The successes of Soviet policy appeared not only in the statistics of industrial production and agricultural yield; in-deed, Soviet leaders had begun to remake an entire society in the interests of economic production, rapidly achieving a high level of mechanization and of the "standardization of human beings."[64]

Whereas Chase and others attributed these achievements to central planning, Hoover dismissed planning as inefficient. Gosplan was less use-ful as a coordinating body, Hoover argued, than as a means to "interfere authoritatively in the economy." Brute force, not careful coordination, lay at the root of the planning system, according to Hoover. His onetime col-league Alvin Hansen similarly attributed Soviet planning successes to regi-mentation, not rationality. Hoover indicated that the greatest victories of the Soviet plans, particularly in the realm of regimentation, could be found in the countryside. Imposing collective agriculture on the peasantry re-quired coercion, Hoover wrote, but it was nevertheless the most "striking proof [in all history] of the power of the human intellect over the material world."[65] Higher praise of collectivization would be hard to come by.

Were the Russian peasants, the principal targets of collectivization, part of "human intellect" or the "material world"? Hoover's view of the peas-antry suggests the latter. Collectivization necessitated the peasants' "be-ing torn up by the roots and transplanted into a totally new and strange soil." This metaphorical repotting would change the nature of the plant it-self. Peasants had been superstitious and helpless—"immensely inert"—thereby slowing the pace of economic change.[66] Only by overcoming this inertia would Russia have an economic future. Although this assessment of the peasantry shared much with Perlman's, it was hardly limited to the Marxian left. The technocratic Tugwell, for instance, employed similar lan-guage when he termed the peasantry "a heavy amorphous mass." Karl Bor-ders, a Chicago sociologist and settlement worker, wrote of the "sleepy outward inertia" of the peasants. Others used stronger terms. The journalist Louis Fischer referred offhandedly to Russians' "bovine equanimity," repeating a centuries-old barnyard comparison.

Hoover applied his assessment of peasant passivity to Soviet policy. He concluded that the Party knew that the typical peasant was "so congenitally lazy that if he did not have the immediate stimulus of hunger, he would not work." But this hardly worried Soviet planners: "The Party is determined that the Revolution shall not perish, even if a few peasants starve." Samuel Northrop Harper offered a similar analysis, indicating that collectivization might lead to the death of four out of five peasants, but that Russians' enthusiasm for industrialization remained strong.[67] If Chase thought the costs of modernization were calculated in bloodshed, Hoover calculated the costs in terms of starvation—less messy, perhaps, but no less deadly.

For Hoover, as for most of those who derided peasant capabilities, the peasants themselves represented a significant impediment to the Soviet plans for industrialization. A stultifying calm dominated the countryside; the only activity to interrupt it came in the form of rare "wild and planless outbursts" rather than rational effort. But most of the time, peasant passivity and fatalism—what Hoover termed the peasants' "reserve of Asiatic resignation to the inscrutable decrees of Fate"—held sway. This resignation could nevertheless serve Soviet aims. The endurance of the peasants, together with the centralization of political power, yielded an impressive national savings rate; capitalist nations with higher standards of living could not match Soviet levels of savings—which provided funds for investment. The recent past served to support this claim: only people with "the predominantly Asiatic character which the Russians have," Hoover concluded, could have survived the tumult of the preceding decades. Hoover valued at least one ostensibly Asian trait. Like China, he wrote, "Soviet Russia may be expected to endure also, because the population has the same Asiatic capacity to endure suffering."[68] Thanks to this trait, Soviet plans had a good chance of success.

Hoover's references to peasant endurance were right in line with the thinking of the Russia experts whom he met in Moscow, or whose works he had read. For instance, the journalist William Henry Chamberlin—who along with his wife, Sonya, frequently hosted Hoover in Moscow—offered numerous appraisals of the peasantry that paralleled his guest's. Hoover's writings neatly echoed Chamberlin's invocation of the "tenacious vitality of the semi-Asiatic peasantry." Hoover also wrote appreciatively of Chamberlin's books, which "made plain the character of the sacrifices which the people have had to bear in order to attain . . . [the present] degree of industrial progress." Similarly, Bernard Pares, the long-time friend of Samuel Harper's, argued that "the concrete achievements [of the Five-Year Plan] . . . simply prove that no regime on earth could ever rob the Russian soul of its capacity for self-sacrifice, idealism and suffering."[69] Hoover was hardly alone in his assessment of Russian character.

Like those in the pro-Soviet camp, Hoover believed that the Soviet economic project would succeed; unlike that group, he feared this prospect. As he candidly wrote to Harper, he shared with Communists the view that the USSR represented a threat to capitalism, but he diverged from them in assessing the implications of that threat. To Hoover, the Communist threat called for a reinvigoration of capitalism before it was too late.[70] This position—joining with the left in his predictions about Soviet prospects, but with the right in fearing the implications of Soviet success—even earned Hoover a cameo role in a classic Soviet satire, *The Golden Calf*. In that novel an American professor attends the opening ceremonies for the Turk-Sib Railway:

> "I am delighted," said the professor. "All of the construction which I have seen in the USSR is so grandiose! I have no doubt that the Five-Year Plan will succeed. I will write about this."
>
> Half a year later, he really did write a book on this, in the first 200 pages of which he proved that the Plan would be fulfilled on schedule, and that the USSR would become one of the most powerful industrial countries. But on the 201st page, the professor proclaimed that exactly for this reason, the Land of the Soviets must be eliminated as quickly as possible, for otherwise it would bring about the natural death of capitalist society.[71]

This rendition is accurate in all but page number.

Hoover's work won not just satirists but also many admirers. State Department personnel, in particular, shared his distaste for the prospects of Soviet rule. The director of the East European Division, Robert F. Kelley, cited approvingly Hoover's projections about comparative standards of living. More important, Kelley commended *Economic Life* to his State Department superiors. Undersecretary of State William Phillips called the book "the most scholarly study on economic conditions which has appeared in any language" before passing it along to Secretary of State Cordell Hull.[72]

But by the time the book made its way to the top of the State Department, Hoover had moved on to other European topics. His interest in Germany was piqued by his hope that it might represent an effective counterpoise to rising Soviet power. Living in Berlin during the fateful winter of 1932–1933, though, disabused Hoover of this notion. He soon became convinced that Fascism, despite its declarations against Communism, presented an equally grave threat to western societies. Hoover then began to sound the alarm about the rise of a new kind of nation, one with its society and economy under total state control. In articles for both scholarly and popular audiences, he warned of the danger of totalitarian states in the USSR, Germany, and Italy.[73]

Through the 1930s, Hoover also progressed quickly through the academic ranks at Duke. He served in intelligence during World War II and thereafter frequently interrupted his academic work with "summer jobs" in economic policy for the CIA, the Council of Economic Advisors, and the Economic Cooperation Administration. In 1953, he served as president of the American Economic Association. Although he is remembered today for building Duke's economic department, for his studies on the Southern economy—in which he endorsed a more active role for the federal government—and for his formulations of the concept of totalitarianism, Hoover's writings on the Soviet Union are long forgotten. His analyses of the USSR were nonetheless pathbreaking for their detailed empirical work as well as their success in uniting disparate strands of social thought.

Hoover represents the romance of economic development in full bloom. References to Russians' endurance and passivity date back many centuries; allusions to Asiatic Russia were no more novel. But in the context of the Five-Year Plans, such invocations took on new meanings. Passivity no longer explained the reasons for Russians' poverty and stagnation; it now explained the price of Russian economic progress. Hoover offered this new argument in the most direct and specific terms: Soviet modernization would be costly, though the famous Russian ability to endure hardship would make it possible.

Focusing on material considerations rather than on political ideology—much like his mentor John Commons's institutionalist analyses of pragmatic American workers—Hoover described the economic benefits of Soviet political organization. He concluded that only hunger could rouse the peasantry, and that the Politburo would countenance starvation in order to meet its goals. Only months later, Soviet leaders would follow his claims to their logical, if catastrophic, endpoint.

Others who started from similar premises about Russian national character reached a different conclusion: that the national character traits themselves could and should be changed. John Dewey, the philosopher, educator, and activist who dominated American intellectual life in the early twentieth century, thought that the economists had it wrong when it came to understanding the Soviet Union: the real revolution in Russia was "psychic and moral rather than merely political and economic." The Bolsheviks, Dewey argued, sought a new economic organization in order to enact "an enormous psychological experiment in transforming the motives that inspire human conduct."[74] Along with his epigone George Counts of Columbia University's Teachers College, Dewey argued that Americans needed to learn from the Soviet example in education and cultural transformation. Their arguments were based on a combination of universalism and particularism that closely resembled the ideas of economists. The Soviets had developed an approach to social organization that merited close attention from Americans seeking to improve their own nation. At the same time, though, experts needed to account for the dramatic differences between the United States and the Soviet Union in economic base, in culture, and in character. These differences could eventually be overcome, the educators argued. A rising industrial society, properly managed, would transform pre-modern peasants into modern citizens.

George Counts represents, even more clearly than Dewey, the logic of industrialism and its connections to education. Counts's own personal trajectory—from rustic Kansas to the hallowed halls of the University of Chicago to the bright lights of New York—recapitulated in some ways the process of social transformation he described in his scholarly writings. Proud of his frontier roots, Counts attended a one-room schoolhouse before matriculating at the local Methodist college in 1907. He abandoned his pioneer dreams to confront modern industrial society, a process whose impact on education he would study for much of his career.[75]

By the time Counts began his graduate study at the University of Chicago, Dewey had been gone for nearly a decade, replaced by a scholar whose interests differed quite substantially from Dewey's Progressive pedagogy. Dewey's principal aim had been to bring school and society into a closer and more mutually beneficial relationship. But his successor at the helm of the education program, Charles Hubbard Judd, focused primarily on building up the "science of education" and enforcing the professional boundaries of education research.[76] Judd's professionalism was hardly the only influence on Counts, who sampled liberally from the course offerings of Chicago's extraordinary group of social scientists, including the political scientist Charles Merriam and the sociologists Robert Park, William I. Thomas, and Albion Small. To expand beyond Judd's focus on professional standards, Counts broke away from tradition and took sociology as his minor field—and in fact ultimately had more courses in his minor than in his major.[77] This experience in Chicago's pioneering sociology department gave his writings on the social impact of education a Deweyan cast. During the itinerancy of his early career—at five universities in ten years—Counts negotiated a middle road between Judd and Dewey, writing technical quantitative analyses (à la Judd) of Deweyan topics like the relationship between education and social circumstances. For example, Counts paid Dewey a high compliment by calling his own book *School and Society in Chicago,* incorporating the title of Dewey's classic work. But in this book Counts took a narrower view of society than Dewey had in *School and Society.* While aiming to study "the play of social forces on the school," Counts limited such forces to institutions like business associations, labor unions, elected officialdom, and civic organizations. In the end, Counts called for educators to free the school from the clutches of politics.[78]

Counts maintained this interest in professional control of education throughout his career. By the time he arrived at Columbia in 1927, his field of vision had grown more international. He had already made his first trip to Russia as a member of Stuart Chase's expert delegation. Like most of his fellow travelers, Counts was impressed by Soviet cultural activities, especially in the Commissariat of Enlightenment. He appreciated the Soviet Union's broad conception of education, which, he wrote, "exceeds that found in any other great country." From children's homes and youth clubs to factory schools and classrooms for political literacy, Soviet education reached well beyond schools. The tremendous diversity in Russia, which contained "every stage of culture from semi-nomadism to the highest type of western civilization," necessitated such broad measures, according to Counts. Soviet authorities were meeting this challenge by ensuring that material conditions and educational programs stayed in sync. Counts also cherished the Soviet education establishment's receptivity to Progressive theories from the west: "there is no place in the world where new educational ideas receive a warmer welcome." His mentor Dewey was similarly impressed.[79]

Counts worked hard to apply the lessons from the "sociological laboratory" he observed in Russia.[80] This was especially evident in his many writings on American education in the late 1920s. In outlining the major ideas shaping American instruction, Counts relied heavily on Dewey's belief that social and economic progress required cultural adjustments. He argued that the American educational system "reflected the conditions, the ideals and the aspirations of a pioneering and agrarian society." Twentieth-century life was no longer so simple, but the theory and practice of schooling had not yet adapted to the new world in birth. Americans, he complained, were reluctant to use planned and coordinated activities to shape their increasingly complex industrial surroundings. Russia's transformation, in contrast, "challenged [his] thinking on both educational and social questions." It persuaded him that comprehension and control of industrial society were not just possible but imperative. Counts wanted educators to lead the movement to place American society under more direct human control.[81]

In a lecture read while he was preparing his first book on the USSR, Counts predicted that historians in the year 2000 would criticize his generation for "the absence of any vigorous and concerted effort to discover the educational implications of the new industrial civilization which is rapidly overwhelming and transforming the traditional social order." Part of the problem lay in the domination of instruction by political forces. Since American politics stood on the brink of "ideological bankruptcy," modern education needed to operate outside the political realm. Although Counts maintained some of Charles Judd's professionalizing zeal, his overall vision owed more to Dewey's concern with developing an educational system adequate for its time and place.[82] Indeed, Counts dedicated a book to Dewey.

Like Counts, Dewey found much to admire in Soviet education. After garnering an invitation from the education minister, Anatolii Lunacharskii, Dewey set out in June 1928 with a group of two dozen or so American educators, including researchers, college presidents, and a handful of teachers.[83] Dewey's reflections on his 1928 trip included an endorsement of Soviet educational methods and an acute awareness of the cultural differences between Russia and America. On the one hand, he greatly admired Soviet educators' Progressive methods—a task made all the easier by the fact that the Russians praised Dewey's own writings on the topic. Inspired by Dewey's *School and Society* (1899), a cohort of Progressive pedagogues in the USSR sought to end the schools' "isolation from life," to link factual learning to actual experience, and to inculcate an attitude of inquisitiveness and social connectedness in students.[84] While conceding that Dewey was a "defender of the bourgeois system," Soviet educators nevertheless found "much that is healthy and reliable" in the American's writings.[85] It is hardly a great surprise, then, that Dewey enjoyed an enthusiastic reception among one important circle of Soviet educators. This in turn contributed to his hopefulness about the Soviet Union in general. As he told his host, Stanislav Shatskii (also one of the leading Russian interpreters of his thought), upon leaving Moscow, "I depart from you with great sympathy for a country in which such profound pedagogical works are possible."[86]

Dewey had been especially impressed with Soviet efforts to use schools as instruments in the reorganization of society and culture. Soviet educators, moreover, adapted tools of western Progressive education, from classroom architecture to the so-called project system, which taught abstract principles through hands-on activities. Indeed, he boasted that Americans "may feel a certain patriotic pride" in seeing the adaptation of their own ideas in Soviet education—but then cautioned that they should also be "humiliated" that those ideas were applied so much more thoroughly in the USSR than in the United States.[87] Soviet education had caught up with and even surpassed western education in the application of American educational theories, or so Dewey believed.

True to his distaste for political theories, Dewey insisted that the Soviet Union must be understood not in terms of politics but in terms of technique. The ideological rigidities of Marxism, Dewey wrote, mattered less than the "experimental factor that is flexible, vital, creative." By the early 1930s, as he grew increasingly enthusiastic about Soviet planning within and beyond the economic sphere, Dewey applied this perspective to a broader range of Soviet activities. In a ringing endorsement of central planning and social control—here sounding more like a Veblenesque technocrat than an educator—Dewey argued as follows: "The point for us is not this [Soviet] political setting nor its communistic context. It is that by the use of all available resources of knowledge and experts an attempt is being made at organized social planning and control."[88] Soviet techniques could be abstracted from their specific political circumstances and applied to very different societies.

Dewey insisted that Soviet education and planning could be analyzed independent of Communist politics, but he argued that Soviet social organization was dependent on Russian national character. This perspective is evident from his first writings on the Soviet Union, in which he applied his own version of cultural relativism to Soviet events. For instance, Dewey described how Soviet schools relied more heavily on indoctrination than American schools. This was acceptable because it was "in consonance with the conditions of national life." In a preface to a book by the journalist Maurice Hindus, Dewey dismissed the notion that Soviet Communism was universally applicable, instead pointing to the "thoroughly Russian character of this upheaval of institutions." Such upheavals, Dewey wrote (closely paralleling Chase), might be necessary in backward societies like Russia, with its "comparatively simple social structure" and its ideas drawn from the "Oriental world." But such a violent revolution had no place in "a modernized society" like the United States; it could result in "chaos" or even a "blood bath."[89] Dewey's assessment of Russia's distinctiveness incorporated universal economic terms—especially backwardness—as well as traits of Russian character.

Counts resolved Dewey's dilemma—balancing the universality of the Soviet experience with the effects of peculiarly Russian culture and character—on his own travels to the USSR. Seeking a broader perspective, Counts embarked on a grand tour of the Soviet Union by automobile in 1929. Perhaps his long drives gave him more opportunity to ponder Dewey's theories. In any case, his close relationship to Dewey's ideas about education in a modern society is all the more evident in his subsequent writings. Taking the rise of industrialism to be the central fact of the twentieth century, Counts admired the Bolsheviks for "wrestling with certain of the most fundamental problems of industrial civilization." In trying to "lift" Russia "into the modern world," Soviet leaders had to confront the principal problems of industrial society, but they had unprecedented opportunities to do so through conscious design rather than haphazard adjustment.[90]

The principal challenges facing modernization efforts in the USSR were related to the present capabilities of its population. Rural-dwellers, in their state of cultural backwardness, were not ready for industrial society. Counts catalogued the failings of Russian peasants: they were passive and overly deferential, unwilling to further even their own interests. They had no sense of time, impeding any efforts to impose work discipline.[91] Counts also invoked another longstanding characterization: Russians were natural and instinctual, not civilized and rational. Just as American experts had used such characterizations to justify military intervention in the Russian Civil War, Counts and his colleagues in the 1930s applied the notion of Russians' instinctual behavior to the Soviets' campaign for collectivization. Counts's arguments were echoed elsewhere. The education specialist Thomas Woody concluded that peasant resistance to collectivization did not take the form of "'thought out' objections," but was instead the result of "a 'feeling' that it was not right."[92] Russians, as children of nature, were unable to make rational decisions.

How did Russians obtain these traits? Here Counts's argument borrows from another well-pedigreed notion of Russian character: the idea that it was shaped by the land. Counts believed so staunchly in the topographical origins of the Russian temperament that he spent much of his 6,000-mile trip searching for the vast Russian plains, which he had heard were the crucible of the Russian character. Counts had very likely taken this theory from the writings of the Yale geographer Ellsworth Huntington, whose book *Civilization and Climate* combined the climatic/geographic determinism of Montesquieu with American social-scientific confidence. Huntington attributed Russians' nature—especially lethargy and passivity—to the country's topographic "monotony." Or, in the words of the Columbia historian J. Bartlett Brebner, one of Chase's three musketeers, "Flat lands . . . lead to placid lives."[93] Ignoring strongly worded warnings from a friend, the iconoclastic historian Charles Beard, Counts persisted in using geography to describe national traits.[94]

Counts's search for the "vast monotonous plains" that had defined Russian character came up empty. He speculated facetiously that perhaps the plains had been abolished by the Five-Year Plan.[95] Counts should have taken his own jokes more seriously; his argument implied that Russian traits (created by the plains) could be overcome by the Five-Year Plan. If the Plan eliminated the defects of the Russians, their great potential might be realized. Slavs, Counts wrote, had "all of the abilities which are needful in building a great industrial civilization"; the challenge was to tap the Russians' "reservoir of talent," which Counts called the largest "among the white-skinned races." But using this reservoir would require the machinery of industrialism. Industrialization had already helped modern nations conquer their natures; it could do the same in Russia. Until that point, however, the country would remain a "civilization of the earth and the elements."[96] National character did not prohibit industrialization, though it made the process more difficult.

Similarly, the Russian peasantry's condition was not innate but circumstantial. There was, Counts argued, a "perfect correlation between living conditions and degree of enlightenment." Thus, eradicating Russian poverty would also eliminate cultural backwardness. Although peasants were "inured by privation," an improvement in their conditions would allow them to outgrow their character. Like Dewey, Counts saw the fruits of industrialism in broad terms. Within a generation, he predicted, the old peasant "will have disappeared, and there will take his place a new type of peasant, brought up . . . with a different philosophy of life." Industrial society would spell the end of national particularity.[97]

Counts praised Soviet efforts to abolish the remnants of Russian character (if not its ostensible geographic origins), hardly limiting himself to educational institutions. He described most of the changes he saw in terms of their contribution to creating a new psychology, one suited for industrial life. Among the most important prerequisites to creating an integrated society, Counts argued, was psychological. Specifically, industrialism would require the elimination of peasants' deeply rooted "individualistic tradition." The industrial future required not individualism, he argued, but integration. Already the Soviet government was promoting collective enterprises over private ones, Counts observed. But the issue went deeper than that: a collective economy would contribute to building a society far more integrated than anything possible under capitalism.[98] Socialist economic organization, then, was not just about efficiency (as Chase and the technocrats insisted) but also about a communal society.

The claim that peasants were individualistic might seem unusual to readers in the early twenty-first century. Indeed, the scholarly field of peasant studies has emphasized peasants' collective institutions and communalism.[99] The majority of America's Russia experts in the 1920s and 1930s, however, blamed the slow pace of Russian economic progress on peasant individualism. Some of these reports did not place a strong value judgment on individualism over collectivism but rather framed the issue in terms of the aims of Soviet policy. To these writers—among them the journalist William Henry Chamberlin and the economists Arthur Feiler and Lazar Volin—individualism presented a problem only to the extent that it conflicted with Soviet power.[100]

But another strand of thought—closer to Counts's own meanings—sheds light on the reconsideration of individualism in interwar American thought. A wide range of American intellectuals in the 1920s sought to establish a new, less absolute form of individualism. In the words of the historian Wilfred McClay, this new post-war individual was "a permeable entity with indistinct boundaries" between self and society. Even Herbert Hoover, the Republican president who resisted any governmental role in countering the effects of the market crash, called for a "better, brighter, broader" individualism, one that "invites responsibility and service to our fellows." The scale of economic enterprises, Hoover hypothesized, rendered the disconnected individual useless in modern society; only through participation in associations and organizations could a modern person achieve individual goals.[101] Far more influential and radical was John Dewey's call for a new American ideology. Mocking the "rugged—or is it *ragged?*—individualism" of America's pioneering days, Dewey dismissed such models as irrelevant in the "collective age" brought about by modern industry. He instead called for an "integrated individuality," an identity well connected to others through a range of social networks. Those who existed outside any networks, "whether domestic, economic, religious, political, artistic or educational," the philosopher concluded, were "monstrosities."[102] To call Russian peasants individualists, then, was to assert their unpreparedness for the modern age.

Dewey's call for a new and more collective individualism inspired many Russia experts beyond those, like Counts, who had worked directly with him. Sherwood Eddy, the Christian socialist who had sponsored the early studies of Jerome Davis and Reinhold Niebuhr, asked rhetorically, "Must not all life be both individualized and socialized . . . for the potential personality and the great society?" Observers defined industrial-age individualism in terms of its collective elements.[103]

Many Americans shared Counts's excitement about remaking human nature. Thomas Woody, an education professor at the University of Pennsylvania who spent a year in Moscow on a Guggenheim Fellowship, for instance, had similar goals. Citing Dewey's work on individualism, Woody devoted a whole chapter of his book to explaining how to turn Russia's individualistic tendencies into more modern—that is, collectivist—ones. Woody noted with approval the harsh means of social as well as psychological transformation, praising the "frankly avowed dictatorship" in Soviet education.[104] This interest in remaking Soviet culture through education attracted not just Deweyans like Counts and Woody but also observers like Samuel Harper. Harper offered great praise for Soviet efforts to address the "psychological factor," even recognizing the force it entailed. Although he did not go so far as Woody in praising coercion, Harper nevertheless insisted that it did "not destroy entirely the positive value of this factor." Compulsion, especially when "coated with the sugar of propaganda," served useful purposes in Soviet education.[105] Counts freely used the term "indoctrination," implying no disapproval. All societies needed to impart their own conventions and rules, he argued, thus the principal difference between the American and Soviet systems was that Soviet schools used "modern techniques and methods" rather than relying on a disorganized complex of traditions and rituals.[106]

Making a psychological revolution alongside an economic one was no easy task, Counts believed. Unsure of its eventual success, he was nevertheless sure that human knowledge would benefit from the very attempt. Like many other Americans in the 1920s, he viewed the search for solutions to the problems of industrial society as part of an ongoing experiment; this view of Soviet policy as an experiment was widely shared in the 1920s. The ubiquity of the phrase "Soviet experiment" indeed testifies to the popularity of Dewey's language, if not necessarily his epistemology, in interwar America. Soviet educational and cultural policies, in his analysis, were experimental and experiential. Dewey had no higher form of praise than terming an endeavor experimental rather than ideological.

In addition to celebrating the experimental nature of Soviet education, Dewey also endorsed what he saw as its flexibility. He attributed Progressive education's successes in the USSR to a willingness to fit theories to local contexts and needs. Emphasizing—indeed, overemphasizing—the autonomy of local districts in establishing their own programs, Dewey praised the range of activities across the Soviet Union seeking to realize similar goals through diverse means.[107]

Counts and Dewey were among those promoting the view that the Soviet Union in the 1920s was defined by experimental flexibility rather than ideological rigidity. Dewey, for instance, summarized his initial impressions of Russia by asserting that "the Revolution was a great success, while Communism was a frost." Soviet efforts to remake the "mental and moral disposition of a people" were working because of a general willingness to try out new theories and practices—even if that meant putting Marxian ideas on ice.[108] Counts extended this argument into the Five-Year Plan era, praising the frequent changes in Plan targets as indications of flexibility rather than chaos. By the same token, variation in collective-farm arrangements revealed not disorganization but a willingness to modify goals—"almost daily" if necessary—"in the light of experience."[109] Portraying Soviet policies as experimental rather than ideological, then, offered an implicit criticism of the rigidity and stagnation American observers saw in their own country.

But Dewey's conception of experimentation also had a broader vision. In seeking an antidote to absolutism, or the derivation of practices from *a priori* principles, Dewey placed experimentalism at the center of his epistemology. Philosophers seeking to elaborate theories of the world had for too long treated experience as "the germ of a disease to which [one] needs to develop resistance." Dewey wanted philosophers to recognize that they derived their "material and . . . issues from the currents of life" around them. More important, philosophers had to work with social scientists to move beyond mere observation of social phenomena to evaluation followed by intervention.[110] Pragmatists, in other words, must be deeply engaged in the world around them, withholding judgment about human practices until the success or failure of such practices became clear. Dewey's insistence that social policies must be treated as an experiment flew in the face of those who assessed the policies on the basis of the principles from which they derived. As applied to the Soviet Union, experimentalism led to an interpretation of events in terms of practices rather than principles. But it also demanded that intellectuals detach themselves from the high costs of the experiment, at least until such costs could be compared to potential benefits.

When could an experiment be judged successful? Or, more pointedly, at what point could it be deemed a failure? Social scientists writing about Soviet policies often struck this experimental theme to defer (or perhaps even duck) judgment on success. The sociologist Edward Alsworth Ross went so far as to question the ultimate success of Communism in Russia, though he nevertheless called for patience: "I am inclined to think that on many matters the Russians are pushing up the wrong trail, but I am intensely curious as to how they actually come out." Counts offered a time frame: it would take a generation to discern the success of the Soviet experiment, he argued in 1931; until then, the American expert "would do well to reserve his judgment."[111]

An emphasis on the accumulation of experimental evidence contributed to Americans' detachment from the costs of the Soviet experiment. Although experts catalogued and occasionally celebrated the extraordinary dislocations and sacrifices that accompanied Soviet policy, they insisted that the experiment itself was nevertheless worthwhile and perhaps even essential. One economist suggested that Russia's experiment provided western social scientists with a foolproof cure for physics envy, the desire to replicate laboratory conditions when studying human behavior. By observing Russia, American scholars could experience the "intellectual enjoyment which economists have had in contemplating a closed system."[112] Bryce Hoover tallied the costs but argued for the experiment to continue all the while. The "human blood, sacrifice and suffering" in the USSR might ultimately contribute to a "fund of human experience and knowledge" from which all social scientists could presumably withdraw. Hoover later called on Americans to "adapt such experimental data as have been developed in Russia" to help solve the problems of capitalist societies. But Dewey's summation remains perhaps the most notable statement of the costs of Soviet policy:

> I find it instructive to regard it [the USSR] as an experiment whose outcome is quite undetermined, but that is, just as an experiment, by all means the most interesting going on upon our globe—though I am quite frank to say that for selfish reasons I prefer seeing it tried out in Russia rather than in my own country.[113]

Dewey's protégé, Counts, meanwhile continued his Russia studies but focused increasingly on American education. In the early 1930s Counts applied lessons from the Soviet experiment to the United States. He began by arranging for translations of two Soviet works on pedagogy. In his introductions, Counts revealed his desire to spur Americans to action. "Can we not in some way harness the school to the task of building a better, a more just, a more beautiful society?" he asked plaintively. In the meantime, American educators must devote themselves to "doing for our society what Russian educators have done and are doing for theirs." Foremost among such measures were Soviet inquiries into "the possibility of directing the course of social evolution through control of educational agencies."[114] The central moral of Soviet schooling was the notion that schools could be effective instruments of social control.

Counts expanded on this vision of social control in a provocative 1932 pamphlet, "Dare the School Build a New Social Order?" Although this piece made no direct references to Soviet education, it was nevertheless framed around the failure of western education to match Soviet achievements. Counts denigrated western pedagogy for ignoring questions of how schools shaped society. The issue was not whether "the child will be imposed upon," he wrote; imposition was a common and essential means of imparting social norms. But would American norms be set by random factors from all over the social system, or would they be shaped by a rational and organized educational effort? In promoting the latter, Counts called on educators to take an active role in "social regeneration": "If schools are to be really effective, they must become centers for the building, and not merely the contemplation, of our civilization."[115] Counts's desire to see social scientists take a direct role in shaping society was shared by Dewey, who praised Counts's hope that "the development of human society can be made subject to human will."[116] Others also shared Counts's desire to learn from Soviet methods of education. For instance, the entry for "Social Control" in the landmark *Encyclopedia of the Social Sciences* reported that the Soviet Union "has contributed enormously in making vivid the possibility of a deliberate change . . . in both the instrument and aim of control."[117] Counts hoped that Soviet schooling could provide not just inspiration for but also instigation to American educators.

While using Soviet education to goad fellow pedagogues into seeing education's potential for social transformation, Counts also worked within the community of Russia experts. He gave one of the key papers at the 1932 Institute of Politics—an annual symposium bringing together leading specialists in a Chautauqua-like environment—in which he described not just education but planning in general. According to the transcript of the subsequent discussion, Counts's notion that the Five-Year Plan was about social and not just economic transformation garnered wide acceptance from the assembled specialists.[118] Counts also was part of two different proposals for Russian studies programs, one at the University of Chicago (organized by Paul Douglas), the other at Johns Hopkins. Counts himself proposed a summer-long study in the Soviet Union for 1934, though the proposal foundered, perhaps because of high expenses.[119] Not just fellow scholars but also policy-makers in the State Department and White House sought out Counts's views on Soviet events.[120] Counts believed that he could learn from—and explain to others—the Soviet experiment of modernization and indoctrination. The Soviet Union was so important that Counts, presumably referring to himself and his colleagues, contended that it "should be watched by the most intelligent observers that our country can provide."[121] This early cohort of the best and the brightest grew excited about Russia for the same reasons Counts had. They were less inspired by Marxist slogans than by the challenge of building a new industrial society—and the role in that society for experts like themselves.

In the mid-1930s, though, Counts had begun to distance himself from

American radicals, and eventually from the Soviet experiment. Like so many of his contemporaries, he turned against American Communists as a result of working closely with them in the labor unions. He opposed an effort to expel a Communist faction from the American Federation of Teachers (AFT) in the mid-1930s. But afterward, watching the Communists' repeated efforts to take over the union one local at a time, Counts came to resent Communist involvement. Affiliated with the American Labor Party in the 1930s, he joined the growing ranks of left-wing anti-Communists. Counts's prominence and political activism soon thrust him into the AFT's national leadership. He campaigned for the presidency of the AFT against the incumbent, the sociologist Jerome Davis, who had just been fired by Yale for his anti-capitalist statements. Fulfilling his campaign promise to rid the union of Communists, Counts steered the AFT on the anti-Communist course it maintained for decades.[122]

By the time Soviet-American tensions built up in the 1940s, Counts was already a veteran anti-Communist. In one curious way, though, his argument about Soviet education survived this political shift. Writing about Soviet education in 1949, he castigated as "mind control" what he had earlier celebrated as "indoctrination." Soviet schools were no longer the crucible of a progressive new society, but instead the site of "an all-inclusive system for positive moulding of the mind." In 1957 Counts wrote a book entitled *The Challenge of Soviet Education*—and in doing so revealed the interpretative distance he had traversed since writing *The Soviet Challenge to America* in 1931. The later book described the role of Soviet education in inculcating obedience to Marxism-Leninism as well as the means for technological mastery. Soviet education no longer served as an inspiration for American educators (as he had argued in the 1930s), but was in the Cold War a grave threat that "free peoples can ignore only at their peril."[123] Counts had come a long way politically, yet his view of the effectiveness and comprehensiveness of Soviet education had changed little.

Counts need not have worried, as he did in 1929, about how future scholars would treat the ideas of his generation. A small but dedicated group of education theorists still carries a torch for Counts, arguing for the applicability of his work today. For these supporters, Counts's decade-long fascination with the USSR is something of a lodestone, the weight of which is only partially alleviated by his later anti-communism. Seeking to explain his enthusiasm for the USSR, these writers insist that Counts was inspired not by communism but by the prospects of Soviet modernization.[124] Although supporters accurately describe Counts's main focus, they do not explore the full meanings of his argument. Establishing an industrial society, as Stalin had called for in the first Five-Year Plan, would not only put peasants on tractors but would also make them into modern individuals. Industrialism could eliminate the natural traits of the Russians, which in the past had limited them. Remaking Russians—like remaking Russian society—was no simple or painless task. But Counts had as much confidence in the power of modernity as he did in the willingness of Soviet leaders to impose modern ways. Always more comfortable than Dewey with indoctrination, Counts did not shrink from the coercive aspects of this revolution. Like Chase, he abstracted Soviet technique from Soviet ideology, putting politics to the side. Yet Counts differed from Chase by asserting that age-old Russian traits could be reforged in the furnace of industrial life.

Some American scholars made parallel claims about Russia's ostensibly Asian disposition, suggesting that Asiatic characteristics might also disappear during industrialization. Asia, in the writings of these scholars, no longer defined an immovable continent or an inborn character trait. Instead it became a stage of economic and social development.

Bruce Hopper, a political scientist at Harvard, made seemingly fixed geographic categories more fluid. He had aimed to be one of the first university-trained Russia experts in the United States. Hopper's career was launched by Archibald Cary Coolidge, who supervised his undergraduate and graduate work, engineered his only significant appointment outside Harvard (as a researcher in Moscow in the late 1920s), and arranged for his first Harvard appointment. Hopper used his Moscow stint to research a dissertation on Soviet economic policy. By the time his fellowship expired and his dissertation was completed, Coolidge had died. Appointed to Harvard's Government Department in 1930, Hopper would remain there for three decades. As his junior colleague Adam Ulam kindly noted, Hopper's "scholarship was rarely of the obsessive footnote-gathering variety." Indeed footnotes (or even facts) rarely impeded the flow of Hopper's writing. His strength lay in his lecturing; his students—among them John F. Kennedy—flocked to his courses. Such pedagogical talents were insufficient for advancement at Harvard in the 1930s. In spite of the best efforts of well-connected friends like Walter Lippmann and Hamilton Fish Armstrong, Hopper never received a long-sought promotion to full professor.[125]

Notwithstanding these difficulties at his own university, Hopper made extensive and enduring contacts among that group he called the "esoteric cult" of Russia specialists. Well integrated in the social whirl of expatriate Moscow, Hopper frequented the home of William Henry and Sonya Chamberlin, as well as the bachelor apartments of Walter Duranty (Moscow) and H. R. Knickerbocker (Berlin).[126] Even before George Frost Kennan made his first trip to Moscow in 1933, he and other diplomats had been in close touch with Hopper, who sent confidential and informative missives to State Department officials Kennan, John Wiley, and Loy Henderson. When Kelley, the chief of the Eastern European Division, convened an "expert roundtable," Hopper was among those featured.[127] In addition, Hopper maintained close contacts with wide-ranging journalists like Armstrong, who asked him to vet manuscripts on Russia for *Foreign Affairs,* and Lippmann.[128] These contacts did not spare Hopper from criticism of his scholarly work; indeed, one scholar called his work "frivolous." Most members of the expert cult, however, were more generous.[129]

Perhaps this wide network of acquaintances distracted Hopper from serious scholarly work. In any case, his principal book derived not from his research in Moscow but from a series of lectures given in 1930. That book, along with articles in *Foreign Affairs* (edited by Armstrong after Coolidge's death in 1928), emphasized the problems of industrialization among a "backward people" such as the Russians. Very much like Coolidge's argument that Peter the Great replaced centuries of "Asiatic despotism" with a modern state, Hopper argued that the Bolsheviks were bringing European modernity to backward Asia. But whereas Coolidge had argued that Peter had "Europeanized" a small stratum of elites, Hopper noted the Bolsheviks' efforts to bring European ways to the entire population of the Soviet Union.

Although the category of Asia ostensibly implied fixed racial categories, Hopper employed a far less rigid cognitive geography, one in which the classifications related to development and not just geography. Coolidge had used Asia to stand for a political system; his student used it to mean an economic one. Soviet Russia, to Hopper, represented the "halfway station between the advanced West and the backward East"—though it was moving, through a continental shift of sorts, in a westerly direction. Russia, situated between the industrial nations of the west and the backward nations and colonies of the east, was especially well suited to bring industrialism to backward peoples. With Soviet-led industrialization, Hopper continued, "the old East becomes the new West." Nations once part of Asia could enter the west by industrializing.

As for nations, so for individuals. To Hopper, the transformation of backward Asia was social as well as economic. He offered a variation on Counts's view that Russia's psychological revolution would accompany its economic one, but he did so in geographic terms. The Russians were poorly suited for industrial life, Hopper wrote, because of their eastern dispositions. To make Russia western and modern, then, was tantamount to changing "the spirit of the people of the East." Hopper never confronted the paradox in his own thinking. Like Huntington, he attributed national character to climate and topography—and yet he expected it to change with economic circumstances.

The spread of industrialization came with its own dangers for the United States. Like Bryce Hoover, Hopper both predicted and feared the rise of Soviet economic power, seeing it as a threat to American political and economic interests in Asia. He nevertheless predicted boldly that Soviet industrialization would succeed, eventually making Asia the battleground between economic systems.[130]

Hopper's fusion of geography and economic development was carried even further by Hans Kohn. Kohn, a Czech refugee, arrived in the United States in 1933 after a tumultuous youth that included service with the Czech Legion in Siberia during the Russian Civil War. Before writing his classic work on nationalism in 1944, Kohn wrote widely on both Asian and Soviet affairs. His work in the mid-1930s focused on what he called the "Europeanization of the Orient." Although he admitted that the phrase had critics, Kohn insisted upon its utility in describing the arrival of rationality, individualism, and industrialism to formerly backward nations. Elsewhere Kohn celebrated the transformation of Asian cultures along putatively western lines, calling the process "a spiritual victory of the dynamic civilization of the West over the static civilization of the East." He cited the Marxian narrative through which the bourgeoisie spreads industrialization globally, extinguishing or incorporating traditional societies the world over.[131] Unlike Marx, Kohn expressed this transformation using supposedly geographical categories. Thus he prefaced his first full-fledged analysis of the USSR with his own definition of terms: "'East' and 'West' are not intended here as racial or geographical distinctions . . . but as particular stages of historical, social and cultural development."[132]

Kohn's arguments, in many ways, paralleled those of Counts as well as Hopper. Kohn noted that the Five-Year Plans would bring about not only economic and technological but also cultural westernization. Ultimately the Plans would produce not just industrialism but also people equipped for industrial work. Once again, geographic categories held economic meanings; creating industrial workers meant the elimination of "Asian" traits. In order to succeed, Soviet plans needed to produce not just steel but a "new human type, more disciplined and more controlled than the 'natural' man, than the Russian or the Oriental." The industrialization that Kohn described would bring Russia into the advanced west while transforming once-"Asiatic" Russians into rational, work-oriented westerners. Like other American experts, Kohn described the high costs of economic and cultural modernization but saw it in a positive light. Whereas Hopper expressed his concern that the spread of Soviet influence across Asia would damage American interests, Kohn took a broader and more enthusiastic view. Soviet-style industrialization would reach across Europe's colonies, he wrote, and initiate the "re-awakening of the whole earth under the irresistible compact of Western civilization."[133] The spread of industrialization would create a unified, westernized world.

Hopper's and Kohn's efforts to turn Asia into an economic category did not win universal acceptance among those writing about Russia in the early 1930s. Some scholars maintained their emphasis on Russia's eternal and unchanging difference. This theme appears prominently in the writings of Rev. Edmund Walsh, the founding dean of Georgetown University's School of Foreign Service (now named in his honor). Walsh's Jesuit training distinguished him from other American experts. There were also parallels, however: Walsh worked in the burgeoning wartime bureaucracy; he served on a relief mission in Russia in 1921–1922; and he too invoked "Asiatic" Russia.[134]

Walsh's writings emphasized continuities of Russian history. Bolshevism, he suggested, was merely a phase of Russian history. Given the uninterrupted legacy of barbarism, from Rurik to Stalin, the Bolsheviks became only the latest installment of Russian tyranny: "Bolshevism is a natural phase of a strictly historical process originating in the soil, the culture, and the politics of Russia itself." The Bolsheviks might be excused for their behavior; they were, after all, only "the fruits of barbarian practices in government extending through three centuries." Even the seemingly chaotic events of 1917 could be explained in terms of Russian character: the Provisional Government was handicapped by the Russian proclivity for debate rather than action. The role of the peasants that year was determined by their tendency toward procrastination, "dreamy idealism," and "self-immolation."[135] Russian history, in this reckoning, was simply the continued elaboration of a genetic code of character traits.

Like so many other observers, Walsh traced this code back to Russia's geographic position. Suspended between continents, Russia incorporated tendencies of both Europe and Asia. Walsh ultimately resolved this tension by citing Rudyard Kipling, who called Russia not "the most easterly Western country" but "the most westerly Oriental one." Russia, born more Asian than European, became even more "orientalized" through the long period of Tartar rule.[136] Russia's Asian traits, in turn, contributed to Russian brutality, both before and during Bolshevik rule: "Human life and human rights were always cheap in the East and still are in Russia to-day, a relic, doubtless, and a blending of two influences that cut themselves deep into the character of the ruling classes—Asiatic callousness and Byzantine haughtiness."[137] Invoking this explanation for the violence of the Russian past and present—while at the same time implying that geography was destiny—Walsh continued a longstanding theme in western writings about Russia. This sort of argument, once found frequently among America's best trained and most notable experts on Russia, had become marginal by the 1930s.[138] Indeed, Walsh himself sat on the sidelines of his field; he was specifically excluded from an effort to create an interdisciplinary Soviet studies program at Johns Hopkins University in the early 1930s.[139]

In the 1930s, most invocations of particularism—reference to specific qualities of the Russians—were directly connected to explanations of the costs of modernization. Few American experts drew the same conclusions as Walsh did. Russia experts who were influenced, directly or indirectly, by what the philosopher Morton White called the "revolt against formalism" did not dispense with the notion that Russians were different from Americans.[140] Challenging fixed and formal hierarchies, these thinkers argued that human behavior was context-specific and that human capacities were not rigidly set. These intellectual revolutionaries set the stage for new notions of society and social change. Yet they incorporated those differences into broader arguments that saw Russia as one more nation undergoing the universal process of modernization.

The steady professionalization of American studies of the Soviet Union helped spread this universalist perspective. As more and more Russia experts received formal academic training, they introduced broad sociological concerns—planning, industrialization, and education—into their analyses of Russia. A new generation of Russia experts, including Bryce

Hoover and George Counts, traveled often enough with social scientists that they too began carrying social-scientific baggage.

These broader concerns shaped analyses of the Soviet Union in two significant ways. First, America's Russia experts expressed increasing interest in gleaning from the Soviet Union ideas for reshaping American society. American social scientists who confronted the problems and prospects of modern societies often sought solutions from the Soviet experience. Problems such as inefficiency, economic inequality, isolation, and disorganization, they hoped, could be solved by learning from the USSR. Soviet practices—not Soviet political ideology—might teach the rest of the world how to plot a route toward modernity.

Second, the encounter with professional social science contributed to the marginalization of political concerns in American studies of the USSR. Insisting that key Soviet techniques, from central planning to Progressive education, could be adapted to the United States implied that political ideologies were irrelevant. This thinking was consistent with the shift in American social science toward the study of behaviors rather than ideas. Scholars from Counts to Douglas to Chase gave primacy to economic organization rather than political system. "Industrialism" was a social type, with variants such as Bolshevism, Fascism, and capitalism. Industrial societies, they suggested, had common traits even if their members espoused different (even antithetical) political theories.

The received historical wisdom that American pro-Soviet thought was doctrinal or naive is thus misguided on both counts.[141] Observers were well aware of the costs of Soviet industrialization, but they considered them worthwhile. The idea that those who cheered Soviet policy did so out of political commitments is contradicted by that cheerleading squad's general ignorance of the writings of Marx and Lenin. (Paul Douglas may be something of an exception here, though his attraction to the USSR was not based on doctrine.) Indeed, observers like Chase went to great lengths to declare their distance from ideological issues; they disdained political theory in favor of economic practice. Soviet techniques, they hoped, would provide solutions to American problems of the day.

In this vision of a universal modernity, national particularities no longer determined national destinies. But ideas of national character still had their place in American analyses of the Soviet transformation of the early 1930s. Particularist arguments supported rising social-scientific universalism. American observers saw traits of Russian character as obstacles to be overcome in the process of industrializing. The eradication of undesirable characteristics, they suggested, might even require the eradication of some undesirable characters. But the end result, either way, would be a suitably modern population. In addition, traits like Russians' famed endurance could work to the advantage of the modernizers; thus Russians' ability to endure privation became an explanation of present conditions. Even if such traits did not in fact facilitate modernization, they certainly made it more palatable for western experts. Diminishing Russians' capabilities went hand-in-hand with extolling Soviet modernization, however grotesque the consequences.

The particularism of the interwar years, though it derived from earlier western analyses, contained some significant new elements. Gone were formalist strictures that condemned the Russians to their own past by blaming economic stagnation on Russian character. In their place appeared a new argument: Russian national character meant that economic progress would come at a high cost, but a cost that could and should be borne. Hence Calvin Bryce Hoover—no friend of the Soviet Union—recognized starvation as a motivational technique. Stuart Chase asserted the value of remaking the economy, even if bloodshed resulted. George Counts turned the issue into one of cultural transformation: the Soviet efforts at economic revolution supported a salutary psychological revolution— and again, one that would inflict heavy casualties. Bruce Hopper, ever the wordsmith, coined the phrase that accounted for gains and losses: Russia was ready to "starve itself great."[142] That the Russians might be destined for greatness was an innovative element of American thought. But acceptance of the idea that such greatness was best achieved through starvation offers a frightening picture of social change—and an ominous foreshadowing of the American response when famine devastated Russia.

CHAPTER

9

Starving Itself Great

The Soviet famine of 1932–1933 had calamitous results. Leaving as many as eight million dead, it devastated the principal breadbaskets of the Soviet Union: Ukraine, the Volga Valley, the North Caucasus region, and Kazakhstan.[1] Its legacy ultimately exceeded even this gruesome death toll, marking the final victory of central Soviet authorities over the peasantry.[2] While poor weather may have contributed to the problems of the countryside, the famine was in no way a natural disaster. In the simple words of a Russian peasant adage, "God makes a poor harvest, but human beings make a famine." Recent scholars agree; as Nobel Laureate Amartya Sen put it, "Starvation is the characteristic of some people not *having* enough to eat. It is not the characteristic of there not *being* enough to eat."[3]

The famine originated in the Soviet leadership's desire to bring the countryside under economic and political control. The central instrument in this campaign was the collective farm. In the cleverly brutal phrase of one western economist, the purpose of collectivization was not to build a collective but to collect, to gather the grain and its growers under central control.[4] Official efforts to create these farm units in the rural districts, replacing village structures, accelerated and intensified with the first Five-Year Plan. The claim that Russian peasants entered the farms voluntarily was one of the many cruel fictions circulated during the Soviet drive to industrialize. The most effective recruiting tools were not dreams of mechanized farms or promises of higher production but the threat and application of violence.

Soviet collectivization was the most comprehensive and effective weapon in the battle over rural Russia. The battle, fought on various fronts for the Soviet Union's first decade, grew more fierce as it continued. The

194

famine was a result of this battle. Rural Russians wanted to maintain control over a portion of their harvest (for personal use and local sale), while central Soviet authorities insisted that the harvest was needed to advance the economic goals of the Five-Year Plans. The grain could feed the growing number of workers, in burgeoning cities as well as in the new industrial enterprises growing out of the steppe. At the same time, grain exports could help purchase foreign machinery to further the industrialization effort.[5]

Soviet officials also recognized the political benefits of collectivization. The countryside, after all, was not only the main source of food for the USSR but also home to many of those least enthusiastic about collectivization. By disrupting local structures and turning agriculturalists into workers employed by the collective farms, central Soviet authorities took unprecedented control over the countryside. Rural-dwellers, well aware of the threat that collective farms posed to their political independence and economic well-being, offered concerted resistance to collectivization—what one leading historian of the phenomenon called a "grain strike."[6]

The authorities resorted to extraordinary measures to force an increasingly recalcitrant peasantry into collective farms. Peasants paid a heavy price for resisting the imposition of Soviet power. Soviet authorities declared war on *kulaks,* a term that once meant rich peasants but by the late 1920s referred to opponents of collective farms. Equating resistance to collectivization with backwardness, and collective farms with modernity, authorities dispatched cadres of armed workers and soldiers to the "grain front" and denied necessary supplies to shrinking and beleaguered "individual" farms. Soviet authorities eventually requisitioned all the grain in the countryside—including not just seed grain but food—in order to further what one agricultural official called "the colossal program of construction" in the industrial sector.[7] The unattainable targets for industrial growth, in short, would be funded in part by involuntary reductions in living standards. Although all Russians (except for a small Party elite) suffered from the shortages, rural Russia was devastated. The treatment of peasants was so brutal that one asked a Soviet official whether "Soviet authorities consider the peasants human." And there was plenty of reason for doubt.[8]

Word of these horrendous conditions spread slowly if at all. The crisis remained, in the words of one Russian historian, a "top-secret famine." Internal Soviet documents avoided the term *golod* (meaning "famine" or "starvation"), referring instead to "well-known events" or "difficulties on the grain-requisition front."[9] Stalin disdained such euphemisms, instead blaming peasants for initiating an *ital'ianka* (slow-down strike), sabotage, and a "secret war."[10] The famine generated little interest from western news outlets. How could such a momentous tragedy receive such limited attention?

Censorship clearly played a role, as the Press Office of the NKID (the People's Commissariat for Foreign Affairs) worked assiduously to shape coverage of Soviet events. The four multilingual censors working in the early 1930s approved every telegram or telephone report before transmission. They also received after-the-fact summaries of articles that had escaped censorship. Soviet officials were also proactive, exploiting their contacts with American editors to lobby for a different slant on coverage, or occasionally for different reporters. Their contacts included editors at the *New York Times* and the United Press syndicate.[11] Censorship, of course, was not a Soviet innovation. A whole section of the tsar's Interior Ministry had spent its time monitoring and controlling both domestic and international press coverage of internal events, deleting even the most innocuous references to anything slightly controversial. Bolshevik censorship, instituted in the first days of Soviet power, sharply limited foreign dissemination of news about Russia.

Soviet censorship was far from leakproof, even during a crisis like the famine. A scattering of western newspaper articles described conditions in rural regions of the USSR in 1932 and 1933. However sketchy, they were full of explanations that drew attention away from the famine and toward its causes.

Many of those who have written about the famine blame this coverage on a combination of ideological commitment and individual treachery. A handful of western journalists, these authors allege, were either enthralled by Communism or induced by bribes to lie about Soviet events, covering up rather than covering the famine.[12] And indeed, there is an element of validity to this claim.

But if the blame for covering up the famine rests with a handful of corrupt or compromised journalists, then what explains the coverage that the famine did receive in some western newspapers, and the many American experts who knew about conditions in the countryside? The answer lies beyond individual politics and individual perfidy, and gets at the root of some of the long-standing (even well-worn) aspects of western understandings of Russia. Journalists like Walter Duranty (*New York Times*), Maurice Hindus (a freelancer), and Louis Fischer (*The Nation*) did indeed soft-pedal crucial information about the famine. Yet their reports differed little from those of other journalists who later condemned the famine: Eugene Lyons (United Press) and William Henry Chamberlin (*Christian Science Monitor*).

All five of these journalists shared two basic assumptions about Russian and Soviet life that helped them understand the famine. First, they generally expressed great enthusiasm for the Soviet Union's program of rapid modernization, turning a backward agricultural nation into a modern industrial one. Like their academic counterparts, they recognized that this program entailed high costs, but they explained these as the price of Russia's bid for industrial greatness. Second, the journalists' calculations of these costs were discounted by their low estimation of Russian national character. Western journalists disparaged the peasantry almost as much as Soviet officials did. This group of journalists employed national-character stereotypes to suggest that Russians and especially peasants were ill-equipped for the modern age. Western experts expected little from Russians other than passivity, conservatism, and apathy.[13] Any changes that took place, then, would come at a high cost—but even this could be explained with reference to the Russians' ostensible hardiness and endurance.

But what of journalistic standards of objectivity and professionalism? Changing notions of journalism promoted not objectivity but interpretation as an essential aspect of reporting. Good journalism demanded contextualization of events, and notions of national character and difference provided such a context. Assumptions about Soviet modernization and Russian character dominated American reports. Just as the professionalization of academic expertise still incorporated older, amateur ideas of alien Russia, so too did the professionalization of journalistic practice leave plenty of room for the amateur exoticism of nineteenth-century reporting. Indeed, professional journalists had even more opportunity than academic experts to dwell on Russian particularities. Ostensibly Russian qualities, reported by journalists meeting the highest standards of their profession, suggested the inevitability and even the desirability of Russian hardships on the way to modernity. These new professional standards in journalism, furthermore, themselves emerged out of controversies over American reporting from Russia.

Well before the Bolshevik takeover in 1917, westerners fought with Russian authorities, and among themselves, about the news coming from the empire of the tsars.[14] After the publication of his incendiary criticisms of Siberian exile, for instance, the Russian government barred George Kennan from Russia. And throughout the Russo-Japanese War and the revolutionary struggles of 1905, the imperial government maintained tight control over good news and bad. In the midst of this crisis, Melville Stone of the Associated Press engineered a short-lived liberalization of foreign censorship. Stone hoped that these new rules would permit coverage from St. Petersburg, supplanting the disparaging coverage of Russia from immigrant journalists in the United States. The Russophile Charles Crane applauded Stone's efforts to supplant the "Jewish elements in New York" who had provided only "hostile [and] estranging" news about St. Petersburg.[15] Getting news out of Russia had its own politics.

The high point of political reporting from Russia, not surprisingly, came with the revolutionary tumult of 1917. Most notable was John Reed's epic work *Ten Days That Shook the World,* originally serialized in 1919. Reed's contemporaries had much less success on their Russian sojourns than he had. Of the seven reporters working for U.S. newspapers in revolutionary Russia, four were asked to leave, while another was formally expelled. The other two fared worse, facing arrest and imprisonment as spies. By the end of the Civil War in 1920, no western journalists reported from Russia.[16]

The absence of on-the-spot reporting hardly diminished the quantity of news coverage about the Russian Civil War. But quality suffered, as a devastating study by the journalists Walter Lippmann and Charles Merz revealed. Most western reports about the events of the Civil War emerged from highly partisan groups in Riga, the Baltic center of anti-Soviet activity. Lippmann and Merz followed these reports over three years of recent history, showing how the *New York Times* and its correspondents in Riga and Paris turned every event into a sign of imminent Bolshevik defeat. A White Army retreat from Perm' to Irkutsk, which the *Times* had termed "strategic," could hardly be considered as such. No retreat from Sante Fe, New Mexico, to the Bahamas would ever be strategic, rebutted Lippmann and Merz, superimposing a North American map over a Russian one. As the critics summarized, the *Times* issued a constant refrain that Bolshevik collapse was just around the corner:

Thirty different times [between 1917 and 1920] the power of the Soviets was definitely described as being on the wane. Twenty times there was

news of a serious counter-revolutionary menace. Five times was the explicit statement made that the regime was certain to collapse. And fourteen times that collapse was said to be in progress. Four times Lenin and
Trotzky were planning flight. Three times they had already fled. Five
times the Soviets were "tottering." Three times their fall was "imminent"
. . . Twice Lenin had planned retirement; once he had been killed; and
three times he was thrown in prison.

These were indeed interesting times, the authors observed—but could they
have been *that* interesting? Lippmann and Merz did not accuse the *Times*
editors of intentional deceit, but instead argued that they had been misled
by anti-Bolshevik propagandists. Censorship was not a major factor, Lippmann and Merz insisted: "the chief censor and the chief propagandist were
hope and fear in the minds of reporters and editors."[17]

The solution to this reporting fiasco, Lippmann and Merz proposed, was
to build up the capacity and corporate identity of the journalistic profession. Only after establishing "tradition and discipline" for the "newspaper
guild" could Americans expect more reliable news. With that discipline
came an appreciation of scientific thinking, without which the reporter
would be as irrelevant to American society as "an astrologer or an al-
chemist."[18] Indeed, working journalists themselves had similar goals. The
newly formed American Society of Newspaper Editors, for instance, pro-
mulgated a set of professional standards in 1922.[19] Elsewhere Lippmann
broadened his program, calling not only for a new reportorial ethic but
also for a new regulatory apparatus. Only the "power of the expert," en-
sconced in a federal agency, could ensure that democracies got the news
they needed to function properly. Lippmann was proposing a journalistic
equivalent of Thorstein Veblen's "soviet of engineers" to regulate the production of news and, ultimately, public opinion.[20]

Lippmann and Merz's attack had a direct effect on news reporting from
Soviet Russia. Officials with the American Relief Administration, astute
shapers of American public opinion, insisted that American reporters accompany ARA workers into Russia in 1921. The journalists included Walter Duranty, a *New York Times* reporter who had spent the war reporting
from the front lines in the Baltics as well as France before settling into a
sullen belligerence in Paris. Deeply stung by Lippmann and Merz's criticisms of the previous summer, *Times* editors hoped to relieve the tensions
in the newspaper's Paris office while improving its representation, and per-

haps even its reputation, in Moscow. Duranty longed to return to the glamorous and independent life of a battlefield correspondent. Heading to Soviet Russia to cover the ARA would give him the autonomy and excitement he desired. No wonder that Duranty later recalled, with typical callousness and bravado, "luck broke my way in the shape of the great Russian famine" of 1921–1923. His editors may also have felt lucky by the turn of events.[21]

Duranty found Moscow much to his liking. He affected insouciance at the famine conditions he observed, considering himself duly hardened by his wartime duties. An author's note later claimed that Duranty's wartime experience provided "such a baptism of fire that nothing he saw afterwards in the Soviet Union made him turn a hair."[22] After his first tour through the afflicted areas, he reported that Russians had the same detached attitude toward their own suffering that he himself had: "The Russian people, ever patient, are dying quietly, but they are dying." They showed little emotion other than a "despairing fatalism" as they starved.[23] Of course, as a foreign journalist, Duranty himself was protected from most hardships. He lived a comfortable bachelor existence in Moscow for the next dozen years. Frequent trips to France, to the United States, or to his native England provided respite from the rigors of Russian life.

Duranty's reportage through the 1920s reached a broad audience, attracting strong reactions along partisan political lines. One Soviet sympathizer, Alexander Gumberg, accused Duranty of using vinegar for ink when writing about Russia. Others, though, accused him of using too much honey, as Duranty quickly earned a reputation for sympathetic views of the Soviet Union. One wag renamed the *Times*, at least in its Russian coverage, "The Uptown Daily Worker."[24]

Thinking of Duranty's reporting in narrowly political terms is somewhat misleading. From his first days in Russia, he denied any political motives. In 1924, while on vacation in Paris, Duranty seriously injured his leg, necessitating a partial amputation—though he would later claim the injury was a war wound. While recuperating, the reporter contemplated his future. Duranty told his editor of his earnest desire to return to Moscow. He admitted that Bolshevism amounted only to a bunch of "wild economic theories," and Communism was merely a "facade." But behind these lay the "fret and turmoil of a great young nation" and the dramas of rapid change in a country "newly freed from . . . feudalism." Later he called himself "as anti-Bolshevik as anyone could wish."[25] Whatever his flaws as a reporter (more on which below), not politics but personality was the driving force. Even the illustrious Harrison Salisbury, who later reported from Russia for the *Times,* called him "simply amoral" and insisted that "Machiavelli, rather than Marx" was Duranty's private god.[26]

Some of Duranty's colleagues in Moscow did worship Marx and Lenin, viewing their assignments as pilgrimages to the promised land of Communism. William Henry Chamberlin, for instance, left for Russia at the urging of the ubiquitous Gumberg, a fellow traveler-about-town who befriended Chamberlin and his wife, Sonya, in Greenwich Village. Shortly after his graduation from Haverford College, Chamberlin went to the Village to immerse himself in its socialist politics. His first exposure to socialism had come from his middle-class parents; his father was one of the many who voted socialist not out of belief in Marxism but out of disgust with the other candidates. William Henry found socialism especially useful in understanding the World War.[27] Once in the Village, Chamberlin wrote articles for a variety of left-wing periodicals, including *The Call* (a Socialist Party organ) and *Soviet Russia Today.*[28] He served on the staff of the *New York Herald-Tribune,* working under the legendary book-review editor Heywood Broun. His onetime boss later remembered Chamberlin's boasts about "boring from within" the capitalist system. Broun mocked his assistant's disappointment that his desire to "overthrow the government of the U.S. . . . through the medium of the book columns" did not ignite fear in the hearts of the bourgeoisie.[29] Chamberlin's book reviews captured both the themes and the fiery language of the Soviet propagandist. Even working with such limited human resources as prevailed in Russia, Chamberlin wrote, the Bolsheviks were in the midst of a "great and heroic effort to shorten the dragging march of time."[30] Tired of viewing the revolution from afar, Sonya and William Henry set sail for Moscow in 1922, arriving full of hopes but empty-handed. After working as a freelance writer, Chamberlin found a position as the *Christian Science Monitor* correspondent. The job, Gumberg joked, would serve as the "Money-tor," providing the steady income he needed to support his unpaid political writing. Chamberlin apparently agreed; his editors later described his relationship with the *Monitor* as existing on a strictly "bread-and-butter basis."[31]

Chamberlin continued to praise Bolshevism through the 1920s. In an article tellingly entitled "The Amazing Bolshevik," he repeated sympathetically one Bolshevik's claim that the peasant was "little more than an animal." He praised Bolshevik leaders of the day: Leon Trotsky had a "mighty genius for organization," Karl Radek for argument, and Lenin for leadership. No wonder that Soviet police officials called him a "very friendly" reporter in 1923.[32] At the same time that he wrote for the *Monitor*, Chamberlin contributed to various left-wing publications, eventually becoming the correspondent for the *Manchester Guardian*, a bastion of British pro-Soviet liberalism. By 1927, some of Chamberlin's early enthusiasm began to fade, a process helped along not just by his wife's criticisms of the USSR but also by the *Monitor*'s insistence that he "avoid saying anything . . . that might be interpreted as complimentary to the present order of things in Russia."[33] Satisfied that his writings in their own publication passed this political test, the editors left alone (either out of ignorance or generosity) his many writings in other periodicals.

Louis Fischer, like Chamberlin, started in Philadelphia and ended up in Moscow. But the intermediate points on his pilgrimage differed from Chamberlin's. Fischer's early Zionism, born of the Jewish ghetto, was cured by service in the Jewish Legion in Palestine. In late 1921, Fischer left for Europe to join his girlfriend, the Latvian-born Philadelphian Bertha Mark, who had just taken a job with the Soviet Foreign Office in Berlin. Fischer did not stay there, but worked as a freelance reporter in Europe, roving through Old World capitals, which seemed to him "dazed and still dripping with blood" years after the war's end.[34] Hearing more and more about the promises of Soviet Russia and especially its new approach to international relations, from his European travels as well as from his girlfriend "Markoosha," he first went to Moscow in fall 1922.

Fischer went to Russia searching "not for a better present but for a brighter future." He was immediately compelled by what he saw in Moscow. In 1922, with the wounds of the Civil War still visible, and in the midst of famine, Fischer reveled in Soviet Russia, that "kingdom of the underdog." He continued working as a freelancer, publishing in the staid *New York Evening Post* as well as the Jewish Telegraphic Agency. On a trip back to New York in 1923, Fischer hustled his way into a position as correspondent of the *Nation*, then full of Soviet enthusiasts. Fischer hoped to parlay the *Nation*'s sympathies, which closely matched his own, into privileged access to Soviet officials. He wrote to Leon Trotsky, "I am not in search of sensations . . . The Nation is a serious publication which has always been friendly towards Soviet Russia." Returning to Moscow, he quickly fell in with the colony of western journalists, especially Duranty, Chamberlin, and Paul Scheffer, the correspondent for the *Berliner Tageblatt*. He continued to place articles in magazines ranging from *Menorah Journal* to *Asia*—and even worked, for four unhappy months, at the official Soviet news agency, TASS. But his post at the *Nation* would be his mainstay for the next two decades.[35]

Fischer's reporting on Soviet Russia indeed lived up to his promises to Trotsky, though he was motivated as much by admiration as by ideological fealty. Like Trotsky himself, Fischer saw the arrival of the New Economic Policy as a retreat, tactically necessary but not ultimately in the best interests of socialism. He called on the Politburo to defend the socialist "commanding heights" from the capitalist-inclined peasants on "the plains." Fischer, like so many Bolsheviks, described the urban-rural divide as a progressive proletariat's straining to overcome a reactionary peasantry. He saw peasants as backward, unproductive, disinclined to socialism, and therefore doomed to eventual extinction. His distrust of the peasantry started under NEP and only grew over time.[36]

Fischer was far harsher about Soviet economic policy than Soviet diplomacy in the 1920s. He devoted much of the mid-1920s to a major study of Soviet foreign policy, interviewing the leadership of the People's Commissariat for Foreign Affairs. Fischer developed an especially close friendship with foreign commissar Georgii Chicherin, benefiting from hours of interviews. The book soon became (in his words) "the story of Chicherin's lifework." Not surprisingly, Fischer explained Soviet diplomacy sympathetically. He stressed the west's missed opportunities to bring the new Soviet state into the international political and economic systems. He boasted to Chicherin that the work "presents your policies and activities in an almost unqualifiedly friendly spirit," and was both hurt and angered when the Soviet official declined to write a preface for the book.[37]

Fischer and Chamberlin, who found their way into foreign reporting through a desire to observe Bolshevik rule first-hand, were joined by Eugene Lyons as the first Five-Year Plan began. Lyons arrived in Moscow in 1928, having spent the previous five years working for Soviet news organs in the United States: first the magazine *Soviet Russia Pictorial* and then a predecessor to TASS. Although he did not join the Communist Party, Lyons's interest in Soviet affairs was more political than journalistic: "emotionally and professionally," he recalled, "I lived close to the new Russia." Hired as the Moscow correspondent for the United Press, he soon would have the chance to live not near but in Russia. Switching from proletarian TASS to bourgeois UP was not, in Lyons's mind, abandoning the Soviet cause, but instead serving it more strategically. Six weeks after Bolshevism's tenth anniversary, Lyons and his family headed to the "land of [their] dreams." Lyons was met in Moscow by the fellow pilgrim Fischer, and he soon settled into Moscow reporting.[38] Working for a wire service came with obligations different from those of other reporters. UP expected its correspondents to produce numerous short news items and to stay near the center of business for fear of missing any breaking stories. While other Moscow journalists worked on extended projects, often involving research travel, Lyons produced a steady stream of unbylined cable reports from Moscow. Perhaps for this reason Lyons and his wife, Billie, quickly became the hub of the foreign colony's social network, running an informal salon for both resident and visiting westerners.[39]

Lyons adopted what he saw as the classic reportorial pose, "faintly cynical and a little bored," not as swashbuckling or romantic as Duranty's performance as a war correspondent on the Soviet front. This detachment soon covered up for Lyons's growing doubts about the Soviet Union; though he had worshipped it from afar, he soon came to question it up close.[40] Yet he stayed at the job, writing straightforward if bland dispatches on major Party events, new showpiece facilities, and the like. Lyons's big break came in November 1930, when the Press Office granted one of his routine—even ritual—requests to interview Joseph Stalin. The interview itself took a casual tone, focusing as much on Stalin's daughter as on his designs for the future of the Soviet economy. Numerous reports of the interview appeared in American news magazines, emphasizing Stalin's ostensibly Georgian traits like "broad oriental gestures." Whereas Lyons considered the interview and reports a success and career boost, the Press Office derided his seriousness compared with Duranty's tone in an interview shortly afterward.[41] Lyons's other reporting gave little indication of any dissatisfaction.

If Chamberlin, Fischer, and Lyons had traveled to the Soviet Union as if on a pilgrimage to a distant mecca, the journalist Maurice Hindus's trip to the USSR in 1923 was instead a homecoming. Born with the surname Gindelovich in the tiny Belorussian town of Bol'shoe Bykov, Hindus spent his teenage years in upstate New York, graduating from Colgate University in 1915. His return to Russia was part of a mission to resuscitate the reputation of the Russian peasant. While studying with the literary scholar Leo Wiener at Harvard after finishing at Colgate, Hindus came across Leo Tolstoy's and Anton Chekhov's portrayals of the peasants wallowing in "mud, drunkenness and brutality [as well as] . . . gloom and savagery."[42] Reading these accounts in the remote recesses of the Harvard library, Hindus grew homesick for his childhood village and resentful of writers who derided the Russian peasants for their supposed lack of intelligence, individualism, and industriousness. He attacked these portrayals in a 1920 book, *The Russian Peasant and the Revolution*. Although Geroid Robinson praised the book's handling of factual material as well as its readability, few others took note.[43] While condemning stereotypes of the Russian peasant, Hindus offered many generalizations of his own: peasants were "provincial" and selfish and lived on a "low cultural plane." But the peasants' greatest problems, Hindus insisted, were based in circumstance, not character: their "primitive" organization and technology held them back.[44]

After a few years of freelance reporting in the United States, Hindus jumped at the opportunity to visit Bol'shoe Bykovo and report on the changes that had taken place there since he had left in 1905. The resulting book, *Broken Earth* (1926), set the model for his future works. Although he wrote widely and frequently for periodicals, Hindus's best work came in the form of three-hundred-page travelogues, light on statistics but full of stories. In a series of anecdotes, Hindus portrayed simple Russians in simple scenes: a wedding, a drinking bout with town elders, a funeral procession, and many tea- or vodka-lubricated conversations with everyday people in train stations, taxis, and other workaday locales.

Just as his Russian peasants cultivated their crops with meager tools and age-old methods, Hindus himself cultivated an image of rustic innocent. He spoke incessantly of the virtues of rural life. His prolific writing covered primarily peasant topics. Louis Fischer offered a romantic depiction of Hindus as a simple man, more at home with rural folk than with urban sophisticates. After a few days in Moscow, Fischer recalled, Hindus would "sling his shoes over his shoulder like the Russian peasant . . . and tour the countryside." Hindus's home on the Upper West Side of New York and his frequent stays at Moscow's Grand Hotel hardly interfered with this image.[45] But even if he differed from Duranty, Chamberlin, and Fischer, all of whom viewed the Russian peasantry with a combination of suspicion and condescension, Hindus nevertheless praised the Bolsheviks for the same reason: their desire to transform the countryside.

Hindus focused on the peasants' "wretched" economic conditions, low education levels, and especially the poor technology that kept rural-dwellers in "darkness." Wooden plows going only four or five inches deep, Hindus complained, left Russian agriculture at the mercy of the harsh climate. The peasant, to Hindus, was hard-working, intelligent ("ignorance does not imply stupidity, any more than a college training implies intelligence"), and, ultimately, "pitifully human."[46] Hindus's writings centered on the "painfully picturesque" scenes of the Russian village: brief sketches described a healthy inventory of human frailties from dishonesty to superstition.[47]

Much had changed since Hindus had left Belorussia in 1905. The Bolsheviks had begun the social transformation of the peasant, a necessary and indeed noble task. Already the peasants had become more articulate than under tsarism, belying "other far-reaching changes in peasant psychology," and even providing a new sense of "personal dignity."[48] Hindus's desire to eradicate the poverty of his birthplace led to his support for the Bolsheviks' broad and increasingly violent efforts to transform the Soviet countryside. As the pace of that transformation accelerated in the late 1920s, Hindus and his journalistic colleagues continued and even intensified their own support for Soviet policies. And they did so in the name of journalistic objectivity.

All five of these reporters, whether arriving in Russia for political or professional reasons, found themselves in a changed environment for reporting. Previous generations of foreign correspondents had followed a strict empirical diet—just the facts—in an effort to achieve journalistic objectivity. Yet after World War I, as the sociologist Michael Schudson persuasively observed, many journalists came to believe that facts were no longer enough. The rise of propaganda, the expansion of censorship, and the invention of public relations meant that news reports were increasingly seen as one-sided. Reporters could no longer simply repeat the news they heard; they now had to evaluate it and place it in a broader context.[49] Practicing journalists and scholars alike expressed this goal in urgent terms: facts without interpretation led to public bewilderment—almost all observers used this word—about international events. In the halcyon days before World War I, wrote one such commentator at the newly created Columbia School of Journalism, any reader could understand news stories "without help from Walter Lippmann." Yet unadorned facts, in the complex world of the late 1920s and early 1930s, no longer sufficed: "To leave the item naked, not clothed in its historical environment, is to invite the reader not to read it at all, because it has little meaning for him . . . No wonder he is bewildered and indifferent." The solution was interpretation: journalists must explain "why and how this happened and what it means."[50] It was time to abandon, another journalist-turned-scholar wrote, the "almost fanatical insistence upon facts served so entirely without background as to be practically unintelligible."[51]

Walter Lippmann himself helped the cause. In a 1931 speech, he focused on the responsibilities of American foreign correspondents with America's newfound role as a "world power in spite of ourselves." U.S. foreign relations were once reducible to simple ideas and phrases—"the Monroe Doctrine" or "no entangling alliances." But such terms could no longer explain the complexity of the post-war world or America's place in it. To penetrate the "thick fog of details" about international relations, Lippmann wrote, required moving beyond facts to interpretation—"an exploration, tentative, sympathetic, and without dogmatic preconception."[52] American reporters in Russia and around the world responded to these calls, offering not merely facts about but interpretations of foreign nations. For most western reporters in Moscow, the nature of Russian national character formed a crucial part of their interpretations of the Soviet Five-Year Plans—an element that made their enthusiasm for the Plan seem not just logical but necessary.

As the Five-Year Plans began in 1928, these five American reporters each had his own reasons for enthusiastically supporting them. Fischer, Chamberlin, and Lyons, all initially attracted to Russia for ideological reasons, praised industrialization for bringing the USSR (and eventually the world) one step closer to socialism. For Duranty, enthusiastic about the rapid economic change and dismissive of the peasantry, the Plan represented a campaign to pull Russia into industrial modernity, one resulting in a series of battles he relished. And despite the torch he carried for the peasantry, Hindus approved of Soviet planning, and especially collectivization, for seeking to modernize the countryside out of its medieval squalor. Although these journalists had different motives and varied in the particulars of their coverage, a number of common themes emerge. All five decried peasants' passivity and praised the Bolsheviks' attempts to spur them to action. Most of them, furthermore, incorporated the familiar language of "Asiatic Russia" into their explanations of both peasants' inactivity and their ability to withstand the high costs of remaking the Soviet countryside. These two trends combined to justify the need for agricultural reconstruction in spite of the high costs. The first Five-Year Plan was, in the eyes of these journalists, part of the Soviet Union's efforts to "starve itself great."

Even Maurice Hindus, that fierce partisan for all things peasant, blamed the peasantry for the sorry state of Russian agriculture. He lauded Soviet efforts in the NEP era for expanding the horizons of the peasantry, bringing rural-dwellers newfound voice and energy in local affairs as well as introducing them to the world beyond the local. "Beneath his crude ancient exterior," Hindus rhapsodized, "there dwelt a changed and shining human being." The subtitle of one of his articles from 1927 summed up his views effectively: "The Russian Peasant Reborn: The Timid but Anarchic Being Made Self-Assertively Articulate by the Revolution." Hindus attributed the changes in peasant behavior to the ascendancy of the Bolsheviks: "the Revolution is slowly but mercilessly jolting him [the peasant] out of his old inertia."[53] Collectivization, in this reckoning, was one of the Bolsheviks' efforts to save the peasants from their own worst traits.

Louis Fischer, wary of peasant conservatism, especially appreciated Maurice Hindus's excitement over the transformation of the Russian peasant. Reviewing Hindus's book *Red Bread*, Fischer praised not just its evocation of rural life—"the book smells of the soil and the sweat of the Russian village"—but also its claims about redirecting human behavior. "If you think that human nature cannot change," Fischer dared, "read Hindus's story." The book is compelling enough, Fischer concluded, that Hindus had "done a great service to the revolution" by demonstrating how "collectivization has immediate advantages over *muzhik* farming."[54] Collectivization, in the context of the broader goals of the Plan, inaugurated what Fischer termed the "heroic stage of the revolution."[55] The Russian village of the 1920s "was so unproductive and unprogressive, so illiterate culturally and agriculturally that almost any change would have been a change for the better." The most damaging flaws of the countryside related to the characteristics of its inhabitants. The famous Russian patience, Fischer argued, was not a virtue but instead "one of the worst curses of this land." Only under the threat of collectivization, he contended, would the Russian village exorcise "Slav sluggishness" in the name of a new god, "Plan Fulfillment." Fischer hoped to overcome the "bovine equanimity" with which peasants accepted their fate.[56]

Eugene Lyons, who would come to share little else with Fischer, did find common ground (pasture?): the use of livestock metaphors. Lyons's memoirs phrased his complaints about Russians' "animal-like indifference" in terms similar to Fischer's. Russian peasants were a "brow-beaten bovine" people facing dramatic changes under collectivization. Lyons condemned "the universal habit of *not* grumbling, of fatalistic submission to suffering and tyranny, of extraordinary meekness," among Russians.[57] Other Russian traits helped define Soviet economic policy. The Russians' lack of "discipline, efficiency and speed" required increasingly harsh measures of incentive and enforcement. At a more trivial level, the tendency to "dramatize the commonplace," along with an abnormal fascination with numbers, Lyons argued, shaped the substance and the style of the Five-Year Plans.[58]

William Henry Chamberlin used similar language and logic when describing the Five-Year Plans and their impact on the Russian peasantry. He, like Fischer, referred to Slavic "sluggishness" and disparaged the peasants' work habits. Chamberlin resented the romantic portrayals of the Russian peasant as "a mysterious idol in a sheepskin coat." His own reports ran little risk of idolizing the peasantry. In one article, for instance, Chamberlin associated peasants and sheep not in terms of clothing but in terms of character: collectivization might succeed, he argued, because the "sheeplike" nature of the peasants meant that they would follow a few leaders into the collective.[59] Elsewhere he emphasized peasants' passivity; they were typically "placid" and "unenterprising," their demeanor "shiftless and indifferent." Chamberlin hoped that the Plans might make up for the absence of initiative by instilling—or if necessary installing—the "capacity for steady, concentrated work which has hitherto never been a conspicuous feature of the national character."[60] Arguing that such deficiencies increased the costs of Soviet policy, he called for balancing means and ends. He praised those analysts, like Bruce Hopper, who did "not underestimate the huge strain and deprivation which have become the inevitable accompaniment of the Russian plunge into quickline industrialization."[61] But Russian traits could work to the advantage of Soviet planners. The "docility" of Russian peasants, Chamberlin argued, left them in a state of resigned acceptance to Soviet policy and led them to accept the hardships and poor living conditions without protest. Russians' legendary endurance thus allowed the Plans to continue.[62]

If Chamberlin accepted the costs of Soviet industrialization, writing them off to inborn hardiness, his colleague Walter Duranty adopted a more celebratory tone. That Bolsheviks required peasants to work themselves to death was no surprise to the war-worn Duranty. "It is a hard and bloody doctrine," he admitted, but "they are a hard people and Russia a hard country." His major concern about collectivization was that its proponents might suffer from "loss of nerve" before bringing the process to completion.[63] His support for radical and violent change was rooted in his derision toward the Russian peasants. Like Chamberlin, he dismissed those who believed Tolstoy's or Feodor Dostoyevsky's descriptions of "soulful" peasants. These fictional characters little resembled the "'dark,' illiterate masses" who composed the bulk of the Russian population. Duranty preferred Gorky to Tolstoy when it came to depicting the Russian peasantry. Gorky, a close friend of the Bolsheviks, demeaned the peasants as "Chinese barbarians . . . uncivilized . . . semi-savage," and even anti-intellectual.[64] In Duranty's estimation at least, the beastly peasants were at least able to contribute to the Plan through their own suffering.

Ideas of exotic Russia appeared so frequently in American writings that they led to a rare moment of agreement between the Soviet Foreign Commissariat and the Soviet arch-enemy Leon Trotsky. In a routine report on American news coverage, one NKID Press Office employee mocked Duranty's reliance on the "hackneyed motif" of the "eastern disposition of the Russian soul." The following year, Trotsky railed against American reporters for explaining away the rising violence in the USSR. He mentioned specifically the *New York Times*'s man in Moscow: "No, the Messieurs Duranty tell us, it is not a madhouse [in the USSR], but the 'Russian soul.'"[65] Indeed, the heavy reliance on exoticism—found especially in Lyons, Chamberlin, and Duranty—defined an important component of American views of the Soviet planning effort.

In spite of some internal disagreements—were peasants individualist or collectivist? was the problem with collectivization peasant recalcitrance or incompetence?—these five journalists all offered explanations of the Five-Year Plan that began with the peasant traits of passivity and endurance. These themes also resonated outside this small but influential group. Even the mild-mannered professor Samuel Harper, hardly prone to reportorial proclamations of cynicism, nicknamed the Five-Year Plan "Build Till It Hurts." And when the German reporter Paul Scheffer was denied re-entry into Russia after a brief trip home, Harper blamed Scheffer's excessive tenderness, not Soviet censorship. The German was, in Harper's words, "too sensitive by temperament to stand the violence and injustice that accompany revolutionary movements."[66] In contrast to Scheffer's rough handling (by Soviet officials and fellow journalists alike), reviewers praised those books that recognized the costs of Soviet industrialization. Hindus's work received special kudos on this score. Bruce Hopper claimed that Hindus's language resonated with "all who have listened to the despairing lament of the dark people who are being violently transformed in Russia." And one sociologist offered the praise of a voyeur: Hindus's writing is so good, the review read, that "one can feel the actual suffering of the people."[67] Of all the problems with the Five-Year Plans, then, the human costs ranked low on American experts' lists.

These high costs could also be explained with the notion that Russia and Russians had "Asiatic" tendencies. The catalogue of Asiatic traits attributed to the Russians had changed little over time, though by the 1920s they were more directly linked to discussions of modernization. Walter Duranty applied the notion of Asiatic Russia comprehensively, situating it at the center of his argument. "Most foreigners who go to Russia," Duranty explained didactically, "fail to understand that Russia is Asiatic." No wonder, then, that Duranty boasted that he learned more about Soviet life from three months in China than he had in six years in Moscow.[68] What was Asia to Duranty? Asia meant fatalism, mysticism, duplicity, despotism, and violence. Duranty insisted that his emphasis on Russians' dissimilarities from westerners did not imply inferiority: "Russia and Russians and Russian logic are different, but the fact that they are different does not mean that they are wrong."[69] The bulk of his writings, however, contradict this disclaimer.

Russia's unique characteristics, Duranty implied, determined the form and ultimately the fate of Soviet ideology and institutions. The revolution of 1917, in this argument, eliminated the "European veneer" of tsarism, allowing "the essential Russianism" to break through from underneath as Bolshevism. Marxist economic doctrine was reconfigured, Duranty reported, to meet Russia's "racial needs . . . [which] are strange and peculiar, and fundamentally more Asiatic than European." These racial needs explained the popularity of central planning in the Soviet Union. The Plan, Duranty wrote as it entered its second year, would be successful because it "provided an esoteric stimulus to a people whose roots are deep in mysticism." As the first Plan turned onto the final stretch, he added that "Russians, ignorant or wise, have a positive passion for plans."[70] Whereas Thorstein Veblen and his technocratic followers admired the planning process for its imposition of rationality, Duranty expressed the opposite conviction: planning appealed to Russians' innate irrationalism and mysticism.

Duranty and other journalists explained Russian political life, especially its tendency toward despotism, in terms of character traits. Duranty traced

the spread of Bolshevism to fatalism. Once Lenin took charge, he suggested, Russians simply accepted his vision as their fate. Stalin's despotism,
similarly, was the eventual outgrowth of Russia's ostensible Asiatic nature:
"with its ancient Asiatic craving for mass action under an absolute ruler
whose word is the law," Russia was fertile ground for Stalin's rule.[71]
Whereas Samuel Harper inferred that Asia meant collectivism, Duranty
himself preferred more lurid tendencies like predispositions to violence,
deceit, and tyranny.[72]

Eugene Lyons offered a similar discussion of Stalinism as a peculiarly
Asian form of rule. Unlike Duranty's vision of a purely Asiatic Russia, Lyons's Russia contained an internal tension between European and Asiatic
elements. Stalin's ascent, therefore, represented the victory of eastern elements over western ones. The result was distinctly eastern: an "Asiatic dictatorship" that established a particular type of "Asiatic horror" in the form
of political repression.[73]

William Henry Chamberlin shared many of Duranty's and Lyons's views
about the political implications of Russia's ostensibly Asian nature. Like
Lyons, Chamberlin saw Russia as torn between east and west:

> Russia has always had a foot in each continent without belonging
> definitely to either. Its cultural forms and aspirations have been Euro-
> pean. Its governmental and living standards have suggested Asia. This du-
> alism has not been removed [in recent years]; in some respects it has
> been intensified by the changes which the Revolution brought about.[74]

Yet he implied that the eastern tendencies were holding sway in Stalin's
USSR, which had turned toward "Oriental despotism." Chamberlin's version of this concept identified despotism with actions "in quantity as opposed to quality," a proclivity fulfilled by the "majestically Asiatic" Soviet
system, replete with its "millions of victims." Asian societies, in short, were
mass-oriented, tyrannical, and violent.[75]

If Russia was prone to violence and hardship, at least (according to
American journalists) Russians were used to paying the price. Indeed, they
seemed to have a special talent for it. Chamberlin argued that "Asiatic"
traits like a general "indifference to suffering" and a "tenacious vitality"
meant that peasants would be able to withstand the numerous hardships
of the first Plan.[76] (Chamberlin also identified many other aspects of
peasant life, from clothing to arranged marriages to farming methods, as
Asian.)[77] But among the most important Asian traits Chamberlin de-

scribed were passivity and fatalism. One 1925 article, for instance, called peasants "sluggish and apathetic" under NEP. Things improved little with collectivization, where under the sway of "oriental fatalistic philosophy," peasants did what they were told with little enthusiasm or energy.[78] Russians' fatalism, furthermore, equipped them to persevere through hard times. In Duranty's phrase, Russians were so fatalistic that in times of crisis they maintained "passive suffering . . . [as] a universal rule."[79] Whether western observers connected fatalism to innate Slavic traits or to ostensibly Asiatic ones, the conclusions were the same: Russians could best contribute to Soviet modernization by enduring its hardships.

Russia's Asian qualities shaped foreign as well as domestic policies. Duranty suggested that Soviet diplomats' violations of protocol and their willingness to break promises were merely symptoms of Russians' "Oriental duplicity." He wrote that Georgii Chicherin, the commissar for foreign affairs, was "an Oriental, or at least Oriental-minded," and therefore "never boggled at any denial if it suited him"—this of a man fluent in English and German as well as Russian, and at home all over Europe.[80] Lyons offered a similar portrayal, especially in his description of working with the NKID censors. "The bargaining [with censors] is truly Oriental," Lyons wrote, "swathed in smiles and leisurely conversation, but sharp and infinitely cautious underneath." It also evidenced a general disregard for human life; he described a hypothetical conversation that combined western reporters' self-conscious toughness with supposed "Asiatic" lack of respect for life. "I am no more upset by the executions than you are—we're both inured to such trivia, of course—but news is news," an imaginary reporter might argue in the process of negotiation with a censor.[81] Russians' Asian natures, and especially the denigration of life supposedly identified with The East, accounted for Soviet economic policy as well as diplomacy.

It is tempting to associate the references to "Asiatic Russia" with either political partisanship or amateur exoticism. Yet politics and amateurism cannot account for the frequency and breadth of the concept's application in western reporting. The term crossed many political boundaries; indeed, both radicals and conservatives referred to "Asiatic Russia" in making their cases about the USSR. Those writers like Chamberlin and Lyons who traversed political boundaries over the course of their own careers used the same concepts with more or less the same meanings whether they were endorsing Soviet policies or criticizing them.[82]

References to "Asiatic Russia," furthermore, are important illustrations of the new journalistic professionalism in post–World War I America. When reporting from places as remote from the American experience as Russia, the argument went, interpretation was essential. Walter Duranty made precisely this claim in an interview with a trade publication after winning a Pulitzer Prize in May 1932: "When you write about Russia, you're writing about a nation and a people whose customs and ideals are as strange to the western mind as are those of the Chinese." The objective of the Moscow correspondents, then, was to offer an interpretation of Russian events, to draw on Russian history and culture to explain the significance of news about the USSR. "Statements of fact," Duranty said, echoing the journalistic theories of the day, "convey no impression of importance" to the American reader. The vast differences between American and Soviet life, he continued, "make it necessary for the correspondent to interpret the news in order to give it value." Apparently many of his fellow journalists concurred. His interview in the trade magazine was published under the headline "Uninterpreted News of Russia Puzzles Prejudiced World, Says Duranty."[83] And even more important, the citation for Duranty's Pulitzer Prize, awarded for his coverage of the first Five-Year Plan, praises the reporter not for research but for interpretation: "Mr. Duranty's dispatches show profound and intimate comprehension of conditions in Russia and of the causes of those conditions. They are marked by scholarship, profundity, impartiality, sound judgment and exceptional clarity and are excellent examples of the best type of foreign correspondence."[84] Judgment, not investigation, earned Duranty his prize.

Duranty's prominence, especially after the Pulitzer, illustrates another aspect of the new styles of journalism in the late 1920s, the rise of the celebrity correspondent. While newspapers had long sent well-known individuals overseas on special assignment, Duranty's popularity indicates that professional journalists could become well known for their reporting. Duranty and the others were aided immeasurably by the rise of the bylined article in the 1920s. News columns, previously printed as the official voice of an institution, now offered its articles as personal items by individual reporters.[85] Wire-service reporters like Eugene Lyons could also get in on the act, writing articles on Russia for popular magazines while filing daily dispatches for the United Press. Even before the Pulitzer, Duranty was a highly sought after interpreter of Russia. In the ballyhoo following his prize, publishers and politicians fell over themselves to fete him. President Hoover's advisors wanted him to go on a weekend fishing excursion with Duranty, though the president apparently did not take the bait. The reporter did meet, however, with candidate Franklin Delano Roosevelt as well as State Department personnel.[86] Celebrations of Duranty brought the *Foreign Affairs* editor Hamilton Fish Armstrong as well as the financiers Felix Warburg and W. Averill Harriman in touch with the reporter.[87] The media critic George Seldes claimed that "we would have nothing but objective and reliable news if all the editors in America chose correspondents of the Duranty caliber." Ralph Barnes (*New York Herald Tribune*) and Oswald Garrison Villard (editor of *The Nation*) praised Duranty's writing—the latter calling it "brilliant" and "scintillating."

Other movers and shakers sought out Duranty's advice and counsel. Walter Lippmann begged for a lunch date, while John Dewey enjoyed a dinner with the reporter. Even Robert F. Kelley from the State Department responded favorably to Duranty's reports.[88] Duranty, it seems, was as much a news items as the events he was covering. Indeed, when Maxim Litvinov sailed to Washington in November 1933 to negotiate for diplomatic recognition, it was unclear whether he was accompanying Duranty or vice versa. It was as if, quipped one friend of the reporter, America "was recognizing both Russia and Walter Duranty."[89] Intellectuals and journalists expected from Duranty not a mere recitation of facts but a broad interpretation of Soviet events. His particular—and particularistic—interpretation drew on Russia's differences from the west to explain Russia's shortages and violence. He was not the first, not the only, and not even the most effective proponent of this view. But his ability to offer this interpretation placed the facts of Russian hardships in the context of Russian culture.

Ultimately, Duranty went beyond interpretation. He used context not merely to explain but to justify the hardships created by Soviet policies. In one private letter he praised Bolshevik leaders for "making a genuine effort to lift the masses out of the appalling misery and ignorance in which they have lived for centuries."[90] Duranty insisted that analysts focus on the future benefits of Soviet industrialization, which was bringing Russia "from oxcart to airplane" in a single generation.[91] As he put it an oft-repeated phrase, "You can't make an omelet without breaking eggs." The phrase, which the reporter incorporated in most of his conversations about the USSR, served two purposes. It was a part of his efforts to balance the benefits of industrialization against the costs; but at the same time, it helped Duranty stake his claim as a dispassionate, hard-boiled reporter who could comment calmly and cynically on any event, no matter how bloody.[92] Human losses were a small price to pay for the potential gains of industrialization—or objective reporting.

Given Duranty's dim views of the Russian peasantry, those who would be most victimized by Soviet-style progress, his calculation of the benefits of collectivization is unsurprising. But even Maurice Hindus endorsed collectivization as a necessary step for his beloved peasants. After traveling through the countryside in 1929 and 1930, Hindus wrote to his friend Samuel Harper enthusiastically: "the spread of the collective farming movement in spite of peasant recalcitrance is one of the most outstanding features of the Revolution."[93] Peasant resistance was far from the only problem collectivizers faced in the rural Soviet Union. In discussing current events with a Soviet official, Hindus listed innumerable problems on the farms he had visited: peasants' frequent and lengthy breaks from work, poorly maintained equipment, malfunctioning tractors, and farm workers' lackadaisical attitudes. Yet, the official accurately concluded, "all of these shortcomings have not kept Hindus from being a genuine enthusiast of the *kolkhoz* [collective-farm] movement. He said that he has not seen literally a single *kolkhoz* in which there was not a new beginning, of either an economic or a cultural character."[94] Hindus did not underestimate the resistance to or the failures of collectivization. But he nevertheless offered his unqualified endorsement of collectivization as "the only thing that can save the farmer from utter ruin"—"however disturbing and upsetting it is to the older generation of peasants." The social and economic dislocations of collectivization were small prices to pay for its "potentialities."[95]

Hindus's trilogy of Plan-era books about Russia all celebrated collectivization as the key to unlocking the human potential of the Russian peasantry. The first and best-selling of these books, *Humanity Uprooted*, appeared in 1929 and was reprinted at least sixteen times in the next three years. Journalists, scholars, and diplomats alike praised Hindus's keen analysis, his attention to detail, and his intimate knowledge of rural Russia; John Dewey even wrote an introduction to the book.[96] Calling Russia's upheavals the "birthing pains of a new society," Hindus remained optimistic about the final results. As he wrote to a friend: "looking at things in perspective, I am heartily convinced that whatever setback collectivization may be countenancing in the villages, it has come to stay and eventually [will be] for the good of the peasants. All doubts of the benefits of the [collective] movement have, for the present at least, disappeared from my mind." Like Woodrow Wilson, who argued for a military campaign "in the best interests of what the Russians themselves desire," Hindus purported to help the Russians by stating opinions on their behalf. And though the price of collectivization was high, it was well worth paying.[97]

Hindus organized his books around the benefits rather than the costs of collectivization. His book *Great Offensive* (1933) discussed the creation of a "new economic order" based on "The Machine," which Hindus saw as both a peculiar fascination of the Russian people as well as a means to modernization. The second section focused on the creation of a "new human personality," with each chapter a celebration of the transformation of one or another social institution (religion, family, schools, armed forces, and jails) and, ultimately, society itself. Other chapters contained cheerful obituaries of bourgeois inhibitions and limitations. Most chapters ended with an italicized paragraph summing up how rural Russians had "lost faith in God . . . lost all fear of parental authority . . . and lost the fear of sex, money, family, and insecurity." Hindus admitted that he stood "in awe of [the Bolsheviks'] transcendent powers" to overcome the limits of human nature. He told one American diplomat that these social improvements alone provided ample justification for the revolution.[98] One widely cited article asked, "Has the Five-Year Plan Worked?" Hindus's answer was an enthusiastic affirmative: the Machine Age did not merely increase agricultural efficiency but also was central to the "remaking of the human personality" that accompanied economic changes. Hindus balanced economic losses against cultural gains: "The peasants are not so well off from the point of view of food as in 1926 . . . but they now have education, entertainment, and care for their children." Educational advances compensated for material losses.[99]

The five most important American journalists in Moscow each had his own reasons for supporting the increasingly brutal Soviet policy in the countryside. Fischer was still offering his fealty to the Party line. Chamberlin and Lyons, no longer committed to the Party, nevertheless held the Russian peasantry in such low esteem that they saw rural transformations as a necessary step. Duranty's leadership in the group's informal cult of suffering led him to endorse Soviet policy to his ever-growing audience. And the pro-peasant Hindus found rural conditions in desperate need of improvement. But what would happen if rural conditions continued to deteriorate? Could there be a famine? *The Great Offensive* opened with just this question, framed as a hypothetical conversation about the costs of collectivization:

"—And suppose there is a famine in Russia?" continued my interlocutor, an American businessman of national renown and known for his liberalism, "what will happen?"

"People will die, of course."

"And supposing three or four million die?" [the businessman queried]

"The Revolution will go on."[100]

The revolution would move forward, visiting havoc on many Russians but continuing through to completion.

Although the perspectives of these five journalists ranged from cavalier calculation of human loss to warm sentimentalism for the peasants' plight, all five found a way to explain the need for dramatic transformations in Russia. Understanding these justifications goes a long way toward explaining western coverage of the rural crisis in the Soviet Union as it reached its apogee in late 1932 and 1933.

Food conditions worsened in the winter, as peasants consumed the last of the meager grain stocks and began killing livestock. By midwinter, death tolls mounted in the major breadbaskets of the USSR—Ukraine, the Volga Valley, the Don region, the Caucasus, and Kazakhstan. Food supplies in Moscow remained stable if hardly copious. Even so, rumors of famine spread through the western colony there in the summer of 1932. Harvard's Bruce Hopper, well-acquainted with the Moscow correspondents, wrote to a friend in the State Department that "there is definite famine" in Ukraine.[101] Other information about rural conditions spread among westerners. German embassy officials had been reporting famine conditions in grain-growing regions of the USSR as early as the summer of 1932. One report by Otto Auhagen, based more on Soviet statistics than on first-hand experience, referred to "famine (*Hungersnot*) in the fullest sense of the word" in Ukraine, the Lower Volga, western Siberia, and Kazakhstan.[102] The German agricultural attaché Otto Schiller, one of the best-informed foreigners in Moscow, spent much of 1932 touring the Soviet countryside. Traveling with the Canadian Andrew Cairns, Schiller detailed the dire conditions in the Soviet countryside in an article that appeared in Germany in February 1933. Cairns's reports reached the British Foreign Office even earlier.[103]

More details about rural conditions reached Moscow in fall 1932. One British diplomat reported in late October 1932 that Duranty "ha[d] at last awakened to the agricultural situation," blaming the severe problems on shortages of labor and draught-power. The diplomat summarized Duranty's analysis: "There are millions of . . . peasants whom it is fairly safe to leave in want . . . [But] is there no limit to people's endurance?" Yet Duranty did not foresee any organized resistance. His articles typically came across as equivocally sanguine. For instance, he reported that the USSR was "in better shape than most of the world" despite serious supply problems that had sapped "peasant energy and initiative." Even an otherwise celebratory article on the fifteenth anniversary of Bolshevik rule closed with mixed optimism. "Times are hard and will not be easy in the near future," Duranty wrote, but the ultimate victory of "socialist building" was assured.[104]

Duranty soon took a markedly less optimistic tone about the situation in Russia. At the end of November, he published a six-part series on the food shortage, mailed out of Moscow to evade censorship. This series established the parameters for his subsequent writings on the food situation. While he dismissed the predictions of famine ("there is no famine or actual starvation, nor is there likely to be"), Duranty did write of the "great and growing food shortage in town and country alike," which was having "ever graver" effects. Only bread was available in reasonable amounts. Dairy products were never seen. Meat and fish appeared only rarely and in quantities "below the people's wants and probably below their needs." The Russians' capacity for sacrifice, however, would carry them through: "Russians have tightened their belts before to a far greater extent than is likely to be needed this Winter." Duranty seemed impressed with Soviet leaders who were "not in the least trying to minimize its [the food shortage's] gravity, its widespread character and its harmful effects," but were not "much alarmed by it." Finally, perhaps to explain his own reluctance to stray from Moscow, Duranty dismissed the need for a foreign observer to tour the villages, "where it commonly happens that disgruntled or disaffected elements talk loudest while others are busy working."[105] The series served Duranty well in New York, where editors praised it as "one of the best stories current." Yet it served him less well in Moscow, as a British diplomat reported:

Shortly after [the series appeared], Duranty was visited by emissaries from governing circles here (not from the Censorship Department of the People's Commissariat for Foreign Affairs but from higher spheres) who reproached him with unfaithfulness . . . [D]id he not realize that the consequences for himself might be serious? Let him take this [as a] warning. Duranty, who was to have left for a short visit to Paris that day, put off his departure to wait further developments. He affects to think it possible that . . . he may not be allowed to return.[106]

Duranty postponed his trip for a few days, eventually leaving in early December. Once in Paris, he gave a report to a group of Americans. A diplomat in attendance summarized Duranty's views as follows:

> The chief reason for his pessimism was the growing seriousness of the food shortage. This he ascribed to difficulties which the Government was having with its scheme of collective farming . . . He described the situation in Russia to-day as comparable to that which existed in Germany during the latter part of the war, when . . . the civil population was living on practically starvation rations.

According to two reports, the Paris speech angered Soviet authorities.[107] By the end of 1932, then, Duranty had set a pattern for describing the rural crisis. He frequently employed military terminology, once again celebrating his wartime exploits. He issued critical and pessimistic reports on the food situation accompanied by denials that "famine conditions" existed. This pattern would continue throughout the famine's duration and beyond.

As Walter Duranty published his November 1932 series on the food shortage in the Soviet Union, Louis Fischer voiced few worries about Soviet conditions: "I feel as if this were the beginning of the end of a long Soviet winter which has lasted several years. Now the earth commences to smell of spring." Perhaps the new springtime provoked Fischer's allergies, as he left Moscow for an extended American tour, from December 1932 until the following June. His final article from Moscow called for easing the pressure on Soviet peasants. That article also noted a decline in grain collections in the North Caucasus region, blaming "bad organization, slack guidance by party members [and] insufficient loyalty to Moscow's instructions." The problems might extend even farther, as "important grain-growing areas like the Ukraine, North Caucasus, the Volga region and the central black-earth district" had no grain on the market. Fischer thus identified food shortages, but only in cryptic phrases containing gross understatements.[108]

Like Fischer, Chamberlin also left Moscow for an extended trip to the

United States, perhaps spurred by the rumors about food shortages. He predicted food-supply problems for the fall and winter of 1932–1933. In early October, he recommended to his replacement that foreigners should consider hoarding nonperishable food for what promised to be a tough winter.[109] Traveling through London *en route* to the United States, Chamberlin gave a standing-room-only talk at the Royal Institute of International Affairs. The overall tone of the speech was quite positive. He lauded the growing strength of the Red Army and criticized those who opposed American recognition of the Soviet Union. He sounded decidedly optimistic about the economic prospects for the USSR. Collectivization had exacted a substantial toll but was making progress. He hesitated to predict the future in the Soviet countryside, but suggested that recent Soviet measures with regard to trade and consumer goods would determine the success or failure of the effort. Chamberlin did, however, warn that a "dual agrarian and food crisis" would be costly in human and financial terms. He shrank from calculating the bottom line on the Five-Year Plan's impact: "It is very difficult to make any sort of arithmetical balance sheet of how much happiness and unhappiness this period of violent and great change has brought in Russia." A Soviet report summarized the talk with apparent relief: Chamberlin "behaved entirely favorably toward the USSR. In fact, in a few cases he resorted to quite original forms of defense of the USSR." Chamberlin also submitted an article to a British magazine; that article praised the "impressive addition to the national industrial capital" but noted that it "has been purchased at an extremely high price in the standard of living."[110]

By New Year's Day 1933, then, both Chamberlin and Duranty had given mixed reports on Soviet conditions. They both remained optimistic about Soviet industrialization efforts while also describing the costs involved. Fischer, by contrast, expressed nothing but optimism and enthusiasm for the coming year. Although talk of a "crisis" appeared in Chamberlin's and Duranty's writings, neither journalist considered the situation a famine.

Reports of actual famine first appeared in the mainstream western press in early 1933, spurred by two news items from the countryside. Eugene Lyons set into motion one set of famine-related articles, which appeared in American newspapers. His secretary read of problems in the North Caucasus, in a local Soviet newspaper article about a secret-police "rampage" in a village near Rostov. This information set the tone for Lyons's dispatches of January and February 1933, which emphasized food shortages and government demands for grain. Lyons often characterized government repression as a response to peasant laziness. Soviet economic policy, he wrote, amounted to various efforts to "overcome peasant apathy."[111] One undated dispatch adopted the Soviet government's viewpoint, applauding improved grain collections, while other dispatches noted the "intense struggle to extract seed grain . . . developing nationwide as the first act of the drama of spring sowing." Lyons reported dire conditions in Ukraine, the North Caucasus, and parts of the Lower Volga, but he maintained optimistically that these conditions were "not typical of the entire country." Lyons's view of peasant character traits—in which apathy played a featured role—thus explained the hardships in the Soviet countryside.

Although Lyons himself apparently did not write a dispatch on the Rostov news item, he did alert two American journalists, William Stoneman of the *Chicago Daily News* and Ralph Barnes of the *New York Herald Tribune*. Stoneman and Barnes quickly hired a translator and bought train tickets to Rostov to "view the performance," as Stoneman later worded it.[112] Stoneman's dispatch of February 6 described "virtual martial law" and army activity in the region despite the absence of collective resistance. He blamed the lack of grain in "one of Russia's richest grain regions" on the central authorities' "taking revenge on the peasants." After a few days of observing conditions in Rostov and environs, the journalists attracted the attention of the secret police, who shipped them back to Moscow. The reporters nevertheless succeeded in smuggling reports to their newspapers. Barnes's article focused on the terror in the Kuban', mentioning the dire food situation there. His reports echoed the claims of Walter Duranty—whom he held in high esteem—in his November 1932 reports. Barnes's article mentioned "only a limited number of cases of deaths due strictly to starvation," but admitted that there were "many deaths resulting from disease attacking constitutions seriously undermined by lack of sufficient food."[113] Even smuggled reports about the famine used evasive language.

After the first of these accounts appeared in the western press, senior Soviet officials moved to reassert control over famine reports. In February 1933 they banned foreigners' travel within the USSR. Although the Press Office was charged with primary enforcement of the new ban, its staff unsuccessfully opposed a blanket prohibition. Censors argued confidently that they could keep foreigners out of the problem areas without calling attention to the situation by announcing a formal prohibition. In a letter to Premier Viacheslav Molotov, the Press Office argued against the travel ban:

The decision on a new arrangement for foreign correspondents' movement in the territory of the Union [the USSR] without the permission of the militia will without any doubt be interpreted by Moscow-based correspondents, and also by the international press, as the denial of freedom of movement for foreigners/journalists for the purpose of hiding from them the "true situation" in the localities . . .

The negative consequences of a general ban on the free movement of foreign correspondents might be averted if the NKID Press Office, together with some general measures, could in each individual case try to obtain voluntary rejections of this or that trip which is undesirable to us. In precisely this way, two trips to Ukraine by foreign correspondents were recently prevented.[114]

The Press Office staff protested the implementation of a full-fledged prohibition on travel, arguing that they could be just as effective in one-to-one conversations, convincing journalists not to visit afflicted areas without raising suspicions of a new policy. Soviet censors, however, grossly overestimated their powers of persuasion. Stoneman (who attempted one of the two trips mentioned in the censors' final sentence) recounted his conversation with a censor in a way that suggests that the censors were heavy-handed, did much to arouse journalists' suspicions, and in no way succeeded in obtaining a "voluntary" change of itinerary. The censor first questioned Stoneman's need to visit Ukraine as opposed to some other rural region. He then pleaded with the reporter "as a friend" before finally declaring unilaterally: "You had better postpone your trip."[115]

News of the travel ban spread quickly through the foreign colony in Moscow. The *New York Times* and other major newspapers, however, printed nothing on either the Stoneman-Barnes reports or the new travel restrictions for foreigners. Duranty, perhaps chastened by his run-in with Soviet authorities in December, changed the focus of his reporting. His articles shifted toward coverage of political events, stopping briefly on economic conditions only long enough to predict a "decisive struggle on the agrarian front" in the spring. Duranty accentuated the poverty and "backwardness" of Russian peasants, comparing them not to farmers but to "farm-cattle" because of their passivity and servile mentality. "I am inclined to think," he concluded, that the Bolsheviks will "win" (defeat the peasants) "in the long run, but it won't be easy." Duranty did not deny peasants' hardships—in fact he rather relished them—and attributed them to peasant character. The picture looked bleak, especially given the peasants' degree of "degeneration and apathy." According to Duranty, the Bolsheviks needed to "swing all the forces in their command into an effort to overcome peasant apathy, individualism, [and] dislike of novel collective methods." Prospects for the current harvest were poor, and the food shortage, "already widespread and serious," would only get worse.[116] Like Lyons, Duranty blamed peasant character—primarily apathy—for the problems with collectivization.

Chamberlin, meanwhile, articulated new concerns about Soviet prospects. His November speech in London seemed relatively sanguine, but he apparently suffered a mood change while at sea. Once in the United States, he emphasized both the rising inequalities and the "food shortage and falling off in agricultural production" that were plaguing Russia.[117] He published an article in the New Republic (at that time sympathetic to the USSR) that described the Five-Year Plan as a "forced, concentrated drive for high speed industrialization, regardless of the cost to the daily standard of living." The article mentioned both domestic food shortages and rising grain exports. But prospects were good, Chamberlin claimed, because Soviet leaders had realized that they had already reached the limits of peasant endurance. In another article, he noted the "considerable strides" the USSR had made "toward its goal of becoming a powerful industrial country." In spite of the destitution, especially for those groups targeted by the Soviets, the Five-Year Plan represented "Russia's extraordinary contribution to economic history." Chamberlin, like Duranty, described the high costs of Russian collectivization and industrialization but nevertheless endorsed the lessons they offered and the achievements they promised.[118]

Chamberlin's temporary replacement in Moscow also wrote his own reports on the famine. The Briton Malcolm Muggeridge arrived in Moscow in fall 1932, full of enthusiasm for Soviet ideals. It quickly dissipated. In spite of his disdain for most foreign journalists in Moscow, Muggeridge took much from them, including their national-character clichés. After hearing of starvation in Kiev, for instance, Muggeridge remarked in his diary that "starvation is in the nature of things" for a Russian. He attempted to apply his "Eastern" experiences—in India—to understanding Russia. In both places, he wrote, "mere brutality . . . [is] not in and of [itself] a condemnation" of official policy.[119]

Muggeridge sent reports on famine conditions to the Manchester Guardian in early 1933. His first leads on the famine came from an anonymous visitor who deposited articles from provincial newspapers on the reporter's doorstep, and also from Dr. Joseph Rosen, an American organizing Jewish agricultural settlements in the USSR. At the end of January, the reporter traveled to Ukraine and the North Caucasus to observe conditions first-hand. The *Manchester Guardian* did not print Muggeridge's dispatches un-til late March 1933, perhaps because they dissented from the newspaper's pro-Soviet editorial stance. The *Guardian's* three-part series reported on "famine conditions" in the North Caucasus, conditions that Muggeridge contended would last at least three to five more months. It also described "hunger in the Ukraine" and the author's pessimistic predictions for the future. Muggeridge blamed heavy grain requisitions for the precarious sit-uation but also mentioned peasant characteristics. Requisitions had left the population with a "characteristic peasant look—half resignation and half cunning." While western journalists in Moscow may follow with curiosity the experiment of collectivization, Muggeridge concluded, "for the partici-pants, [it was] often more disagreeable than interesting."[120] Like Barnes and Stoneman, Muggeridge had provided western newspapers with a clear sense of conditions in the Soviet countryside.

Other Moscow-based writers like Duranty and Lyons were more cir-cumspect. Duranty headed for another European vacation in early March, however, and filed dispatches not subject to direct Soviet censorship. These reports noted the "gloomy picture" in Ukraine as well as the North Cauca-sus and Lower Volga regions. The *Times* reporter saw, however, a "brighter side": new repressive organs, in this case the political departments of Ma-chine-Tractor Stations located throughout the countryside. He blamed a familiar culprit for the food crisis: "what is wrong with Russian agriculture is chiefly Russians."[121] Yet again, national character hindered economic progress.

Muggeridge's *Manchester Guardian* series was quickly followed by a re-port on the famine from Gareth Jones. Jones, a Russian-speaking assistant to British Premier David Lloyd George, learned about the devastation during his brief travels through Ukraine. Jones's articles described how starvation and disease had laid waste to whole villages in the region.[122] These reports appeared within days of stories by Stoneman and Barnes. Perhaps because Jones was not a permanent Moscow correspondent, the NKID targeted him for special treatment and enlisted the help of Moscow regulars in discrediting him. Lyons's version of how the Press Office chief Constantine Oumansky recruited the foreign journalists to "throw down

Jones" is a cliché in those writings that allege a famine cover-up. As Lyons wrote in *Assignment in Utopia* (1937),

> There was much bargaining in a spirit of gentlemanly give-and-take, under the effulgence of Umansky's gilded smile, before a formula of denial was worked out. We admitted enough to soothe our consciences, but in roundabout phrases that damned Jones as a liar. The filthy business having been disposed of, someone ordered vodka and *zakuski* [snacks], Umansky joined in the celebration . . . he had done a big bit for Bolshevik firmness that night.[123]

But plenty of evidence contradicts Lyons's oft-told tale. First, there is some reason to doubt Lyons's chronology. The meeting with the censors, he reported, took place after Jones's *Manchester Guardian* article appeared—therefore, after March 30, 1933. Yet Lyons follows up his description of the gathering for "Bolshevik firmness" with a description of how each journalist was summoned to the Press Office and told not to leave Moscow without official permission. Stoneman's account—corroborated by documents from American, British, and Russian archives—indicates that news of the ban circulated in late February.[124] Furthermore, no other western correspondents—including both Duranty's assistant and Stoneman, who were present in Moscow and were later interviewed about the famine—ever mentioned this party. Lyons himself, finally, was rather sketchy on the details when asked about it decades later. As his recollections were summarized by one historian:

> Lyons remembers little more about the meeting with Oumansky than the description of it in *Assignment in Utopia*. It was not a "general session" of the foreign correspondents, he recalls, nor did [the chief censor] have to do more than "hint" as to what should be done. Lyons cannot remember who attended or . . . where the meeting was held. He adds, however, that "presumably" Duranty was there.[125]

Whether or not this evening affair took place as Lyons described it, Duranty indeed did "throw down" his fellow countryman Jones. In an article that remains a textbook example of double-speak, Duranty criticized Jones's judgment as "somewhat hasty" and based only on minimal travels in Ukraine. (Jones, it might be noted, traveled more than Duranty himself.) Duranty's article, published under the headline "Russians Hungry, but Not Starving," cynically noted the number of times that foreigners had prematurely "composed the Soviet Union's epitaph." Duranty ridiculed Jones's most recent effort, claiming that Jones had "seen no dead or dying human beings" and therefore had little direct evidence of famine. Duranty did not deny the "deplorable" conditions, but he blamed the problems on the "novelty and mismanagement of collective farming." In a justly infamous paragraph, Duranty awkwardly concatenated culinary and military analogies: "But—to put it brutally—you can't make an omelette without breaking eggs, and the Bolshevist leaders are [like military commanders] . . . indifferent to the causalities that may be involved." In words just as infamous if less evocative, Duranty continued with his odd denial:

> There is a serious food shortage throughout the country . . . There is no actual starvation or deaths from starvation, but there is widespread mortality from diseases due to malnutrition . . . These conditions are bad [especially in Ukraine, North Caucasus, and the Lower Volga], but there is no famine.[126]

Duranty's basic formula—shortages, even malnutrition, but no famine—carried over from his November series.

Fischer, who would have missed whatever meeting took place because he was touring the United States, needed little official encouragement to rail against famine reports. He spent spring 1933 campaigning for American diplomatic recognition of the USSR. As rumors of a famine reached American shores, Fischer vociferously denied the reports. He agreed that Russians were "hungry—desperately hungry" but attributed this to the country's "turning over from agriculturalism to industrialism." In each city he visited, Fischer flatly denied that mass starvation existed in Russia. Arguing that there were shortages but no famine, he declared in another speech that the Russian peasant would make the sacrifices "as long as the fulfillment of his objective is visible to the naked eye, in the form of industrial achievement." Upon his return to Russia later that summer, Fischer changed his story only slightly. His first article from Moscow, entitled "Russia's Last Hard Year," stated simply that "the first half of 1933 was very difficult indeed. Many people simply did not have sufficient nourishment." Fischer blamed poor weather and the refusal of peasants to harvest the grain, which then rotted in the fields. Government requisitions drained the countryside of food, he admitted, but military needs (a potential conflict with Japan) explained such deadly thoroughness in grain collections.[127] His story, like Duranty's, had remained the same: tough times, yes, but no famine.

Whereas Fischer used the threat of war as a justification for hardships, Duranty continued to employ war in a metaphoric sense. Perhaps inspired by the Soviets' own rhetoric, he continued to compare collectivization to a battle between the modernizing Bolsheviks and backward peasants. Off on another vacation in April—this time to Greece—Duranty organized the trip so that he could travel through Ukraine. Speaking with peasants at the stations along the way, he concluded that the rumors about a famine were unsubstantiated, always attributed to the next village. Duranty still maintained his optimism for the future: "an end has been made of the muddle and mismanagement of the past two years, and . . . Moscow is taking an interest" in the peasants.[128] In spite of the shortages, Soviet rural conditions were improving.

By late spring, Gareth Jones rebutted Duranty in a stinging counterattack. Jones reiterated his assessment of famine conditions, claiming it was based on conversations with numerous foreign diplomats in addition to peasants in more than twenty villages. He also cited Muggeridge's late-March series in the *Manchester Guardian* as corroboration. Lashing out against the Moscow-based journalists, Jones called them "masters of euphemism and understatement" thanks to ever-stricter censorship. The letter closed on a bitter congratulatory note: the Soviets' spin control—food-distribution policy (so that Moscow remained "well-fed") and censorship—had managed to "hide the real Russia."[129]

After only two months back in Russia, Duranty pleaded with his editors for another respite from the USSR. *Times* editors scotched the trip, so Duranty redirected his complaints to a friend and fellow-journalist, H. R. Knickerbocker. He told Knickerbocker that "the 'famine' is mostly bunk as I told you except maybe Kazakhstan and the Altai where they wouldn't let you go . . . The [NKID] in particular is rather crotchety about reporters traveling these days." Stuck in Moscow, bored, Duranty returned to one of his favorite themes: Russian suffering. He referred to Bolsheviks as "fanatics [who] do not care about the costs in blood or money." Suffering in Russia, he stressed, was not strictly a Soviet phenomenon: "It is cruel . . . but the USSR is near to cruel Asia, and the proverb 'One Life, One Kopeck' was a century-old expression of human values in Czarist Russia." The article closed with the acknowledgment that "life here is hard and menaced by malnutrition and diseases that arise therefrom," but once again underlined the ultimate goal justifying these sacrifices: the leadership's "fanatic fervor" for industrialization.[130]

An early August dispatch dealt once again with rumors of famine. Duranty attributed them to the anti-Bolshevik émigré "rumor factories" in neighboring states. Soviet authorities, Duranty wrote, had inadvertently abetted their enemies by adopting an "ostrich policy . . . in trying to hide [the food shortage] and some of its consequences." Such shortages had taken "a heavy toll on Soviet fortitude and even Soviet lives," reducing the food supply "below what are generally regarded as the minimum requirements." Shortly thereafter, Duranty cabled his editor that notwithstanding hearsay to the contrary, the word "famine" should be avoided in news coverage—in favor of the above formulation about minimum requirements. In an article headlined "Famine Report Scorned," Duranty praised the new harvest without denying past problems: "Until this harvest the picture was dark enough. The Kremlin had ruthlessly carried through the agrarian revolution of collective farming, and the costs had been heavy for the Russian people, but it looks now as if the revolution is complete because the harvest is really good."[131]

Over the summer Duranty's optimism about Soviet agriculture had returned. Given the improved conditions, Duranty expressed his consternation about the travel ban: "The poor goofs [in the NKID Press Office] have chosen this moment, when the harvest REALLY IS GOOD, to forbid foreign correspondents to travel." He once again denied that there was a famine *per se,* "but there was a heavy loss of life and much suffering and now of course is the moment to see and say that things are better. But the [NKID] doesn't seem to understand that." Ignoring Duranty's repeated injunctions against the word "famine," the *Times* editors printed articles from Vienna and Berlin that used the word. They even printed one of Duranty's own articles under the headline "Famine Toll Heavy in South Russia." That article continued his usual themes: there was loss of life not from starvation but from diseases "due to lower resistance." The death rate was three times normal in Ukraine, North Caucasus, and the Lower Volga, Duranty wrote, but no "famine" existed.[132]

The deterioration of Soviet conditions seemed to affect Duranty's mood if not his published reports. He complained to his editors that he had tired of working overseas, especially in Moscow. Duranty distinguished himself from those whose future happiness justified present suffering. The USSR "may someday be a paradise for a future generation of Russians," he wrote, "but I am not a future generation, nor, thank God, a Russian." He proposed working only part-time in Moscow, writing primarily feature articles. The *Times* senior editors, all dissatisfied with Duranty's frequent absences from Moscow, were happy to accept this arrangement.[133]

The NKID gave Duranty one last scoop before he stepped down. The Press Office informed him in late August that he could travel through the Ukrainian countryside. Permission to travel, however, did not imply that he could travel freely. The restrictions on his itinerary perplexed Duranty. According to one skeptical diplomat, "Mr. Duranty professed to be much irritated by this action, which he felt had cut the ground from under his feet by obliging him to recognize a ban upon his movements."[134] Duranty did not mention the restrictions to his editors. He instead boasted that he and the Associated Press correspondent Stanley Richardson soon would be taking a trip to Ukraine and the North Caucasus to challenge the "campaign about the alleged famine."

Once under way, Duranty and Richardson traveled first to Rostov and then to Kharkov. Duranty's reports echoed the arguments of his November 1932 series on food shortages. The first report began by asserting that "the use of the word 'famine' in connection with the North Caucasus is a sheer absurdity." After gloating that "even a child can see that this is not famine but abundance," Duranty revised downward his earlier estimate that mortality had trebled. Yet his giddiness quickly dissipated when he reached Ukraine. Duranty resorted again to wartime analogies: the Kremlin "has won the battle with the peasants," though "the cost has been heavy." The whole episode could be summed up briefly, Duranty wrote: "Hunger had broken [the peasants'] passive resistance—there in one phrase is the grim story of the Ukrainian Verdun." Here Duranty wrote more explicitly about the costs: "hard conditions . . . had decimated the peasantry."[135] Even the hard-bitten war correspondent was struck by what he saw that summer.

In his private conversations, Duranty described the famine's results graphically. In an oft-cited incident reported by Eugene Lyons, Duranty apparently stopped by Lyons's apartment upon returning from his travels in the south. Lyons recalled:

> He gave us his fresh impressions in brutally frank terms and they added up to a picture of ghastly horror. His estimate of the dead from the famine was the most startling I had as yet heard from anyone.
>
> "But, Walter, you don't mean that literally?" Mrs. [Anne O'Hare] McCormick exclaimed.

"Hell I don't . . . I'm being conservative," he replied, and as if by way of consolation he added his famous truism: "But they're only Russians . . ."

While Lyons did not repeat Duranty's mortality figure in this 1937 recollection, other sources suggest that Duranty estimated a toll of seven to ten million deaths "directly or indirectly from lack of food."[136]

Duranty and Richardson's trip to Ukraine soon sparked resentment from other journalists. The NKID chief, Maksim Litvinov, called for the end of a blanket restriction on travel, in part to reduce foreign correspondents' jealousies. As he wrote to the head of the secret police:

> After foreign correspondents Duranty and Richardson set out, with our permission and your agreement, on their trip to Ukraine, many other foreign correspondents asked for permission for trips to the south . . . Since I cannot be up-to-date (*v kurse*) on conditions in the various regions to which the foreign correspondents would like to go, I am asking you to give us your conclusions after weighing all of the circumstances. Personally, it seems to me that the moment has come when we can be more liberal on the issue of foreign correspondents' movements, that is, on the extremely irritating strict application of the rules about their trips outside Moscow.[137]

Litvinov was most likely referring to William Henry Chamberlin, whose petition to travel into the famine areas was refused in late August. The *Christian Science Monitor* printed an Associated Press story about this denial, referring to its own desire to report on the impact of the food shortage that had occurred "last winter."[138] Shortly afterward, Chamberlin wrote a friendly letter to Bryce Hoover which explained that the travel ban was related to "what has happened rather than . . . what is happening now" in the countryside. He went on in an optimistic tone, predicting that "this year's crop . . . is exceptionally good, and, while there are familiar difficulties in harvesting and transporting it, the signs seem to point to an easier winter. Everything in this world is, of course, highly relative." At the same time, Chamberlin published a report on contradictory rumors about rural conditions floating around Moscow. On the basis of a report from "a foreign agricultural expert with a knowledge of the Russian language and long experience in various parts of the country" (perhaps his friend Otto Schiller?), Chamberlin announced that events in Russia gave "some measure of confirmation to both the optimistic and the pessimistic reports." This unnamed expert "confirmed the prevalent stories of widespread acute distress and hunger in the southern and southeastern parts of the country." Still, Chamberlin optimistically insisted that "there would be some increase in the agricultural production, measured by [last year's] extremely low level." Better weather fueled Chamberlin's hope for improvement, as did the "fear of hunger" and the effectiveness of new repressive machinery. The section closed with the observation that Muscovites were choosing vacation spots far from Ukraine, in part because of the reports of poor conditions there.[139]

After the Duranty-Richardson trip, Chamberlin finally received permission to travel through the afflicted regions in late September. The journalist William Stoneman sent the first word back to the States about their travels: "Chamberlin says after a two week trip . . . that 30% of the people in some villages died of typhus & famine. It must have been a ghastly spring in the villages." Stoneman did report one note of optimism, though: central authorities "have plenty [of grain] to support the cities, to replenish the army stores and to give more to the villages." Shortly after returning to Moscow, Chamberlin visited his friend William Strang in the British Embassy. According to Strang, Chamberlin "often asked himself why the population did not flee *en masse* from the famine areas. He could only attribute [inaction] to the characteristic Russian passivity of temperament. In the Ukraine he had the impression that the population could find nothing better to do than die as a protest."[140] Chamberlin thus explained the course (if not the cause) of the famine in terms of peasant passivity.

Although the *Monitor* did not print Chamberlin's reports from Ukraine, the *Manchester Guardian* ran them as a five-part series under the rubric "The Soviet Countryside: A Tour of Inquiry." Early articles referred to "famine" conditions and actions that were "no less ruthless than those of war," but also noted the "excellent crop" for 1933 and closed with a familiar statement about Russia as a "land of paradoxes." In the final article, Chamberlin mused about peasant inaction, searching for a "psychological explanation of this curious fatalism." He concluded that "those who died were . . . old-fashioned peasants who simply could not conceive of life without their individual farm." Although Chamberlin discussed famine conditions openly, his reporting placed much of the blame on the peasants' conservatism and recalcitrance.[141]

Reports filed by Duranty and Chamberlin in autumn 1933 sounded quite similar. The *Times* reporter, for instance, tallied the results of the Five-Year Plan in an article entitled "Russia's Ledger." The costs of industrialization had been "prodigious, not only in lowered standard of living but in human suffering, even in human lives." Yet Duranty did not blame Soviet policy; the fault lay instead with the "innate conservatism of the farmer." Political liberties had been trampled by the "attempt of the Bolsheviks to submerge the individual in the state"—but such should be expected of Russia's political tradition, which so closely resembled the "despotism of Asia." Duranty did not dwell on his latest travels, but he did assess Russian sufferings as did Chamberlin: the previous year had "tightened the belts of the Russian people to an almost, but not quite, intolerable degree."[142] In reports based on their respective trips through the famine regions, Duranty and Chamberlin both emphasized the human costs. Both remained optimistic that the worst had passed; and both blamed peasants' hardships on their own passivity as much as on Soviet policy. Most strikingly, both gave the clear sense that peasant life was cheap.

The famine of 1932–1933 eventually led these five American journalists from a loose consensus toward sharply divergent views of the Soviet Union. Chamberlin and Lyons broke definitively with the positions they had expressed before and during the famine. In doing so, they also broke with journalists like Hindus, Duranty, and Fischer, all of whom continued to soft-pedal aspects of the famine well into the 1930s.

Chamberlin's trip into the countryside marked the most important stage of his quickening estrangement from the Soviets. While most of the reports filed before his trip—and even immediately afterward—shared much with Duranty's and Fischer's, his observations soon led him to reconsider Soviet policy. In articles appearing in the months after his harrowing trip through the devastated countryside, Chamberlin still expressed ambivalence about collectivization. After detailing, in one widely circulated article, the destruction wrought by famine, he sounded a note of optimism: the "tenacious vitality [of] the semi-Asiatic peasantry" ensured that "recovery [would come] more easily than might be the case in a softer country." Similarly, in one 1934 article containing his estimate of four million famine-related deaths, Chamberlin repeated his earlier argument that "the poor harvest of 1932 was attributable in some degree to the apathy and discouragement of the peasants." National character remained a crucial factor in Chamberlin's explanations of Soviet events, even as his political position began to shift.

Signs of this shift appeared first in his analyses of peasant responses to industrialization. Earlier he had considered peasant "backwardness" an impediment to collectivization. Later he came to believe the opposite: "It was not the more backward peasants, but the more progressive and well-to-do, who usually showed the greatest resistance to collectivization, and this not because they did not understand what the new policy would portend, but because they understood too well."[143] This view, appearing in Chamberlin's articles and books published in 1934, amounts to a recantation of his earlier ideas.

Chamberlin—like many others—also argued that the benefits of collectivization might outweigh the costs. Reviewing a book of Duranty's collected dispatches, Chamberlin defended the legitimacy of the *Times* reporter's claims:

> Duranty consistently takes the line, a perfectly logical and defensible one, that the sufferings which, as he recognizes, have been and are being imposed on the Russian people in the name of socialism, industrialization, and collectivization are of small account by comparison with the bigness of the objectives at which the Soviet leaders are aiming.

Other reviewers joined Chamberlin in praising Duranty's collected works. Journalists admired Duranty's ability to make sense of Soviet chaos. As the day's leading scholar of journalism put it, Duranty's "interpretations of Russian characters and customs and attitudes add much to the value of his book, for after all the Russian takes a good deal of explaining to an American audience."[144]

Unlike Chamberlin or Duranty, Fischer did not mention Soviet agricultural problems for the remainder of 1933. A letter to a friend in November promised only "I will give you the [lowdown] when I see you." Fischer's first mention of "the Ukrainian famine of 1933"—in an April 1934 article from and about Spain—connected it to "prodigious efforts, now already crowned with considerable success, to give the country a new and permanently healthy agrarian base." Fischer did not directly address the "difficulties" of 1933 until well after the fact, in a June 1934 *Nation* article entitled "In Russia Life Grows Easier." His articles focused on the USSR's "bright prospects" and improved supplies of clothing and food in major cities. These economic improvements had led to a decline in political opposition, said Fischer, which he hoped would lead to a curtailment of secret-police activities.[145]

Fischer maintained his general optimism about the Soviet Union through the publication of his travelogue *Soviet Journey* in 1935. The book devoted three pages to a discussion of the famine of 1932–1933, in which Fischer described his October 1932 travels through Ukraine. He told of food left rotting in the fields as the result of peasants' "passive resistance." Fischer blamed the peasants directly for having "brought the calamity upon themselves":

> It was a terrible lesson at a terrific cost. History can be cruel. The Bolsheviks were carrying out a major policy on which the strength and character of their regime depended. The peasants were reacting as normal human beings would. Let no one minimize the sadness of the phenomenon. But from the larger point of view the effect was the final entrenchment of collectivization. The peasantry will never again undertake passive resistance.[146]

Like Duranty and Chamberlin, Fischer stressed the positive results ensuing from Bolshevik victory in the countryside and connected the famine to peasant behavior.

The reporters' interpretations of the famine resurfaced in 1935, when Chamberlin and Fischer traded blows over their reporting of the famine. After a week-long series on a famine raging in the USSR appeared in Hearst newspapers, Fischer published a rebuttal of these claims in *The Nation*.[147] Fischer, Lyons, and Chamberlin all agreed that there was no famine in Russia in 1935; Lyons, for instance, called the Hearst series "patently doctored." But Chamberlin used the occasion to blast Fischer, attacking him for ignoring the famine of 1932–1933, which (according to Chamberlin) ravaged "Ukraina [*sic*], the North Caucasus, considerable districts of the Lower and Middle Volga, and Turkestan." Claiming that Fischer had yet to make any "single, forthright unequivocal recognition of the famine," Chamberlin accused him of using "misleading euphemistic terms" to describe Soviet events. In his reply to Chamberlin, published in the same issue, Fischer defended his treatment of the famine and then turned the tables by accusing Chamberlin of one-sidedness for blaming only the Soviet government. If the famine was "man-made," as Chamberlin had charged, then "the peasants were the men who made it," wrote Fischer.[148] Evenhandedness required spreading the blame to the peasants.

By the time of this dispute over the 1935 famine hoax, the five protagonists sharply diverged. Although they had all started the decade positively inclined toward the Soviets, Lyons and Chamberlin had grown disen-

chanted with and disgusted by the "Soviet experiment." These two had issued slashing criticisms of both the Soviet Union and its American supporters. Hindus, Duranty, and Fischer quickly became targets, especially
for their coverage of the famine of 1932–1933.

Hindus spent the famine year shuttling between his Manhattan apartment and his upstate farm. His publications in 1933 mentioned the shortages in rural Russia, though in cryptic phrases. One article, for instance,
lingered on the issue of famine, mentioning that agriculturalists were "often without bread and without feed for their stock"—but quantified only
losses of livestock. In *The Great Offensive,* which opened with a dialogue
about famine, Hindus warned that 1932–1933 brought "distress and privation" to many areas of the USSR. "The fault," he continued, echoing
Duranty, "is not of Russia but of Russians."[149] Perhaps chastened by the
famine, Hindus turned to fiction for two years, though he told his nephew
about the rural crisis in an effort to sway him from Communism.[150] Hindus returned to his reporting only in 1936, when he made his third ances-
tral pilgrimage. Returning to Moscow after visiting his birthplace, Hindus
nevertheless found much to admire in Soviet policy. As he told a Press
Office official, "The fact that a peasant in the Soviet Union can plow fifteen
centimeters deeper than before the Revolution overcomes (*perekryvaet*) everything else that has happened in the country."[151] At last, in 1937, he acknowledged a deadly famine, attributed "exclusively" to collectivization.
Yet he continued to balance benefits and costs: "in spite of its enormous
cost in substance and in human and animal life, collectivization in my
judgment constitutes the most triumphant achievement of the revolution."[152] Even the death of some of his adored peasants did not dampen his
enthusiasm for collectivization.

Merely acknowledging the famine hampered Hindus's career. The pro-
Soviet British publisher Victor Gollancz rejected Hindus's next book
proposal on political grounds. Hindus rebutted that he could better serve
the revolution by writing about the famine, which he called "one of the
greatest tragedies in the history of mankind."[153] And after publishing an article entitled "The Triumph of Collectivization" in *Soviet Russia Today,*
Hindus angrily withdrew its sequel after differing with the editor about
how to describe the famine.[154] On top of these publishing setbacks, the
NKID prevented him from returning to the USSR in 1937.[155] Reflecting on
the Soviet Union a quarter-century later, Hindus argued that its history
was quintessentially Russian: whatever it had created had come "in a tradi-

tional Russian way, by iron rule from above and in complete disregard of human cost and the freedoms that the West cherishes."[156] Hindus endorsed economic and cultural development while documenting the costs that peasants would pay.

Duranty, similarly, never recanted outright his earlier views. Later writings mentioned the famine, calling it "man-made" but wavering as to its origins. Duranty's final book (in 1949) offered an apology of sorts: "Whatever Stalin's apologists may say, 1932 was a year of famine." While the widespread suffering may have appeared unintentional to those "on the spot," he explained, he now believed that authorities should be blamed for their actions. Duranty's final proof came from a speech of Stalin's: "Why blame the peasant? . . . For we [the Party] are at the helm."[157] Although his celebration of violence lost some of its energy, Duranty never shrank from describing the costs of Soviet industrialization. And in this, he differed little from his journalistic contemporaries, at least as they reacted to the agrarian crisis.

Fischer did, belatedly, reconsider his views about the Soviet Union, writing about his new perspective with more thoughtfulness and considerably less venom than Lyons and Chamberlin had. Fischer's essay in the widely read book *The God That Failed* (1950) attributed the famine to "Bolshevik haste and dogmatism." Reflecting on his fifteen years of enthusiastic support for the USSR, Fischer concluded that he had been "glorifying steel and kilowatts and forgetting the human being."[158] But this was long after the events had taken place.

Fischer's recantation of his enthusiasm for the Soviets included a telling description of the crucial events leading to an individual believer's apostasy against the USSR. Fischer called the defining moment a "Kronstadt," referring to the Bolsheviks' suppression of the sailors' uprising there in early 1921. If the Kronstadt Rebellion itself was the cause of some radicals' disillusionment, Fischer wrote, other westerners found theirs in the 1930s. That decade brought a plethora of potential Kronstadts, each of which shook the faith of pro-Soviet Americans: intra-leftist factionalism, the purges, and eventually the Nazi-Soviet Pact of 1939.[159]

For both Chamberlin and Lyons, who had arrived in Moscow as if pilgrims approaching Mecca, the famine of 1932–1933 was their Kronstadt.[160] Even if Chamberlin had been ambivalent earlier, the famine hastened his "retreat from Moscow."[161] By 1934, he and his family had relocated to Berlin, where they used his Guggenheim Fellowship to complete the two-volume history of the Russian Revolution on which he and Sonya had been intermittently working for the previous decade. That book remained in print for more than sixty years.[162] Whereas Chamberlin's account of the revolution revealed both its passion and its drama, his writings on contemporary events in the Soviet Union became increasingly polemical and predictable. Writing a series of articles in late 1934, Chamberlin bade "Farewell to Russia," but also to his own ideas about what Soviet policy might achieve. Early in his career, writing as A. C. Freeman, Chamberlin had described the Russian past as an enemy that the Soviets hoped to vanquish. But a dozen years later, he argued that the Soviet Union represented the fulfillment, not the negation, of Russia's despotic past.[163]

After Chamberlin relocated to Tokyo as the *Christian Science Monitor*'s correspondent there, his output on Russia and Communism slowed but did not stop. He published two books of collected essays, many of which attacked Communism and the Soviet Union. While Chamberlin had always invoked stereotypes of Russian character, especially in its Asian aspects, he had by the 1930s turned Asia into his central category for analyzing the Soviet Union. He attributed everything that had gone wrong in Russia—a lengthy list by his reckoning—to Russia's Asian traits, most notably "ruthlessness [and] contempt for the individual." The Soviet Union, he wrote in 1941, "possesses most of the characteristics of the Asiatic absolutist state."[164] The faults of the USSR, Chamberlin concluded, grew out of Russia's (and Russians') flaws. Yet whereas his attack on the Soviet Union relied on national character, his increasingly fierce assault on that country's western supporters was strictly political. He indicted left-wing critics in the United States and the United Kingdom for applying a double-standard as well as for their willful ignorance of conditions in the Soviet Union.[165]

Lyons's writings in the late 1930s complemented Chamberlin's. Both argued forcefully against the Soviet Union and its western supporters, but Lyons took aim primarily at American adherents while Chamberlin focused on Soviet policies. Lyons also left Moscow shortly after American recognition in November 1933. Yet his departure, unlike Chamberlin's, was not voluntary. Soviet press officials had, months earlier, gotten wind of Lyons's plans to write a "deeply hostile" book about the Soviet Union. Waiting until just after Maxim Litvinov and Franklin Roosevelt had agreed upon diplomatic recognition, the Press Office—so Lyons plausibly claimed—manipulated him into sending a false dispatch.[166] Such maneuvers erased any last traces of the pro-Soviet sentiment Lyons had brought to Moscow in 1928.

Even after his unceremonious departure from the Soviet Union in 1934, Lyons, like Chamberlin, wrote ambiguously about the famine. He avoided the word "famine," for instance, though he referred (in early 1934) to a "heavy toll of life taken in the first part of last year by food shortage and industrial backwardness." He still held Russian character responsible for Soviet disasters: "Meekness and patience and a capacity for suffering in silence are still pre-eminently Russian attributes . . . and their effect in molding the Soviet experiment cannot be overestimated." He also confessed privately that he had "lied and exaggerated on things Soviet" in the course of his six years with United Press in Moscow. These lies, which amounted to "ton[ing] down distressing facts and pull[ing] my punches," were not responses to Soviet requests or threats but attempts to offer maximum support for the pro-Soviet cause in the United States.[167] In his *roman à clef* about westerners in Moscow, as in an autobiographical account, *Assignment in Utopia* (1937), Lyons pulled few punches; in fact he was more prone to sucker punches and after-the-bell jabs at Duranty, Fischer, Hindus, and other American enthusiasts of the USSR.

Lyons's attacks on American leftists reached a high point in his 1941 book *The Red Decade: The Stalinist Penetration of America.* Calling his effort "frankly journalistic and polemic," Lyons hoped in print that he had succeeded in his effort to "understand the social phenomenon rather than to lambaste its dupes," though he admitted the possibility that he had "not always succeeded in this feat of fairness."[168] His concern was a legitimate one, as Lyons eagerly pilloried those who sympathized with the Soviet Union. Deeming the rise of pro-Soviet radicalism a grave danger to the United States, he began his book with a chapter entitled "In Defense of Red-Baiting." Perhaps afraid it would soften his tone, Lyons nowhere acknowledged directly his former connections to Communism.[169]

With its staunchly critical tone, *The Red Decade* traced the tortured history of American radicalism in the 1930s.[170] Maintaining a pro-Soviet position, Lyons recounted gleefully, required steering a path around an ever-denser collection of Kronstadts. For Lyons and Chamberlin, the famine they observed became (albeit well after the fact) a turning point. For many others, it was the Soviet turn toward political and social conservatism in the early 1930s that changed their opinion of the USSR. Western enthusiasts for the radical and experimental forms of art and literature, for instance, found the Stalinist cultural straitjackets of Socialist Realism all too restricting. Max Eastman, whose own enthusiasm for the USSR had long since waned, aptly described "Artists in Uniform." Those pro-Soviet Americans who greatly admired the first generation of Bolsheviks found their Kronstadt in the waves of purges that began in 1936. Watching brilliant thinkers like Nikolai Bukharin mouth scripted apologies for their ostensibly counter-revolutionary acts pushed Fischer and others away from the Soviet cause. True believers in the Popular Front against Fascism, these leftists often admitted problems in the USSR but argued that it provided the last best hope against Nazi Germany at a time when western governments pledged neutrality in the looming European wars. As France, Great Britain, and the United States washed their hands of the Spanish Civil War, only the USSR and the Comintern seemed ready to fight Fascism. But as Lyons pointed out, Soviet involvement in Spain served Stalinist, not Loyalist (that is, anti-Franco), interests. Lyons saved his harshest words, but also his strongest pity, for those stalwarts whose commitments to the Soviet Union survived all these potential Kronstadts only to face their gravest challenge in the Nazi-Soviet Pact of 1939. Intellectuals' support for the Soviet Union, already reeling from earlier events in the USSR, disintegrated in the aftermath of this pact. What did it mean to join a Popular Front against Fascism if the Front's vanguard had just signed an agreement with the Fascists?

Although the pact marked the end of Communist sympathies among all but a few American intellectuals, Lyons, writing in 1941, did not rest easy. His targets were both historical and contemporary. While acknowledging that many radicals had since changed their minds, he defiantly listed the names of those involved in the Communist Party or one or another of its front organizations. At the same time, Lyons warned that the Communists' drive to keep the United States out of the European war was harming its defense efforts, especially through disruptive strikes in defense industries. Lyons and Chamberlin here diverged; though both argued fiercely against the Soviets, Chamberlin took a stance of international wariness, hoping to keep the United States isolated from the European conflict. Lyons, by contrast, wanted the United States isolated from the Soviet contagion but not from the war itself. Even the most basic civil rights, Lyons insisted, might need to be limited in order to fight the Communist menace within the United States. Although such energetic pursuit of the Communists brought dangers—"innocent bystanders may get hurt"—Lyons called upon Americans to stand up to the Communist "menace of today."[171]

Both Chamberlin and Lyons maintained their staunch anti-Communism after the war. They became, in the taxonomy of Hannah Arendt, "ex-

Communists" rather than "former Communists." That is, they defined their professional goals around challenging their former affiliations rather than returning to the commitments that had led them to radical politics in the first place.[172] Chamberlin worked as an editor of anti-Soviet standard-bearers, *The New Leader* and (later) *Human Events,* as well as a new U.S.-based journal on Russian affairs, *The Russian Review.*[173]

After the war Lyons and Chamberlin continued their aggressive anti-Communism. Both contributed to a pamphlet series sponsored by the Catholic Information League, advertised with the slogan "Face these facts, Mr. America, and act while you are still free." These pamphlets, along with their other post-war writings, occupied an extreme position within a rapidly expanding anti-Communist network.[174] Chamberlin took the stance that the Russian past was responsible for the Soviet present. Soviet tendencies toward an autocratic or absolutist state, he wrote, dated back not to Lenin's theories but to the rise of the medieval Russian state.[175] For that reason, the American policy of containment was insufficiently assertive. Chamberlin, then, had brought the particularist argument about Russia into the Cold War. Rather than using claims about Russia's backwardness or Asian aspects to justify the high costs of modernization—as he once had—Chamberlin by the 1950s invoked these claims to demonstrate the gravity of the Russian threat. If he often attributed the Soviet threat to deep historical and geographic forces, Chamberlin also noted the ideological threat. He devoted energy to attacking Communism as a set of principles.[176] Even longtime particularists like Chamberlin made tentative gestures toward universalist arguments.

Lyons, meanwhile, drifted away from foreign policy and into other corners of the conservative movement. He turned after World War II to writing a biography of the conservative icon Herbert Hoover, eventually completing a total of three authorized biographies of the former president. Lyons's anti-Communism, more than Chamberlin's, took a universalistic tone. In making a sharp distinction between the Russian people and the Soviet state, he overturned the long-running claim that the state had emerged out of the particular traits of the Russian people. Instead, he argued in a 1953 tract, assumptions that the Russian past explained the Soviet present amounted to "racist drivel." *Homo Sovieticus,* in this analysis, was an entirely different species from the Russian. There were uniquely Russian characteristics—he mentioned "broad nature" and patience—but these only served to protect Russians from the daily depredations of Soviet life.[177] The Russian population, Lyons concluded, could become America's allies against the Soviet regime. Understanding the Soviet Union as an ideological construct, and not as an outgrowth of Russian history, character, or geography, marked one of the central tenets of Cold War thought and shaped the intellectual life as well as the formulation of and reactions to American policy during the Cold War.

Lyons's and Chamberlin's rancorous anti-Communism occasionally covered up their own actions and writings during the famine year—many of which bore marked similarities to those of their targets, Duranty, Fischer, and Hindus. In 1932–1933, all five authors portrayed the conflict between the Party and the countryside as a battle between determined modernizers and recalcitrant, fatalistic peasants. While reporting—and regretting—the loss of peasant lives, all five authors framed the loss of life as a necessary cost in the struggle for economic progress. All five journalists, furthermore, deployed stereotypes about Russian peasants in order to explain peasant actions (or inaction). Fischer and Chamberlin explicitly linked the horrible fate of the Soviet peasantry to visions of a modern, industrial society. The expression, repeated by these two, among others, that the Five-Year Plan represented Russia's attempt to "starve itself great" emphasized the hoped-for ends of industrialization over the brutal means.[178]

Enthusiasm for Soviet economic development led American Russia-watchers of all political persuasions to support, or at least withhold judgment on, Soviet Five-Year Plans. This "romance of economic development" explains the widespread American support for the USSR far better than Lyons's harangues about "the Stalinist penetration of America." Many commentators approved of Soviet-style industrialization while denouncing Communism. Their support for Soviet efforts to modernize quickly a "backward" nation came in spite of their recognition of the tremendous human costs entailed.

American observers found the sacrifices worthy because they considered the people sacrificed so unworthy. Common stereotypes of national character explained Russians' struggles and suffering. Conservative and apathetic peasants could be trusted to resist (but only passively) Soviet plans. To bring about important changes, the logic went, required significant force and loss of life—which the peasants, fatalistic and inured to suffering, were especially well-suited to endure. National-character stereotypes thus combined with enthusiasm for economic development to resolve the tensions between ends and means of modernization. As the anti-Communist economist Calvin Bryce Hoover put it, Russian peasants would not rise from their "Asiatic" laziness unless prompted by the "immediate stimulus of hunger."[179] The end of modernization, Hoover and others implied, justified violent means.

Most western journalists in Stalin's Moscow, spared the high price paid by the Russians, cheered on Soviet collectivization by connecting it to industrialization. These reporters placed the tragic events of 1932–1933 in a broad context that crossed the line from description to explanation and perhaps to justification. In doing so, they used the newfound liberties of interpretive rather than empirical reporting, as well as their rising status as public experts. Chamberlin, for instance, noted the great loss of life but placed it in the context of Soviet goals: the villages he visited in the famine's aftermath, he wrote at the time, stood as "grim symbols of progress." Duranty, for his part, insisted that the peasants who died in the battle for control of the countryside had become "victims on the march toward progress."[180] That the march was a forced one, prodded by Soviet bayonets, concerned these journalists less than the ostensible destination.

Ultimately, the USSR's *annus horribilis* of 1932–1933 left its own, far less disastrous, mark in the United States. It contributed to the increasing polarization of political debates over the USSR and the fate of radicalism. But even outside of the increasingly factional public discourse, in the Foreign Service's self-fashioned refuge from politics, American assessments of the USSR offered some sympathy for Soviet industrialization.

CHAPTER

10

Scratch a Soviet and You'll Find a Russian

As partisan political disputes about the Soviet Union intensified in the 1930s, the State Department's new Russia experts maintained a diplomatic detachment. These new specialists, the products of a recent drive to professionalize the diplomatic corps, were both better trained and less public than their predecessors. Unlike their contemporaries in the field of journalism, who were encouraged to offer interpretation and personal perspective in the move toward professionalization, the newly minted cadres at the State Department were taught to adhere to rigid notions of a diplomat in the nation's service. Expression of domestic political differences and personal opinion was proscribed. Their training covered more than discretion, though, as they received formal instruction about international relations as well as about specific regions. Yet in other ways the professionalization impulse among diplomats and journalists had similar effects. State Department officials sought to instill an *esprit de corps* among the diplomats, just as Walter Lippmann had hoped to do for the journalists. Lippmann, in fact, had called for the reconstruction of diplomacy half a dozen years before his manifestoes on journalism.

Lippmann's short volume *The Stakes of Diplomacy* (1915) came at a peculiar moment in the debates over America's overseas representation. A flurry of articles between the outbreak of the European war in 1914 and America's entry into combat in 1917 insisted upon the need for American diplomacy to adopt the European model of apolitical professionalism. This movement gained additional energy from Secretary of State William Jennings Bryan's partisan purge of experienced diplomats in late 1913.[1] Bryan's 1915 resignation renewed the charge for taking American diplomats out of the political realm, while the crush of war-related activity demonstrated the need for experienced and capable personnel at the American embassies.[2]

The turn toward professionalization gathered steam after World War I, though without Lippmann's involvement. The Rogers Act in 1924 reorganized America's overseas representatives, creating the Foreign Service. The Rogers Act also created a Foreign Service School (FSS). This institution provided new Foreign Service Officers (FSOs) with a general background in international affairs, free from what departmental leaders dismissed as universities' "utopian" musings about world peace. In contrast to such idealists, FSS instructors described international relations as an ongoing contestation over political and economic interests. These deeply held interests, as well as the different "psychologies" of the nations fighting for them, outlasted superficial shifts in government as well as the wholesale replacement of political regimes. One distinguished historian told students at the Foreign Service School in 1926 that recent revolutions in Germany and Russia had not shaken the deep-rooted "psychology" of either nation's inhabitants. Robert Kelley, the head of the Foreign Service's Eastern European Division, reinforced this when discussing his regional expertise. He opened his lectures at the FSS by claiming that "a most important role in the evolution of the Russian state has been played by the physiography of the habitat of the Russian people."[3] Geography shaped character, and character shaped diplomacy.

For many FSOs, this lesson about the permanence of national character reinforced what they had already learned in college. George Frost Kennan recalled the major theme of his Princeton history courses as "the effect of such things as climate, geography, and resources on the character of human civilizations." His readings likely included the books of the Yale geographer Ellsworth Huntington, who strenuously argued for links among character, climate, and geography. Such messages, repeated in FSS courses, certainly would have resonated for a class of young diplomats taken almost entirely from these universities. These ideas implied that behaviors derived from geography would be more stable than those derived from government.[4] The school aimed to teach not only an approach to foreign relations but also standards of professionalism and personal behavior. These standards served (in the words of one historian) "to initiate a process of identification with the diplomatic profession." The Rogers Act reforms, especially the provisions for in-service education, thus promoted both the intellectual and the professional development of America's overseas representatives.[5]

International events also led to dramatic changes in the State Department's Russia staff. The department's experts on Russia moved around, administratively speaking, in a dramatic fashion, as if the victims of frequent continental shifts. From 1909 until the end of World War I, Russia experts were members of the Division of Near Eastern Affairs. Between 1919 and 1922, a quick succession of directors (including the gentleman socialist Arthur Bullard) ran a stand-alone Division of Russian Affairs. Only in 1922, with the creation of a Division of Eastern European Affairs (EE in the State Department's succinct jargon), did the internal situation stabilize. The division was headed in its early years by various officials with Baltic, not Soviet, experience. This was in large part the result of the government's refusal to recognize the USSR until 1933. Well into the 1920s, the department credentialed the emissaries of the long-defunct Provisional Government. With the appointment of Kelley in 1925, however, the division finally acknowledged Bolshevik Russia as a serious force in the region. Kelley quickly became a legend, one diplomat's "Mr. Eastern Europe," during his twelve years at the helm of EE. But perhaps the most telling indication of his importance to the division appears in his own papers. Filing his own brief description of the division's history under "Autobiographical Statement," Kelley showed just how much his identity had merged with his job's.[6]

Kelley cut an unusual figure in the State Department of the 1920s. Unlike 85 percent of his fellow diplomats, he had not attended a private high school. His Irish Catholic background, furthermore, set him apart from the overwhelmingly WASP corps of FSOs.[7] Kelley took a scholarly approach to diplomatic topics, one he learned from his mentor at Harvard, Archibald Cary Coolidge. After earning his B.A. in 1915, Kelley began graduate study in history, researching a dissertation on Russian-English relations before the Crimean War. He earned his M.A. in 1917 but then abandoned Harvard for the army. After the war, Kelley served with the State Department in the Baltic states and Finland, returning to Washington in 1923. Once back, he wrote a handful of narrow and technical articles for Coolidge's journal, *Foreign Affairs,* and contributed to the professionalization of Russian studies.[8]

Well-versed in Russian affairs, Kelley expected similar levels of technical and linguistic mastery from his subordinates in EE. He insisted that they acquire a thorough knowledge of Russian language, culture, and history. Toward this end, Kelley successfully lobbied to expand the department's language-training program, originally designed for envoys to Asia, to include Slavic languages. This program sent selected FSOs to European universities to study Russian. Taught primarily by Russian émigrés and native scholars, the courses maintained a determined ignorance of the Soviet Union's existence. Kelley favored this emphasis, insisting that trainees' interest in current Soviet affairs be relegated to their free time. In 1929 the first cohort of so-called language officers in training included two brilliantly successful career diplomats, George Frost Kennan (named after his great-uncle the adventurer-journalist) and Charles Bohlen. Whereas most trainees (including Bohlen) went to Paris, the Germanophile Kennan opted for Berlin. In either location, FSOs received an education appropriate for Silver-Age Russian nobility, imbuing in them nostalgia for a life they never knew.

This training also reinforced, at least for Kennan, the lessons of Princeton and the FSS. He credited one of his Berlin teachers, Anton Palme, for teaching him much about Russian national character. Invoking the language of German historicism, with its emphasis on concrete historical forces as opposed to ethereal ideas, Kennan recalled that Palme explained how the "*Realien*" of geography shaped the Russian character.[9] *Realien*, like character and national interests—and not ephemera like governments and ideologies—defined the proper subject for Kelley's FSOs. Through this training program, Kelley also imparted to his protégés his appreciation for tsarist Russia, his distrust of and distaste for the Bolsheviks, and his own scholarly attitude toward the object of his study. The lapsed graduate student Kelley had such success in this last aim that one colleague later complained that the EE staff exhibited the narrow and pedantic "habit of mind of a Ph.D. candidate."[10]

With that serious cast of mind, Kelley sought to learn as much as possible about the Soviet Union—in spite of his staunch opposition to official American diplomatic recognition. He built up the department's Soviet "listening post" in Riga, the capital of then-independent Latvia. The small staff there devoted themselves to analyzing Russian events using newspaper reports and interviews with foreign visitors to the USSR.[11] Kennan, Bohlen, and the other participants in the language program joined the post for summer internships during their training period. There they perfected their language skills and learned the ways of the professional Russia-watcher.

Just as the FSS sought to instill a sense of corporate identity among the Foreign Service as a whole, so did Kelley's smaller program do the same for "his boys" in EE. Trainees and other FSOs who studied Russia circulated through Washington, Riga, Berlin, Paris, and eventually Moscow, and came to know one another well. The camaraderie extended to other Russia hands, like Loy Henderson, who had not gone through the European program. They all studied Russia with great enthusiasm, debating their ideas in meeting rooms, restaurants, and bars around the world. As a German diplomat noted, the American Russia experts shared a "unanimous obsession" with their subject.[12]

Although the three most successful young staffers in EE in the 1930s shared common views of Russia, they differed greatly in personality and politics. Chip Bohlen, related to a family of German industrial magnates, socialized energetically with Americans and Russians alike. Kennan, a brilliant if brooding young man, cultivated his outsider status well before joining the Foreign Service and even before enrolling at Princeton; his high school yearbook listed his pet peeve as "the universe." Henderson surpassed Kennan in stiffness; for instance, the chapter of his memoirs describing his courtship and marriage bears the distinctly unromantic title "Change in Marital Status and Transfer to the State Department."[13] Yet the three shared not just their obsession with Soviet events but also common notions of social hierarchy and national character. These common ideas received frequent reinforcement through the Foreign Service School, the language-training program, and the intensely serious atmosphere of EE.

Even before the establishment of formal American-Soviet relations in 1933, American diplomats stationed overseas had some opportunities to interact with scholars and journalists writing about Russia. Many nongovernmental experts visited American embassies in Berlin, Riga, or Warsaw after leaving the Soviet Union; their thorough debriefings were widely circulated through EE. Those experts based at headquarters met frequently with their academic and journalistic counterparts, often forging friendships that stretched over long distances and many years. Bruce Hopper stayed in close touch with Kelley and Kennan as well as their colleague John Wiley, a Baltic specialist. Wiley also maintained a friendship with Walter Duranty; through him, the reporter met periodically with Robert Kelley—in spite of their disagreements over American policy.[14] The State

Department alumnus Samuel Harper maintained especially close connections with many EE officials, even as his enthusiasm for the Soviet Union grew after 1927. He remained in frequent contact with Kelley through the early 1930s, and his correspondence with Loy Henderson, then based in Moscow, touchingly reveals the intertwining of international politics and personal friendships.[15] Kelley himself remained an active member of scholarly associations, participating in the 1924 Slavicists' meeting in Richmond as well as maintaining his membership in the American Historical Association.[16] He also brought many experts to Washington for informal consultations; a 1929 roundtable, for instance, featured Harper, Hopper, Louis Fischer, and Leo Pasvolsky in addition to State Department officials.[17] Kelley and his EE colleagues, barred from the country on which they reported, were hardly isolated from the dense networks of America's Russia experts.

Diplomats' close contacts with other experts shaped their analyses of Russia. Parallels between American diplomats and other observers are visible, for instance, in a group dispatch from Riga in spring 1932. When Robert Skinner, the head of the Riga legation, asked his staff to reflect on recent Russian events, the responses overlapped considerably. All the respondents expressed dissatisfaction with Soviet foreign policy, yet many noted improvements in Soviet conditions. Kennan combined these two trends in his conclusion that internal developments, however promising, should not affect the American diplomatic position. Another diplomat sounded like Bryce Hoover when he admitted that "Russia is going through a period of national upbuilding [which] can't but meet with sympathy on the part of all unbiased observers," while nevertheless condemning the methods employed. Skinner himself balanced the "great and terrible wrongs" in Russia with the slow improvement of the "ponderous machinery of state." He also noted how Soviet economic policy had adapted production methods to "the Russian temperament and the backward state of the Russian people."[18] Like so many journalistic and academic observers, American diplomats connected national traits with the national economy.

Other assessments from the early 1930s emphasized the economic benefits more directly. The longtime EE staffer Earl Packer, for instance, appreciatively saw the first Five-Year Plan as a signal of the Bolsheviks' intention to raise the nation out of its "primitive agricultural" state into an industrial power.[19] Packer's boss, Kelley, put the matter even more strongly in 1932: "The Government and people of the United States look with sympathy upon the aspirations of the Russian people to develop their national economy."[20] Kelley's assessment may well be in reference to the prospect of increased trade with the Soviet Union as it developed, though Kelley had long expressed the view that commercial concerns—like internal political affairs—were completely independent of diplomatic relations. From a suitably professional distance, Kelley and his staff offered moderate endorsements of Soviet economic aspirations.

Still forbidden to travel to the Soviet Union, these diplomats made the most of careful reading and close contacts with western Russia-watchers. Through such diligence, the staff wrote informed reports about conditions within the Soviet Union, including the agricultural crises of the early 1930s. The University of Chicago's Samuel Harper, for instance, spoke with American officials in Riga in October 1932, warning of growing shortages. Urban industrial workers were "undernourished," he said, and "worst of all is the situation in the Ukraine, which last year [had] been milked dry by the excessive government grain procurements." The steep decline in agricultural productivity demonstrated to Harper that collectivization was an economic failure; it was maintained solely "on political and military grounds." Yet Harper concluded that this repression was the unavoidable result of "industrialization under Russian conditions," in which great suffering would accompany great progress. And worse was yet to come, he warned presciently: "the food shortage has become very serious and may become catastrophic in a year from now." But even these hardships did not dim the appeal that "turning Russia into a powerful modern industrial nation" had for "a great many of its inhabitants."[21] Russians were ready for the sacrifices at hand.

State Department outposts farther afield also sent reports of a looming food crisis in the USSR. Missives from Berlin and Belgrade in the summer and fall of 1932 mentioned famine conditions.[22] From Paris came a diplomat's debriefing of Walter Duranty, who had arrived there in mid-December. Duranty appeared increasingly pessimistic about Soviet prospects, in large part because of the "growing seriousness of the food shortage." Yet Duranty closed by mentioning the youths, especially in Russian cities, who were "as enthusiastic as ever and determined to push ahead . . . in the hope of better times to come."[23] Into the winter of 1932, then, State Department officials had word of famine conditions but were encouraged by experts like Harper and Duranty to consider the hardships in the context of Soviet goals.

By April 1933, a new flood of reports appeared from European embassies, many related to efforts to assist Ukrainians suffering from the famine. Relief groups and ethnic organizations called on the United States to provide food aid (or at least to promote private relief) to Ukraine. Yet the official response was restrained. The EE director Kelley, no friend of the Soviets, responded to pleas for help in straitened and evasive diplomatic prose: "it is the opinion that there are no measures this Government may appropriately take at this time." Secretary of State Cordell Hull echoed this language in a letter to an inquiring senator.[24] The issue here was hardly about Soviet sympathies. Kelley remained hostile to the USSR, yet his professional standards called for an apolitical stance. What he called "accepted practices in the field of international relations" precluded any official American position on internal Soviet affairs. As Kelley told an anti-Soviet congressman in 1929, "The domestic aims and policies of the Soviet government have nothing to do with" American policies toward that government—including even recognition.[25] Or, in the words of another EE official in response to a request from the United Ukrainian Organizations of the United States: because possible famine conditions "do not appear directly to affect American citizens or interests, this Government is not in a position to take any action in the matter."[26] Professional diplomacy, then, called for careful contemplation of and studied agonisticism toward other nations' internal arrangements, a balance meticulously maintained by Kelley and his staff.

Through the winter of 1932–1933, the State Department remained well-informed about the deepening agricultural crisis in the Soviet Union. Yet such concerns seemed increasingly irrelevant to public discussions about America's Soviet policy. The landslide electoral victory of Franklin Delano Roosevelt over President Herbert Hoover in November 1932 completely transformed debates over the Soviet Union. Even before his inauguration in March 1933, the president-elect sent strong signals that he hoped to end the sixteen-year policy of official nonrecognition. With typical vagueness, Roosevelt asked two advisors, Henry Morgenthau and William Bullitt, to investigate (as he put it in a campaign statement) "different angles of this question" of recognition. The selection of these two advisors, each of whom favored diplomatic ties, suggests both FDR's leanings and his logic. Morgenthau, just appointed to head the Farm Credit Administration, explored the possibilities of expanded Soviet-American trade. Bullitt, a newspaperman who had served as an emissary to the Bolsheviks in 1919, had

long lobbied for recognition on economic grounds. Geopolitical considerations also played a role, as Roosevelt expressed his concern over the Japanese invasion of Manchuria in 1931; the Soviet Union, stretching all the
way to the Pacific (and bordering Manchuria), might be able to help stem
Japanese expansion. Looking to personal acquaintances for advice, the
president ignored the State Department experts on Russia and their wariness about recognition.[27]

When the White House finally called on EE to evaluate the prospects of
recognition in summer 1933, it did so with the assumption that recognition talks would begin soon. Kelley's reply, not surprisingly, emphasized
the obstacles to recognition. Without first establishing "mutual understanding," Kelley wrote, "official intercourse . . . is bound to lead to friction
and rancor." He specified three major issues likely to create such rancor.
Most important to Kelley was concern over the "Communist World Revolutionary Activities." Violating Kelley's notion of acceptable diplomatic
practice, Soviet officials openly interfered in the domestic affairs of other
nations through the Communist International and local Communist
Parties. Economic issues also played a role; Kelley highlighted Soviet debts
to western governments and businesses. The Soviet regime's repudiation of
debts incurred by the Provisional Government amounted to nearly $300
million, while the confiscation of property under War Communism, Kelley
alleged, added another $330 million. While most western European gov-
ernments had stopped paying American banks, they had at least acknowledged the existence of the debts. Finally, Kelley expressed his concern over
the differences in legal and economic systems in the two nations. The state
monopoly on foreign trade, for instance, precluded granting a favored
trade status to the USSR. And the USSR's "broad conception of espionage"
might well endanger American visitors there.[28] True to the dictates of diplomacy, Kelley made no reference to internal circumstances in the Soviet
Union except as they might affect official relations. Thus the food crisis
went unmentioned. In any case, Kelley's prescient warnings about the
problems of Soviet diplomacy received little attention from a White House
staff already intent on recognizing the Soviet Union.

In November 1933, sixteen years after the Bolshevik ascent to power and
one year after Roosevelt's election, Soviet foreign minister Maxim Litvinov
departed for negotiations in Washington. In spite of the State Department's last-ditch efforts to sidetrack recognition by leaking allegations of
subversive Soviet activities in Cuba, Litvinov and Roosevelt exchanged

notes of recognition on November 17. The president named Bullitt the first American ambassador to the Soviet Union.[29] The professional diplomats' view is perhaps best summed up by the way the *American Foreign Service Journal* covered recognition. The story was tucked quietly into a section entitled "Washington News Items," behind a riveting report on marine insurance and the reminiscences of a retired diplomat.[30] The State Department's celebration of recognition was understated to say the least.

Ambassador Bullitt, eager to establish good relations with EE as well as with Soviet officials, soon asked Kennan, then based in Riga, to set up the American Embassy in Moscow. Kennan had long sought to visit Russia, the country to which he had devoted the previous five years of study. As 1933 drew to a close, he finally had his chance. He later recalled the excitement of his initial entry into Soviet territory. Unable to sleep, he busied himself scratching the ice off the train windows and peering excitedly out into the darkness. His tale of entry took the form of an extended apostrophe:

> Russia, Russia—unwashed, backward, appealing Russia, so ashamed for your own backwardness, so orientally determined to conceal it from us by clever deceit, so sensitive and so suspicious in the face of the wicked civilized west. I shall always remember you—slyly, touchingly, but with great shouting and confusion—pumping hot water into our sleeping-car in the frosty darkness of a December morning, in order that we might not know, in order that we might never realize, to how primitive a land we had come.[31]

In this tale of entry Kennan, with typical elegance and compactness, summarized his views of the Soviet Union: backward and primitive, oriental and deceptive—but at the same time appealing and touching.

With Kennan as the vanguard of an official American presence in Moscow, the networks of the American colony quickly expanded to encompass the embassy staff. In his first three weeks there, Kennan met the American reporters Ralph Barnes, William Henry Chamberlin, and Walter Duranty as well as Harvard's Bruce Hopper. Kennan enthused that the journalists—also including Eugene Lyons and William Stoneman—"had all gone Russian in a big way, and lived a life which was the most genuine approach I have ever seen to the true Boheme." The Friday-afternoon teas hosted by William Henry and Sonya Chamberlin provided a further venue for journalists and diplomats to compare notes. Journalists frequently attended embassy events as well.[32]

By the time the American Embassy in Moscow began operating in early 1934, the famine conditions had subsided. The passage of this immediate crisis hardly made life "more joyous," as Stalin had proclaimed to a group of workers in 1935.[33] Shortages were the rule in major cities, in the countryside, and in the newly emerging industrial settlements in the Urals. One diplomatic report from 1934 alluded to "a situation closely resembling famine" that had plagued the Soviet countryside the previous year.[34] Another report, from Loy Henderson in Moscow, ducked any queries about the food crises by noting that no famine conditions had prevailed since the establishment of the Moscow embassy. Henderson came close to replicating Duranty's description of the famine's effects: while there had been no famine *per se*, "the health of many persons [had] been seriously undermined" by food shortages.[35] The strictures of professional diplomacy, which encouraged knowledge about other nations but sharply limited the applications of that knowledge, precluded more direct action. Whatever American diplomats knew about Soviet conditions, they maintained a public silence.

But the buttoned-up manners of professional diplomats cannot explain the lack of a stronger official American response to famine conditions. A close assessment of American diplomats' reports shows that they, like the journalists and scholars they knew, balanced the costs of Soviet economic development against potential benefits. This balancing act hardly altered their opposition to the Soviet rulers or to American recognition, but it does offer insights into American perspectives on Soviet development. Indeed, Kennan himself provided the most vivid description of enthusiasm for economic development in the Soviet Union. His observations on this topic came in response to a question from his boss while he was still based in Riga, in summer 1932. Asked to evaluate the popular mood in the Soviet Union, Kennan was at a strong disadvantage; unable to visit, he based his analysis on official Soviet accounts as well as on western reports on the USSR. He derived from these reports the extent of regimentation of Soviet life and the discontent of Soviet citizens. But one western analysis, a book on Soviet youths by the German sociologist Klaus Mehnert, convinced Kennan that the Soviet regime had a dedicated group of supporters, indeed enthusiasts. Mehnert had expressed both surprise and respect for the ability of Soviet citizens to "come to grips with the new and gigantic difficulties" of the first Five-Year Plan. Mehnert refused to dismiss the Plan's successes as "merely" the results of "savage terrorism [or] merely the Rus-

sian people's renowned capacity for suffering." Instead, he attributed Soviet success to the "heroic sacrifice" that "exacts the greatest devotion"
from its citizens. Kennan elaborated on Mehnert's analysis in his official
report:

> [Mehnert] shows a certain portion, at least of young people, as extremely
> enthusiastic and as happy as human beings can be only when they are
> completely wrapped up in tasks which have no relation to their personal
> life. There is no reason to doubt this. The romance of economic develop-
> ment has been known to inspire young people in other countries than
> Russia. This inspiration is all the greater in Russia, where the government
> has encouraged young people to ignore all other questions in favor of
> economic progress . . . [This inspiration] has relieved these young people
> to a large extent of the curses of egotism, romanticism, daydreaming, in-
> trospection, and perplexity which befall the young of bourgeois coun-
> tries.[36]

Aside from its material goals, therefore, Kennan saw industrialization as a
useful distraction from the typical problems of western youths—the very
same problems, perhaps, that had plagued Kennan's own youth. His recognition of the "romance of economic development," then, was part of his
critique of the egoism and isolation of bourgeois life, both of which he
himself felt keenly. This longing for a great task to which he could commit
himself extended even to Soviet industrialization. His quest for a larger
cause overcame, in this instance, his opposition to the USSR and to cultural and economic modernization in general.

But if Kennan's argument reflects a certain self-absorption, he was
hardly alone in identifying—and perhaps even identifying with—popular
enthusiasm for Soviet industrialization. Kennan's claims closely paralleled
Duranty's from late 1932. And eighteen months before Kennan wrote
about this romance, his fellow diplomat John Wiley approvingly repeated
one western engineer's assessment that enthusiasm for the Plan had
reached "super-human" proportions and had become "the most important
factor for its eventual success."[37] In Washington, State Department officials
solicited Samuel Harper's views on popular morale, distributing them
widely within the department. In one such report, written a few months
after Kennan's, Harper identified "economic patriotism" as a central element in Soviet life. The Chicago scholar's next report, which reached the
highest echelons of the government, described the widespread appeal of

"the idea of turning Russia into a powerful modern industrial nation." The popularity of this idea, Harper concluded, was essential to "help [the population] beat the sacrifices which they are being compelled to make."[38] Similarly Chip Bohlen, writing home from his post in the Moscow embassy, described how Soviet citizens' "hope for the future" and "glorification of work" distinguished them from the rest of the world's population.[39] Finely attuned to popular mood, Kennan's colleagues viewed Soviet hardships as unfortunate but necessary; Kennan, for his part, found personal virtue in their collective sacrifices.

In spite of their general distaste for the Soviet regime, EE experts found a bright spot amid the chaos and shortages of the early Five-Year Plans. Although these efforts to balance the costs and benefits of the early Plans hardly constitute an unqualified endorsement of Soviet policy, they do nevertheless suggest some sympathy with Soviet economic aims. As the Soviet Union passed from the first Plan through the famine to the second quinquennium, American diplomats' perspective on the economic costs and benefits of Soviet industrialization changed little. Economic modernization was costly but ultimately useful. Loy Henderson, based in Moscow, assessed Soviet agricultural policy in such terms after a trip through the countryside in 1937. Echoing the journalist Maurice Hindus, Henderson described the "new vitality" of the villages and credited the Soviet leaders' "genuine efforts" to improve the moral as well as the material conditions of the countryside.[40] Kennan, while composing his first memoirs (at the age of thirty-four), separated political issues like Soviet propaganda in the United States from economic issues like industrialization. In doing so, he expressed guarded approval of Soviet policy: "Whatever we may have thought of Soviet machinations in the United States, we wished the Kremlin no ill in its efforts toward the modernization of Russia, in its program of internal development." He went on to acknowledge the "unquestionable desire to modernize a backward country." But Kennan, like his colleagues in Riga and Moscow, recognized the costs of industrialization. He described the determination of Soviet leaders to industrialize and predicted success; they were a "tough lot," he wrote, "strong-nerved, lean, [and] ruthlessly competent." Economic success, he implied, depended on such ruthlessness.[41] Norris Chipman, who went through the same training program as Bohlen and Kennan, extolled the efforts of the Soviets to transform a "backward agricultural nation" into an "advanced industrial State," even while allowing that their principal methods were "fear and force."[42]

In 1934 Ambassador Bullitt, whose brief tenure in Moscow quickly shattered his previous sympathies for the Soviet Union, told the secretary of state that the first Plan had been a success. Confidence was the mood of the day, even if purchased at a heavy price: "The present optimism has many roots. Stalin's agricultural policy, however appalling its cost in human suffering, has been successful. The peasants have been starved, shot and exiled into submission. The new harvest is adequate."[43] Bold visions came with high costs.

State Department experts, like their journalistic and academic counterparts, frequently referred to mitigating factors in calculating the high cost of modernization: ostensible traits of Russian national character. True to their collegiate and professional education, the diplomats remained heavily indebted to notions of national character rooted in the Russian soil. During the early Five-Year Plans, diplomats attributed the harshness of Soviet life as well as the manifold problems with industrialization to alleged features of Russian character. Kennan's recap on the Soviet economy, for instance, blamed the costs of collectivization on, among other things, "lethargy and indifference on the part of the peasants."[44] Elbridge Durbrow, another language trainee, blamed Soviet industrial failures on the "primitive" nature of the "human material" used.[45] Durbrow's Moscow boss, Loy Henderson, stated the case even more strongly. Writing privately to his friend Samuel Harper in 1939, the *chargé d'affaires* confided, "I do not believe that it is necessary for me to go into the reasons for what may be called the present industrial stagnation of the economy. You are sufficiently acquainted with the defects of the Russian people."[46] Recalling his activities in Stalin's Moscow, Bohlen expressed similar sentiments: the hardships of Soviet industrialization resulted from the "primitive nature of Russian society."[47] And Chipman considered the lack of managerial abilities one of the "main weaknesses" of the USSR—an opinion also shared by Ambassador Bullitt.[48] Such sentiments also appeared among the top echelons of the foreign-policy apparatus. President Roosevelt endorsed a report, which he sent to the State Department experts, stating that the Soviets' principal obstacle was the "lack of dependability of the Russian people and their incapacity for organization."[49] The enduring Russian character, ill-suited for industrialization, would impede Soviet progress and increase its costs.

Other aspects of Russian character appeared in diplomats' assessments of Soviet events. Kennan described, in his early memoirs, his role as a Russia expert in terms echoing his instructors at Princeton, Berlin, and the

Foreign Service School: "I had to weigh the effects of climate on character, the results of century-long conflict with the Asiatic hordes, the influence of medieval Byzantium, the national origins of the people, and the geographic characteristics of the country." These characteristics, he concluded, were "little favorable to normal administrative control [or] to national self-confidence."[50] Speaking at the FSS in 1938, Kennan elaborated on the economic impacts of the Russian climate as it shaped character. He described the Russian economic cycle as an alternation between long periods of inactivity and short-lived frantic action—much like the first Plan. Such a cycle, Kennan argued, reflected the harsh Russian seasons: long winters of lethargy followed by intense summer flurries of activity. Bohlen, in his memoirs, made an identical argument.[51]

But the economic effects of Russian character went beyond the cycle of energy and apathy. Focusing on rural life, Kennan celebrated the Russian peasant as a "long-suffering and patient soul," inured to the material deprivations that defined Soviet life. Other EE staff held similar views about the Russian peasants' endurance and fatalism, allowing an explanation of the sacrifices involuntarily made in the drive for industrialization. Robert Kelley, Norris Chipman, and Earl Packer all attested to the peasants' remarkable knack for surviving great hardship.[52] Kelley even wondered, in the midst of the first Plan, whether it was possible that the Soviet leadership had exhausted the population's "Slavic capacity for suffering."[53] While the diplomats celebrated the activism and energy of a small group of Soviet youths, they nevertheless saw such energy as an unusual trait in Russia. The lethargic and inert peasantry proved both an obstacle and a boon for Soviet industrialization: the lack of energy slowed plans for economic expansion, but the boundless reserves of endurance meant that the peasants could contribute to economic progress through their own suffering.

Notions of national character, so deeply rooted in the Foreign Service's corps of Russia experts, also shaped the diplomats' analysis of political trends. In one famous report from 1937, Kennan described the show trials of the Old Bolshevik Lev Kamenev (who headed relief efforts in the famine of 1921–1923) and others, concluding with a Kennanesque paragraph about Russian thought. These trials featured the debasement of dedicated revolutionaries, forced to confess their complicity in outrageous, illogical, and indeed impossible schemes of treason. They eliminated Stalin's present and past rivals, along with millions of other citizens. Kennan concluded that the trials illustrated a peculiarly Russian kind of logic, one that long preceded Stalin: "The Russian mind, as Dostoyevsky has shown, knows no moderation; and it sometimes carries both truth and falsehood to such infinite extremes that they eventually meet in space, like parallel lines, and it is no longer possible to distinguish between them."[54] Cleansed of its literary allusions, Kennan's argument appeared also in his colleagues' writings about the purges. John Wiley, for instance, described the previous round of show trials as "gloriously Russian" for many of the same reasons, most notably the irrelevance of truth in the American sense of the term.[55] And Loy Henderson expanded the analysis of Russians' "lethargy and apathy" to explain the Soviet Union's political—and not just its economic—failings.[56]

National character shaped the diplomats' perception of Russian foreign policy as well. Kennan and his colleagues suggested that Soviet diplomacy was deeply Russian in both manner and direction. The Russians' need for display, Kennan told students at the FSS, had been raised in the USSR to "a policy and a passion." In both public pronouncements and private correspondence, Kennan highlighted the Russianness of Soviet diplomatic practice. Soviet representatives shared with their tsarist predecessors a suspiciousness, fear of foreigners, jealousy toward the "cultivated" nations of Europe, and general insecurity. To this list, one ambassador added that the Soviets, like other "primitive" peoples, might overreact when threatened.[57]

Kennan often tapped directly into the argument he had learned in college: climate and geography shaped character. He addressed this issue most directly in a 1938 essay. "Fundamentals of Russian-American Relations," as the piece was titled, related to fundamentals of character. These, in turn, related to the fundament itself: "Between any two of the great world powers, relations are always governed in the long run by certain relatively permanent, fundamental factors, arising out of geographical and historic conditions." He described aspects of Russian character that resonated with Americans—their "unrestrained expressions," generosity, and willingness to defy tradition. "America's greatest assets in Russia," Kennan concluded, were rooted in "qualities of American character." This document differs from Kennan's other writings of that era, few of which expressed any optimism about American-Russian relations. Yet, strikingly, his argument for rapprochement is framed in terms of the same national-character logic as his argument about Russian-American hostilities—in terms of the *Realien* he had studied in Princeton, Washington, and Berlin.[58]

The notion that Russian national character defined Soviet life is perhaps made most clearly in one of Kennan's rare practical jokes. When Kennan was bedridden in Moscow in 1936, his friends dug up, for his amusement, some dispatches from the American diplomat Neill Brown in the 1850s. Kennan found that his own life in Soviet Moscow in the 1930s shared a great deal with those of his predecessors in St. Petersburg eight decades earlier. To prove his point, Kennan sent to Washington some of Brown's dispatches—as if they depicted present Soviet events—changing only names and dates. Russian character and Russian life, he implied, survived even the most dramatic political and economic changes.[59]

Events in the Soviet Union, so directly shaped by Russian character, prompted for Kennan (as he put it in his early memoirs) "a startling revelation of how little communism had affected Russia, [and] how much Russia had affected communism." Ambassador Bullitt took a more moderate approach to the question but clearly shared Kennan's opinion: "There is much in this regime of terror and suspicion which is communist," he wrote to Secretary Hull, "but there is also much which is Russian."[60] The Soviet Union, in short, was as much Russian as it was Communist. As Ambassador Bullitt reported to Washington, paraphrasing the Russian quip, "Scratch a Russian and you'll find a Tatar": "Scratch a Soviet and you'll find a Russian."[61] Under the patina of Soviet modernity lay eternal Russianness.

Notions of Russianness built on ostensibly Slavic traits as well as on traits associated with Asia. Kennan himself described the original Slavic racial stock as European rather than Asian, but he also found that Russian traits—especially the less desirable ones—had much in common with "Asiatic" traits. The so-called Mongol hordes, Kennan claimed, left their imprint on Russian character. Acutely aware of their physical insecurity after such invasions, Russians grew xenophobic and obsessively secretive, ultimately leaving them with "dismal ignorance of the outside world." At the same time, these foreign depredations transplanted "Oriental" elements into Russian political culture. These elements long outlived the demise of Tatar rule in the late fifteenth century. In their business dealings, Kennan reported, Russian diplomats had an acute need to maintain "face and dignity." Kennan appreciated the irony: "in a state which comprises a good part of Asia geographically, ethnologically, and psychologically, there is no greater insult than to accuse a person or an institution of being Asiatic."[62] Nonetheless Kennan and his colleagues made such insults a regular theme in their diplomatic reporting. John Wiley, for instance, agreed that knowledge of "Asiatic philosophy" was indispensable for understanding Soviet

policy as well as Russian life more generally. Earl Packer described the So-
viet population as "more Asiatic than European." He meant this (as Bruce
Hopper had) in behavioral, not ethnic terms, noting the ubiquity of the
"Asiatic" tendency toward violent extremes.[63]

Russia's ostensibly Asian nature shaped the political and economic life
of the Soviet Union. Many diplomats, for instance, agreed with the journalist Walter Duranty and the academic Rev. Edmund Walsh that Russians
had little respect for human life.[64] This familiar line offered a powerful
statement of cultural relativism, emphasizing the importance of understanding Russia on its own terms, rather than imposing American values.
First Lady Eleanor Roosevelt spoke in such terms when she criticized anti-
Soviet diplomats for falling prey to the "western obsession with freedom"
rather than recognizing Russia's differences.[65] But this superficial appraisal
also cut short any effort to analyze the tumult of early Stalinism. There was
little need to explain or understand Soviet events if they were merely expressions of a character forged half a millennium ago.

American diplomats also frequently referred to Asia when explaining
the nature of Stalinism and its leader. For Henderson, the purge trials
proved Stalin's "semi-Oriental" nature—"vengeful, jealous, suspicious, ca-
pricious."[66] Most common was the claim that Russians had no historical or
temperamental inclinations to liberty. Kelley's public lectures, for instance,
called attention to the "racial and historical background" of the Russians
when explaining their lack of interest in individual freedoms. Evaluating
Soviet repressions in the mid-1930s, Bohlen emphasized that the "Russian
people have no conception of individual liberty." Similarly, the ambassador
in Moscow on the eve of World War II, Laurence Steinhardt, based his description of Russian politics on the Soviet Union's "Asiatic" orientation—
meaning not its Pacific interests but its brutal internal politics.[67] Once
again it was Bullitt who most emphatically connected Soviet behavior
and the Asian aspects of Russian character: "To speak of the Russians as
'Asiatics' is unfair to the Asiatics. Both China and Japan created mag-
nificent civilizations. The Russians have never created a civilization. They
have never emerged wholly from the status of barbarians. Progress in this
unhappy land has always been made by spasmodic and dreadful jerks."[68]
Russia, the onetime Soviet enthusiast wrote, had no place among civilized
nations, even Asian ones. It instead represented the worst qualities of Asian
societies: backward and brutal. Overall, the references to national character, whether defined as Russian or Asian, appeared in diplomatic reports as

regularly as they did in journalistic and academic writings. From the lowest level of EE staffer up through the White House, participants in American foreign-policy debates employed notions of national character to understand and evaluate the Soviet Union's tumultuous 1930s.

These notions of national character formed the basis for interpretations of Soviet international intentions until the escalation of the Cold War. Even the briefest of summaries of Kennan's wartime writings, like the one undertaken here, demonstrates his reliance on particularistic arguments: the Soviet Union is what it is because it is Russian. Defining the USSR in national more than ideological terms, Kennan traced the origins of Soviet diplomacy and politics to early modern Russia. Over his long career devoted to understanding the Soviet Union, Kennan has shown a willingness to shift his positions, emphasizing different causes at different moments. He continually returns, however, to the notion that Russian character defined Russian and Soviet life. This mix of views, as well as the continuing emphasis on national character, is visible through Kennan's rapid advancement in the 1930s and 1940s.

After establishing the Moscow embassy in 1934, Kennan remained there for three years, returning to EE in Washington just in time for the "purge" of that division. In a move much bemoaned by EE members, the Division of European Affairs subsumed their organization, dissolving a center of anti-Soviet sentiment within the State Department—but also dispersing the staff and library resources that Kelley had so effectively nurtured for fifteen years. Kelley himself was exiled to a diplomatic post in Turkey.[69] Kennan, meanwhile, went back to Europe. His nose for drama took him to Prague in 1939 (in the wake of Nazi occupation there) and then Berlin. Shortly after Germany declared war on the United States in December 1941, Nazi officials confined American diplomats to a former spa, Bad Neuheim. Restricted to this sleepy town for an undetermined period, some of the internees established a small university, at which Kennan offered a course in Russian history. His hastily prepared lectures on the full sweep of Russian history proved popular, attracting as many as half of the 123 Americans in town.[70]

In his Bad Neuheim lectures, Kennan placed Russian national character in a prominent role. Character, he said, was based on physical environment. "I am a great believer," Kennan began, "in the power of the soil over the human beings who live above it." Inhospitable conditions led to Russians' legendary endurance, he continued. A volatile climate created a volatile economy. The invasions of the "Asiatic hordes" only made matters worse: they created a spate of problems in Russian political life, including "the lack of loyalty in politics, the venality of officials, the arbitrariness of justice, the cruelty of punishments . . . and the widespread exploitation of the peasant population by the state."[71] These conditions led Kennan to take a dim view of Peter the Great's attempts to "Europeanize" Russia. The westernized contingent in imperial Russia, he wrote, never amounted to more than a delicate "upper crust" with little success at remaking the country. Thus with the collapse of tsarism in 1917, Russians "appeared before the world again as what they were: a seventeenth-century semi-Asiatic people." The return of Stalin, "a native of the Asiatic country of Georgia, holding court in the barbaric splendor of the Moscow Kremlin," confirmed that the Bolshevik revolution had stripped Russia of its brittle veneer of European culture.[72] Russia's innate qualities, growing out of the soil, had outlasted Peter and his westernizing successors, eventually allowing Stalin to return to Russia's true roots. Only by understanding those Russian roots could one make sense of recent events in the USSR.

After leaving Bad Neuheim, Kennan served in a variety of diplomatic posts, returning to Russia only in 1944 at the request of Ambassador Averill Harriman. He celebrated his return in a document entitled "Russia—Seven Years Later."[73] Arriving in the midst of the war, Kennan found Russian character fundamentally unchanged—not just since 1937, but over a longer period. "Through war, through peace, through drama, through suffering," Kennan dramatized, Russian life remained the same. Russians maintained the same "passion for display" they had inherited centuries ago, as well as those traits that made diplomatic dealings in the Soviet Union so frustrating. Soviet leaders of 1944 exhibited the "traditional mistrust of the foreigner," as well as the "traditional Russian preoccupation with the *interpretation* rather than the *letter* of an agreement." And as he had observed during the purge trials, Russians know "no objective criteria of right and wrong . . . of reality and unreality." He closed the memorandum with a melodramatic plea that foreign–policy makers listen to those few experts who knew Russia like he did. Experts such as himself, he worried, would enjoy only "the lonely pleasure of one who stands at long last on a chilly and inhospitable mountaintop, where few have been before, where few can follow, and where few will consent to believe that he has been." Only from atop a high peak, peering back into the distant past, could the true Russia expert understand contemporary events there. Yet that vantage point, which itself required a thorough knowledge of Russian character, was likely to remain uninhabited. Few people properly understood Russia as he did.

Kennan's policy-oriented writings, penned at the close of the war, similarly emphasized national character. Asked to explain the Soviet Union's goals after defeating Germany, for instance, Kennan cited "age-old [Russian] insecurity" as evidence that the USSR would endeavor to expand eastward, an urge that was "a permanent feature of Russian psychology."[74] Another essay the following winter once again stressed how Russian national character shaped Soviet foreign policy: "For [the Soviets], all foreigners are potential enemies. The technique of Russian diplomacy, like that of the Orient in general, is concentrated on impressing an adversary with the terrifying strength of Russian power, while keeping him uncertain and confused as to the exact channels and means of its application." The United States, he warned, must remain a tough negotiator, sure of its own goals. "Firmness" must be the name of the American game. And once again, he closed with a plea for more attention to Russia experts.[75]

Kennan's famous "Long Telegram," written in early 1946, echoed the character-based logic and conclusions of his wartime essays. In it, he explained Soviet diplomacy in terms of Russia, not Communism. Marxism, he summarized, provided Soviet leaders with only a "fig leaf of their moral and intellectual responsibility."[76] And national character also helped explain the popularity of Marxism in Russia: only in such an inherently insecure country could the Bolsheviks find justification for "the dictatorship without which they did not know how to rule, for the cruelties they did not dare not to inflict, for the sacrifices they felt." What might seem at first glance like Bolshevik traits, Kennan argued, had Russian origins. Soviet diplomatic tactics similarly derived from age-old Russian characteristics such as "oriental secretiveness" and a skepticism about the existence of truth. Most significant for the Americans, though, Soviet leaders were (as Russians) "impervious to the logic of reason" but "highly sensitive to the logic of force." American policies needed to account for the USSR's Russian qualities.

American discussions about Soviet policy coalesced around the Long Telegram as much for its policy implications as for its authoritative tone. Kennan's timing was also fortuitous, as the telegram circulated alongside accounts of dramatic events. News of Soviet international activities and assertive western responses piled up in 1946: reports of Soviet troop movements in northern Iran, the arrest of atomic spies in Canada, Winston Churchill's evocation of an "Iron Curtain" across Europe, and hard-line speeches by the Republican Party leaders John Foster Dulles and Arthur Vandenberg. This confluence of events provoked just the sorts of questions that Kennan's telegram sought to answer. The attention paid to the Long Telegram (and its author) derived from its depiction of Soviet foreign policy—aggressive and unresponsive to everything but countervailing force—and its proposals for action. Kennan's ascription of the Soviet threat to Russianness rather than to Communism played little role in the telegram's warm welcome in Washington amid the growing springtime frost that became the Cold War.

Kennan became a sensation in Washington. His Long Telegram circulated widely among senior officials in the departments of State, War, and Navy. Secretary of the Navy James Forrestal was especially thrilled by Kennan's work, arranging Kennan's appointment to the staff of the National War College. In that capacity, the diplomat also provided formal and informal advice to policy-makers.

The opportunity to expound on Russia before a conscripted audience allowed Kennan (as it had in Bad Neuheim four years earlier) the liberty to lay out carefully his views and assumptions about Soviet policy. In these lectures, Kennan continued to apply the logic of national character and Russian traditions to the Soviet Union. He explained that understanding the Soviets required psychological tools, particularly familiarity with psychopathologies.[77] At a talk at Yale University in fall 1946, for instance, he criticized those who wanted to expend American goodwill on the Soviets. Kennan derided this approach because it "was not based on a real understanding of Russian character." He insisted that ideology was not irrelevant to Soviet leaders; it provided a "figleaf of respectability." Nevertheless, he concluded, "there's a lot of good old Russian tradition in their system." Kennan shifted between ideology and tradition by invoking psychology: "these people are essentially fanatics." Kremlin rulers inherited the extremism and dissimulation that had defined Russian foreign policy for centuries.[78] Communism was simply the latest form of extremism.

Psychology also played a prominent role in Kennan's speech before the prestigious Council of Foreign Relations (CFR), "The Soviet Way of Thought and Its Effect on Soviet Foreign Policy." In that address, Kennan identified key tendencies of Soviet policy—xenophobia, messianism, and adherence to the principle that "the ends justify the means." Although Soviet officials might express these tendencies using the language of Communist ideology, Kennan insisted that they ultimately derived not "from Marx but rather from the recesses of the Russian mind." In general, he concluded, "Russian traditions and attitudes dovetail conveniently with the Soviet ideology."[79] Or, as he put it in a speech at his home institution, the ends-means principle "was something born out of the dark and pagan recesses of the Russian soul itself." While Americans might naively hope to wean the Soviets from their ideological commitments, Kennan dismissed this possibility: "when people speak in terms of overcoming or altering these ideological convictions which animate Soviet thought, they are in reality speaking of overcoming or altering some of the most basic and deep-seated traits of traditional Russian psychology."[80] Even when ideology mattered, it did so by expressing essential Russianness.

Given the intractability of Russian traits—and therefore Soviet policy—the western response must be firm. Kennan concluded the lecture by coining one of the most significant and controversial concepts of the Cold War: the Kremlin's "inherent expansive tendencies must be firmly contained at all times by counter-pressure which makes it constantly evident that attempts to break through this containment would be detrimental to *Soviet* interests." Other lectures of Kennan's employed a similar range of references to timeless national character rather than to epiphenomenal trends like ideology. One presentation on foreign relations, for instance, devoted three typescript pages to inventories of Teutonic, Anglo-Saxon, and Slavic traits.[81]

Kennan's newfound prominence extended well beyond Washington. The young diplomat caught the attention of Hamilton Fish Armstrong, the editor of *Foreign Affairs*. Armstrong invited Kennan to submit an article to that journal, preferably along the lines of his Yale or CFR presentations.[82] After winning his superiors' approval to publish an anonymous article, Kennan sent a manuscript entitled "The Psychological Background of Soviet Foreign Policy." This paper surprised the editors, who were disappointed that it did not maintain the "tone of a personal inquiry into the Russian character which [they] thought so effective in the earlier addresses." Yet the article would eventually be one of the most famous documents of the early Cold War, "The Sources of Soviet Conduct" by "X." It differed substantially from the thrust of Kennan's writings in the decades—even the months—before its appearance.

Kennan's submission to *Foreign Affairs* emerged out of a set of concerns wholly different from those addressed in his previous work.[83] His Yale and CFR speeches elaborated on themes of Russian character and Soviet policy that had long been part of Kennan's repertoire, from the War College addresses (1946) and the Bad Neuheim lectures (1942) to his telegrams, long and short, from Moscow (1944–1946). But the "Psychological Background" paper began as a response to another analysis of the Soviet Union, done at the behest of Navy Secretary Forrestal. That analysis, by the Smith College professor Edward Willett, explained Soviet foreign policy in terms of ideology rather than national character. Willett's background in finance made him an improbable advisor on Soviet affairs, a circumstance confirmed by his amateurish and poorly argued ideas. Captivated by Willett's derivative claim that the Soviets were leaders of a "militant religion," Forrestal solicited formal analyses of Soviet policy from Willett. The result, "Dialectical Materialism and Russian Objectives," reveals Willett's (and Forrestal's) focus on Marxist ideology as the key to understanding the USSR. Forrestal then invited commentary on the paper from diplomats and scholars, including Kennan. Initial comments were harsh; one commentator diplomatically derided Willett's piece as "suitable only for use with religious groups." Kennan delayed responding, perhaps hoping to duck the assignment, but Forrestal insisted.

Kennan's reply to Willett became the "Psychological Background" paper and eventually the X-article. Because it was organized around Willett's piece, Kennan had only a narrow latitude for response. He did not want to contradict directly Forrestal's ideological emphasis. Although the historian Lloyd Gardner may be exaggerating when he claims that Kennan and Forrestal "collaborated" on the X-article, his basic point is on the mark; Kennan's article, originally written for Forrestal, contained many elements of Forrestal's thinking. Kennan himself later hinted at this relationship. He once explained some of the article's limits with reference to "what I felt to be Mr. Forrestal's needs at the time when I prepared the original paper for him." At a 1985 lecture at the National Defense University, Kennan was even more explicit: "This piece was not originally written for publication; it was written privately for . . . James Forrestal."[84] Well aware of his superior's views, Kennan expressed Forrestal's ideas with his usual elegance.

Recognition that the X-article served "Mr. Forrestal's needs" explains that document's divergence from Kennan's notions of the Soviet Union.[85] Kennan's newfound emphasis on ideology as a factor in Soviet foreign policy is easily explained by Forrestal's predispositions in that direction.

Maintaining the psychological language so common in his 1940s writings, Kennan argued that the "political personality of Soviet power" was shaped by two competing forces: Marxist-Leninist ideology and "the circumstances of the power." The opening paragraphs of the article go on to describe the key facets of Marxian ideology, liberally quoting Lenin. Kennan also attributed Soviet foreign policy to two factors—a belief in the "innate antagonism between capitalism and Socialism" and the "infallibility of the Kremlin"—both of which were ideological rather than national, Communist rather than Russian.

Even while writing for Forrestal, Kennan did not completely abandon Russian national character. He argued that Marxist ideology exerted such an influence on Soviet leaders because it was "so congenial to their own impulses and emotions." The Bolsheviks, for instance, exhibited their "particular brand of fanaticism unmodified by any of the Anglo-Saxon traditions of compromise." Similarly, while Bolshevik ideology "taught them that the outside world was hostile," the "powerful hands of Russian history and tradition reached up to sustain them in this feeling." The Soviet belief that all other nations were hostile flowed as much from Marxism as from "the Russian-Asiatic world from which they [the Soviets] had emerged." Soviet "precepts of caution and flexibility," Kennan wrote, had been "fortified by the lessons of Russian history." The importance of these tactics "finds natural appreciation in the Russian or the oriental mind." Soviet ideology drew additional sustenance from aspects of Russian character.

Kennan's policy prescriptions in the X-article differed little from those in the Long Telegram, in spite of the differences in their arguments. Dealing with the USSR should be a "test of national quality," Kennan wrote, echoing Woodrow Wilson's exhortation that the American response to the Bolshevik revolution was "an acid test of our goodwill." The post-war situation required Americans to "be all that they can be"—a phrase that he later used, appropriately enough, in a presentation to the Armed Forces Film Forum.[86] If American citizens stood together, he claimed, they could limit and eventually eliminate the Soviet Union. But if the nation were riven by disunity, that would "have an exhilarating effect on the whole Communist movement." In more concrete terms, Kennan called for American policy to act firmly, forcefully, and rationally to Soviet advances. Given Soviet sensitivity to force rather than logic, the United States should start on a "policy of firm containment."

The X-article, published in the summer of 1947, soon took Washington and the nation by storm. A *New York Times* columnist quickly unmasked its author. Excerpts appeared in *Reader's Digest* and *Life.* The idea of containment appealed to a wide segment of informed American opinion. In 1947, after two decades of quiet ambition in the Foreign Service, Kennan became the subject of adoring profiles in major magazines. These articles usually focused on the policy recommendations of "The Sources of Soviet Conduct," but at the same time touched on American diplomats' professional ethos and their particularistic understandings of the Soviet Union as Russian. *Newsweek,* for instance, described how Robert F. Kelley's trainees insisted that the Soviet Union must be understood in Russian, not Western, terms. The *New York Times* attributed the cogency of Kennan's analyses to his knowledge of "the Russian people." And both sources mentioned Kennan's adherence to the professional Foreign Service doctrine of "effacement."[87] The popular acclaim must certainly have seemed a mixed blessing to the scholarly and elitist Kennan, whose approach to diplomatic realism called for insulating foreign policy from the whims of a fickle public.[88] Unlike his earlier arguments, though, Kennan's X-article adumbrated an ideological explanation of Soviet behavior. In that article it was Communism, not Russia, that required containing.

Not everyone was convinced by Kennan's logic. Walter Lippmann wrote a particularly effective broadside against the X-article in the *New York Herald-Tribune.* His principal accusation, ironically enough, was that Kennan had ignored Russian national character.[89] Lippmann did not pick up on Kennan's ambivalent views about Soviet ideology. He attacked Kennan for misguided policies based on a misguided understanding of the USSR: "Mr. X has neglected even to mention the fact that the Soviet Union is the successor of the Russian Empire and that Stalin is not only the heir of Marx and Lenin but of Peter the Great and the Tsars." Seeing the Soviets as Russians, rather than as Communists, Lippmann argued, explained the Soviets' westward expansion better than any ideological factors. Ideology mattered less than long-term Russian interests and characteristics. Kennan, recently appointed to a sensitive State Department post, could not reply publicly to Lippmann's commentary. But he did offer a cryptic retort to the columns in a speech back at the National War College that fall. Kennan claimed, with some merit, that Lippmann had missed the article's references to Russian national traditions. But at the same time he rebuked Lippmann for falling into "the pitfall of identifying Soviet policy with Russian national tradition. Soviet policy exploits that tradition for its purposes." This rebuttal suggests a reversal for Kennan. From his bed in Moscow, writing the Long Telegram, he had described ideology as the "fig leaf" covering up the Russians' national traditions. Soviet leaders espoused Communism, in other words, to obscure national aims. But only seventeen months later, at the center of a swirling debate in Washington about the USSR, Kennan inverted the argument: Soviet leaders exploited national traditions to further their ideological goals.[90]

The X-article weathered Lippmann's withering criticisms and offered powerful support for those favoring a more assertive international role for the United States. Kennan quickly complained that proponents of a military buildup who used his article misunderstood him, a move many historians take as a disingenuous effort to distance himself from a geopolitical situation he came to regret.[91] Given how the X-article diverged from his own ideas, perhaps Kennan, in this case, did not protest too much. In both public and scholarly addresses throughout the 1950s, Kennan stressed the continuities between tsarist and Soviet foreign policy—much as he had in most of his writings aside from the X-article.[92] For instance, speaking to the assembled students and faculty of Columbia University's new Russian Institute in 1950, Kennan made the claim, couched in contrived melodrama, that "communists are human beings." By this he meant that Communists in the Soviet Union were shaped by the same forces as everyone else. Kennan's enumeration of these forces had changed little from the factors he had studied in the 1920s: climate, topography, and tradition. In the case of Russia, he told the Columbia group, these *Realien* conspired to create "an almost wearisome regularity of the triumphs of violence over moderation in Russia." Stalinism was simply one more chapter in that long tale of despotism and destruction that is Russian history.[93]

The early Cold War played cruel games with the notions and nomenclature put forth by Kennan and Lippmann. Kennan recanted the vision of Soviet foreign policy and American response (containment) that he had made famous in his X-article. And Lippmann, whose responses to the X-article brought the term "Cold War" into wide use, saw his own criticisms of Kennan's ideological focus fall on deaf ears. The common ground between the two thinkers—that the Soviet Union was more Russian than it was Communist—had less and less currency in a world increasingly defined in inflated ideological terms. The X-article offered an ideological view of the rising world conflict: the United States and the Soviet Union represented systems of belief. Yet both Kennan and Lippmann understood

American-Soviet antagonisms as rooted in immutable factors of culture and interests, not ephemeral beliefs espoused by impermanent governments. Almost inadvertently, Kennan and Lippmann provided new language for one of the central paradigms of United States foreign policy: the notion that the Cold War was an ideological conflict.

The escalation of Cold War tensions coincided with a dramatic change in paradigms for understanding the Soviet Union. Decades of American commentary on the USSR, most of which focused on Russians' national differences from Americans, had little place in a new framework that defined the Soviet Union in ideological terms. This transformation was not the natural result of the professionalization of knowledge in the United States. In diplomacy, as in journalism, the interwar drive to professionalization had reinforced notions of Russian uniqueness. The professionalization of diplomacy had gone further, enthroning particularism as a central tenet in diplomatic analysis. Yet these notions were soon overtaken by claims that Soviet-American conflict was ideological. The rapid rise of universalistic social science, combined with a dramatic shift in political sensibilities, relegated particularist claims to the margins. By this token, George Kennan becomes—as he has long sought—not the diplomat responsible for anti-Communism but one overtaken by it, "a guest in [his own] time rather than a member of its household."[94]

Epilogue: Russian Expertise in an Age of Social Science

The newfound attention to Communist ideology, symbolized by George Frost Kennan's X-article, jarred with Kennan's belief that the *Realien* of geography and national interest, and not impermanent and intangible political ideas, properly shaped relations between nations. Kennan and his cohort continued to evaluate the Soviet Union in the particularist framework that placed Russia and Russian character at the center of understanding Soviet policy.

In academic discourse, meanwhile, scholars focused more on Soviet ideology than on Russian history. This shift was in keeping with broader changes in the social sciences. Conceptual and methodological innovations of the interwar era reached their fruition in the booming universities of post-war America. Charles Merriam's interest in behaviorism had transformed political science. Talcott Parsons's interpretations of social structure and function, inspired in part by Max Weber's work, quickly took hold in American sociology. A new generation of scholars focused on commonalities across societies more than on differences between them. Celebrating their scientific worldview, they developed universal theories of society, economics, and politics. In doing so, they took pleasure in violating W. H. Auden's commandments to American college graduates: "Thou shalt not sit / With statisticians nor commit / A social science."[1]

The rise of universalism also revealed the sharp distinctions between professional writings in the spheres of journalism and diplomacy—both of which stressed particularism—and scholarship, which embraced universalism. A broad shift in mid-century American thought discredited some forms of particularism and created space for more universalistic approaches to the study of national and cultural difference. Some of these changes were in response to the events of the moment. The rise and defeat of Nazism, for instance, put certain biological arguments about national character beyond the pale.[2] This trend made the prior work of cultural anthropologists led by Columbia University's Franz Boas all the more relevant. Arguing in the 1920s and 1930s that social differences were rooted in culture, not biology, Boas and his students Margaret Mead and Ruth Benedict described cultural differences in the context of a universal humanity. As Mead herself put it in a study of the USSR, the anthropologist "lays stress upon differences between cultures, upon the basis of an acceptance of a common humanity . . . and upon a recognition of the diffusion of ideologies, such as Communism, beyond the limits of one's culture."[3] Explorations of social difference, then, relied increasingly on notions of malleable cultures, not ones made by permanent factors like inheritance or geography.

Mead joined with many social psychologists to explore differences in "character," yet this work differed substantially from early invocations of national character. Some of the most notable social-psychological studies focused on extreme ideologies—especially Communism—as a symptom of psychopathology, if not a form of pathology itself. Nathan Leites, for instance, undertook a psychological study of Bolshevism that focused on its ideological and political aspects and had little discussion of Bolshevism's Russian context. "I should like to state emphatically," he declared in the introduction, "that in this book I do not make any affirmations about Russian 'national character.'" Leites concluded that Bolshevik character was shaped by two drives absent from Russian character: a preoccupation with death (neatly inverting the Russian attitude on the subject) and "latent passive homosexual influences."[4] The Bolshevik, not the Russian, was the relevant personality type.

Scholars who focused on national character *per se* worked within a similar psychological worldview. The same psychological tools used to analyze western societies applied with equal explanatory power to Russia. Particularities, when they were defined at all, were rooted not in history but in contemporary evaluations of individual behavior and pathology.[5] This Freudian tilt was also evident in other works, such as Geoffrey Gorer's infamous correlation between tight swaddling of infants and future despotism.[6] Furthermore, as the sociologist Daniel Bell noted pointedly, the studies focused on individuals—a society's "modal personalities"—without any explicit connection to what made certain tendencies national. Freed from earlier models of national character rooted in race or geography, psychological studies of national character could explore symptoms but not causes. In sum, studies of national character offered inadequate definitions of its key terms, "nation" and "character."[7] These studies offered no indication why a set of traits, however defined, should correspond with national or ethnic boundaries. They instead presented broad generalizations of cultural differences in varying degrees of social-psychological jargon. But in any case, these researches quickly became marginal to serious scholarship on the USSR. It was this brief psychological turn that the historian Carl Schorske lamented as the "dehistoricization" of the social sciences in the 1950s.[8]

If the experience of World War II helped discredit biological theories of human difference, it also offered some inklings of what would follow, at least in ideas about Russia. The wartime alliance between the United States and the Soviet Union called forth a set of arguments about the similarities between the two societies. Joseph Davies, the American ambassador to Moscow in the late 1930s, contributed a self-serving autobiography, *Mission to Moscow*. This book, which wiseacre subordinates nicknamed "Submission to Moscow," argued for the commonality of spirit, and not just purpose, in the American-Soviet wartime alliance.[9]

From the groves of academe came a similarly pro-alliance book by the Russian-born sociologist Pitirim Sorokin, *Russia and the United States* (1944). It gathered together between its covers an impressive range of arguments that Russian and American societies were meant to be allies rather than enemies. The arguments included biological claims that the Russian and American racial stocks differed little. Sorokin also made, along the lines of Mead and Benedict, culturally inclined arguments about the "congeniality of the American and Russian mentalities." Finally, he highlighted a sociological argument that would receive increasing prominence in the post-war era: the notion that Soviet and American societies were converging, along with all other "highly industrialized societies," into a common type of modern society.[10] Sorokin's determination to marshal such a wide range of ideas into his call for a post-war American-Soviet alliance perhaps reveals Harvard's wisdom in naming him director of its Research Center in Altruistic Integration and Creativity.[11] Sorokin brought together particularistic and universalistic frameworks. *Russia and the*

United States thus reveals a transitional moment in American thought about the USSR, caught between arguments of national character and general theories about industrial societies. But the latter soon came to dominate.

The conceptual innovations of post-war American scholarship focused on developing universal theories of social behavior. Disentangling the various conceptual novelties would present a serious challenge. Explanations based on ideology and power overlapped with those centered on modernization and totalitarianism. Yet these ideas gained wide currency in the 1950s, and all of them helped shift understandings of national difference away from particularism. For the purposes here, it is less important to devise precise categories than to suggest how each of these concepts emphasized universal attributes of modern societies and dismissed the view of earlier observers who had focused on the USSR's uniquely Russian qualities.

Defining the Soviet Union as shaped predominantly by its official political **ideology** diminished the importance of the USSR's Russian heritage. As Walter Lippmann noted in his criticism of Kennan's X-article, the question revolved around whether Stalin was an heir to Lenin or to Tsar Peter. Many Russia experts who had previously emphasized the Petrine heritage begin in the 1940s and 1950s to stress the Leninist one. Former particularists like the diplomat Charles Bohlen and the historian Geroid Tanquary Robinson defined Soviet ideology as the principal factor shaping Soviet international behavior. In late 1945, Bohlen and Robinson co-authored a policy proposal that addressed many of the same issues that Kennan's X-article would eighteen months later. While offering a substantially different set of recommendations—geared more toward a fluid American response capable of adjusting to shifts in Soviet policy—the Bohlen-Robinson memorandum shared the X-article's claim that Soviet policy originated in Communism rather than in Russian character. Their memo, in fact, contained little of the X-article's ambiguity on this score. Soviet aggression, they wrote, was not a relic of Russian hostility to foreigners but derived from "the Marxian ideology of inevitable conflict." Similarly, Soviet suspiciousness in diplomatic relations was shaped in part by "an official Soviet ideology of a very special character."[12] Communism, not character, determined Soviet policy.

This emphasis on ideology stayed with Robinson after he returned from his wartime government service. He became the founding director of Columbia University's new Russian Institute. Like Bohlen, Robinson had gone through the 1920s and 1930s insisting that understanding the Soviet Union required understanding Russia. The "Communist experiment," he had written in 1922, was a "Russian problem." In contrast, his few publications after returning to Columbia in 1946 focused on the Soviet Union as an ideological threat. His only major article, entitled "The Ideological Combat," addressed the American-Soviet conflict solely in political terms. It is an unusual piece, revealing Robinson's earlier immersion in the Progressive milieu of *The Dial*. The article starts with a point reminiscent of John Dewey (who was at last slowing in productivity as he entered his ninety-first year). Robinson worried that economic conditions had long outstripped American notions of an individual's place in society. Yet unlike Dewey, Robinson wanted to reinvigorate rather than redefine individualism. Robinson continued that a renewed individualism was essential in the looming ideological struggle, for America's lack of self-definition left it ill-prepared for the Soviet Union's ideological challenges.[13] Political beliefs, not national characteristics, would be the battleground of the Cold War.

When explaining Soviet behavior, as he did frequently in speeches in the mid-1940s, Robinson stressed ideological over national concerns. For instance, speaking to the Amy War College, he criticized earlier scholars for neglecting Communist ideology as a force in Soviet history. His talk "Factors in Soviet Intentions Abroad" to the Council of Foreign Relations in late 1946 emphasized ideology and power—with no reference to the Soviet Union as a Russian problem.[14] In speaking before scholarly audiences, however, Robinson allowed that Russian traits shaped some aspects of Soviet life. But even there, he insisted that ideology played the dominant role. Soviet irrationalism, for instance, came about "*in part*" because of Russia's past, which "*helps* to explain . . . the immaturity of the Bolshevik ideology."[15] Russian heritage could have only a minor role in shaping Soviet power.

American social scientists in the 1950s drew new attention to the pitfalls of ideology. Celebrating their own pragmatism and objectivity, they insisted that ideologies caused trouble for other nations—but not their own. Ideologies were systems of total thought, they implied, that could exist only in the minds of intellectuals. They were ineffective and indeed impossible guides to present and future action. Daniel Bell's well-known essay from 1960, "The End of Ideology in the West," made this point. Ideologies had emerged in the eighteenth and nineteenth centuries, Bell wrote, to challenge an all-encompassing religious worldview. Successful at replacing faith in divinity with faith in rationality, ideologies had in the twentieth century run aground. They "lost their 'truth' and their power to persuade," Bell wrote, and left serious doubts about the possibility of creating new worlds of perfect harmony. He blamed the exhaustion of ideologies on the recognition that future promises would entail present hardships. In this Bell both evoked and invoked Alexander Herzen's argument of a century earlier. Ideologies, with their focus on the future over the present, had run their course. The Soviet Union, the living embodiment of ideology, was also the living proof of ideology's failures.[16] Bell rested his case against modern ideologies by quoting Herzen's powerful lines about caryatids.

The critique that ideology was faulty because ideologues created the Soviet Union appeared alongside its inverse: the Soviet Union was faulty because it was ruled by ideology. Post-war Soviet studies, dominated initially by political scientists, devoted much attention to the nature of Soviet ideology.[17] In doing so, social scientists helped lay to rest American ideas of Russia that focused on the peculiarities of the Russians. The work of their students, while innovative, informed, and often erudite, stressed Communism over Russianness, ideology over history.

Other ways of understanding Soviet policy also downplayed the Russian context. Two of the most important analyses of the early 1950s, for instance, both studied Soviet politics in terms of the exigencies of **power**. The sociologist Barrington Moore described the aims of his book, *Soviet Politics—The Dilemma of Power* (1951), in terms of its contributions to social theory. He hoped to shed light on "social behavior and institutions" as well as "the relationship between various aspects of a going social system." The book's secondary objective, he continued, was to "test prevailing general theories concerning the role of ideas in organized human behavior." The Soviet Union was merely an interesting case in a larger project to analyze the components and functions of human societies. Moore's study concluded that Bolshevik ideology, which contained both anti-authoritarian and authoritarian elements, abandoned the former as it came to power. While maintaining some of their earlier language of political participation and social equality, the Bolsheviks in power readily employed the practices of absolute control. The exercise of power and the existence of inequality, Moore continued, were necessary to rule modern industrial states, and required the marginalization of their earlier "utopian" beliefs.[18] The implications of Moore's work called for combining an ideological emphasis with a sociological one. The ideas of the Bolsheviks shifted as a result of their assumption of power as well as their drive to become industrial. Once these had taken place, the Soviet Union, like other modern nations, was shaped by the forces of modern life.

In centering on power, scholars often dismissed notions of national character as unscholarly. The Harvard political scientist Merle Fainsod, for instance, explicitly rejected national character. His industry standard, *How Russia Is Ruled* (1953), derided the argument that "there is some mystic substance in the Russian soul which breeds submission." Instead he called for new scholarly efforts to determine the structure of totalitarian states. "The problem of the origins of Communist totalitarianism is too complex to be disposed of by impressionistic judgments of Russian national character," he insisted.[19]

Interest in the operations of Soviet power, as Fainsod demonstrated, also emerged from studies of the Soviet Union as an example of **totalitarianism**. This well-used addition to social science's conceptual toolbox emphasized structural similarities over national differences. The most erudite use of the concept, by Hannah Arendt, offered a powerful theory of totalitarianism—"radical evil" manipulating an atomized and uprooted society—which was of questionable utility for explaining Soviet politics. In spite of her pretensions to universalism, she offered few systematic comparisons.[20] Carl Friedrich, one of the most energetic academic promoters of this new category, developed a checklist of sociological trends that defined totalitarian societies: an official ideology; a single party of dedicated believers; the "near-complete monopoly of control" of both weapons and the means of communication; and "terroristic police control." Friedrich ducked efforts to describe the specific historical origins of totalitarian societies, insisting instead that they were "historically *sui generis*," but "why they are what they are we do not know."[21] The intellectual power of that category derived from its focus on institutional similarities in the present. This focus, however, left little room for a discussion of history, either the historical forces leading to that type of society, or the evolution of totalitarian societies.[22]

Speaking at a conference on totalitarianism, Friedrich presented these ideas to an audience including likeminded social scientists as well as older Russia experts like Chamberlin and Kennan. Yet these observers did not share Friedrich's interest in theorizing. In his own presentation at the conference, Kennan specifically addressed the question of history, insisting that "the Russian and German phenomenon [*sic*] were highly disparate things, in nature as in origin."[23] Chamberlin, like Kennan, explained the

Soviet Union, as he always had, in terms of the Russian past. He invoked nineteenth-century writers like the Marquis de Custine and the American diplomat Neill Brown for their insights into Soviet society—and even cited Sigismund von Herberstein's sixteenth-century observations. All these writings, he said, pointed to traits of Russian national character—specifically, the lack of "instincts for relativity and moderation"—that shaped Soviet authority.[24] Yet these particularist concerns ran against the grain of the conference. Chamberlin's essay, in fact, was not published with the conference proceedings, which focused more on describing the structures and functions that united totalitarian societies than on exploring historical antecedents particular to each example of a totalitarian society.

The totalitarian paradigm illustrates another aspect of the turn toward universalism in the 1950s. Whereas the first step for universalism was to abandon history in favor of ideology, the next step was to throw over ideology in favor of social structure. This shift, traced most readily by the spread of Talcott Parson's ideas through the social sciences, emphasized the commonalities among all industrial societies, regardless of the political beliefs their leaders expressed. In his influential but turgid prose, Parsons declared that ideology mattered less than social organization, and that the common features of modern industrial society mattered as much as any superficial differences in political beliefs. Even in their 1945 memorandum, Bohlen and Robinson had offered an inkling of this conception well before it climbed the ivory tower; they wrote that all societies, irrespective of form of government, were subject to the same factor of change: "a technology of machine production."[25] History mattered less than sociology. Parson's insights, joined to a dynamic theory of social development, were central to the rising tide of modernization theory.[26]

The promises and the perils of universalism were nowhere more visible than in **modernization** theory of the 1950s. Unlike the previous three concepts, modernization had a clearly specified place for national character: in the past. Modernization involved overcoming—or overthrowing—national characteristics as a prerequisite to becoming modern. As Bruce Hopper and George Counts had argued in the 1930s, national differences were effaced during the process—indeed, as a result—of modernization. While there was room for national differences in so-called traditional societies, theorists argued, modernization had a homogenizing effect. Thus the claim of modernization theory's most energetic impresario, Walt Whitman Rostow, was that every country could reach the American stage of "high-mass consumption" if it only followed his five-step program. His simplest statement of his hopes for modernization came in a book arguing for a significant expansion of American development aid for the newly independent nations of Asia and Africa. He closed with a wish expressed by his namesake a century earlier:

> One thought ever at the fore—
> That in the Divine Ship, the World, breasting Time and Space,
> All peoples of the globe together sail, sail the same voyage, are bound
>   to the same destination.[27]

Rostow's own name and career trajectory mirrored his hopes for the world. Born into a family of poor but ambitious Jewish immigrants, Rostow and his two brothers were named after great Americans, Ralph Emerson and Eugene Victor (for the perennial socialist candidate Debs). From their earliest days, they hoped to transcend any taint of ethnic particularism as they scaled the heights of American society. It is hardly surprising that Rostow downplayed his ethnic roots once he reached the top. As with the nations that had achieved take-off, there was no looking back.[28]

Such invocations of a budding universalism also took place far outside academic conference halls. An exhibit curated by the photographer Edward Steichen, *The Family of Man,* first displayed at the Museum of Modern Art but then sent around the world by the United States Information Agency, purported to celebrate common elements of the human experience. All manner of scholars, writers, and commentators defined the United States and the world in terms of an eternal present and a bright future common to all, rather than as entities that differed by nationality, race, or class.[29] Overcoming cultural and political differences along these lines was optimistically—even naively—anticipated by much of post-war American social thought.

Rostow's best-known book, *Stages of Economic Growth* (1960), combined his Whitmanesque universalism with a theory of economic and social change. All nations, he insisted, could be located on a single five-stage path from traditional to modern. Once on the path, there was no backtracking; some cases (including Russia) might see progress halted temporarily, but eventually the travels toward modernity would resume. Russia fit well in Rostow's view of modernization, tracking the United States from a third to half a century behind. The important differences between the two countries, Rostow continued, related to their starting points.

Whereas Russia struggled to "overcome a traditional society," the United States had been "born free." But this sort of difference, he insisted, did not put the USSR on a fundamentally different path: "there is nothing mysterious about the evolution of modern Russia," which will soon enough "create a modern economy and a modern society."[30]

Rostow's earlier monograph on the USSR included a similar narrative of modernization. His CIA-funded book *The Dynamics of Soviet Society* placed great stress on Soviet ideology and the Bolsheviks' pursuit of power. He acknowledged certain Russian characteristics that shaped the USSR but reduced them to quirks or atavisms: "The Russian mannerisms of the Soviet regime are . . . to be regarded as the consequence of the tactics of pursuing power from a Russian base . . . [and not] a direct national phenomenon determined by the aspirations of the Russian peoples." Even while acknowledging that aspects of Leninism resonated with Russian traits, Rostow had two counter-arguments. First, Russian traits did not determine Soviet history, for other paths were equally likely to emerge from imperial Russia; and second, Soviet ideology had suppressed Russian character.[31]

Other applications of modernization theory to Soviet Studies made similar claims about the USSR. That theory's leading proponent among professional Sovietologists, Cyril Black, proposed a major conference with the title "The Modernization of Russian Society."[32] The conference, in 1958, included an opening address from Parsons. The Harvard sociologist diagrammed the common structures of all industrial societies and found that even apparent differences—for instance, conflicting ideologies—ultimately served to "legitimize change in values and in institutional structure." Ideologies ultimately smoothed institutional change and soothed discontent.[33] In his concluding essay, Black presented a similar picture of a world growing together as it grew modern. Here he offered a narrative of modernization that portrayed the rise of modern society overcoming cultural and historical particularities: "values and traditions that had stood the test of centuries"—he specifically mentioned fatalism—"have been cast aside."[34] Describing the "destructiveness of modernization," Black noted the demise of particularism in the face of a new industrial society. In a broader study in the mid-1960s, he predicted that the global "revolution of modernization" would lead to the end of international conflict and eventually to the end of national governments themselves.[35] Modernization was the path to a single type of social organization.

The rise of modernization theory and the abandonment of history in early Sovietology were important parts of a broad trend that reverberated throughout the academy: the rise of a universalistic vision of human society and behavior. This vision contained within it a remarkable liberation from earlier scholarly failings. Biology or culture would no longer limit the possibilities of persons or nations. People or peoples could reach—eventually and in principle—the state of industrial modernity that the United States had already attained. But that form of modernity required shedding the cultural particularities that defined traditional societies.

The rampant universalism of American thought in the Cold War, so effectively illustrated by changing views of the Soviet Union, marginalized those determined to explore cultural and historical roots of human behavior. Thus Kennan's own claims that he was out of the American mainstream in the 1950s have some merit. Praised for the X-article's attention to ideology, Kennan himself continued to describe the USSR in particularist terms, as inescapably Russian. This distinction helps account for Kennan's dissatisfaction with his own famous article, as well as for his lament that he was born in the wrong era, an "expatriate" in his own time.[36]

Having outlined the foreign-policy implications of universalist thought in the early Cold War, Kennan soon found himself in a familiar place: on the margins. In a world differentiated not by national characteristics but by degrees of industrialization—a process Kennan viewed warily—the reception of his X-article signaled a step toward the demise of particularistic understandings of the Soviet Union.[37] In this new age of universalism, studies of the Soviet Union would focus on social structure, economic production, and ideology. Although the shift to universalism was hardly complete in 1950s Sovietology, it had progressed sufficiently to leave the misunderstood Cold Warrior Kennan out in the cold.

With Kennan, the ideas of a generation of professional diplomats, well-versed in the language of geography and national character, shifted to the sidelines of intellectual debate. The heightened attention to the USSR did not bring American Foreign Service Officers (even those with regional training) into the broader public debate. The dictates of professional diplomacy prevented this. In the academy, post-war Sovietologists ignored most pre-war work, with its particularistic tone. There were a handful of exceptions to this: Geroid Robinson's book *Rural Russia* and William Henry Chamberlin's volumes on the Russian Revolution remained frequently and fruitfully read in the post-war era. But the new direction of Soviet Studies itself relied on the narrative of modernization, a field that had risen above its particularistic roots to embrace general theories of society.[38]

Proof of the new direction is visible, ironically, the republication of Marquis de Custine's famous nineteenth-century travelogue. The former Moscow ambassador Walter Bedell Smith and his friends were swayed by Custine's argument that tsarist despotism was the result of Russian character. These diplomats believed that Custine's experiences in Russia paralleled their own a century later. Kennan himself invoked Custine frequently in public lectures in the early Cold War.[39] Publishing the work with a doggedly conservative publisher, Ambassador Smith insisted that the French nobleman's ideas still applied—a point further underscored by the new title, *Journey for Our Time*. Smith chastised those who believed that "the Russian people are like people everywhere and only the Government is different." Not true, insisted the former ambassador: "The people, too, are different . . . set apart from other civilizations."[40] Yet the book met with a resounding thud. The only scholarly review, a brief note in a sociology journal, praised the book's translation but thought its utility circumscribed. It "throws light only on social continuities," wrote the young scholar Alexander Vucinich; understanding the full nature of "Soviet society as a historically unique structure" would require other sources. Responses in the popular press were similar. Hans Kohn emphasized that the resemblances between nineteenth- and twentieth-century Russia were merely "external." *The Nation*'s reviewer claimed that the book's discussion of eternal Russian traits was "more likely to obscure than to illuminate" current Soviet affairs. And Louis Fischer's son George, a historian, feared that Custine's work would become "a storehouse for foolish analogies." Only Chamberlin offered his unqualified enthusiasm for the book.[41] Kennan remained unswayed by these criticisms, returning to Custine's work in the late 1960s. His historical researches led him to doubt the accuracy of the work's description of 1839, yet he found it a compelling depiction of the Russia he knew in the 1930s.[42] Only among particularists did Custine's work seem relevant for the Cold War.

The rising ideological fervor of the early 1950s left arguments like Custine's—and along with it, Kennan's, Smith's, and Chamberlin's—as historical curios. Understanding the Soviet threat in the 1950s would require the latest tools of social science, which devoted itself to adapting universal theories of social structure, political ideology, and economic production to the Soviet Union. The insights of one German universalist, Max Weber, became essential to studying a regime claiming its origins in the writings of another, Karl Marx. The American academy's turn to Weber in the post-war years, of course, went well beyond the study of the USSR. But the impact was especially striking in Sovietology because of its long tradition of particularism.

Yet if this universalism offered opportunities for liberation—a point often lost in today's age of identity—it also came with its own significant shortcomings. Viewing all people and peoples as capable of great achievements left little room for explorations of historical differences, and ultimately, of history itself. Whether relying on psychological concepts like those Mead and Leites had adopted in the late 1940s, or on ideology (like Robinson), or on modernization (like Black), scholars placed less emphasis on the role of history in shaping contemporary societies.

By the early 1950s, the notion of the Soviet Union as a chapter in Russian history no longer stood at the center of American thought. Those arguing for peculiarly Russian modes of behavior and social organization became, in their own ways, peculiarities in an age of universalism. Gone were the traps of particularism, especially the invocations of national character that diminished the prospects for Russian progress and even the value of Russian life. Newly arrived, though, were a whole new set of pitfalls: those derived from believing, with a potent mixture of post-war optimism and social-scientific confidence, that a single set of theories could explain a world of difference.

SOURCES
ABBREVIATIONS
NOTES
ACKNOWLEDGMENTS
INDEX

Sources

In the process of turning an unwieldy dissertation into a slightly-less-unwieldy book, I have made significant, even drastic, cuts to the notes. Those interested in additional citations can find them in that original document: "America, Russia, and the Romance of Economic Development" (Ph.D. diss., University of California-Berkeley, 1998). I would like to identify here a number of works whose importance to my thinking is not fully reflected in these pared-down notes.

Previous historians' scholarship on American ideas of Russia proved very helpful. Peter Filene's study of the first years of Soviet rule was similarly useful: *Americans and the Soviet Experiment, 1917–1933* (Cambridge, Mass.: Harvard University Press, 1967). Eduard Mark's article on the 1930s and 1940s is admirably broad and inclusive: "October or Thermidor? Interpretations of Stalinism and the Perception of Soviet Foreign Policy in the United States, 1927–1947," *American Historical Review* 94 (October 1989); for a view of the subsequent years, see David S. Foglesong, "Roots of 'Liberation': American Images of the Future of Russia in the Early Cold War, 1948–53," *International History Review* 30 (March 1999). Robert F. Byrnes, a distinguished historian of the Soviet Union, also made numerous forays into the history of Soviet Studies, collected in *A History of Russian and East European Studies in the United States: Selected Essays* (Lanham, Md.: University Press of America, 1994). Christopher Lasch's first book was incisive and thought-provoking: *American Liberals and the Russian Revolution* (New York: Columbia University Press, 1962).

There is a larger and more developed literature on European ideas about Russia. Most recent is Martin Malia's erudite work *Russia under Western Eyes: From the Bronze Horseman to the Lenin Mausoleum* (Cambridge, Mass.: Harvard University Press, 1999); its early sections especially are full of brilliant insights and incisive phrases. Coming from a rather different perspective, and focusing on the transmission of economic ideas, is Esther Kingston-Mann, *In Search of the True West: Culture, Economics, and Problems of Russian Development* (Princeton: Princeton University Press, 1999). Larry Wolff's book on Enlightenment views of Russia was especially important to my thinking; it appeared just as I embarked on dissertation research: *Inventing Eastern Europe: The Map of Civilization on the Age of Enlightenment* (Stanford: Stanford University Press, 1994).

With the exception of Lasch, most of the historians writing about Russia in the American mind isolate their subject from broader streams of American thought. I have learned American intellectual history from overviews as well as from more specialized works. Dorothy Ross's wise and weighty book contains brief summaries of key social scientists as well as an overarching approach to understanding their work—*The Origins of American Social Science* (Cambridge: Cambridge University Press, 1991). More specialized works on individual disciplines have proved similarly helpful: George W. Stocking, Jr., *Race, Culture and Evolution: Essays in the History of Anthropology* (New York: Free Press, 1968); Robert C. Bannister, *Sociology and Scientism: The American Quest for Objectivity, 1880–1940* (Philadelphia: Temple University Press, 1987); David M. Ricci, *The Tragedy of Political Science: Politics, Scholarship and Democracy* (New Haven: Yale University Press, 1984); and Michael A. Bernstein, *A Perilous Progress: Economists and Public Purpose in Twentieth-Century America* (Princeton: Princeton University Press, 2001). For a useful if episodic history of American scholarship on the rest of the world, see Robert A. MacCaughey, *International Studies and Academic Enterprise: A Chapter in the Enclosure of American Learning* (New York: Columbia University Press, 1984).

Historians of American thought have also written a number of influential books on intellectual currents outside the academy. The most important of these for the early twentieth century are Morton White, *Social Thought in America: The Revolt against Formalism* (1949; Boston: Beacon, 1957); Edward A. Purcell, Jr., *The Crisis of Democratic Theory: Scientific Naturalism and the Problem of Value* (Lexington: University Press of Kentucky, 1973); and John Jordan, *Machine-Age Ideology: Social Engineering and American Liberalism, 1911–1939* (Chapel Hill: University of North Carolina Press, 1994). David Hollinger's essays on modern American thought have been widely influential among historians, and deservedly so; they are conveniently collected in two books: *In the American Province:*

Studies in the History and Historiography of Ideas (Bloomington: Indiana University Press, 1985) and *Science, Jews, and Secular Culture: Studies in Mid-Twentieth-Century American Intellectual History* (Princeton: Princeton University Press, 1996). Hollinger's historical and programmatic work on dilemmas of ethnic diversity has also been influential in a broader setting; see *Postethnic America: Beyond Multiculturalism* (New York: Basic Books, 1995). Abbott Gleason follows one crucial concept from its scholarly and political roots to its propagandistic expression in *Totalitarianism: The Inner History of the Cold War* (Oxford: Oxford University Press, 1995).

The role of the Soviet Union in the promises and tragedies of the American left is hard to underestimate. While I have generally steered clear of Party politics here, left-wing debates over the Soviet Union are central to American interwar political and intellectual life. The contentiousness of historical scholarship suggests that the fierce debates of the 1930s have not yet lost their power. Judy Kutulas, *The Long War: The Intellectual People's Front and Anti-Stalinism, 1930–1940* (Durham: Duke University Press), packs much more than its title indicates. See David Caute, *The Fellow-Travellers: A Postscript to the Enlightenment* (New York: Harper and Row, 1973), for a cosmopolitan argument about one group of Soviet sympathizers. John Patrick Diggins offers his usual combination of insight and provocation in *The Rise and Fall of the American Left* (New York: W. W. Norton, 1992). Paul Hollander's analysis of American travelers to the Soviet Union is harsh—*Political Pilgrims: Travels of Western Intellectuals to the Soviet Union, China, and Cuba, 1928–1978* (Oxford: Oxford University Press, 1981). Hollander takes much of his Soviet material from a monograph—Sylvia R. Margulies, *The Pilgrimage to Russia: The Soviet Union and the Treatment of Foreigners, 1924–1937* (Madison: University of Wisconsin Press, 1968). Recent work in Soviet archives should offer a much-needed perspective on these events; Michael David-Fox is currently writing a history of VOKS, and Shawn Salmon's dissertation on Intourist should also prove useful. Daniel Aaron's classic work on left-wing writers still offers measured and thoughtful views; see *Writers on the Left: Episodes in American Literary Communism* (New York: Harcourt, Brace and World, 1961). The crucial decade of the 1930s is also covered in Richard Pells, *Radical Visions, American Dreams: Culture and Social Thought in the Depression Years* (New York: Harper and Row, 1973); and Frank A. Warren, *Liberals and Communism: The "Red Decade" Revisited* (New York: Columbia University Press, 1966).

Monographs on specific aspects and episodes of Russian-American relations also provided insight and perspective. Norman Saul's thorough volumes on American-Russian contacts were especially important reference works: *Concord and Conflict: The United States and Russia, 1867–1914* (Lawrence: University Press of Kansas, 1996), and *War and Revolution: The United States and Russia, 1914–1921* (Lawrence: University Press of Kansas, 2001). Saul also cites widely from the secondary literature. David A. Mayers, *The Ambassadors and America's Soviet Policy* (Oxford: Oxford University Press, 1995), covers a similarly broad span but focuses on a narrow range of contacts. And in spite of the controversies surrounding his later work, William Appleman Williams began his career with an important book on Russia: *American-Russian Relations, 1781–1947* (New York: Rinehart, 1952). Benjamin M. Weissman's short book, *Herbert Hoover and Famine Relief to Soviet Russia, 1921–1923* (Stanford: Hoover Institution Press, 1974), was the standard published work, but Nana Tsikhelashvili's dissertation ("Amerikanskaia pomoshch' narodam Rossii v nachale 20-kh godov XX veka," Russian State Humanities University, 1997) and Bertrand M. Patenaude's book *The Big Show in Bololand: The American Relief Expedition to Soviet Russia in the Famine of 1921* (Stanford: Stanford University Press, 2002) offer far more detail and nuance.

Work on other aspects of American foreign relations has generally provided a stronger interpretive edge. Frank Ninkovich's recent books are especially important in this regard: *Modernity and Power: A History of the Domino Theory in the Twentieth Century* (Chicago: University of Chicago Press, 1994) and its "son," *The Wilsonian Century: U.S. Foreign Policy since 1900* (Chicago: University of Chicago Press, 1999). Michael H. Hunt's work is well worth (re)visiting: *Ideology and U.S. Foreign Policy* (New Haven: Yale University Press, 1987).

While my interests in Russian history go well beyond what is covered in this book, I found a few works absolutely indispensable while writing it. On nineteenth-century currents, particularly involving economic thought, Andrzej Walicki's work is of the highest significance; see especially *The Controversy over Capitalism: Studies in the Social Philosophy of the Russian Populists* (Oxford: Clarendon, 1969). A similarly broad take on Marxist currents is Adam Ulam, *The Unfinished Revolution: An Essay on the Sources of Influence of Marxism and Communism* (New York: Random House, 1960). Alexander Gerschenkron's work is especially important for understanding both historical and historiographic trends; his essays are conveniently collected as *Economic Backwardness in Historical Perspective: A Book of Essays* (Cambridge, Mass.: Harvard University Press, 1964) and *Continuity in History and Other Essays* (Cambridge, Mass.: Harvard University Press, 1968). For thoughtful reflections on Gerschenkron's ideas and legacies, see the essays in *Patterns of European Industrialization: The Nineteenth Century*, ed. Richard Sylla and Gianni Toniolo (New York: Routledge, 1991). Cathy Frierson's analysis of changing Russian views of the peasantry offers fruitful comparisons: *Peasant Icons: Representations of Rural People in Late Nineteenth Century Russia* (Oxford: Oxford University Press, 1993). Among the most productive areas of scholarship using newly opened Soviet-era archives have been studies of the Soviet manmade disasters in the countryside. Important analyses of the famine of 1932–1933 include unpublished work by Viktor Kondrashin and D'Ann Penner: Kondrashin, "Golod 1932–33 godov v derevne Povol'zhia" (diss., Russian Academy of Sciences, 1991), and Penner, "The Agrarian 'Strike' of 1932–1933," Kennan Institute for Advanced Russian Studies, Occasional Paper no. 269 (1998). Recent work in quantitative economic history of the USSR has also proven helpful: *From Tsarism to the New Economic Policy: Continuity and Change in the Economy of the USSR*, ed. R. W. Davies (Ithaca: Cornell University Press, 1991) and *The Economic Transformation of the Soviet Union, 1913–1945*, ed. R. W. Davies, Mark Harrison, and S. G. Wheatcroft (Cambridge: Cambridge University Press, 1994).

Last but hardly least are biographies of some of the Russia experts dealt with in *Modernization from the Other Shore*. These works range from incisive ruminations on major figures (like Anders Stephanson's work on George Frost Kennan) to careful reconstructions of more obscure figures (like Frederick Travis on the elder George Kennan). Glenn Altschuler's biography of Andrew Dickson White is broad and deep, as is Robert Byrnes's on Archibald Cary Coolidge. Whitman Bassow's collective biography *The Moscow Correspondents: Reporting on Russia from the Revolution to Glasnost* (New York: William Morrow, 1988) is all the more useful for the fact that Bassow admirably turned over his interview notes to the Library of Congress. S. J. Taylor's biography of one of Bassow's subjects, Walter Duranty, is (for the time being) the last word on him. Robert Westbrook's remarkable biography of John Dewey presents a compelling depiction of its subject and many of his most important arguments.

Although I do not agree with every aspect of the books listed here, I have learned from all of them, and also from those cited in the notes.

Private Archival Collections

American Peace Commission to Versailles Papers, Library of Congress
American Relief Administration—Europe Unit Records, Hoover Institution Archives
American Relief Administration—Russia Unit Records, Hoover Institution Archives (Unless otherwise noted, citations to "ARA Papers" refer to this collection.)
American Relief Administration Papers, Bakhmeteff Archive, Columbia University
Hamilton Fish Armstrong Papers, Mudd Library, Princeton University
Joseph Barnes Papers, Columbia University Library
Whitman Bassow Papers, Library of Congress
Luther Bernard Papers, University of Chicago Library
Charles E. Bohlen Papers, Library of Congress
Stuart Chase Papers, Library of Congress
Christian Science Publishing Society, Church History Office, First Church of Christ, Scientist
Archibald Cary Coolidge Papers, Harvard University Archives
George S. Counts Papers, Columbia University Teachers College Library
George S. Counts Papers, Southern Illinois University Library
Charles R. Crane Papers, Bakhmeteff Archive, Columbia University
Richard T. Crane Papers, Georgetown University Library
Crane-Lilly Family Papers, Chicago Historical Society
Vera Micheles Dean Papers, Schlesinger Library, Radcliffe Institute
Louis Fischer Papers, Mudd Library, Princeton University
Louis Fischer Papers, Yale University Library
Harold H. Fisher Papers, Hoover Institution Archives
Raymond H. Fisher Papers, Bancroft Library, University of California—Berkeley
William Dudley Foulke Papers, Library of Congress
Alexander Gerschenkron Papers, Harvard University Archives
Frank A. Golder Papers, Hoover Institution Archives
James P. Goodrich Papers, Herbert Hoover Presidential Library
Alexander Gumberg Papers, State Historical Society of Wisconsin
Samuel Northrop Harper Papers, University of Chicago Library
Loy W. Henderson Papers, Library of Congress
Maurice Hindus Papers, Colgate University Archives
Milton Hindus Papers, Brandeis University Archives
Calvin Bryce Hoover Papers, Duke University Library
Herbert Hoover "Bible" (ten-volume collection of publications and speeches), Herbert Hoover Presidential Library and Hoover Institution Archives

Bruce C. Hopper Papers, Harvard University Archives

Isaac A. Hourwich Papers, Yivo Institute

Colonel Edward Mandell House Papers, Yale University Library

Lincoln Hutchinson Papers, Hoover Institution Archives

Inquiry Papers, Yale University Library

Edwin L. James Papers, *New York Times* Archive

Alvin Aaron Johnson Papers, State Historical Society of Wisconsin

Robert F. Kelley Papers, Georgetown University Library

George Kennan Papers, Library of Congress

George Kennan Papers, New York Public Library (Astor, Lenox, and Tilden Foundations)

George Frost Kennan Papers, Mudd Library, Princeton University

Robert J. Kerner Papers, Bancroft Library, University of California—Berkeley

Freda Kirchway Papers, Schlesinger Library, Radcliffe Institute

H. R. Knickerbocker Papers, Columbia University Library

Robert E. Lansing Papers, Library of Congress

Walter Lippmann Papers, Sterling Library, Yale University

Eugene Lyons Papers, Hoover Institution Archives

Eugene Lyons Papers, University of Oregon Library

John van Antwerp MacMurray Papers, Firestone Library, Princeton University

Cyrus McCormick Papers, State Historical Society of Wisconsin

George von Lengerke Meyer Diary, Library of Congress

Malcolm Muggeridge Diary, Hoover Institution Archives

Alfred Ochs Papers, *New York Times* Archives

Office of the Messrs. Rockefeller Records (Record Group 2), Rockefeller Archive Center

Raymond Robins Papers, State Historical Society of Wisconsin

Geroid Tanquary Robinson Papers, Columbia University Library

Joseph A. Rosen Papers, Yivo Institute

Edward Alsworth Ross Papers, State Historical Society of Wisconsin

W. W. Rostow Papers, John F. Kennedy Library

Maud Russell Papers, New York Public Library (Astor, Lenox, and Tilden Foundations)

Henry Shapiro Papers, Library of Congress

William Stoneman Papers, Bentley Historical Library, University of Michigan

Arthur Hays Sulzberger Papers, *New York Times* Archive

Rexford Tugwell Papers, Franklin Delano Roosevelt Presidential Library

University of Chicago Board of Trustees Papers, University of Chicago Library

University of Chicago Presidents' Papers, University of Chicago Library

Oswald Garrison Villard Papers (bMS Am 1323 [1705]), Houghton Library, Harvard University

George Vincent Diary, Rockefeller Foundation Records (Record Group 12.1), Rockefeller Archive Center
William English Walling Papers, State Historical Society of Wisconsin
Rev. Edmund Aloysius Walsh Papers, Georgetown University Library
Allen Wardwell Papers, Bakhmeteff Archive, Columbia University
Andrew Dickson White Papers, Cornell University Library
John X. Wiley Papers, Franklin Delano Roosevelt Presidential Library
J. Butler Wright Papers, Record Group 200, Gift Collections, U.S. National Archives

Official American Collections

Herbert Hoover Presidential Library

Commerce Papers
PSF   President's Secretary's Files

Franklin Delano Roosevelt Presidential Library

PSF   President's Secretary's Files
OF   Office Files

Record Group 59—U.S. Department of State

SDDF   State Department Decimal Files

Decimal files at National Archives II
"Records of the Department of State Relating to Political Relations between the United States and the Soviet Union, 1930–1939" (Microfilm T1241)
"Records of the Department of State Relating to the Internal Affairs of Russia and the Soviet Union, 1910–1929" (Microfilm M316)
"Records of the Department of State Relating to the Internal Affairs of the Soviet Union, 1930–1939" (Microfilm T1249)

SDR   State Department Records (general)

Records of the Division of Eastern European Affairs
"Despatches from U.S. Ministers to Russia, 1808–1906" (Microfilm M35)
"Personal and Confidential Letters from Secretary of State Lansing to President Wilson, 1915–1918" (Microfilm M743)

Record Group 84—U.S. Department of State—Post Files

Moscow Post Files

Record Group 256—Inquiry Records

"Inquiry Documents: Special Reports and Studies" (Microfilm M1107)

Official Russian Collections

Unless otherwise noted, citations to Russian archival materials are in the form fond/opis'/delo/list' (collection/ inventory/file/page).

AVPR   Arkhiv vneshnei politiki Rossii

f. 170   Posol'stvo v Vashingtone

AVPRF   Arkhiv vneshnei politiki Rossisskoi Federatsii (cited as fond/opis'/papka/ delo/list [collection/inventory/folder/file/page])

f. 04   Sekretariat Chicherina
f. 05   Sekretariat Litvinova
f. 0129   Referantura po SShA
f. 508   Informatsionnoe biuro v Vashingtone (cited as fond/opis'/poriadok/ papka/list [collection/inventory/sequence/folder/page])

GARF   Gosudarstvennyi arkhiv Rossiiskoi Federatsii

f. 1058   Polnomochnoe predstavitel'stvo pravitel'stv RSFSR i UkSSR pri vsekh zagranichnykh organizatsii pomoshchi golodaiushchim Rossii
f. 1064   Tsentral'naia komissiia pomoshchi golodaiushchim pri VTsIK
f. 1065   Tsentral'naia komissiia po bor'be s posledstviami goloda pri VTsIK
f. 1235   Vserossiiskii tsentral'nyi ispolnitel'nyi komitet (VTsIK) (s.ch. = sekretnaia chast')
f. 5283   Vsesoiuznoe obshchestvo kul'turnoi sviazi s zagranitsei (s.ch. = sekretnaia chast')

RGAE   Rossiiskii gosudarstvennyi arkhiv ekonomiki

f. 4372   Gosudarstvennyi obshcheplannovaia komissiia (Gosplan)
f. 8040   Komitet po zagotovkam sel'sko-khoziaistvennykh produktov pri STO

RGASPI   Rossiiskii gosudarstvennyi arkhiv sotsial'no-politicheskoi istorii

f. 5   Sekretariat Lenina
f. 17   Tsentral'nyi komitet KPSS (cited as fond/opis'/delo/punkt [collection/
         inventory/folder/point])
         op. 3—Politbiuro
         op. 84—Orgbiuro
f. 76   Fond F. E. Dzerzhinskogo
f. 158   Fond A. D. Tsiurupy
f. 558   Fond I. V. Stalina

RGIA   Rossiiskii gosudarstvennyi istoricheskii arkhiv

f. 1204 Osobii komitet dlia pomoshchi nuzhdaiushchemusia naseleniiu v
         mestnost'iakh, postignutykh neurozhaem

Abbreviations

Journal titles include the dates consulted.

AER   *American Economic Review* (1911–1940)

AHR   *American Historical Review* (1894–1940)

AJS   *American Journal of Sociology* (1895–1940)

Annals   *Annals of the American Academy of Political and Social Science* (1890–1940)

APSR   *American Political Science Review* (1906–1940)

ARA   American Relief Administration

AVPR   Arkhiv vneshnei politiki Rossii (Archive of Russian Foreign Policy)

AVPRF   Arkhiv vneshnei politiki Rossiiskoi Federatsii (Archive of Foreign Policy of the Russian Federation)

CDN   *Chicago Daily News*

CSM   *Christian Science Monitor*

DVP   *Dokumenty vneshnei politiki,* 21 vols. (Moscow: Ministerstvo innostrannykh del, 1957–1977)

EE   Eastern European [Division of the U.S. Department of State]

EJ   *Economic Journal*—U.K. (1891–1940)

FA   *Foreign Affairs* (1922–1940)

FPA   Foreign Policy Association

FRUS   *Papers Relating to the Foreign Relations of the United States* (Washington: Government Printing Office, 1870–)

FRUS: RL   *Papers Relating to the Foreign Relations of the United States: The Lansing Papers, 1914–1920* (Washington: Government Printing Office, 1939)

FRUS: SU   *Foreign Relations of the United States: Diplomatic Papers: The Soviet Union, 1933–1939* (Washington: Government Printing Office, 1952)

FSO   Foreign Service Officer [in the U.S. Department of State]

FSS   Foreign Service School [of the U.S. Department of State]

GARF   Gosudarstvennyi arkhiv Rossiiskoi Federatsii (State Archive of the Russian Federation)

HBR   *Harvard Business Review* (1922–1940)

HH   Herbert Hoover

JDC   Joint Distribution Committee

JPE   *Journal of Political Economy* (1892–1940)

JSS   *Journal of Social Science,* originally *American Journal of Social Science* (1869–1909)

LW   John Dewey, *The Later Works, 1925–1953,* ed. Jo Ann Boydston et al., 17 vols. (Carbondale: Southern Illinois University Press, 1981–1990)

MECW   Karl Marx and Friedrich Engels, *Collected Works,* 49 vols. (New York: International Publishers / Progress Publishers, 1975–)

MW   John Dewey, *The Middle Works, 1899–1924,* ed. Jo Ann Boydston et al., 15 vols. (Carbondale: Southern Illinois University Press, 1976–1983)

NEA   National Education Association

NEP   New Economic Policy

NKID   Narodnyi komissariat po inostrannym delam (People's Commissariat for Foreign Affairs)

NYHT   *New York Herald Tribune*

NYPL   New York Public Library

NYT   *New York Times*

OF   Office Files, Franklin Delano Roosevelt Presidential Library

PSF   President's Secretary's Files, Herbert Hoover and Franklin Delano Roosevelt Presidential Libraries

PSQ   *Political Science Quarterly* (1886–1940)

PSS   Vladimir Il'ich Lenin, *Polnoe sobranie sochinenii,* 55 vols. (Moscow: Gosudarstvennoe izdatel'stvo politicheskoi literatury, 1958–1970)

PWW   *Papers of Woodrow Wilson,* ed. Arthur Link et al., 69 vols. (Princeton: Princeton University Press, 1966–1994)

QJE   *Quarterly Journal of Economics* (1886–1940)

RGAE   Rossiiskii gosudarstvennyi arkhiv ekonomiki (Russian State Economic Archive)

RGASPI   Rossiiskii gosudarstvennyi arkhiv sotsial'no-politicheskoi istorii (Russian State Archive for Social-Political History)

RGIA   Rossiiskii gosudarstvennyi istoricheskii arkhiv (Russian State Historical Archive)

RR   *Russian Review*—U.K. (1912–1914)

RSFSR   Russian Soviet Federated Socialist Republic

SDDF   State Department Decimal Files

SDR   State Department Records (general)

SEER   *Slavonic and East European Review,* originally *Slavonic Review*—U.K. (1922–1940)

SF   *Social Forces* (1922–1940)

SSR   *Sociology and Social Research* (1927–1940)

TASS Telegrafnoe agentstvo Sovetskogo Soiuza (Telegraph Agency of the Soviet Union)

UP   United Press syndicate

VOKS Vsesoiuznoe obshchestvo kul'turnoi sviazi s zagranitsei (All-Union Society for Cultural Connections Abroad)

VSNKh Vysshii sovet narodnogo khoziaistva (Supreme Council of the National Economy)

WRP Frank A. Golder, *War, Revolution, and Peace in Russia: The Passages of Frank Golder, 1914–1927,* ed. Terence Emmons and Bertand M. Patenaude (Stanford: Hoover Institution Press, 1992)

Notes

Introduction

1. Herzen, *From the Other Shore* (New York: George Braziller, 1956). Background information on Herzen comes from Isaiah Berlin, *Russian Thinkers,* ed. Henry Hardy and Aileen Kelley (New York: Penguin, 1979); Berlin's introduction to *From the Other Shore;* Martin Malia, *Alexander Herzen and the Birth of Russian Socialism, 1812–1855* (Cambridge, Mass.: Harvard University Press, 1961); Franco Venturi, *Roots of Revolution: A History of the Populist and Socialist Movements in Nineteenth Century Russia,* trans. Francis Haskell (London: Weidenfeld and Nicolson, 1960), chap. 1; and Abbott Gleason, *Young Russia: The Genesis of Russian Radicalism in the 1860s* (New York: Viking, 1980), chap. 2.

2. The phrase was coined before the famine; for an early use, see Bruce Hopper to Hamilton Fish Armstrong, 18 January 1930, Hamilton Fish Armstrong Papers, box 35.

3. Herzen, *From the Other Shore,* 158.

4. It should be obvious from what follows that my reporting of these and other stereotypes of national character, whether or not enclosed in quotation marks, does not constitute my endorsement of them.

5. Herzen, "The Russian People and Socialism: An Open Letter to Jules Michelet" (1851), in *From the Other Shore,* 175–176, 180.

6. Larry Wolff, *Inventing Eastern Europe: The Map of Civilization on the Mind of the Enlightenment* (Stanford: Stanford University Press, 1994); Martin Malia, *Russia under Western Eyes: From the Bronze Horseman to the Lenin Mausoleum* (Cambridge, Mass.: Harvard University Press, 1999); Donald M. Lowe, *The Function of "China" in Marx, Lenin, and Mao* (Berkeley and Los Angeles: University of California Press, 1966); Karl Wittfogel, *Oriental Despotism: A Comparative Study in Total Power* (New Haven: Yale University Press, 1957).

7. Marx and Engels, "Manifesto of the Communist Party" (1848), *MECW* 6:481; Marx, "Preface to the First German Edition of *Capital*" (1867), *MECW* 35:8.

8. Kennan, "Memorandum for the Minister," 19 August 1932, SDDF 861.5017 Living Conditions/510.

9. Herzen, *From the Other Shore*, 36–37, 159 (ellipses in original); Berlin, introduction to ibid., xv.

10. John M. Jordan, *Machine-Age Ideology: Social Engineering and American Liberalism, 1911–1939* (Chapel Hill: University of North Carolina Press, 1994); Guy Alchon, *The Invisible Hand of Planning: Social Science and the State in the 1920s* (Princeton: Princeton University Press, 1985).

11. David R. Shearer, *Industry, State, and Society in Stalin's Russia, 1928–1934* (Ithaca: Cornell University Press, 1996); Lynne Viola, *The Best Sons of the Fatherland: Workers in the Vanguard of Soviet Collectivization* (Oxford: Oxford University Press, 1987).

12. Hans Rogger, "*Amerikanizm* and the Economic Development of Russia," *Comparative Studies in Society and History* 23 (1981): 383–420; Thomas P. Hughes, *American Genesis: A Century of Invention and Technological Enthusiasm, 1870–1970* (New York: Viking, 1989), chap. 6; Jeffrey Brooks, "The Press and Its Message: Images of America in the 1920s and 1930s," in *Russia in the Era of NEP: Explorations in Soviet Society and Culture*, ed. Sheila Fitzpatrick, Alexander Rabinowitch, and Richard Stites (Bloomington: Indiana University Press, 1991).

13. For key works on professionalization in the social sciences, see Thomas L. Haskell, *The Emergence of Professional Social Science: The American Social Science Association and the Nineteenth-Century Crisis of Authority* (Urbana: University of Illinois Press, 1977); and Dorothy Ross, *The Origins of American Social Science* (Cambridge: Cambridge University Press, 1991). On the Foreign Service, see Robert D. Schulzinger, *The Making of the Diplomatic Mind: The Training, Outlook, and Style of United States Foreign Service Officers, 1908–1931* (Middletown, Conn.: Wesleyan University Press, 1975); and Hugh De Santis, *The Diplomacy of Silence: The American Foreign Service, the Soviet Union, and the Cold War, 1933–1947* (Chicago: University of Chicago Press, 1979). On journalists, see Michael Schudson, *Discovering the News: A Social History of American Newspapers* (New York: Basic, 1978).

14. Werner Sombart, *Why Is There No Socialism in the United States?*, trans. Patricia M. Hocking and C. T. Husbands (1906; White Plains, N.Y.: M. E. Sharpe, 1976). Works dealing with western European views of modern Russia include Malia, *Russia under Western Eyes;* A. N. Zashikhin, *Britanskaia Rossica vtoroi poloviny XIX-nachala XX veka: uchebnoe posobie* (Archangel: Izdatel'stvo Pomorskogo mezdunarodnogo pedagogicheskogo instituta, 1995); Stephen R. Graubard, *British Labour and the Russian Revolution, 1917–1924* (Cambridge, Mass.: Harvard University Press, 1956); Troy R. E. Paddock, "German Perceptions of Russia before the First World War" (Ph.D. diss., University of

California-Berkeley, 1994); Michael Burleigh, *Germany Turns Eastward: A Study of Ostforschung in the Third Reich* (Cambridge: Cambridge University Press, 1988); and Martha Helms Cooley, "Nineteenth-Century French Historical Research on Russia—Louis Leger, Alfred Rambaud, Anatole Leroy-Beaulieu" (Ph.D. diss., Indiana University, 1971).

For stimulating comparisons outside of Europe, see Tadashi Anno, "The Liberal World Order and Its Challengers: Nationalism and the Rise of Anti-Systemic Movements in Russia and Japan, 1860–1950" (Ph.D. diss., University of California-Berkeley, 1999); Anno, "*Nihonjinron* and *Russkaia Ideia: The Transformation of Japanese and Russian Nationalism in the Postwar Era and Beyond*," in *Japan and Russia: The Tortuous Path to Normalization, 1949–1999*, ed. Gilbert Rozman (New York: St. Martin's, 2000); and Haruki Wada, *Rossiia kak problema vsemirnoi istorii,* ed. G. A. Bordiugova (Moscow: Airo-XX, 1999), chap. 12. For an interesting comparison of notions of cultural and economic difference within another empire on Europe's borders, see Ussama Makdisi, "Ottoman Orientalism," *AHR* 107 (June 2002): 768–795.

15. These paragraphs build especially on Cathy A. Frierson, *Peasant Icons: Representations of Rural People in Late 19th Century Russia* (Oxford: Oxford University Press, 1993), quoted pp. 45, 159. On the populists, see also Richard Wortman, *The Crisis of Russian Populism* (Cambridge: Cambridge University Press, 1967); Andrzej Walicki, *The Controversy over Capitalism: Studies in the Social Philosophy of the Russian Populists* (1969; Notre Dame, Ind.: University of Notre Dame Press, 1989). The theme of growing gulfs within Russian society is explored in Nicholas V. Riasanovsky, *A Parting of Ways: Government and the Educated Public in Russia, 1801–1855* (Oxford: Clarendon, 1976), and in Leopold Haimson's influential articles, "The Problem of Social Stability in Urban Russia, 1905–1917," *Slavic Review* 23 (December 1964): 619–642, and 24 (March 1965): 1–22.

16. Edward W. Said, *Orientalism* (New York: Random House, 1978). My critique has been informed by Michael Adas, "'High' Imperialism and the 'New History,'" in *Islamic and European Expansion: Toward a Global Order,* ed. Adas (Philadelphia: Temple University Press, 1993); Yuri Slezkine, *Arctic Mirrors: Russia and the Small Peoples of the North* (Ithaca: Cornell University Press, 1994), epilogue; and Gyan Prakash, "*Orientalism* Now," *History and Theory* 34 (1995): 199–212.

17. Eugene Lyons, *The Red Decade: The Stalinist Penetration of America* (1941; New Rochelle: Arlington House, 1971), remains an important starting point. See also Sylvia R. Margulies, *The Pilgrimage to Russia: The Soviet Union and the Treatment of Foreigners, 1924–1937* (Madison: University of Wisconsin Press, 1968); Paul Hollander, *Political Pilgrims: Travels of Western Intellectuals to the Soviet Union, Cuba, and China, 1928–1978* (Oxford: Oxford University

Press, 1981); and William L. O'Neill, *A Better World: The Great Schism, Stalinism and the American Intellectuals* (New York: Simon and Schuster, 1982). More sympathetic accounts still interpret the episode in primarily political terms—Richard H. Pells, *Radical Visions and American Dreams: Culture and Social Thought during the Depression Years* (New York: Harper and Row, 1973); and Judy Kutulas, *The Long War: The Intellectual People's Front and Anti-Stalinism, 1930–1940* (Durham: Duke University Press, 1995). David Caute's book on Soviet enthusiasts, *The Fellow Travellers: A Postscript to the Enlightenment* (New York: Harper and Row, 1973), takes a broader perspective.

18. On engineers, see Shearer, *Industry, State and Society;* and Kendall E. Bailes, *Technology and Society under Lenin and Stalin: Origins of the Soviet Technical Intelligentsia, 1917–1941* (Princeton: Princeton University Press, 1978). On economists, see Esther Kingston-Mann, *In Search of the True West: Culture, Economics, and the Problems of Russian Development* (Princeton: Princeton University Press, 1999). On ideas about rural Russia, see George L. Yaney, *The Urge to Mobilize: Agrarian Reform in Russia, 1861–1930* (Urbana: University of Illinois Press, 1982); Frierson, *Peasant Icons;* and Yanni Kotsonis, *Making Peasants Backward: Agricultural Cooperatives and the Agrarian Question in Russia, 1861–1914* (New York: St. Martin's, 1999). Lars Lih, "Experts and Peasants," *Kritika* 2 (Fall 2001): 803–822, challenges Kotsonis and Kingston-Mann.

19. Scott, *Seeing Like a State: Why Certain Schemes to Improve the Human Condition May Fail* (New Haven: Yale University Press, 1998); see also Kate Brown, "Gridded Lives: Why Kazakhstan and Montana Are Nearly the Same Place," *AHR* 106 (February 2001): 17–48. For precedents, see Michael P. Adas, *Machines as the Measure of Man: Science, Technology, and Ideologies of Domination* (Ithaca: Cornell University Press, 1989). For links to the Cold War, see Odd Arne Westad, "The New International History of the Cold War: Three (Possible) Paradigms," *Diplomatic History* 22 (Fall 2000): 551–565.

20. Bilahari Kausikan, "The 'Asian Values' Debate: A View from Singapore," *Democracy in East Asia*, ed. Larry Diamond and Marc F. Plattner (Baltimore: Johns Hopkins University Press, 1998), 20; Kishore Mahbubani, *Can Asians Think?* (Singapore: Times Books International, 1998); Lee Kuan Yew, "The East Asian Way," *New Perspectives Quarterly* 9 (Winter 1992): 4–13. Important challenges have come from Amartya Sen, "Human Rights and Asian Values," *New Republic* 217 (14–21 July 1997), and William Theodore de Bary, *Asian Values and Human Rights: A Confucian Communitarian Perspective* (Cambridge, Mass.: Harvard University Press, 1998).

21. Robert J. Shiller, Maxim Boycko, and Vladimir Korobov, "Popular Attitudes towards Free Markets: The Soviet Union and the United States Compared,"

AER 81 (June 1991): 399; also in "Hunting for *Homo Sovieticus:* Situational versus Attitudinal Factors in Economic Behavior," *Brookings Papers on Economic Activity,* no. 1 (1992): 179; Boycko, "Price Decontrol: The Microeconomic Case for the 'Big Bang' Approach," *Oxford Review of Economic Policy* 7 (Winter 1991): 42. Boycko, Andrei Shleifer, and Robert Vishny, *Privatizing Russia* (Cambridge, Mass.: MIT Press, 1995), 9–10.

22. Marshall I. Goldman, *Lost Opportunity: Why Economic Reforms in Russia Have Not Worked* (New York: W. W. Norton, 1994), 16–18; Richard Pipes, "Russia's Past, Russia's Future," *Commentary* 101 (June 1996): 35; Pipes, "A Nation with One Foot Stuck in the Past," *Sunday Times* (London), 20 October 1996. Compare to Padma Desai, "An Interview with Martin Malia," *Problems of Post-Communism* 47 (November-December 2000): 52–59.

23. This argument is hardly novel; in quite different contexts, it appears in the writings of two of the most influential thinkers in American universities: Richard Rorty, *Achieving Our Country: Leftist Thought in Twentieth-Century America* (Cambridge, Mass.: Harvard University Press, 1998), and Benedict Anderson, *Imagined Communities: Reflections on the Origins and Spread of Nationalism* (New York: Verso, 1983).

24. Herzen, *From the Other Shore,* 3. Retranslated from A. I. Gerzen, "S togo berega" (1850), *Polnoe sobranie sochinenii i pisem,* ed. M. K. Lemke, 22 vols. (Petrograd: Literaturno-izdatel'skii otdel NKProsa, 1919–1925), 5:382.

25. Recently anthropologists have argued the opposite: that deeming some societies backward—what one calls "allochronism"—is a form of othering; see Johannes Fabian, *Time and the Other: How Anthropology Makes Its Object* (New York: Columbia University Press, 1983).

26. Marx and Engels, "Manifesto," *MECW* 6:494.

1. An Empire of Climate

1. These paragraphs build on the summary accounts in Ronald Grigor Suny, *The Soviet Experiment: Russia, the USSR, and the Successor States* (Oxford: Oxford University Press, 1998), chap. 1; and Nicholas V. Riasanovsky, *A History of Russia* (Oxford: Oxford University Press, 1993).

2. Marshall T. Poe, *"A People Born to Slavery": Russia in Early Modern European Ethnography, 1476–1748* (Ithaca: Cornell University Press, 2000), chap. 5; Herberstein quoted at p. 164.

3. Ibid., 165; Larry Wolff, *Inventing Eastern Europe: The Map of Civilization on the Mind of the Enlightenment* (Stanford: Stanford University Press, 1994), 11.

4. Wolff, *Inventing Eastern Europe,* 204–205. Montesquieu, *The Spirit of the Laws,* trans. Thomas Nugent (1748; New York: Hafner, 1949), 1:59, 1:298–299.

5. Rousseau, *The Social Contract,* in *The Social Contract and the Discourse on the Origin of Inequality,* ed. Lester G. Crocker (1762; New York: Pocket Books, 1967), 46–48; Wolff, *Inventing Eastern Europe,* 199.

6. Martin W. Lewis and Kären E. Wigen, *The Myth of Continents: A Critique of Metageography* (Berkeley and Los Angeles: University of California Press, 1997), chaps. 1–2; Mark Bassin, "Russia between Europe and Asia: The Ideological Construction of a Geographic Space," *Slavic Review* 50 (Spring 1991): 2–3.

7. Nicholas V. Riasanovsky, *Russia and the West in the Teaching of the Slavophiles: A Study of Romantic Ideology* (Cambridge, Mass.: Harvard University Press, 1952), 171–174; Martin Malia, *Russia under Western Eyes: From the Bronze Horseman to the Lenin Mausoleum* (Cambridge, Mass.: Harvard University Press, 1999), 130–133, 207.

8. The use of "civilization" to exclude Russia in early periods is suggested in Gerritt W. Gong, *The Standard of "Civilization" in International Society* (Oxford: Oxford University Press, 1984), 100–106.

9. Marquis de Custine, *Journey for Our Time: The Journals of Marquis de Custine,* ed. and trans. Phyllis Penn Kohler (1843; New York: Pellegrini and Cudahy, 1951), 21–22, 254, 137; George F. Kennan, *The Marquis de Custine and His "Russia in 1839"* (Princeton: Princeton University Press, 1971), chap. 2.

10. Aksakov quoted in Cathy A. Frierson, *Peasant Icons: Representations of Rural People in Late Nineteenth-Century Russia* (Oxford: Oxford University Press, 1993), 102.

11. Baron August von Haxthausen, *The Russian Empire: Its People, Institutions and Resources,* 2 vols., trans. Robert Farie (1847; London: Chapman and Hall, 1856), 1:66, 2:233; S. Frederick Starr, "August von Haxthausen and Russia," *Slavonic and East European Review* 46 (July 1968): 477.

12. Herzen here is agreeing with the historian Jules Michelet; Herzen, "The Russian People and Socialism: An Open Letter to Jules Michelet" (1851), in *From the Other Shore* (New York: George Braziller, 1956), 203.

13. Geroid Tanquary Robinson, *Rural Russia under the Old Regime: A History of the Landlord-Peasant World and a Prologue to the Peasant Revolution of 1917* (1932; Berkeley and Los Angeles: University of California Press, 1969), 12; Jerome Blum, *Lord and Peasant in Russia: From the Ninth to the Nineteenth Century* (Princeton: Princeton University Press, 1961), chap. 24. Although there are important distinctions between the *mir* and *obshchina* (a related form of peasant collective life), they are left aside here—few foreign experts before World War II observed the differences; see Steven A. Grant, "Obshchina and Mir," *Slavic Review* 35 (December 1976): 636–651, and Francis M. Watters, "The Peasant and the Village Commune," in *The Peasant in*

Nineteenth-Century Russia, ed. Wayne C. Vucinich (Stanford: Stanford University Press, 1968).

14. The literature on Marx's encounters with Russia is huge. I have been guided especially by Andrzej Walicki, *The Controversy over Capitalism: Studies in the Social Philosophy of the Russian Populists* (1969; Notre Dame: University of Notre Dame Press, 1989), 179–194 (quoting Marx on p. 187); Esther Kingston-Mann, *In Search of the True West: Culture, Economics and the Problems of Russian Development* (Princeton: Princeton University Press, 1999), chap. 6; James D. White, "Marx and the Russians: The Romantic Heritage," *Scottish Slavonic Review* 2 (Autumn 1983): 51–81; Bruno Naarden, "Marx and Russia," *History of European Ideas* 12:6 (1990), 783–797; and *Late Marx and the Russian Road: Marx and the "Peripheries of Capitalism,"* ed. Teodor Shanin (London: Routledge and Kegan Paul, 1983).

15. D. MacKenzie Wallace, *Russia* (London: Cassell, Petter and Galpin, 1877), 179, 209, 231, 263–264, 334–335, 339; Kingston-Mann, *In Search of the True West,* 169–170.

16. Alfred Rambaud, *The History of Russia from the Earliest Times to 1877,* trans. Leonora B. Lang, 2 vols. (1878; New York: Hovendon Company, 1886), 2:265; Martha Helms Cooley, "Nineteenth-Century French Historical Research on Russia—Louis Leger, Alfred Rambaud, Anatole Leroy-Beaulieu" (Ph.D. diss., Indiana University, 1971), 204.

17. Anatole Leroy-Beaulieu, *The Empire of the Tsars and the Russians,* 3 vols., trans. Zénïade A. Ragozin (New York: Knickerbocker Press, 1902); Cooley, "Nineteenth-Century French Historical Research," 290–291.

2. Endurance without Limit

1. Hans Rogger, *Russia in the Age of Modernisation and Revolution, 1881–1917* (New York: Longman, 1983), 15, 22.

2. Daniel Walker Howe, "American Victorianism as a Culture," *American Quarterly* 27 (December 1975): 528.

3. Peter Gay, *Schnitzler's Century: The Making of Middle Class Culture, 1815–1914* (New York: Norton, 2002), is an erudite effort to describe a single Victorian culture across the (north) Atlantic basin—but he too runs up against national differences; see, for example, pp. xxv, 4 n., 21.

4. John P. Desmarais, "Slavic Studies in France, 1840–1910," *New Review* (Toronto) 9 (December 1969): 264–266; A. N. Zashikhin, *Britanskaia Rossica vtoroi poloviny XIX–nachala XX veka: uchebnoe posobie* (Archangel: Izdatel'stvo Pomorskogo mezhdunarodnogo pedagogicheskogo instituta, 1995), 15–18; Troy R. E. Paddock, "German Perceptions of Russia before the

First World War" (Ph.D. diss., University of California-Berkeley, 1994), chap. 7.

5. This material is based on a comprehensive and reliable biography—Frederick F. Travis, *George Kennan and the American-Russian Relationship, 1865–1924* (Athens: Ohio University Press, 1990), 17–18.

6. George Kennan, *Tent Life in Siberia and Adventures among the Koraks and Other Tribes in Kamtchatka and Northern Asia* (New York: G. P. Putnam's, 1870), 465, 196, 64, 233.

7. Anna Laurens Dawes, "George Kennan," *Century* 36 (August 1888): 631; Warren I. Susman, "'Personality' and the Making of Twentieth-Century Culture," in *Culture as History: The Transformation of Russian Society in the Twentieth Century* (New York: Pantheon, 1984).

8. George Kennan, "The Mountains and Mountaineers of the Eastern Caucasus," *Journal of the American Geographical Society of New York* 5 (1874): 171, 176, 187.

9. The exchange appeared in the *New York Tribune,* 27 July 1878 and 2 August 1878, and in the *Nation* 29 (29 July 1878): 134–135. Kennan's letter to his father is quoted in Sue Skaggs Fowler, "Eugene V. Schuyler: First American Specialist on Eastern Europe" (M.A. thesis, Georgia State University, 1972), 123.

10. James M. Hubbard, "The Late Eugene Schuyler" [letter to the editor], *Nation* 51 (4 September 1890): 190; Ralph P. Rosenberg, "Eugene Schuyler's Doctor of Philosophy Degree," *Journal of Higher Education* 33 (October 1962): 381–386.

11. Evelyn Schuyler Schaeffer, "Eugene Schuyler: A Memoir," in Eugene Schuyler, *Selected Essays, with a Memoir by Evelyn Schuyler Schaeffer* (New York: Charles Scribner's Sons, 1901), 17; Schuyler, "Count Leo Tolstoy Twenty Years Ago" (1889), in ibid., 207–209.

12. All quotations from Schuyler, "The Russian Peasant," *Hours at Home* 9 (May 1869): 14–22.

13. Schuyler, *Turkistan: Notes of a Journey in Russian Turkistan, Khokand, Bokhara, and Kuldja,* 2 vols. (New York: Scribner, Armstrong, and Co., 1877), 1:iii, 1:vi; James Seay Brown, Jr., "Eugene Schuyler, Observer of Russia: His Years as a Diplomat in Russia, 1867–1975" (Ph.D. diss., Vanderbilt University, 1971), 165.

14. Schuyler to State Department, 17 February 1873, in SDR, "Despatches from US Ministers to Russia, 1808–1906," no. 61. His sharpest criticisms appeared in Schuyler's Turkestan dispatch, published in Marshall Jewell to Hamilton Fish, 10 March 1874, *FRUS 1874,* 823–824; also Schuyler to Hamilton Fish, 21 December 1872, *FRUS 1873,* 766; Schuyler, *Turkistan,* 2:388.

15. Schuyler, *Turkistan,* 1:38, 1:147–148, 1:172, 1:271, 2:118; Schuyler, "On the

Steppe," *Hours at Home* 9 (August 1869): 327; Schuyler to Fish, 21 December 1872, *FRUS 1873,* 766.

16. Brown, "Eugene Schuyler," 38; Nicholas V. Riasanovsky, *The Image of Peter the Great in Russian History and Thought* (Oxford: Oxford University Press, 1985), 192–195; Norman E. Saul, *Concord and Conflict: The United States and Russia, 1867–1914* (Lawrence: University Press of Kansas, 1996), 122.

17. The first installment appeared in *Scribner's Monthly* 19 (January 1880): 545–564; subsequent pieces appeared more or less monthly for the next two years.

18. Schuyler, *Peter the Great, Emperor of Russia: A Study of Historical Biography,* 2 vols. (London: Sampson, Low, Marston, Searle, and Rivington, 1884), 1:26, 1:175, 1:186, 1:264, 1:329–330, 1:336; also Schuyler, *Turkistan,* 1:153.

19. J. B. A. (James B. Angell), book review, *AHR* 6 (July 1901): 839. An anonymous reviewer, however, wished that Schuyler had moved beyond his "journalistic" work—*Sewanee Review* 9 (July 1901): 372–374.

20. Schuyler, *Peter the Great,* 2:644.

21. See the exchange in the *New York Tribune*—27 July 1878 and 2 August 1878.

22. Travis, *George Kennan,* 25–26.

23. George Kennan, "Siberia: The Exiles' Abode," *Journal of the American Geographical of New York* 14 (1882): 48–58; Travis, *George Kennan,* 39–40.

24. George Kennan to Charles A. Dana, n.d. (1881?), George Kennan Papers (NYPL), box 1.

25. George Kennan, *Siberia and the Exile System,* 2 vols. (New York: Century, 1891), 1:iii, 1:iv, 1:3.

26. Ibid., 1:174, 1:186, 1:234; Kennan to Roswell Smith, 26 August 1885, in ibid., 1:350–351.

27. Ibid., 1:364–370, 2:144; Travis, *George Kennan,* 126; Michael Willrich, *City of Courts: Socializing Justice in Progressive Era Chicago* (Cambridge: Cambridge University Press, 2003), chap. 3.

28. William Dudley Foulke, *A Hoosier Autobiography* (Oxford: Oxford University Press, 1925), 85, 106, 94.

29. Foulke, *A Random Record of Travel during Fifty Years* (Oxford: Oxford University Press, 1925), 99.

30. Foulke, *Slav or Saxon: A Study of the Growth and Tendencies of Russian Civilization* (New York: G. P. Putnam's, 1887), 13, 14, 85.

31. Ibid., 13, 33, 14, 36.

32. For references to French historians, see ibid., iii, 28, 29.

33. Ibid., 72, 22.

34. Foulke, *Random Record,* 9, 99, 108; Foulke, *Slav or Saxon,* 62, 82–83.

35. Foulke, *Slav or Saxon,* 37, 134, 144, 61, 2–3. See also Foulke's 1887 letter to Kennan, cited in Aurele J. Violette, "William Dudley Foulke and Russia," *Indi-*

ana Magazine of History 82 (March 1986): 80. I am grateful to David S. Foglesong for bringing this article to my attention.

36. Brooks Adams, *America's Economic Supremacy* (1900; New York: Harper and Brothers, 1947), 177–179; Adams, *The New Empire* (New York: Macmillan, 1902), 181–182. Adams details the Asian origins of the Russian state in letters to his brother Henry, cited in Thornton Anderson, *Brooks Adams, Constructive Conservative* (Ithaca: Cornell University Press, 1951), 73–74.

37. Foulke, *Slav or Saxon,* 58–59.

38. Ibid., 144.

39. George Kennan to Foulke, 4 February 1888, and Stepniak to Foulke, 9 March 1888, both in William Dudley Foulke Papers, box 3; Anonymous book review, *North American Review* 146 (February 1888): 233–234.

40. On Chautauqua, see "Makers of Recent Russian Literature," *The Chautauquan* 35 (July 1902): 327.

41. Hapgood, "Tolstoi's 'Kreuzer Sonata,'" *Nation* 50 (17 April 1890): 313; Saul, *Concord and Conflict,* 326–327.

42. Hapgood, *A Survey of Russian Literature, with Selections* (New York: Chautauqua Press, 1902), 250.

43. Hapgood, *Russian Rambles* (Boston: Houghton Mifflin, 1894), xi, 64, 89, 159.

44. Ibid., 108–109.

45. John David Smith, *An Old Creed for the New South: Proslavery Ideology and Historiography, 1865–1918* (Westport, Conn.: Greenwood, 1985), chap. 2 (quoted p. 52).

46. Arcadius Kahan, "Natural Calamities and Their Effect upon the Food Supply in Russia," *Jahrbücher für Geschichte osteuropas* 16 (September 1968): 353–377.

47. T. M. Kitanina, *Khlebnaia torgovlia Rossii v 1875–1894 gg. (Ocherki pravitel'stvennoi politiki)* (Leningrad: Nauka, 1978), chap. 3.

48. P. Kh. Shvanebakh, *Denezhnoe preobrazovanie i narodnoe khoziaistvo* (St. Petersburg: D. V. Chichinadze, 1901), 21. On liberal economists and the famine, see James Young Simms, Jr., "The Impact of the Russian Famine of 1891–1892: A New Perspective" (Ph.D. diss., University of Michigan, 1976), 115–130.

49. S. G. Wheatcroft, "The 1891–92 Famine in Russia: Towards a More Detailed Analysis of Its Scale and Demographic Significance," in *Economy and Society in Russia and the Soviet Union, 1860–1930: Essays for Olga Crisp,* ed. Linda Edmondson and Peter Waldron (New York: St. Martin's, 1992).

50. Ibid., 60–61; Richard G. Robbins, Jr., *Famine in Russia, 1891–1892: The Imperial Government Responds to a Crisis* (New York: Columbia University Press, 1975), chap. 7.

51. One relief worker estimated the deliveries to Russia at $100,000 plus five

shiploads of flour—see John Hoyt Report, 25 December 1892, in V. I. Zhuraleva, "'Eto vopros ne politiki, eto vopros ekonomiki': dokumenty o pomoshchi amerikanskogo naroda vo vremia goloda v Rossii, 1891–1892 gg.," *Istoricheskii arkhiv*, no. 1 (1993): 207–208; John W. Hoyt, *Report of the Russian Relief Committee of the United States* (Washington: Rufus H. Darby, 1893), iii–iv. On the Imperial Committee's debate about foreign aid, see N. K. Girs to P. N. Durnovo, 19 December 1891, RGIA, f. 1204, op. 1, d. 548, ll. 1–1ob.

52. Paul Boyer, *Urban Masses and Moral Order in America, 1820–1920* (Cambridge, Mass.: Harvard University Press, 1978), 41.

53. Quoted in Glenn Altschuler, *Andrew D. White—Educator, Historian, Diplomat* (Ithaca: Cornell University Press, 1979), 32; White, *The Autobiography of Andrew Dickson White*, 2 vols. (New York: Century, 1896), 1:38.

54. See the essays in *Russia's Great Reforms, 1855–1881*, ed. Ben Eklof, John Bushnell, and Larissa Zakharova (Bloomington: Indiana University Press, 1994); P. A. Zaionchkovskii, *The Abolition of Serfdom in Russia*, ed. and trans. Susan Wobst (1954; Gulf Breeze, Fla.: Academic International Press, 1978); and Stephen G. Wheatcroft, "Crises and the Condition of the Peasantry in Late Imperial Russia," in *Peasant Economy, Culture, and Politics of European Russia, 1800–1921*, ed. Esther Kingston-Mann and Timothy Mixter (Princeton: Princeton University Press, 1991).

55. Andrew Dickson White, "The Development and Overthrow of the Russian Serf System," *Atlantic* 10 (November 1862): 539, 552, 548, 551; he sounds similar themes in his syllabus "The Greater States of Continental Europe" (1874), Andrew Dickson White Papers, box 198, p. 44.

56. Smith to Secretary of State James Blaine, 28 November 1891, SDR, "Despatches from U.S. Ministers to Russia," no. 130. Similar statements from diplomatic correspondence are cited in George S. Queen, "American Relief in the Russian Famine of 1891–1892," *Russian Review* 14 (January 1955): 140, 149.

57. W. Barnes Steveni, *Through Famine-Stricken Russia* (London: Low, 1892), 28–34.

58. Francis B. Reeves, *Russia Then and Now, 1892–1917: My Mission to Russia during the Famine of 1891–1892 with Data Bearing upon Russia of To-Day* (New York: Knickerbocker Press, 1917), 10.

59. William Edgar, "The Last of the Romanoffs," *Bellman* 22 (28 April 1917): 465.

60. "The Famine in Russia," *NYT*, 3 January 1892.

61. White to Secretary of State, 21 July 1894, cited in Altschuler, *Andrew D. White*, 198–199; White, *Autobiography*, 2:30, 2:54.

62. Murat Halstead, "Politics of the Russian Famine," *The Cosmopolitan* 13 (May 1892): 82.

63. Reeves, *Russia, Then and Now,* 99. This argument is consistent with Queen, "American Relief."

64. *Northwestern Miller,* 18 December 1891, quoted in W. C. Edgar, *The Russian Famine of 1891 and 1892* (Minneapolis: Millers and Manufacturers Insurance Co., 1893), 7.

65. Serge Stepniak, "The Impending Famine," *Free Russia* 2 (August 1891): 1.

66. W. T. Stead, "The Czar and Russia of Today," *Review of Reviews* (New York) 4 (January 1892): 670.

67. Isabel Hapgood, "A Journey on the Volga," *Atlantic Monthly* 69 (February 1892): 234.

68. Charles Emory Smith, "The Famine in Russia," *North American Review* 154 (May 1892): 551.

69. Edgar, *Russian Famine,* 47–48; Edgar, "Russia's Land System: The Cause of the Famine," *Forum* 13 (July 1892): 579. While this article in its title seems to blame the famine on communal land tenure (which "will not bear the test of practical experience"), it has a longer and more detailed discussion about peasant character (especially its flaws) as an obstacle to change.

70. Barton circular, 29 January 1892, in AVPR f. 170, op. 512/1, d. 737, ll. 130–131.

71. Thomas Stevens, "Russia's Famine: The Moujik's Evil Genius," *Frank Leslie's Weekly* 74 (21 April 1892): 198–199.

72. Wurts to Secretary of State James Blaine, 16 May 1892, *FRUS 1892,* 384; Wurts to Wharton, 7 August 1890, SDR, "Despatches from U.S. Ministers to Russia," no. 27; Allan Spetter, "The United States, the Russian Jews, and the Russian Famine of 1891–1892," *American Jewish Historical Quarterly* 64 (December 1974): 237–238.

73. Edgar, *Russian Famine,* 42–44; Edgar, "Russia's Land System," 579–581; W. C. Edgar, "Russia's Conflict with Hunger," *Review of Reviews* (New York) 5 (July 1892): 698; William Harbutt Dawson, book review, *Annals* 5 (July 1894): 118–120. On structural similarities between the emancipations of the 1860s, see Peter Kolchin, "Some Thoughts on Emancipation in Comparative Perspective: Russia and the U.S. South," *Slavery and Abolition* 14 (December 1990): 351–367.

74. Lille B. Chace Wyman, "Peasant Life in Russia," *The Chautauquan* 15 (April 1892): 61.

75. Vicomte Combes de Lastrade, "The Present Conditions of Peasants in the Russian Empire," *Annals* 2 (April 1892): 225–226; Edgar, "Russia's Land System," 576, 581.

76. Smith, "Famine in Russia," 542.

77. "George Kennan upon the Russian Situation," *Free Russia* 2 (February 1892): 7. Predictably enough, Kennan blamed the Russian government for peasants' dire straits.

78. "What Is to Be Done?" [editorial], *Free Russia* 2 (December 1891): 5; "The Famine in Russia" [editorial], *Review of Reviews* 4 (October 1891): 378.

79. "The Precautions against Famine in Russia and India" [editorial], *Nation* 53 (20 August 1891): 137–138.

80. Edgar, *Russian Famine*, 6, 4; Edgar quoted in Shannon Lee Smith, "The Politics of Progress and the American-Russian Relationship, 1867–1917" (Ph.D. diss., Cornell University, 1994), 131; "Russia's Scourge" [editorial], *Review of Reviews* (New York) 5 (February 1892): 1.

81. On American Populists, see Lawrence Goodwyn, *Democratic Promise: The Populist Moment in America* (Oxford: Oxford University Press, 1976); on Russian Populists, see especially Richard Wortman, *The Crisis of Russian Populism* (Cambridge: Cambridge University Press, 1967). For comparative material, see Paul Taggart, *Populism* (Buckingham: Open University Press, 2000), chaps. 3–4; and Norman Pollock, *The Populist Response to Industrial America: Midwestern Populist Thought* (Cambridge, Mass.: Harvard University Press, 1962), chap. 5.

82. Isaac A. Hourwich, *The Economics of the Russian Village* (New York: Columbia University Faculty of Political Science, 1892). For Lenin's use of this book, see "Ot izdatel'stva," in I. A. Gurvich, *Ekonomicheskoe polozhenie russkoi derevni* (Moscow: Gospolizdat, 1941), 4–6; Lenin, *The Development of Capitalism in Russia* (1899; Moscow: Progress, 1956), 185–186; Jesse J. Dossick, *Doctoral Research on Russia and the Soviet Union* (New York: Columbia University Press, 1960).

83. Some biographical details come from Melech Epstein, *Profiles of Eleven* (Detroit: Wayne State University Press, 1965), chap. 8; Kennan, *Siberia*, 2:449.

84. Hourwich, *Economics*, 164n; Engels, "Socialism in Germany" (1892), *MECW* 27:247; also Engels to Danielson, 15 March 1892, *MECW* 47:383–384.

85. Isaac A. Hourwich, "The Crisis of Russian Agriculture," *Yale Review* 1 (February 1893): 432–433.

86. This is a theme in most of Hourwich's articles for *Progress;* see, for instance, I. G. (Hourwich), "Krest'ianskii vopros v politseiskom gosudarstve," *Progress* (New York) 11 (19 February 1892); I. G. (Hourwich), "Golod v Rossii," *Progress* (New York) 3 (20 December 1891).

87. Mary Kingsbury Simkhovitch, *Neighborhood: My Story of Greenwich House* (New York: W. W. Norton, 1938), 50–51, 87; Daniel T. Rodgers, *Atlantic Crossings: Social Politics in a Progressive Age* (Cambridge, Mass.: Harvard University Press, 1998), 85–86.

88. Simkhovitch, *Marxism versus Socialism* (New York: Henry Holt, 1913).

89. Wladimir Gr. Simkhowitsch, *Die Feldgemeinschaft in Russland: Eine Beitrag zur Sozialgeschichte und zur Kenntnis der gegenwärtigen wirtschaftlichen Lage des russischen Bauernstandes* (Jena: Verlag von Gustav Fischer, 1898), 12; Simkhovitch, book review, *PSQ* 18 (December 1903): 703; Simkhovitch, "Re-

cent Works on Russian Economic Conditions," *Yale Review* 8 (February 1900): 384; Simkhovitch, "Hay and History," *PSQ* 28 (September 1913): 398.

90. Simkhowitsch, "Die sozial-ökonomischen Lehren der russischen Narodniki," *Jahrbücher für Nationalökonomie und Statistik* 3. Folge, 14. Band (August 1897): 678.

91. Simkhovitch, "Recent Works," 384.

92. Hourwich, book review, *PSQ* 14 (September 1899): 541–544; Simkhovitch to Hourwich, 24 November 1897, in Isaac A. Hourwich Papers, folder 113.

93. Hourwich, "The Russian-American Extradition Treaty," *Yale Review* 3 (May 1894): 87, 94; Hourwich, "The Russian Judiciary," *PSQ* 7 (December 1892): 673.

3. Studying Our Nearest Oriental Neighbor

1. N. Tourgeneff, "Economic Results of the Emancipation of Serfs in Russia" [letter], *JSS* 1 (June 1869): 141–149.

2. His student Robert Kerner called Coolidge the founder of Russian studies, while the Provisional Government's ambassador in Washington, Boris Bakhmeteff, called Coolidge the dean of the field. Kerner quoted in Harper to Cyrus McCormick, 14 May 1917, in Cyrus McCormick Papers, box 117; Bakhmeteff to Coolidge, 9 January 1925, Archibald Cary Coolidge Papers, series HUG 1299.5, box 1.

3. Peter Novick, *That Noble Dream: The "Objectivity Question" and the American Historical Profession* (Cambridge: Cambridge University Press, 1988), chap. 2; Dorothy Ross, *The Origins of American Social Science* (Cambridge: Cambridge University Press, 1991), chap. 3.

4. Isabel Hapgood, "A Russian Professorship," *Nation* 54 (16 June 1892): 447; also Norman E. Saul, *Concord and Conflict: The United States and Russia, 1867–1914* (Lawrence: University of Kansas Press, 1996), 392–395.

5. Letters from Nathan Haskell Dole and L. S. Wiener, "The Russian Professorship," *Nation* 54 (30 June 1892): 484–485.

6. Hapgood, "The Russian Professorship," *Nation* 55 (14 July 1892): 29.

7. Robert F. Byrnes, *Awakening American Education to the World: The Role of Archibald Cary Coolidge, 1866–1928* (Notre Dame, Ind.: University of Notre Dame Press, 1982), 51.

8. Minister Andrew Dickson White also hoped to hire Coolidge to replace Wurts. See White to John Foster, 24 August 1892, SDR, "Despatches from U.S. Ministers to Russia," no. 230; Coolidge to father, 11 April 1891, in Harold Jefferson Coolidge and Robert Howard Lord, *Archibald Cary Coolidge: His Life and Letters* (Boston: Houghton Mifflin, 1932), 30 (hereafter cited as *Life and Letters*).

9. Byrnes, *Awakening American Education,* 52–53; *Life and Letters,* 20–38 (quoted in Coolidge to his father, 18 March 1891, p. 26); Coolidge, *Theoretical and Foreign Elements in the Formation of the American Constitution* (Freiburg: Universitäts-Buchdrukerei von Chr. Legmann, 1892).

10. Coolidge to Charles R. Crane, 8 March 1893 and 18 June 1893, both in Charles R. Crane Papers, reel 2; Byrnes, *Awakening American Education,* 26.

11. Ephraim Emerton and Samuel Eliot Morison, "History, 1838–1929," in *The Development of Harvard University since the Inauguration of President Eliot, 1869–1929,* ed. Samuel Eliot Morison (Cambridge, Mass.: Harvard University Press, 1930), 166; Coolidge, "A Plea for the Study of the History of Northern Europe," *AHR* 2 (October 1896): 34–39; lecture notes for History 19, Coolidge Papers, series HUG 1299.10, box 2. Coolidge's article and syllabus run counter to the claim that the division of northern/southern Europe was supplanted by an east/west line in the eighteenth century—see Larry Wolff, *Inventing Eastern Europe: The Map of Civilization on the Mind of the Enlightenment* (Stanford: Stanford University Press, 1994), esp. 4–5.

12. Robert F. Byrnes, "Russian Studies in the United States before World War I," in *A History of Russian and East European Studies in the United States: Selected Essays* (Lanham, Md.: University Press of America, 1994), 8. On the German model, see Anton Palme, "The Progress of Russian Studies in German," *RR* 3 (February 1914): 131–136.

13. Dole, "A Plea for the Study of Russian," *Harvard Graduates' Magazine* 3 (December 1894): 180–181.

14. Norbert Wiener, *Ex-Prodigy: My Childhood and Youth* (New York: Simon and Schuster, 1953), 29, 123; Albert Parry, *America Learns Russian: A History of the Teaching of the Russian Language in the United States* (Syracuse: Syracuse University Press, 1967), 51.

15. Leo Wiener, *An Interpretation of the Russian People* (New York: McBride, Nast, 1915), 1–3, 12, 37; his list of traits is similar to that of the British journalist E. J. Dillon in E. B. Lanin [pseud.], *Russian Characteristics* (London: Chapman and Hall, 1892).

16. Leo Wiener, *Anthology of Russian Literature from the Earliest Period to the Present Time,* 2 vols. (New York: G. P. Putnam's Sons, 1902); *The Complete Works of Count Tolstoy,* trans. and ed. Leo Wiener, 24 vols. (Boston: D. Estes and Company, 1902–1904); Norbert Wiener, *I Am a Mathematician: The Later Life of a Prodigy* (Garden City, N.Y.: Doubleday, 1956), 20; Norbert Wiener, *Ex-Prodigy,* 235.

17. These achievements are recorded in Robert F. Byrnes's useful biography, *Awakening American Education.* Pushkin cited in Roderick Thaler, introduction to A. N. Radishchev, *Journey from St. Petersburg to Moscow,* trans. Leo Wiener (Cambridge, Mass.: Harvard University Press, 1958), 35.

18. *Life and Letters,* 139; Byrnes, *Awakening American Education,* 26–27.

19. John Higham, *History: Professional Scholarship in America* (1965; Baltimore: Johns Hopkins University Press, 1989), 6–25; Emerton and Morison, "History," 159.

20. Coolidge, *Origins of the Triple Alliance* (New York: Charles Scribner's Sons, 1917).

21. Coolidge, article dated 5 May [late 1890s?] *[New York?] Evening Post,* Scrapbook, Coolidge Papers, series HUG 1299.17.

22. Anatole Leroy-Beaulieu, preface to Coolidge, *Les Etat-Unis, Puissance Mondiale,* trans. Robert L. Cru (Paris: Librairie Armand Colin, 1908), v.

23. Coolidge, *The United States as a World Power* (New York: Macmillan, 1909), 216, 219.

24. Coolidge, "The Expansion of Russia," Coolidge Papers, series HUG 1299.15, box 1, chap. 2, p. 26; chap. 3, p. 1. (Subsequent citations will be in the form "Expansion of Russia," chapter: page.)

25. Ibid., 8:35, 8:34, 8:39–40.

26. Coolidge to father, 11 April 1891, *Life and Letters,* 31.

27. Coolidge, "Expansion of Russia," chaps. 11–14; Coolidge, "The Expansion of Russia in the Nineteenth Century," *The Nineteenth Century: A Review of Progress,* ed. A. G. Sedgwick (London: G. P. Putnam's Sons, 1901), 63, 64, 70.

28. Coolidge, "Expansion of Russia," 1:1–2, 1:23–25; Coolidge to brother Julian, 6 September 1890, *Life and Letters,* 21–22.

29. Coolidge, "Expansion of Russia," 3:14–15, 12:37; Coolidge, "Nationality and the New Europe" (1915), in *Ten Years of War and Peace* (Cambridge, Mass.: Harvard University Press, 1927), 223–224.

30. Coolidge, "Expansion of Russia," 1:3; also Coolidge, "Russia and the Present War," lecture to the Commercial Club and Algonquian Club, 4 March 1904, Coolidge Papers, series HUG 1299.10, box 1.

31. Jonathan Haslam, *No Virtue Like Necessity: Realist Thought in International Relations since Machiavelli* (New Haven: Yale University Press, 2002); Joel H. Rosenthal, *Righteous Realists: Political Realism, Responsible Power, and American Culture in the Nuclear Age* (Baton Rouge: Louisiana State University Press, 1991); E. H. Carr, *The Twenty Years' Crisis, 1919–1939: An Introduction to the Study of International Relations* (London: Macmillan, 1940).

32. See the list in *Life and Letters,* 139 n. 1; Byrnes, *Awakening American Education,* 263–264.

33. Robert A. MacCaughey, *International Studies and Academic Enterprise: A Chapter in the Enclosure of American Learning* (New York: Columbia University Press, 1984), 80.

34. Byrnes, *Awakening American Education,* 161–162, 263–264; Emerton and Morison, "History," 166n; Bruce Hopper, class of 1918 fiftieth anniversary report, in Hamilton Fish Armstrong Papers, box 35. Only two of Coolidge's

students, Henry Shipman and Frank Golder, focused primarily on Russia—see Terence Emmons, "Russia Then and Now in the Pages of the *American Historical Review* and Elsewhere," *AHR* 100 (October 1995): 1139–1140.

35. Melech Epstein asserts a political motive, though his inaccuracy with dates hardly invites confidence; see his *Profiles of Eleven: Biographical Sketches of Eleven Men Who Guided the Destiny of an Immigrant Jewish Society* (Detroit: Wayne State University Press, 1965), 258. On Hourwich's appointment, see University of Chicago Board of Trustees Minutes, vol. 1, pp. 102, 191, 248, 302. On a possible turf war, see the letters from J. Laurence Laughlin, the chair of Political Economy, to William Rainey Harper, 5 January 1894 and 22 December 1894, both in University of Chicago Presidents' Papers, box 17, folder 14. On the Bemis case in 1895, see Mary O. Furner, *Advocacy and Objectivity: A Crisis in the Professionalization of American Social Science, 1865–1905* (Lexington: University of Kentucky Press, 1975), chap. 8.

36. Crane Memoirs, ed. Walter S. Rogers, Crane Papers, reel 3, p. 18 (hereafter cited by title and page number).

37. Leo J. Brocage, "The Public Career of Charles R. Crane" (Ph.D. diss., Fordham University, 1962), 7–8; Saul, *Concord and Conflict*, 392.

38. Archibald Cary Coolidge to Crane, 18 June 1893, Crane Papers, reel 2; George Harris (Knickerbocker Press) to Andrew Dickson White, 23 March 1894, Andrew Dickson White Papers, reel 61; Coolidge to Charles Crane, 7 April 1896, Crane Papers, reel 2.

39. Crane Memoirs, 54, 63, 64, 74; Saul, *Concord and Conflict*, 462.

40. Albert Parry, "Charles R. Crane, Friend of Russia," *Russian Review* 6 (Spring 1947): 28.

41. Parry, "Charles R. Crane," 28; Crane quoted in John Charles Chalberg, "Samuel Harper and Russia under Tsars and Soviets, 1905–1943" (Ph.D. diss., University of Minnesota, 1974), 288 n. 39.

42. See the correspondence in Crane-Lillie Family Papers, box 2, folder 9.

43. Sir Bernard Pares, foreword to *The Russia I Believe in: The Memoirs of Samuel Harper, 1902–1941*, ed. Paul V. Harper (Chicago: University of Chicago Press, 1945), viii.

44. Parry, *America Learns Russian*, 58; Parry's information on Harper apparently came primarily through personal conversations.

45. A copy of the official program syllabus is in Samuel Northrop Harper Papers, box 1, folder 2.

46. "Uel Harper to Write History," undated clipping (1906?) and penciled agreement for Crane's funding position in Russian language—both in Harper Papers, box 1, folder 8.

47. Harper to Gertrude, 30 April 1903, Harper Papers, box 1.

48. See, for instance, Albion Small to Edward Alsworth Ross, 28 April 1917, Edward Alsworth Ross Papers, box 9, folder 2.

49. Parry, *America Learns Russian*, 82–84, 94.

50. Pares to Harper, 14 March 1910 and 18 March 1910, both in Harper Papers, box 1; Harper, *Russia I Believe in*, 67–81.

51. Harper, *Russia I Believe in*, 61–66; D. P. Keppel to Harper, 20 April 1909, Harper Papers, box 1; Harper to Crane, 13 October 1909, Crane Papers, reel 2.

52. Reference letter from Charles Beard, 23 November 1910, Harper Papers, box 1.

53. See Harper's lectures on Russia given in 1906 and 1907, in Harper Papers, box 32, folders 20–22; Harper, *Russia I Believe in*, 12.

54. In untitled lectures from 1907, 1910, and 1915—see Harper Papers, box 31, folders 8, 23, and 45. On pessimism, see Harper to Crane, 23 May 1906, in Harper Papers, box 1; Harper, "Exceptional Measures in Russia," *RR* 1 (November 1912): 103.

55. All quotations in this paragraph come from the untitled lecture in Harper Papers, box 32, folder 22.

4. Little above the Brute

1. Samuel N. Harper, *The Russia I Believe in: The Memoirs of Samuel N. Harper, 1902–1941*, ed. Paul V. Harper (Chicago: University of Chicago Press, 1945), 27.

2. This background is culled primarily from Abraham Ascher, *The Revolution of 1905*, 2 vols. (Stanford: Stanford University Press, 1988–1992); and Andrew M. Verner, *The Crisis of Russian Autocracy: Nicholas II and the 1905 Revolution* (Princeton: Princeton University Press, 1990).

3. George von Lengerke Meyer Diaries, 14 May and 15 July 1906. On Roosevelt, see Arthur W. Thompson and Robert A. Hart, *The Uncertain Crusade: America and the Russian Revolution of 1905* (Amherst: University of Massachusetts Press, 1970), 54–63.

4. See especially the rewritten conclusion of Miliukov's Chicago lectures, originally given in 1903—Paul Miliukov, *Russia and Its Crisis* (Chicago: University of Chicago Press, 1906).

5. Norman E. Saul, *Concord and Conflict: The United States and Russia, 1867–1914* (Lawrence: University Press of Kansas, 1996), 490–491, 564–566.

6. Hapgood, "The Russian Peasant," *Craftsman* 9 (February 1906): 647–648, 661.

7. Hapgood, "Sergei Iulitch Witte: Russia's Man of the Hour," *Craftsman* 9 (November 1905): 162.

8. Rambaud, "What Is Passing in Russia," *The Independent* 58 (23 March 1905): 663.

9. White, "The Situation and Prospect in Russia," *Collier's Weekly* 34 (11 February 1905): 8–9.

10. "A Day with Andrew D. White at His Home in Ithaca," *Craftsman* 8 (September 1905): 733–734.

11. White, "Prospects of Freedom in Russia," lecture given 11 January 1906, Andrew Dickson White Papers, reel 147, pp. 3, 8–9.

12. Meyer wrote one friend that he thought White "a much-overestimated man and without much tact"—letter to Judge Francis C. Lowell, 19 February 1906, in M. A. DeWolfe Howe, *George von Lengerke Meyer: His Life and Public Services* (New York: Dodd, Mead, 1920), 258.

13. On Coolidge connections, see Robert F. Byrnes, *Awakening American Education to the World: The Role of Archibald Cary Coolidge, 1866–1928* (Notre Dame, Ind.: University of Notre Dame Press, 1982), 129; Wayne A. Wiegand, *Patrician in a Progressive Era: A Biography of George von Lengerke Meyer* (New York: Garland, 1988), 6.

14. Meyer to Henry Cabot Lodge, 9 July 1906, quoted in Wiegand, *Patrician,* 114.

15. Meyer Diary, 15 July 1906.

16. Ibid., 15 July 1906 and 30 May 1905.

17. Quoted in Frederick F. Travis, *George Kennan and the American-Russian Relationship, 1865–1924* (Athens: Ohio University Press, 1990), 178.

18. George Kennan, "Cuban Character," *Outlook* 63 (23 December 1899): 962; Kennan, "Cuban Character, II," *Outlook* 63 (30 December 1899): 1016; Kennan, "The Korean People: The Product of a Decayed Civilization," *Outlook* 81 (21 January 1905): 411, 413.

19. George Kennan, "Which Is the Civilized Power?" *Outlook* 78 (29 October 1904): 519, 515.

20. Kennan to Roosevelt, 1 April 1905, in George Kennan Papers (LC), box 5.

21. The characterizations of Russian nature appear relatively constant throughout this part of Kennan's career, as revealed in correspondence: Kennan to Drake, 2 June 1885, Kennan Papers (LC), box 6; Kennan to Mrs. Jackson, 20 February 1905, Kennan Papers (LC), box 7; and Kennan to Lyman Abbott, 8 May 1914, Kennan Papers (LC), box 8. See also Kennan, "A Russian Experiment in Self-Government," *Atlantic Monthly* 80 (October 1897): 496. Subject files on Russian character—which include Kennan's notations—are in Kennan Papers (LC), box 95—quoted from items dated 6 May 1911, 2 March 1901, and 27 November 1893. These files also contain Kennan's notes on Leroy-Beaulieu.

22. Kennan, "Which Is the Civilized Power?" 520.

23. Harper, *Russia I Believe in,* 27, 44. On other embassy meetings, see Harper to Dear People, 5/19 January 1905, Samuel Northrup Harper Papers, box 1; Meyer Diary, 21 April 1906.

24. Harper to C. S. Eaton, 24 July 1906, Harper Papers, box 1.

25. Harper, "Russia's Second Douma," *World To-Day* 13 (July 1907): 696.

26. Samuel N. Harper, *The New Electoral Law for the Russian Duma* (Chicago: University of Chicago Press, 1908).

27. Harper, "Budget Rights of the Second Duma," *JPE* 16 (March 1908): 156; Harper, "Russia's Persecution of the Duma," *World's Work* 15 (January 1908): 9802.

28. Harper, review of *Le Parlement Russe,* by Pierre Chasles and Anatole Leroy-Beaulieu, *PSQ* 25 (March 1910): 163; Dorothy Ross, "Historical Consciousness in Nineteenth-Century America," *AHR* 89 (October 1984): 919–926.

29. Samuel N. Harper, "The Present Situation in Russia," *World To-Day* 13 (November 1907): 1116.

30. Thompson and Hart, *Uncertain Crusade,* 37.

31. Walling to his parents, 29 January 1906, cited in Jack Meyer Stuart, "William English Walling: A Study in Politics and Ideas" (Unpublished Ph.D. diss., Columbia University, 1968), 36.

32. N. I. Stone in *William English Walling: A Symposium* (New York: Stackpole Sons, 1938), 61, 64–65; also Strunsky Walling's contribution—pp. 7–8, 10–11. Subsequent citations will appear as *Symposium,* page number (author). James Boylan, *Revolutionary Lives: Anna Strunsky and William English Walling* (Amherst: University of Massachusetts Press, 1998), chap. 22.

33. James Gilbert, *Designing the Industrial State: The Intellectual Pursuit of Collectivism in America, 1880–1940* (Chicago: Quadrangle Books, 1972), 209.

34. Walling, *Russia's Message: The True Import of the Revolution* (New York: Doubleday and Page, 1908), 329, 163, 260.

35. Ibid., 152.

36. Ibid., 3. See also Walling, *Progressivism—And After* (New York: Macmillan, 1914), 276–277.

37. Reviews (all anonymous) include *Independent* 65 (10 September 1908): 611; "Russia in Revolution," *NYT Saturday Review of Books,* 25 July 1908; *Outlook* 89 (1 August 1908): 765; *Nation* 87 (8 August 1908): 121.

38. Walling, *Russia's Message,* 145–148, 210, 154, 152; Walling, "Will the Peasants Act?" *Independent* 61 (6 December 1906): 1317–1318.

39. Walling, *Socialism As It Is: A Survey of the World-Wide Revolutionary Movement* (New York: Macmillan, 1912), 390; Walling, *Russia's Message,* xii.

40. *Symposium,* 35 (Howard Brubaker); Albert Edwards [Bullard], "The Russian Revolution," *International Socialist Review* 8 (October 1907): 196–198; Walling to father, 11/24 February 1906, William English Walling Papers, box 1.

41. Ernest Poole, *The Bridge: My Story* (New York: Macmillan, 1940), 85, 103, 113, 124; Truman Frederick Keefer, *Ernest Poole* (New York: Twayne Publishers, 1966), 33–34; *Symposium,* 27–28 (Poole).

42. See, for instance, Poole, "St. Petersburg Is Quiet," *Outlook* 79 (18 March 1905): 680–690; Poole, "The Night That Made Me a Revolutionary," *Everybody's Magazine* 13 (November 1905): 635–640.
43. Poole, "The Russian Bastille," *Saturday Evening Post* 178 (12 May 1906): 7; Poole, "'Peasant Cattle': What the Cossacks Think of the Peasants," *Everybody's Magazine* 13 (October 1905): 497.
44. Poole, *Bridge*, 311.
45. Melech Epstein, *Profiles of Eleven: Profiles of Eleven Men Who Guided the Destiny of an Immigrant Society and Stimulated Social Consciousness among the American People* (Detroit: Wayne State University Press, 1965), 259–260.
46. Hourwich, "Russia as Seen in Its Farmers," *World's Work* 13 (December 1906): 8681.
47. Simkhovitch, "The Russian Peasant and the Autocracy," *PSQ* 21 (December 1906): 570–571, 595.
48. Simkhovitch, "Russian Autocracy: An Interpretation," in *The Case of Russia: A Composite View* (New York: Fox, Duffield, 1905), 274.
49. The authors of *The Case of Russia* included Alfred Rambaud, J. Novicow, Peter Roberts, Hourwich, and Simkhovitch. All but Rambaud's essay appeared first in *International Monthly* or its successor *International Quarterly*.
50. See, for instance, Harper to John R. Mott, 1 May 1917, Harper Papers, box 4.

5. Sheep without a Shepherd

1. Crane to Wilson, 1 August 1918, *PWW*, 49:154.
2. This chapter cannot go into the same level of detail about the American-Russian relations that the best histories do. Recent works on the topic include Norman E. Saul, *War and Revolution: The United States and Russia, 1914–1921* (Lawrence: University of Kansas Press, 2001); David S. Foglesong, *America's Secret War against Bolshevism: U.S. Intervention in the Russian Civil War, 1917–1920* (Chapel Hill: University of North Carolina Press, 1995); and David W. McFadden, *Alternative Paths: Soviets and Americans, 1917–1920* (Oxford: Oxford University Press, 1993). Still of lasting value is George F. Kennan, *Soviet-American Relations, 1917–1920*, 2 vols. (Princeton: Princeton University Press, 1956–1958). On American intellectuals' ideas about revolutionary Russia, see especially Christopher Lasch, *American Liberals and the Russian Revolution* (New York: Columbia University Press, 1962).
3. Crane to Wilson, 18 May 1914, *PWW*, 30:46.
4. Kennan, *Soviet-American Relations*, 2:331.
5. Leonid I. Strakhovsky, *American Opinion about Soviet Russia, 1917–1920* (Toronto: University of Toronto Press, 1961), 22.
6. Inquiry scholars freely admitted their lack of area knowledge: see Preston W.

Slosson, "Historical Note on the Russian Cessions in Asia Demanded by Germany" (8 March 1918), Inquiry Papers (Yale), series III, box 20, folder 296, p. 1; Frank Golder, "The Don Province" (2 April 1918), in American Peace Commission to Versailles Papers, box 29, p. 51; Lawrence E. Gelfand, *The Inquiry: American Preparations for Peace, 1917–1919* (New Haven: Yale University Press, 1963), 54–57.

7. Kennan, "The Victory of the Russian People," *Outlook* 115 (28 March 1917): 546–547; *The Cabinet Diaries of Josephus Daniels, 1913–1921,* ed. E. David Cronon (Lincoln: University of Nebraska Press, 1963), 119–120.

8. Harper, "The Present Situation in Russia," *World To-Day* 13 (November 1907): 1116; other examples in Peter G. Filene, *Americans and the Soviet Experiment, 1917–1933* (Cambridge, Mass.: Harvard University Press, 1966), 15. Because the Russian calendar ran thirteen days behind the western one, what the Russians called the February Revolution happened, by western datebooks, in March 1917; similarly, the Great October Socialist Revolution occurred on November 7.

9. Wilson, Address to Joint Session of Congress, 2 April 1917, *PWW,* 41:524; Harper to Richard Crane, 4 April 1917, Samuel Northrup Harper Papers, box 3.

10. The final roster was Crane, Root, John Mott (YMCA), Cyrus McCormick (International Harvester), James Duncan (AFL), General Hugh Scott, and the banker Samuel Bertron. See the correspondence in *PWW,* vol. 42; also Harper to Roger Williams, April 1917, Harper Papers, box 3; Kennan, *Soviet-American Relations,* 1:20, 2:331.

11. Wilson to Provisional Government, 22 May 1917, *PWW,* 43:365–367; on Golder, see *WRP,* 70 n. 73; Root address, 15 June 1917, *Russian-American Relations, March 1917-March 1920,* ed. C. K. Cumming and Walter W. Pettit (New York: Harcourt, Brace and Howe, 1920), 28–31.

12. Root to Lansing, 17 June 1917, *FRUS 1918,* 1:120–122. On lobbying see, for instance, Mott to Lansing, 22 August 1917, *PWW,* 44:66–69; Crane to Wilson, 23 July 1917, and Mott to Wilson, 24 July 1917, both in *PWW,* 49:62–63, 77–79; Saul, *War and Revolution,* 132–133.

13. Root statement on the work of the Mission, 10 July 1917, *Russian-American Relations,* 32.

14. Report of the Special Diplomatic Mission, August 1917, in *FRUS 1918,* 1:143; *PWW,* 43:416 n. 1.

15. Russell to Wilson, 7 November 1917; Wilson to Creel, 10 November 1917; Wilson to Russell, 10 November 1917, all in *PWW,* 44:557–558.

16. Charles Crane to Richard Crane, 21 July 1917, Richard T. Crane Papers, series II, box 1, folder 5; Harper notes, July-August 1917, in Samuel N. Harper, *The Russia I Believe in: The Memoirs of Samuel N. Harper, 1902–41,* ed. Paul V. Harper (Chicago: University of Chicago Press, 1945), 102; Harper to Richard

Crane, 5 September 1917, Richard Crane Papers, series II, box 1, folder 13; John Charles Chalberg, "Samuel Harper and Russia under Tsars and Soviets, 1905–1945" (Ph.D. diss., University of Minnesota, 1975), 163.

17. Wilson to Lansing, 14 August 1917, *PWW*, 43:460 n. 1.

18. The Russian word *sovet* means "council"; the first such organs sprung up during the 1905 revolution. I use the term "Soviet" (with initial capital) to mean central elements of the Bolshevik system, especially the Petrograd Soviet from which the leadership emerged. Without initial capitalization, soviets refer to councils, a form of local government after 1917.

19. John Reed, *Ten Days That Shook the World* (New York: Boni and Liveright, 1919); Robert A. Rosenstone, *Romantic Revolutionary: A Biography of John Reed* (Cambridge, Mass.: Harvard University Press, 1975); Christine Stansell, *American Moderns: Bohemian New York and the Creation of a New Century* (New York: Metropolitan Books, 2000), 318–323; Lasch, *American Liberals*. On the Socialist Party, see James Weinstein, *The Decline of American Socialism, 1900–1925* (New York: Monthly Review Press, 1967); Theodore Draper, *American Communism and Soviet Russia: The Formative Period* (New York: Viking, 1960).

20. See, for instance, W. C. Huntington, "The Russian Tragedy," *Annals* 84 (July 1919): 95. Lasch, *American Liberals*, 57, cites the correction by the St. Louis *Post-Dispatch* that Bolshevik meant "most demandful" and certainly not "majority," as one impudent reader had claimed.

21. Robins, Union Club Speech, March 1919, Raymond Robins Papers, box 43, folder 3, p. 8; others writing along these lines include Lincoln Colcord and Albert Rhys Williams. This tendency is exaggerated in the historical literature; see Lasch, *American Liberals*, 3, 135; David Brion Davis, *Revolutions: Reflections on American Equality and Foreign Liberations* (Cambridge, Mass.: Harvard University Press, 1990), 82–83. But Lasch's claims that Harper, Walling, and Ross made such statements are not substantiated; see Harper, "The Bolsheviks and the Land Question" (December 1919), Harper Papers, box 63, folder 3, p. 17; Walling, *Sovietism: The A B C of Russian Bolshevism—According to the Bolsheviks* (New York: E. P. Dutton, 1920), 6–7; Ross, "Russian Character in Transition," *Asia* 18 (September 1918): 762–764. For close analyses of the connections, see Dorothy Atkinson, *The End of the Russian Land Commune, 1915–1930* (Stanford: Stanford University Press, 1985), 196–205.

22. Harper to William Phillips, 14 December 1917, Harper Papers, box 4; [Harper,] "Russian Delay Explained," *CSM*, 15 December 1917; this uncredited article appears in a file of Harper's articles in the *CSM* archives.

23. Michael Kazin, *The Populist Persuasion: An American History* (1995; Ithaca: Cornell University Press, 1998), 34–37.

24. Golder to J. Franklin Jameson, 23 March 1917, *WRP*, 53–54.

25. Francis to Richard Crane, 29 August 1918, Harper Papers, box 5.

26. Jerome Landfield, quoted in Foglesong, *America's Secret War*, 177; Saul, *War and Revolution*, 346–347.

27. J. Butler Wright to Harper, 20 June 1918, Harper Papers, box 5.

28. Crane to Wilson, 1 August 1918, *PWW*, 49:154; Kennan to Lansing, 26 May 1918, *PWW*, 48:184; Crane to Wilson, 21 June 1917, *PWW*, 43:13–14; John Caldwell to Lansing, December 1917, SDDF, 861.77/281; Lloyd C. Gardner, *Safe for Democracy: The Anglo-American Response to Revolution, 1913–1923* (Oxford: Oxford University Press, 1984); Michael H. Hunt, *Ideology and U.S. Foreign Policy* (New Haven: Yale University Press, 1987), chap. 4.

29. A. Bullard, "Memo on the Bolshevik Movement in Russia" (January 1918), Edward M. House Papers, series III, folder 1/131, p. 3.

30. Ibid., 4, 7.

31. "Address by George Kennan," *Art World* 2 (June 1917): 258. Kennan had railed against American strikes in 1877 and 1919—see Frederick F. Travis, *George Kennan and the American-Russian Relationship, 1865–1924* (Athens: Ohio University Press, 1990), 298–299; and Kennan to Townsend, 5 October 1919, George Kennan Papers (LC), box 8.

32. *War Memoirs of Robert Lansing, Secretary of State* (Indianapolis: Bobbs-Merrill, 1935), 340–341; Lansing to Kennan, 3 January 1918, Robert Lansing Papers, vol. 33.

33. E. A. Ross, *Social Control: A Survey of the Foundations of Order* (New York: Macmillan, 1901); E. A. Ross, *The Old World in the New: The Significance of Past and Present Immigration to the American People* (New York: Century, 1914), chap. 6; Dorothy Ross (no relation), *The Origins of American Social Science* (Cambridge: Cambridge University Press, 1991), 240–242; E. A. Ross, "In Darkest Russia," *Independent* 94 (11 May 1918): 249.

34. Crane to Wilson, 27 June 1918, *PWW*, 48:459; Nathaniel Pratt to Elihu Root, 1 May 1917, SDDF, 763.72/4832.

35. Ross, "Russian Character," 763; Ross, *The Russian Bolshevik Revolution* (New York: Century, 1921), v–vi.

36. "Notes by Professor Harper" (7 February 1918), Harper Papers, box 4.

37. Poole, *"The Dark People": Russia's Crisis* (New York: Macmillan, 1918), x, 171, 226.

38. Huntington, "Memorandum on the Russian Situation," enclosed in William Cox Redfield to Wilson, 22 November 1918, *PWW*, 53:169–180; [Harper,] "How Russia Can Be Helped by the U.S.," *CSM*, 15 April 1918.

39. Huntington, "The Russian Tragedy," *Annals* 84 (July 1919): 90–97; Huntington, "What the Russian Situation Means to America," *Scribner's Magazine* 65 (March 1919): 369–373; Harper to Huntington, 4 January 1918, and Phillips to Harper, 14 January 1918, both in Harper Papers, box 5.

40. White, "Russia," *Cornell Era* 50 (December 1917): 139. White's own copy of

this article contains notes from White blaming the magazine for errors of transcription; it is not clear whether he was referring to the section quoted— Andrew Dickson White Papers, box 199.

41. Harper report, 25 March 1918, Harper Papers, box 62, folder 17; Moser to Lansing, 23 May 1918, and Wright to Lansing, 26 March 1918, both in *FRUS 1918*, 2:179, 2:91.

42. Harper, "Is Russia Playing Germany's Game," *Independent* 91 (15 December 1917): 507, 535; Harper to Henry Judson, 14 December 1917, Harper Papers, box 4.

43. Lansing to Wilson, early December 1917, in Lansing, *War Memoirs*, 341; Summers to David Francis, 14 January 1918, *FRUS 1918*, 1:338.

44. Walling, *Sovietism*, 7, 94–95; Walling, *Russia's Message: The People against the Czar* (New York: Knopf, 1917); it apparently came out before the fall of the tsar.

45. [Harper,] "Russian Soviets and Bolsheviki," *CSM*, 12 July 1918; Crane, "Present Conditions in Russia" (speech to the Army War College, 2 February 1922), Charles R. Crane Papers, reel 4.

46. Richard Polenberg, *Fighting Faiths: The Abrams Case, the Supreme Court, and Free Speech* (New York: Viking, 1987).

47. [Harper,] "German Intrigue upon U.S.," *CSM*, 17 April 1917; "New Russian Rule Is Upheld," *CSM*, 22 May 1917; "Playing German Game," *CSM*, 19 November 1917. Coolidge was originally appointed to the expert committee to evaluate the documents but did not participate. On the Sisson documents, see Kennan, *Soviet-American Relations*, 1:441–457; Harper, *Russia I Believe in*, 123.

48. Walling memorandum, enclosed in Samuel Gompers to Wilson, 9 February 1918; Wilson to Lansing, 13 February 1918; Lansing to Wilson, 15 February 1918, all in *PWW*, 46:310–313, 334, 349–350. See also Lasch, *American Liberals*, 83–84.

49. [Harper,] "Russia and 'Intervention,'" *CSM*, 5 July 1918; see also Harper quoted in Foglesong, *America's Secret War*, 159.

50. Harper to Crane, 8 July 1917, Harper Papers, box 4.

51. Lansing to Wilson, 10 December 1917, *FRUS: RL*, 2:343–345.

52. David R. Francis, *Russia from the American Embassy: April 1916—November 1918* (New York: Charles Scribner's Sons, 1922), 213, 188, 330, 348. Francis's views went through a number of changes between 1917 and the publication of these remarks in 1922; see David S. Foglesong, "A Missouri Democrat in Revolutionary Russia," *Gateway Heritage* 12 (Winter 1992): 39–40. I am grateful to David S. Foglesong for providing me with a copy of this article.

53. Bullard to Col. House, 12 December 1917, *The Intimate Papers of Colonel House*, ed. Charles Seymour (Boston: Houghton Mifflin, 1928), 3:388.

54. Walling, "The Parting of the Ways," *NYT*, 19 April 1919.

55. White, "Russia," 138.

56. Huntington to Richard Crane, 28 April 1918, Richard Crane Papers, box 2. For other examples along the same lines, see Major General William Crozier, "Trusteeship for Russia Proposed," *NYT*, 12 January 1919; Filene, *Americans*, 17.

57. Sir William Wiseman to Sir Eric Drummond, 30 May 1918; Wilson draft of aide-mémoire, 16 July 1918, both in *PWW*, 48:204, 626. The phrase was omitted from the eventual press release, c. 3 August 1918, *PWW*, 49:172.

58. See especially Leo J. Bacino, *Reconstructing Russia: U.S. Policy in Revolutionary Russia, 1917–1922* (Kent, Ohio: Kent State University Press, 1999).

59. Kennan, "Can We Help Russia," *Outlook* 119 (22 May 1918): 141.

60. Kennan to Lansing, 26 May 1918; Lansing to Wilson, 28 May 1918, both in *PWW*, 48:183–187; Kennan to Lansing, 18 August 1918; Lansing to Wilson, 22 August 1918; Wilson to Lansing, 24 August 1918, all in *PWW*, 49:320–323, 346–347.

61. Crane to Wilson, 9 July 1918, and Wilson to Crane, 11 July 1918, both in *PWW*, 48:573, 590; Ross, *Seventy Years of It: An Autobiography of Edward Alsworth Ross* (D. Appleton-Century, 1936).

62. Coolidge, "The Expansion of Russia," Archibald Cary Coolidge Papers, series HUG 1299.15, box 1, chap. 15, p. 9; Dixon, "The Kirgiz-Kazak and the Steppe Region of Western Siberia" (8 August 1918), Inquiry Papers (Yale), box 21, folder 303.

63. Summers to Francis, 14 January 1918, *FRUS 1918*, 2:28; also J. Butler Wright memorandum, 3 June 1918, in J. Butler Wright Papers, box 17.

64. Crane to Wilson, 23 July 1918, *PWW*, 49:122.

65. Lansing's reliance on Harper began only days after the February revolution— see Lansing to Wilson, 16 March 1917, SDR, "Personal and Confidential Letters from Secretary of State Lansing to President Wilson, 1915–1918," no. 331; Harper, *Russia I Believe in*, 126.

66. Harper, *Russia I Believe in*, 112; Coolidge to Root, 29 April 1918; Coolidge to Harper, 3 June 1918; Coolidge, "Archangel and Murmansk," all in Coolidge Papers, series HUG 1299.5, box 2, folders 12, 15.

6. Feeding the Mute Millions of Muzhiks

1. Quoted in Robert K. Murray, "Herbert Hoover and the Harding Cabinet," *Herbert Hoover as Secretary of Commerce: Studies in New Era Thought and Practice* (Iowa City: University of Iowa Press, 1981), 30.

2. Statistics are culled from H. H. Fisher, "The History of Relief" (June 1926), Harold H. Fisher Papers, box 30; Herbert Hoover, *An American Epic*, 4 vols.

(Chicago: Henry Regnery, 1959–1964), 3:448–462; Frank M. Surface and Raymond L. Bland, *American Food in the World War and Reconstruction Period* (Stanford: Stanford University Press, 1931), 243–264. For background on the famine, see Harold H. Fisher, *The Famine in Soviet Russia, 1919–1923: The Operations of the American Relief Administration* (New York: Macmillan, 1927); Benjamin M. Weissman, *Herbert Hoover and Famine Relief to Soviet Russia, 1921–1923* (Stanford: Hoover Institution Press, 1974); N. Sh. Tsikhelashvili, "Amerikanskaia pomoshch' narodam Rossii v nachale 20-kh godov XX veka" (Dissertatsiia na soiskanie uchenoi stepeni kandidata istoricheskikh nauk, Rossiiskii gosudarstvennyi gumanitarnyi universitet, 1997); and Bertrand M. Patenaude, *The Big Show in Bololand: The American Relief Expedition to Soviet Russia in the Famine of 1921* (Stanford: Stanford University Press, 2002).

3. Walling, "The Parting of the Ways," *NYT,* 19 April 1919; Hoover to Wilson, 30 August 1919, quoted in David S. Foglesong, *America's Secret War against Bolshevism: U.S. Intervention in the Russian Civil War, 1917–1920* (Chapel Hill: University of North Carolina Press, 1995), chap. 8 (quoted p. 232); Hoover to Wilson, 28 March 1919, excerpted in Harold H. Fisher, *The Famine in Soviet Russia, 1919–1923: The Operations of the American Relief Administration* (New York: Macmillan, 1927), 10–14.

4. Alfred L. P. Dennis, "The Genoa Conference," *North American Review* 215 (March 1922): 289. See, for example, Major General William Crozier, "Trusteeship for Russia Proposed," *NYT,* 12 January 1919; for other examples, see Peter G. Filene, *Americans and the Soviet Experiment, 1917–1933* (Cambridge, Mass.: Harvard University Press, 1967), 17.

5. Arcadius Kahan, "Natural Calamities and Their Effect upon the Food Supply in Russia," *Jahrbücher für Geschichte Osteuropas* 16 (September 1968): 374–375.

6. Lars Lih, *Bread and Authority in Russia, 1914–1921* (Berkeley and Los Angeles: University of California Press, 1990), 263; Esther Kingston-Mann, *Lenin and the Problem of Marxist Peasant Revolution* (Oxford: Oxford University Press, 1983), chaps. 8–10; Lih, "Bolshevik Razverstka and War Communism," *Slavic Review* 45 (Winter 1986): 673–688.

7. Paul Avrich, *Kronstadt* (Princeton: Princeton University Press, 1970).

8. E. H. Carr, *The Bolshevik Revolution, 1917–1923,* 3 vols. (New York: Macmillan, 1951–1953); Bertrand M. Patenaude, "Bolshevism in Retreat: The Transition to NEP, 1920–1922" (Ph.D. diss., Stanford University, 1987); and the contributions to *From Tsarism to the New Economic Policy: Continuity and Change in the Economy of the USSR,* ed. R. W. Davies (Ithaca: Cornell University Press, 1991).

9. Lenin, "Zametki o merakh bor'by s golodom i ob usilenii khoziaistvennoi

raboty," 9 July 1921, *Leninskii sbornik*, 40 vols. (Moscow: Gospolizdat, 1924–1980), 36:275–276; Lenin and Molotov circular, 30 July 1921, trans. in Richard Pipes, *The Unknown Lenin: From the Secret Archive* (New Haven: Yale University Press, 1996), 130–131; Politburo protocol, 7 July 1921, RGASPI, f. 17, op. 3, d. 184, pt. 3.

10. Politburo protocol, 25 June 1921, RGASPI, f. 17, op. 3, d. 179, pt. 3.

11. Politburo protocol, 29 June 1921, RGASPI, f. 17, op. 3, d. 181, pt. 4. The committee membership is given in its short-lived official newspaper: *Pomoshch',* 16 August 1921. Gorky circular, 21 July 1921, in *Soviet Russia and the West, 1920–1927: A Documentary Survey,* ed. Xenia Joukoff Eudin and Harold H. Fisher (Stanford: Stanford University Press, 1957), 73–74. On the committee's dissolution, see Politburo protocol, 20 October 1921, RGASPI, f. 17, op. 3, d. 219, pt. 21; Iu. N. Maksimov, "Komitet pomoshchi golodaiushchim," *Pamiat'* 4 (1979): 382–412; Stuart Finkel, "'The Brains of the Nation': The Expulsion of Intellectuals and the Politics of Culture in Soviet Russia, 1920–1924" (Ph.D. diss., Stanford University, 2001), chaps. 3–4.

12. Hoover to Gorky, 23 July 1921, in *Soviet Russia and the West,* 74–75. On ARA revenues, see Hoover, *American Epic,* 3:448–451.

13. Hoover testimony to Congress, ARA Papers, box 325, folder 4; R. A. Jackson to Clarence Stetson, 10 January 1922, ARA Papers, box 325, folder 1; Surface and Bland, *American Food,* 245 n. 2.

14. Chicherin to Lenin, 7 June 1921, AVPRF, f. 0129, op. 4, pap. 102, d. 18, l. 1; Krasin to Chicherin and Lenin, 19 October 1921, *DVP,* 4:432–433; T. T. C. Gregory, "Stemming the Red Tide," *World's Work* 41 (April 1921): 608–613, and *World's Work* 42 (May 1921): 95–102; Gregory, "Overthrowing a Red Regime: How a San Francisco Attorney Ousted Bela Kun," *World's Work* 42 (June 1921): 153–164; Chicherin to Kamenev, 29 July 1921, GARF, f. 1235 s.ch., op. 140, d. 39, l. 2.

15. Lenin to Molotov, 23 August 1921, in Pipes, *Unknown Lenin,* 144–145; D. A. Volkogonov, *Lenin: Politicheskii portret,* 2 vols. (Moscow: Novosti, 1994), 1:421; Politburo protocol, 25 August 1921, RGASPI, f. 17, op. 3, d. 194, pt. 3; "Doklad o rabote Amerikanskoi administratsii pomoshchi za period c 10 do 25 IX [1921 g.]," RGASPI, f. 5, op. 1, d. 2559, l. 31; Lenin to Chicherin, 5 September 1921, *PSS,* 53:177–178.

16. Hoover, *American Epic,* 3:434; James L. Barton, *The Story of Near East Relief (1915–1930): An Interpretation* (New York: Macmillan, 1930), 124–127; Hoover to Coolidge, 9 August 1921, ARA Papers, box 336, folder 9; Robert F. Byrnes, *Awakening American Education to the World: The Role of Archibald Cary Coolidge, 1866–1928* (Notre Dame: University of Notre Dame Press, 1982), 156.

17. Goodrich preliminary report, 1 November 1921, ARA Papers, box 95, folder

3. Hutchinson made a similar claim in a letter to Walter Lyman Brown (head of ARA's London office), ARA Papers, box 325, folder 10.

18. Undated report in James P. Goodrich Papers, box 15, folder 1; 1921 diary, Goodrich Papers, box 18.

19. Fisher, *Famine in Soviet Russia*, 72, 129, 292, 506.

20. Haskell, "A Russian Panorama," ARA Papers-Bakhmeteff, box 1, folder 3, p. 8; Hoover to Haskell, 18 November 1922, ARA-Europe Papers, box 64, folder 2; Oscar T. Crosby, "The European Tangle and Some Suggestions as to Its Unravelling," *Annals* 108 (July 1923): 8.

21. Goodrich cited in Chicherin to Molotov, 11 March 1922, RGASPI, f. 5, op. 2, d. 316, ll. 64–66.

22. Hoover's strategy is most succinctly outlined in "We'll Have to Feed the World Again" (1942), in *The Organization of American Relief in Europe, 1918–1919*, ed. Suda Lorena Bane and Ralph Haswell Lutz (Stanford: Stanford University Press, 1943), 11–12. On American views of earlier famine relief, see E. T. Devine, *Principles of Relief* (New York: Macmillan, 1904), especially 457–470; one bibliography on relief suggests little besides immediate ameliorative work—"Emergency Relief," *Bulletin of the Russell Sage Foundation Library* 8 (December 1914).

23. Kamenev's remarks were paraphrased by a staff member of Near East Relief, whose report was provided, unsolicited, to Hoover. Diary of 1921 trip, Alvin Aaron Johnson Papers, box 3, folder 22; Near East Relief Russian Commission, *An American Report on the Russian Famine* (New York: Near East Relief, 1921), 25.

24. *Promyshlennost' Povolzh'ia i golod 1921 g.* (Moscow: V. S. N. Kh., 1921), 3.

25. Eiduk quoted in *ARA Bulletin* 19 (December 1921): 7–8.

26. Klishko to Chicherin, 24 August 1921, GARF, f. 1064, op. 6, d. 48, ll. 17–18; "Work Accomplished by the International Committee of Russian Relief Funds, under the Superintendence of Dr. Nansen, from September 1921 to September 1923," annex to *Report on Economic Conditions in Russia with Special Reference to the Famine of 1921–1922 and the State of Agriculture* (Geneva: League of Nations, 1922), 103–106.

27. Agreement between the RSFSR and American Mennonite Relief, 1 October 1921, ARA Papers, box 86, folder 3. On the JDC, see the correspondence in Joseph A. Rosen Papers, folder 10; and in the ARA Papers, box 89, folder 1; box 327, folder 4; box 327, folder 6; and box 344, folder 7. On Quaker relief, see John Forbes, *The Quaker Star under Seven Flags, 1917–1927* (Philadelphia: University of Pennsylvania Press, 1962), 161–166.

28. Cyril Quinn interview, 2 May 1966, cited in Weissman, *Herbert Hoover*, 113; ARA Papers, box 318, folder 20.

29. See, for instance, Fisher, *Famine in Soviet Russia*, chaps. 7–8.

30. Coolidge, "Our Relations with Mr. Eiduk," 26 November 1921, ARA Papers, box 94, folder 11; Coolidge, "Liaison Work with the ARA in Russia, September 1921 to February 1922," ARA Papers, box 52, folder 1, pp. 7–8; Haskell, "Russian Panorama," folder 3, p. 7. *Contra* Coolidge, Eiduk was of Latvian, not Russian, descent.

31. Quarton to Secretary of State, 15 December 1921, SDDF, 861.48/1811; J. C. Lekes, "Interview between A. C. Coolidge and L. B. Kamenev, 15 February 1922," ARA Papers, box 96, folder 3; Leonid Krasin to Maxim Litvinov, 7 January 1922, RGASPI, f. 5, op. 1, d. 2177, l. 5.

32. Fisher, *Famine in Soviet Russia*, chap. 12; Lenin speech, 23 December 1921, *DVP*, 4:584–585; Politburo protocol, 31 December 1921, RGASPI, f. 17, op. 3, d. 247, l. 24; Lenin to Politburo, 22 December 1921, *PSS*, 54:585 n. 154.

33. Fisher, *Famine in Soviet Russia*, 199–201; for other intercepted telegrams, see RGASPI, f. 76, op. 3, d. 220, ll. 21–22; Dzerzhinskii's charge to handle ARA political affairs occurred in early March but did not take immediate effect—Politburo protocol, 9 March 1922, RGASPI, f. 17, op. 3, d. 279, pt. 6.

34. Christian Herter to D. C. Poole, 10 April 1922, SDDF, 861.48/1925; Walter Lyman Brown to Edgar Rickard, 13 April 1922, cited in Weissman, *Herbert Hoover*, 132.

35. Fisher, *Famine in Soviet Russia*, 300–307; Haskell to Hoover, 24 June 1922, SDDF, 861.48/1991; *Documents of the ARA Russian Unit* (Hoover Institution), 1:559–590.

36. Department of Justice to Lawrence Richey (a Hoover aide), 21 March 1922; W. J. Burns to Richey, 12 June 1922; J. Edgar Hoover to Richey, 9 January 1923; Burns to Richey, 15 February 1923, all in ARA Papers, box 324, folder 16.

37. Politburo protocol, 7 September 1922, RGASPI, f. 17, op. 3, d. 311, pt. 6; resolution on Posledgol aims, GARF, f. 1065, op. 1, d. 6, ll. 1–2; Kalinin in *Izvestiia*, 8 October 1922, translated in ARA Papers, box 123, folder 5; A. Vinokurov, "Nashi voprosy," GARF, f. 1058, op. 1, d. 181, ll. 31–32; N. A. Stolypin, "Mery preduprezhdeniia goloda na iugo-vostoke Rossii i rol' v etom dele promyshlennosti," *Posle Goloda* 2 (1923): 12.

38. Kalinin speech in Samara district, 16 August 1921, excerpted in ARA Papers, box 327, folder 8. This report is a very loose interpretation of Kalinin's speech, see M. I. Kalinin, *Za eti gody* (Leningrad: Gosizdat, 1926), 85–86.

39. Letters are reprinted in Fisher, *Famine in Soviet Russia*, 334–342. For internal correspondence, see Haskell to Walter Brown, ARA-Europe Papers, box 67, folder 1; circular memo, 2 October 1922, GARF, f. 1058, op. 1, d. 181, l. 9.

40. Lander to Haskell, 24 October 1922, ARA Papers, box 328, folder 3.

41. "Urozhai: urozhai i ego ekonomicheskie posledstviia," *Izvestiia*, 2 August

1922; Fisher, *Famine in Soviet Russia*, 309–312, 324 n. 1; Kamenev to John Gorvin, 30 September 1922, ARA Papers, box 319, folder 12; Haskell to Herter, 18 October 1922, ARA Papers, box 21, folder 3.

42. Politburo protocol, 30 November 1922, RGASPI, f. 17, op. 3, d. 324, pt. 16; Politburo protocol, 27 December 1922, RGASPI, f. 17, op. 3, d. 327, pt. 15.

43. Litvinov to Kerzhentsev, 17 January 1923, GARF, f. 1235 s.ch., op. 140, d. 104, l. 4.

44. "With Grain to Sell, Russia Asks Help," *NYT*, 30 November 1922.

45. Hoover to Haskell, 18 November 1922, ARA Papers, box 21, folder 3.

46. Undated headline from *Brooklyn Daily Eagle* [March 1923?], Allen Wardwell Papers, box 8, folder 2.

47. "Po povodu vyvoza iz predelov RSFSR khleba," *Izvestiia*, 8 February 1923.

48. O. D. Kameneva, "Itogi rabot Pomgola," *Izvestiia*, 31 October 1922; Kameneva in *Posle goloda* 2 (1923), translated in ARA Papers, box 123, folder 4; Kameneva, "Dva goda zagranichnykh organizatsii pomoshchi," *Itogi Posledgol (s 15/X/1922 g.—1/VIII/1923 g.)* (Moscow: Ts. K. Posledgol, 1923), 32.

49. Lander, "O rabote inostrannykh organizatsii pomoshchi," 1 February 1923, GARF, f. 1058, op. 1, d. 71, l. 23; A. Beliakov, "Nuzhen vtoroi shag," *Izvestiia*, 4 January 1922.

50. John Ellingston, "Supplementary Memorandum to Mr. Quinn re Russian Grain Export," 2 March 1923, ARA Papers, box 21, folder 3.

51. Golder to Herter, 2 December 1922, *WRP*, 244–245; for a more complete description, see David C. Engerman, "Economic Reconstruction in Soviet Russia: The Courting of Herbert Hoover in 1922," *International History Review* 19 (November 1997): 836–848.

52. Hutchinson, "Russia: Intervention, Watchful Waiting, or Recognition?" *University of California Chronicle*, January 1925, 4. On wartime service, see the correspondence with Isaiah Bowman in Lincoln Hutchinson Papers, box 1.

53. Hutchinson to Hoover, 3 August 1922, ARA Papers, box 325, folder 10; no response could be located. On Fisher and Quinn, see Samuel Harper to D. C. Poole, 15 January 1923, Samuel Northrop Harper Papers, box 10.

54. Hutchinson, "Can Russia 'Come Back'?," *PSQ* 38 (June 1923): 256; Hutchinson, "Russia," 4–5, 12, 24; Hutchinson, "What Price Freedom," *University of California Chronicle*, April 1926, 190–192.

55. Golder to H. H. Fisher, 7 October 1922, ARA Papers, box 95, folder 2; Golder to Herter, 16 October 1922, *WRP*, 233–234; D. C. Poole to Charles Evan Hughes, 26 October 1922, SDDF, 861.01/512; John Ellingston to H. H. Fisher, 26 December 1922, HH-Commerce Papers, box 30, folder 511.

56. Golder's letters are printed in *WRP*, 89–303. Copies of Golder's and Coolidge's letters in the State Department files include SDDF, 861.00/9320,

861.00/9423, 861.00/9736, 861.00/9781, 861.00/9851, and 861.00/10427. D. C. Poole to Herter, 16 December 1922, Frank A. Golder Papers, box 12, folder 51.

57. Frank Alfred Golder and Lincoln Hutchinson, *On the Trail of the Russian Famine* (Stanford: Stanford University Press, 1927), 46, 58, 103. In reviewing this book, Samuel Harper had "little to say except that the Russians are ardent questioners"—*AJS* 33 (November 1927): 476. Frank Alfred Golder, "Siberia," in "Inquiry Documents: Special Reports and Studies," no. 187, p. 121. Golder's discussion of the "Asiatic" characteristics of the Volga region seems rooted in perceptions of culture more than demography. According to the data from a 1903 census in the large and diverse city of Samara, more than 85 percent of the population was of European origin. See Orlando Figes, *Peasant Russia, Civil War: The Volga Countryside in Revolution, 1917–1921* (Oxford: Oxford University Press, 1989), 23.

58. Golder and Hutchinson, *On the Trail of the Russian Famine*, 95, 109–110; Golder to Herter, 17 July 1922, and 6 August 1922, *WRP*, 191, 204; Golder to Lutz, 5 November 1922, *WRP*, 235.

59. Goodrich quoted in Frederick C. Griffith, "James Putnam Goodrich and Soviet Russia," *Mid-America* 71 (October 1989): 163, 153.

60. The commission's travels are documented in Wardwell's diary, in Wardwell Papers, Catalogued Materials. On the ARA-NIB meeting, see "Memorandum of a Conference on the Policies of Russian Relief," 19 January 1923, in George Vincent Diary; interestingly enough, a copy of this report was obtained by the Soviet foreign ministry—AVPRF, f. 0129, op. 6, pap. 104, d. 48, ll. 10–11. See also "Memorandum of a Meeting at Secretary Hoover's House," 23 January 1923, ARA Papers, box 21, folder 2.

61. Frank Page to Hoover, 26 January 1923; Page to Wardwell, 3 February 1923, both in ARA Papers, box 97, folder 1; National Information Bureau, Commission on Russian Relief, *The Russian Famines, 1921–1922, 1922–1923* (New York: N. I. B., 1923), 19–21, 38–39.

62. Haskell to Herter, 6 March 1923, ARA Papers, box 340, folder 3.

63. Haskell to Hoover, 7 March 1923, ARA Papers, box 95, folder 4.

64. Ibid.; ARA press release, 8 March 1923, Hoover "Bible," 12:292. My suspicion of Gumberg's involvement is supported by his close connections to reconstruction-oriented ARA staff, especially through Robins. He also had connections to both of the publications involved. Copies of the original and edited telegram, furthermore, appear in Gumberg's files—Alexander Gumberg Papers, box 3, folder 1. "Moskovskii predstavitel' ARA o polozhenii v Rossii," *Izvestiia*, 11 March 1923; "Mr. Hoover Stabs Russia" [editorial], *Nation* 116 (21 March 1923): 327; Hutchinson to Hoover, 3 August 1922, Raymond Robins Papers, box 2, folder 3.

65. Press release, 11 August 1921, cited in Weissman, *Herbert Hoover*, 57; Hoover to Charles Evan Hughes, 6 December 1921, *FRUS 1921*, 2:787–788; Hoover to C. V. Hibbard, 22 March 1923, repr. in *Current History* 18 (December 1923): 289.

66. Quoted in Joan Hoff Wilson, *Herbert Hoover: Forgotten Progressive* (Boston: Little, Brown, 1975), 198. George Frost Kennan made a similar claim in *Russia and the West under Lenin and Stalin* (Boston: Little, Brown, 1961), 180.

67. "Vosstanovlenie sel'skogo khoziaistva v Rossii" (1923?), RGASPI, f. 17, op. 84, d. 383, ll. 21–22ob; George Vaucher to A. D. Tsiurupa, 20 January 1923, RGASPI, f. 158, op. 1, d. 33, ll. 6–7ob; "Dogovor mezhdu RSFSR i Missiei Nansena ob organizatsii opytnykh stantsii dlia vosstanovlenie sel'skogo khoziaistva Rossii," 10 February 1923, RGASPI, f. 158, op. 1, d. 33, ll. 23–27.

68. The post-ARA agreement is in GARF, f. 5283 s.ch., op. 1a, d. 2, ll. 11–14. On the transition to Agro-Joint, see Jonathan Dekel-Chen, "Peddlers and Shop-keepers into Soviet Farmers: Jewish Agricultural Colonization in Crimea and Southern Ukraine, 1924–1941" (Ph.D. diss., Brandeis University, 2001), chaps. 2–3.

69. Hoover to Frank Billings, 17 April 1923, ARA Papers, box 351, folder 10.

70. Christine A. White, *British and American Commercial Relations with Soviet Russia, 1918–1924* (Chapel Hill: University of North Carolina Press, 1992); V. K. Furaev, *Sovetsko-amerikanskie otnosheniia, 1917–1939* (Moscow: Mysl', 1964); Thomas J. O'Neill, "Business, Investment, and Revolution in Russia: Case Studies of American Companies, 1880s–1920s" (Ph.D. diss., McGill University, 1987).

71. S. G. Wheatcroft and R. W. Davies, "Population," in *Economic Transformation of the Soviet Union, 1913–1945*, ed Davies, Mark Harrison, and Wheatcroft (Cambridge: Cambridge University Press, 1994), 63.

72. Kamenev amendments to Trotsky, "Tezisi t. Trotskogo o gosprome," 8 March 1923, RGASPI, f. 17, op. 3, d. 342, ll. 7–9.

73. Hoover speech to American Section of the International Chamber of Commerce, 15 May 1922, abridged in *Nation's Business* 10 (5 June 1922): 14–16.

74. Hutchinson, "Observations on the Present Situation in Russia," 7 December 1927, Hoover-Commerce Papers, box 288; Golder, "The Tragic Failure of Soviet Policies," *Current History* 19 (February 1924): 780, 778, 783.

7. New Society, New Scholars

1. Remarkably, there has been no monographic study of the post-WWI Red Scare since the subsequent (post-WWII) one; see Robert K. Murray, *The Red Scare: A Study of National Hysteria, 1919–1920* (Minneapolis: University of Minnesota Press, 1955). For case studies of organized vigilantism in this era,

see Christopher Capozzola, "The Only Badge Needed Is Your Patriotic Fervor: Vigilance, Coercion, and the Law in World War I America, *Journal of American History* 88:4 (March 2002): 1354–1382.

2. Hourwich, "Bolshevism" (1918?), in Isaac A. Hourwich Papers, folder 123; Melech Epstein, *Profiles of Eleven: Profiles of Eleven Men Who Guided the Destiny of an Immigrant Society and Stimulated Social Consciousness among the American People* (Detroit: Wayne State University Press, 1965), 259–260; Theodore Draper, *The Roots of American Communism* (New York: Viking, 1957), chaps. 9–10.

3. Debs quoted in Nick Salvatore, *Eugene V. Debs: Citizen and Socialist* (Urbana: University of Illinois Press, 1983), 291. On Greenwich Village radicals, see Christine Stansell, *American Moderns: Bohemian New York and the Creation of a New Century* (New York: Metropolitan Books, 2000), 314–326. For overviews of American perceptions of revolutionary Russia, see Peter G. Filene, *Americans and the Soviet Experience, 1917–1933* (Cambridge, Mass.: Harvard University Press, 1967), chaps. 1–2; Christopher Lasch, *American Liberals and the Russian Revolution* (New York: Columbia University Press, 1962), chaps. 6–7; and Norman E. Saul, *War and Revolution: The United States and Russia, 1914–1921* (Lawrence: University of Kansas Press, 2001), chaps. 6–7.

4. These trends are discussed in Dorothy Ross, *The Origins of American Social Science* (Cambridge: Cambridge University Press, 1991), chap. 10; Robert C. Bannister, *Sociology and Scientism: The American Quest for Objectivity, 1880–1940* (Chapel Hill: University of North Carolina Press, 1987), chaps. 12–14; and Michael A. Bernstein, *A Perilous Progress: Economists and Public Purpose in Twentieth-Century America* (Princeton: Princeton University Press, 2001), chaps. 1–2. Discussions of the relationship between partisanship and scholarship in the late nineteenth century are also relevant; see Mary O. Furner, *Advocacy and Objectivity: A Crisis in the Professionalization of American Social Science, 1865–1905* (Lexington: University of Kentucky Press, 1975).

5. Harper, "The Communist Dictatorship in Russia," *International Interpreter* 2 (3 November 1923): 981; Harper, "The Foreign Policy of Moscow," *International Interpreter* 2 (12 January 1924): 1302.

6. Filene, *Americans and the Soviet Experiment,* chap. 4; Joan Hoff Wilson, *Ideology and Economics: U.S. Relations with the Soviet Union, 1918–1933* (Columbia: University of Missouri Press, 1974), chap. 4.

7. Harper to Robert F. Kelley, 7 December 1925, Samuel Northrup Harper Papers, box 12.

8. Samuel N. Harper, *The Russia I Believe in: The Memoirs of Samuel N. Harper, 1902–1941,* ed. Paul V. Harper (Chicago: University of Chicago Press, 1945), 136–140.

9. Barry D. Karl, *Charles E. Merriam and the Study of Politics* (Chicago: Univer-

sity of Chicago Press, 1974), 82, 170, chap. 9; Elizabeth Ann Weber, *The Duk-Duks: Primitive and Historical Types of Citizenship* (Chicago: University of Chicago Press, 1929); David M. Ricci, *The Tragedy of Political Science: Politics, Scholarship, and Democracy* (New Haven: Yale University Press, 1984), chap. 2.

10. Harper, *Russia I Believe in,* 144–145; Harper, *Civic Training in Soviet Russia* (Chicago: University of Chicago Press, 1929), 343; Harper, *Making Bolsheviks* (Chicago: University of Chicago Press, 1931), 157, 90.

11. Charles E. Merriam, *The Making of Citizens: A Comparative Study of Methods of Civic Training* (Chicago: University of Chicago Press, 1931), 222; Dorothy Ross, *Origins of American Social Science,* 458; Marguerite A. Green, *The National Civic Federation and the American Labor Movement, 1900–1925* (1956; Westport, Conn.: Greenwood, 1973), chaps. 8–9.

12. Harper, "Sovs Benefit Russ Peasantry," *CDN,* 16 April 1927; Harper, "Red Schools Put to Political Use," *CDN,* 20 April 1927.

13. Harper, *Russia I Believe in,* 145–146, 151–152.

14. Harper, "Sovs Benefit Russ Peasantry"; Harper, "Reds Need Fresh Economic Ideas," *CDN,* 21 April 1927; Harper, *Civic Training,* 1.

15. Preston Kumler to Harper, 23 April 1927, and 27 April 1927, both in Harper Papers, box 12.

16. The best source on Davis's early career is a brief autobiographical statement (1928?) in the Luther Bernard Papers, hereafter cited as "Davis Autobiography" (here from p. 4). Also William McGuire King, "The Emergence of Social Gospel Radicalism: The Methodist Case," *Church History* 50 (December 1981): 436–439.

17. Davis, "The Russian People and the Soviets," *Nation* 109 (6 September 1919): 345, 349; Davis, "More Light on Russia," *Independent* 97 (15 March 1919): 367; Davis, "What We Can Do for Russia," *Independent* 97 (8 February 1919): 199.

18. Davis, "Should America Recognize Russia?" *Annals* 114 (July 1924): 76–80.

19. Davis, "The Key to the Mystery of Russia," *Travel* 34 (February 1920): 24; Davis, "Ten Years: The Leaders Whose Personalities Span the Russian Revolution," *Survey* 57 (1 February 1927): 572.

20. "Davis Autobiography," 4–5; Davis, *The Russians and Ruthenians in America: Bolsheviks or Brothers?* (New York: George H. Doran, 1922); Davis, "Americanizing the Russians," *Nation* 114 (2 January 1922): 121.

21. "Davis Autobiography," 5; Davis, *A Life Adventure for Peace: An Autobiography* (New York: Citadel Press, 1967), 52; Bannister, *Sociology and Scientism,* 207–210.

22. Quoted in Seymour Martin Lipset, "The Department of Sociology," in R. Gordon Hoxie et al., *A History of the Faculty of Political Science, Columbia*

University (New York: Columbia University Press, 1955), 286–287; Franklin Giddings, *Principles of Sociology: An Analysis of the Phenomena of Association and of Social Organization* (New York: Macmillan, 1911), 18; Ross, *Origins of American Social Science,* 127–130.

23. Davis, "A Sociological Interpretation of the Russian Revolution," *PSQ* 37 (June 1922): 227, 243.

24. Davis, *The Russian Immigrant* (New York: Macmillan, 1922), 211–214, based on Étienne Antonelli, *Bolshevik Russia,* trans. Charles A. Carroll (New York: Alfred A. Knopf, 1920), 72–74.

25. Davis, *Russian Immigrant,* 28, 30, 44, 180.

26. Davis, "Russia Today," *New Republic* 48 (13 October 1926): 211; Davis, "The Constitution of the Russian Communist Party," *Current History* 25 (February 1927): 714.

27. Davis, "The Nature of the Russian Government," and Davis, "The Communist Party," both in *Soviet Russia in the Second Decade: A Joint Survey by the Technical Staff of the First American Trade Union Delegation,* ed. Stuart Chase, Robert Dunn, and Rexford Guy Tugwell (New York: John Day, 1928); Davis, "The Communist Party and the Government," in *The New Russia: Between the First and Second Five-Year Plans,* ed. Davis (New York: John Day, 1933).

28. Davis, "Testing the Social Attitudes of Children in the Government Schools in Russia," *AJS* 32 (May 1927): 947, 949; Davis, "A Study of One Hundred Sixty-Three Outstanding Communist Leaders," *Studies in Quantitative and Cultural Sociology* (Chicago: University of Chicago Press, 1930), 55–56; "Davis Autobiography," 7.

29. Davis, "Should America Quarantine the Russian Soviet Government?" *Annals* 126 (July 1926): 117, 125.

30. Douglas, "The Reality of Non-Commercial Incentives in Life," in *The Trend of Economics,* ed. Rexford Guy Tugwell (New York: Alfred A. Knopf, 1924).

31. Douglas, "Labor Legislation and Social Insurance," and Douglas, "Wages and the Material Condition of the Industrial Worker," both in *Soviet Russia in the Second Decade;* Douglas, *Real Wages in the United States, 1890–1926* (Boston: Houghton Mifflin, 1930).

32. Harper, *Russia I Believe in,* 157; "Proekt nauchnogo issledovaniia sovetskogo khoziaistva i politicheskogo opyta," GARF, f. 5283 s.ch., op. 1a, d. 104, ll. 72–79ob; Litvinov to Politburo, 22 August 1928, and 23 August 1928, both in AVPRF, f. 04, op. 3, pap. 5, d. 217, ll. 8–11. For more on this proposal, see David C. Engerman, "New Society, New Scholarship: Soviet Studies Programmes in Interwar America," *Minerva* 37 (Spring 1999): 33–36.

33. Douglas, "The Russian Economic Situation—A Discussion," *AER* 19 (March 1929, supp.): 111–117; Douglas, "Lessons from the Last Decade," *The Social-*

ism of Our Times, ed. Harry W. Laidler and Norman Thomas (New York: Vanguard Press, 1929).

34. Douglas, *In the Fullness of Time: The Memoirs of Paul H. Douglas* (New York: Harcourt Brace Jovanovich, 1972), 29; Douglas, *The Coming of a New Party* (New York: McGraw-Hill, 1932), 205, 220–221; Karel Denis Bicha, "Liberalism Frustrated: The League for Independent Political Action, 1928–1933," *Mid-America* 48 (January 1966): 19–28.

35. See especially Hewes, "Trade Union Development in Soviet Russia," *AER* 13 (December 1923): 618–637.

36. Daniel T. Rodgers, *Atlantic Crossings: Social Politics in a Progressive Age* (Cambridge, Mass.: Belknap Press, 1998), 376–379; Hewes, "The Russian Labor Code of 1922," *Current History* 18 (June 1923): 460.

37. Pares to Coolidge, 11 May 1924, Archibald Cary Coolidge Papers, series HUG 1299.5, box 1; Pares, *A Wandering Student: The Story of a Purpose* (Syracuse: Syracuse University Press, 1948), 303–305.

38. Kerner's fellow planner was Arthur Andrews, a Coolidge student teaching at Tufts. "Program Adopted at the Boston Luncheon . . . April 1924," enclosed in Andrews to Kerner, 22 May 1924, Coolidge Papers, series HUG 1299.5, box 1; Margaret F. Stieg, *The Origin and Development of Scholarly Historical Periodicals* (Birmingham: University of Alabama Press, 1986), 141.

39. The dissertation eventually appeared as Kerner, *Bohemia in the Eighteenth Century: A Study in Political, Economic, and Social History with Special Reference to the Reign of Leopold II, 1790–1792* (New York: Macmillan, 1932). On Kerner's pro-Czech advocacy during the Inquiry, see Kerner to Woodrow Wilson, 26 April 1919, *PWW,* 58:156; Lawrence E. Gelfand, *The Inquiry: American Preparations for Peace, 1917–1919* (New Haven: Yale University Press, 1963), 57–58; Kerner, "The Social Beginnings of the Czechoslovak Republic," *Survey* 43 (29 November 1919): 171.

40. "The Slavonic Conference at Richmond (Va.)," *SEER* 3 (March 1925): 692.

41. Madison Grant, *The Passing of the Great Race, or the Racial Basis of European History* (New York: Charles Scribner's Sons, 1916), chap. 2; Lothrop Stoddard, *The Rising Tide of Color against White World-Supremacy* (New York: Charles Scribner's Sons, 1920), chap. 1.

42. Kerner, "Racial Foundations of World Politics," Robert J. Kerner Papers, carton 20; also Kerner, "Racial History of Man," Kerner Papers, carton 24.

43. Kerner, "The Importance of Eastern European History," lecture at the University of Michigan, 3 April 1924, Kerner Papers, carton 16, pp. 2, 10–11.

44. Boas, *The Mind of Primitive Man* (New York: Macmillan, 1911), 17. Kerner's access to Boas may have come through the writings of the Australian geographer Griffith Taylor, whom he quoted often; see Taylor, "The Evolution of the

Distribution of Race, Culture, and Language," *Geographical Review* 11 (January 1921): 54–119.

45. Kerner to Harper, April 1917, Harper Papers, box 3; Jonathan M. Nielson, *American Historians in War and Peace: Patriotism, Diplomacy, and the Paris Peace Conference, 1919* (Dubuque, Iowa: Kendall/Hunt, 1994), 68.

46. George Frost Kennan likely had Kerner in mind when he wrote that "the academic world in the San Francisco region" contained many who "had an understandable yearning to be closer to the actual operations of diplomacy and a sneaking suspicion that if they were in on it, they could do it much better." Kennan to Francis Russell, 23 August 1946, George Frost Kennan Papers, box 16, folder 11. Kerner also offered his services to the CIA; see Allen Dulles to Kerner, 14 September 1954, in Kerner Papers, carton 8.

47. Kerner, "The Jugo-Slav Movement," in Alexander Petrunkevitch, Samuel Harper, and Robert Kerner, *The Russian Revolution* (Cambridge, Mass.: Harvard University Press, 1918); Kerner, "The Importance of Eastern European History," Kerner Papers, carton 16, p. 8.

48. Raymond Fisher to Robert Byrnes, 15 November 1977, in Raymond H. Fisher Papers.

49. J. F. J. [J. Franklin Jameson], "The Meeting of the American Historical Association at Ann Arbor," *AHR* 31 (April 1926): 427.

50. Kerner, "Recent Changes in Russian Land Tenure" (1925), Kerner Papers, carton 16; Kerner, "Russian Expansion to America: Its Bibliographic Foundations," *Papers of the Bibliographic Society of America* 25 (1931): 111–129; Kerner, *The Urge to the Sea: The Course of Russian History—The Role of Rivers, Portages, Ostrogs, Monasteries and Furs* (Berkeley and Los Angeles: University of California Press, 1942); Kerner, "Tolstoy's Philosophy of History," *University of California Chronicle*, January 1929, 45.

51. Kerner, *The Foundations of Slavic Bibliography* (Chicago: University of Chicago Press, 1916), 39; Kerner to Harper, 27 January 1916, 28 February 1917, and 22 March 1917, all in Harper Papers, box 3; Kerner, "Our Professional Interest," *NEA Journal* 15 (December 1926): 296–297.

52. Robinson, "Karl Marx and His Theories" (Phoenix Union High School, 1913), in Geroid Tanquary Robinson Papers, box 17.

53. Robinson, "The Abyss of the People," *Dial* 67 (15 November 1919): 435–438; Robinson, "Collective Bargaining in Politics," *Dial* 67 (26 July 1919): 50; Robinson, "Trade Unionism and the Control of Industry," *Dial* 67 (12 July 1919): 6.

54. Robinson, "Russia's Double Experiment" (8 May [1919?]), Robinson Papers, box 16.

55. See, for instance, John Dewey, "Internal Social Reorganization after the War" (1918), *MW*, 11:83–86.

56. See especially Veblen, *Absentee Ownership and Business Enterprise in Modern Times: The Case of America* (New York: B. W. Huebsch, 1923), chaps. 8–9; and Veblen, "Between Bolshevism and War," *Freeman* 3 (25 May 1921), which frames its view of the Bolsheviks around the question of absentee ownership.

57. Robinson to Joseph Barnes, 15 August 1941, Joseph Barnes Papers, Catalogued Correspondence.

58. Robinson, "The New Negro," *Freeman* 1 (2 June 1920): 278–280; Robinson, "Sweatshop or Soviet?" *Freeman* 1 (19 January 1921): 443–445; Robinson, "Racial Minorities," in *Civilization in the United States: An Inquiry by Thirty Americans,* ed. Harold E. Stearns (New York: Harcourt, Brace, 1922); Nicholas Joost, *Years of Transition: The Dial, 1912–1920* (Barre, Mass.: Barre Publishers, 1967), 242.

59. Robinson, "Russia Re-Examined," *Freeman* 1 (21 April 1920): 132, 133.

60. Robinson, "The Decentralization of Russian History," *PSQ* 36 (September 1921): 454–455, 457, 465.

61. Richard Hofstadter, "The Department of History," in *History of the Faculty of Political Science,* 229, 241, 244; Luther V. Hendricks, *James Harvey Robinson: Teacher of History* (New York: King's Crown Press, 1946), 13, 23; Robinson, *Rural Russia under the Old Regime: A History of the Landlord-Peasant World and a Prologue to the Peasant Revolution of 1917* (New York: Macmillan, 1932), viii; James Harvey Robinson, *The New History* (New York: Macmillan, 1912), chap. 1 (quoted p. 21).

62. Robinson, "Decentralization," 468; "Slavonic Conference," 693.

63. This speculation comes from his first graduate student—John Shelton Curtiss, "Geroid Tanquary Robinson," in *Essays in Russian and Soviet History in Honor of Geroid Tanquary Robinson* (Leiden: E. J. Brill, 1963), xi–xii.

64. Robinson, "The Russian Peasant as Revolutionist," *Freeman* 8 (4 March 1924): 615.

65. "Doklad o rabote VOKS po kul'turnoi sviazi s Amerikoi," AVPRF, f. 04, op. 3, pap. 15, d. 215, l. 36; O. D. Kameneva report, 19 March 1927, GARF, f. 5283 s.ch., op. 1a, d. 97, l. 9. On SSRC, see Robinson, *Rural Russia,* viii.

66. Esther Kingston-Mann, "Breaking the Silence: An Introduction," in *Peasant Economy, Culture, and Politics of European Russia, 1800–1921,* ed. Esther Kingston-Mann and Timothy Mixter (Princeton: Princeton University Press, 1991), 3–4.

67. Robinson, *Rural Russia,* 33, 116, 240–241, 245, chap. 6.

68. See the notes about his trip in Robinson Papers, box 65.

69. Curtiss, "Geroid Tanquary Robinson," 16–17.

70. Alan Raucher, "The First Foreign Affairs Think Tanks," *American Quarterly* 30 (Autumn 1978): 494–495; Charles B. Saunders, Jr., *The Brookings Institution: A Fifty-Year History* (Washington: Brookings Institution, 1966).

71. Loy Henderson to Thomas R. Maddux, 19 January 1968, in Loy W. Henderson Papers, Special Correspondence, box 1; Donald T. Critchlow, *The Brookings Institution, 1916–1952: Expertise and the Public Interest in a Democratic Society* (Dekalb: Northern Illinois Press, 1985), 74.

72. [Pasvolsky,] *Economic Russia: Her Actuality and Her Possibilities* (New York: A. B. Leach, 1917), 97–98. He prepared the pamphlet in 1916, but it appeared only in mid-1917.

73. Pasvol'skii, "Natsional'naia programma," *Russkoe slovo,* 23 November 1917; Pasvol'skii, "Bol'sheviki," *Russkoe slovo,* 14 January 1918; Pasvolsky to Senator Robert Owen, 4 March 1918, quoted in David S. Foglesong, *America's Secret War against Bolshevism: U.S. Intervention in the Russian Civil War, 1917–1920* (Chapel Hill: University of North Carolina Press, 1995), 192; Edgar Sisson, *One Hundred Red Days: A Personal Chronicle of the Bolshevik Revolution, 25 November 1917–4 March 1918* (New Haven: Yale University Press, 1931), 370.

74. Pasvolsky, "The Intelligentsia under the Soviets," *Atlantic Monthly* 126 (November 1920): 683.

75. Pasvolsky, "Russian Liquor Prohibition," *Russian Review* (N.Y.) 2 (October 1916): 150; Pasvolsky, *Economic Russia,* 95; Pasvolsky, "Moscow's Bid for World Power," *Saturday Evening Post* 193 (20 November 1920): 6.

76. Pasvolsky to Breckenridge Long, 22 March 1920, in Pasvolsky to Harper, 22 March 1920, Harper Papers, box 7; Pasvolsky, *The Economics of Communism with Special Reference to Russia's Experiment* (New York: Macmillan, 1921), 65, 246; Pasvolsky, *Russia in the Far East* (New York: Macmillan, 1922), 161; Pasvolsky, "Russia's Parliament," *Russian Review* (N.Y.) 2 (September 1916): 102.

77. Pasvolsky, *Russia in the Far East,* 144; Pasvolsky, *Economics of Communism,* vii, 307; Pasvolsky, "The Change in Russia: Its Economic Significance," published with *Economic Russia,* 9; Pasvolsky, "Economic Problems of New Russia," *Russian Review* (N.Y.) 3 (April 1917): 17–18.

78. Pasvolsky and Harold G. Moulton, *Russian Debts and Russian Reconstruction: A Study of the Relation of Russia's Foreign Debts to Her Economic Recovery* (New York: McGraw-Hill, 1924), chap. 7; Pasvolsky, "Underlying Economic Factors in the Russian Situation," *Annals* 114 (July 1924): 59–60; Hutchinson, review of *Russian Debts and Russian Reconstruction, SEER* 4 (June 1925): 244–246; Pasvolsky, "Change in Russia," 9.

79. G. John Ikenberry, "A World Economy Restored: Expert Consensus and the Anglo-American Postwar Settlement," *International Organization* 46 (Winter 1992): 308–315; Warren F. Kimball, *The Juggler: Franklin Roosevelt as Wartime Statesman* (Princeton: Princeton University Press, 1991), 57.

80. Biographical information on Dean comes primarily from Andrew Jewett's

unpublished seminar paper, "Vera Micheles Dean and American Foreign Policy" (University of California-Berkeley, 1997).

81. Dean, "The Struggle in Russia," *New Republic* 62 (5 March 1930): 63; Dean, "The Political Structure of the Soviet State," in Dean et al., *New Governments in Europe: The Trend toward Dictatorship* (New York: Thomas Nelson and Sons, 1935), 315, 318, 341; Dean, review of *Hidden Springs*, by Katherine Breshko-Breshkovskaya, *APSR* 25 (November 1931): 1073; Dean, "The Attack on Democracy," in Dean, *New Governments*, 26.

82. Dean, "Soviet Russia, 1917–1933," FPA World Affairs Pamphlet no. 2 (1933): 4; Dean, introduction to "Present Trends in Russia," FPA Pamphlet no. 66 (29 March 1930): 5, 9; typescript for FPA meeting, 24 October 1933, in Vera Micheles Dean Papers, box 3, folder 32, pp. 4–5.

83. Dean, "Political Structure of the Soviet State," 341–342; Dean, "Soviet Russia," 13.

84. Dean, review of *Soviet Russia in the Second Decade*, *APSR* 23 (February 1929): 216; Dean, "The Struggle in Russia," *New Republic* 62 (5 March 1930): 63.

85. Dean, "Rome and Moscow," FPA Pamphlet no. 75 (29 April 1931): 18.

8. The Romance of Economic Development

1. On economic growth and change, see the essays in *The Economic Transformation of the Soviet Union, 1913–1945*, ed. R. W. Davies, Mark Harrison, and S. G. Wheatcroft (Cambridge: Cambridge University Press, 1994).

2. Michael Reiman, *The Birth of Stalinism: The USSR on the Eve of the "Second Revolution,"* trans. George Saunders (Bloomington: Indiana University Press, 1987); Moshe Lewin, *Lenin's Last Struggle*, trans. A. M. Sheridan Smith (New York: Pantheon, 1968); Lewin, *Political Undercurrents of Soviet Economic Debates: From Bukharin to the Modern Reformers* (Princeton: Princeton University Press, 1974).

3. Joseph Stalin, "A Year of Great Change" (1929), *Works*, 13 vols. (Moscow: Foreign Languages Publishing House, 1955), 12:141.

4. Stalin, "The Tasks of Economic Executives" (4 February 1931), in *Works*, 13:42; E. H. Carr and R. W. Davies, *Foundations of a Planned Economy, 1926–1929*, 2 vols. (London: Macmillan, 1969–1978).

5. For an exemplary and detailed description of the economic situation, see R. W. Davies, *The Industrialisation of Soviet Russia*, 4 vols. (Cambridge, Mass.: Harvard University Press, 1980–1996). On the most important new city, see Steven Kotkin, *Magnetic Mountain: Stalinism as a Civilization* (Berkeley and Los Angeles: University of California Press, 1995). On social impact of the Plans, see the contributions to *Social Dimensions of Soviet Industrializa-*

tion, ed. William G. Rosenberg and Lewis H. Siegelbaum (Bloomington: Indiana University Press, 1993). On the impact in rural Russia, see *Tragediia sovetskoi derevni: kollektivizatsiia i raskulachivanie*, 4 vols., ed. V. Danilov, R. Manning, and L. Viola (Moscow: Rossiiskaia politicheskaia entsiklopediia, 1999–).

6. On material conditions, see E. A. Osokina, *Ierarkhiia potrebleniia: O zhizni liudei v usloviiakh stalinskogo snabzheniia, 1928–1935 gg.* (Moscow: Izdatel'stvo MGOU, 1993). On various types of outcasts, see Sheila Fitzpatrick, *Everyday Stalinism: Ordinary Life in Extraordinary Times: Soviet Russia in the 1930s* (Oxford: Oxford University Press, 1999), chap. 5.

7. See Michael David-Fox, *Revolution of the Mind: Higher Learning among the Bolsheviks, 1918–1929* (Ithaca: Cornell University Press, 1997); and the contributions to *Cultural Revolution in Russia, 1928–1931*, ed. Sheila Fitzpatrick (Bloomington: Indiana University Press, 1978).

8. The historical sources on Soviet agencies dealing with foreigners is somewhat limited and needlessly partisan; see Sylvia R. Margulies, *The Pilgrimage to Russia: The Soviet Union and the Treatment of Foreigners, 1924–1937* (Madison: University of Wisconsin Press, 1968); and N. V. Kiseleva, *Iz istorii bor'by sovetskoi obshchestvennosti za proryv kul'turnoi blokady SSSR: VOKS, seredenia 20-kh–nachalo 30-kh godov* (Rostov: Izdatel'stvo rostovskogo universiteta, 1991). Work-in-progress by Michael David-Fox and Choi Chatterjee promises to rectify this situation. For complaints about Intourist, see virtually any account by a western client; also Umanskii to Astakhov, 20 October 1936, AVPRF, f. 05, op. 16, pap. 122, d. 107, l. 35; Liubchenko to Okoneshnikova, 13 April 1933, GARF, f. 5283, op. 1, d. 173, l. 10.

9. Paul Hollander, *Political Pilgrims: Travels of Western Intellectuals to the Soviet Union, China, and Cuba* (Oxford: Oxford University Press, 1981), chaps. 3–4. The estimate is from V. S. Lel'chuk and E. I. Pivovar, "Mentalitet sovetskogo obshchestva i 'kholodnaia voina,'" *Otechestvennaia istoriia*, no. 6 (1993): 75; also G. B. Kulikova, "SSSR 1920–1930-kh godov glazami zapadnykh intellektualov," *Otechestvennaia istoriia*, no. 1 (2001): 4–24. Similar estimates are cited in Daniel Soyer, "Back to the Future: American Jews Visit the Soviet Union in the 1920s and 1930s," *Jewish Social Studies* 6 (Spring/Summer 2000): 127.

10. William F. Ogburn, *Social Change with Respect to Culture and Original Nature* (1922; New York: Viking, 1950), 200–212, 346.

11. Guy Alchon, *The Invisible Hand of Planning: Capitalism, Social Science, and the State in the 1920s* (Princeton: Princeton University Press, 1985); Ellis W. Hawley, "Herbert Hoover, the Commerce Secretariat, and the Vision of an 'Associative State,' 1921–1928," *Journal of American History* 61 (June 1974): 116–140.

12. Kennan, "Memorandum for the Minister," enclosed in Robert Skinner to Secretary of State, 19 August 1932, SDDF, 861.5017 Living Conditions/510. Kennan offers his own analysis of this document in "Memorandum for the Minister," *New York Review of Books* 48 (26 April 2001): 23.

13. Herzen, *From the Other Shore* (New York: George Braziller, 1956), 158.

14. Alienation is posited by Paul Hollander, *Political Pilgrims*. William O'Neill considers only political motivations in *A Better World: The Great Schism— Stalinism and the American Intellectuals* (New York: Simon and Schuster, 1982). Naiveté is one of the themes in Eugene Lyons, *The Red Decade: The Stalinist Penetration of America* (1941; New Rochelle, N.Y.: Arlington House, 1971). And Edward Shils describes intellectuals' Soviet "fantasies" in "The Intellectuals and the Future" (1967), in *The Intellectuals and the Powers and Other Essays* (Chicago: University of Chicago Press, 1972).

15. Yet, *contra* Lewis Feuer, these intellectuals did not import the New Deal from Moscow; see Feuer, "American Travelers to the Soviet Union, 1917–1932: The Formation of a Component of New Deal Ideology," *American Quarterly* 14 (Summer 1962): 119–149.

16. See Christina D. Romer, "The Great Crash and the Great Depression," *QJE* 105 (August 1990): 597–624. One Russia expert confirmed his sense of this lag—Eugene Lyons, *Assignment in Utopia* (New York: Harcourt, Brace, 1937), 399.

17. Moshe Lewin, *The Making of the Soviet System: Essays in the Social History of Interwar Russia* (New York: Pantheon, 1975), chap. 9; Sheila Fitzpatrick, "The Legacy of the Civil War," in *Party, State and Society in the Russian Civil War*, ed. Diane P. Koenker, William G. Rosenberg, and Ronald Grigor Suny (Bloomington: Indiana University Press, 1989), esp. 390–397; Jeffrey Brooks, *Thank You, Comrade Stalin! Soviet Public Culture from Revolution to Cold War* (Princeton: Princeton University Press, 2000), 23–25.

18. Veblen, *The Engineers and the Price System* (1921; New Brunswick, N.J.: Transaction, 1983), 85–86.

19. Joseph Dorfman, *Thorstein Veblen and His America* (New York: Viking, 1934), 384–386.

20. Ibid., 426; Veblen, "Between Bolshevism and War" (1921), in Veblen, *Essays in Our Changing Order*, ed. Leon Ardzrooni (New York: Viking, 1934), 439, 441; Veblen, "A Policy of Reconstruction" (1918), in *Essays*, 396. Veblen's contributions were collected in *The Vested Interests and the Common Man* (New York: B. W. Huebsch, 1920) and included in later collections. Nicholas Joost, *Schofield Thayer and The Dial* (Carbondale: Southern Illinois University Press, 1964), 8–16.

21. Veblen, "A Memorandum on a Practicable Soviet of Technicians," in *Engineers and the Price System*, 135, 147, 149.

22. Bell, introduction (1963) to Veblen, *Engineers,* 27.
23. William E. Akin, *Technocracy and the American Dream: The Technocrat Movement, 1900–1941* (Berkeley and Los Angeles: University of California Press, 1977).
24. Robert Westbrook, "The Tribune of the Technostructure: The Popular Economics of Stuart Chase," *American Quarterly* 32 (Autumn 1980): 390.
25. Margaret Hatfield Chase and Stuart Chase, *A Honeymoon Experiment* (Boston: Houghton Mifflin, 1916).
26. Chase in "Where Are the Pre-War Radicals?" (ed. Frederic C. Howe), *Survey* 55 (1925): 563; Chase, "Portrait of a Radical," *Century Magazine* 86 (July 1924): 303; Westbrook, "Tribune," 391–392; Chase, foreword to Veblen, *The Theory of the Leisure Class: An Economic Study of Institutions* (New York: Modern Library, 1934), xi.
27. Chase, *The Tragedy of Waste* (New York: Macmillan, 1925), 26–41.
28. Chase, "Industry and the Gosplan," in *Soviet Russia in the Second Decade: A Joint Survey by the Technical Staff of the First American Trade Union Delegation,* ed. Stuart Chase, Robert Dunn, and Rexford Guy Tugwell (New York: John Day, 1928), 15–16, 18.
29. Ibid., 54.
30. Chase, "Russia's 'War Industries Board,'" *New Republic* 53 (4 February 1928): 185–186.
31. Chase, *Prosperity: Fact or Myth* (New York: Charles Boni, 1929), 27, 187–188.
32. Chase, "If I Were Dictator," *Nation* 133 (18 November 1931): 536–538. Other authors in the series were attorney Morris Ernst, editors William Allen White (*Emporia Gazette*), Glenn Frank (*Asia*), and Oswald Garrison Villard (*Nation*), and two Britons: political scientist Harold Laski and polymath G. Lowes Dickinson.
33. Edmund Wilson, "What Do the Liberals Hope for?" *New Republic* 69 (10 February 1932): 345–346; "Mr. Chase Replies," ibid., 349.
34. Chais, "Nebyvalyi v istorii eksperiment," *Pravda,* 7 November 1931.
35. Chase, "A Ten-Year Plan for America: Blueprint for a Peace Industries Board," *Harper's Magazine* 163 (July 1931): 3, 5, 7.
36. Douglas, "The Russian Economic Situation—Discussion," *AER* 19 (March 1929, supp.): 111–117.
37. On Soule's biographical details, see R. Alan Lawson, *The Failure of Independent Liberalism, 1930–1941* (New York: G. P. Putnam's Sons, 1971), 67–72; John M. Jordan, *Machine-Age Ideology: Social Engineering and American Liberalism, 1911–1939* (Chapel Hill: University of North Carolina Press, 1994), 209–211.
38. Soule, *The Useful Art of Economics* (New York: Macmillan, 1929), chap. 10;

Soule, *A Planned Society* (New York: Macmillan, 1932), 205, 228, 210, 229; Soule, *The Future of Liberty* (New York: Macmillan, 1936), 150.

39. Soule, *The Coming American Revolution* (New York: Macmillan, 1934), 64.

40. Soule, *Does Socialism Work?* (New York: New Republic, 1936), 33–34, 42–43, 28–29; Soule, *Future of Liberty,* 157–158.

41. Soule, *The New Economic Constitution* (New Haven: Yale University Press, 1939), 101.

42. Chase, "Collective Industry," 38; Chase, "Russia's 'War Industries Board,'" 185; Chase, "Industry and Gosplan," 50.

43. Chase et al., "Soviet Russia after Ten Years," FPA Pamphlet no. 47 (1928): 15; Chase, "Collectivist Industry in Russia: A Great Experiment in Eliminating the Waste Peculiar to Economic Competition," *Asia* 28 (May 1928): 368; Chase, "Industry and the Gosplan," 50.

44. Chase, "Poor Old Competition," League for Industrial Democracy Pamphlets 1:3 (1931): 36; Chase with Marian Tyler, *Mexico: A Study of Two Americas* (New York: Macmillan, 1931), 325.

45. See, for examples, George S. Counts, "The Soviet Planning System and the Five-Year Plan," in Counts et al., *Bolshevism, Fascism and Capitalism: An Account of Three Economic Systems* (New Haven: Yale University Press, 1932), 39; Karl Scholz, "Industry and the Second Five-Year Plan," *The New Russia: Between the First and Second Five-Year Plans,* ed. Jerome Davis (New York: John Day, 1933), 68; Ellsworth Huntington, "Geographic Background of the Revolution," *New Russia,* 49–50.

46. Chase, *A New Deal* (New York: Macmillan, 1932), 156.

47. Chase claimed to have originated the term; see Chase to Ruth Woodruff, 2 March 1954, in Stuart Chase Papers, box 1. The claim is corroborated in Ann Bremer, "The Conning Tower," *NYHT,* 30 August 1933.

48. "Draft Programme of the First Conference of the Economic Institute . . ." and related correspondence (June 1932–February 1933) in RGAE, f. 4372, op. 30, d. 15, ll. 126, 115–113, 96–94; "Otchet anglo-amerikanskogo sektora, 15–31 marta 1932 g.," GARF, f. 5283, op. 1, d. 219, l. 42.

49. Feuer, "American Travelers," 124; Chase, *New Deal,* 247–252.

50. "Can We Have National Planning without a Revolution?" FPA Pamphlet no. 81 (May 1932); *Annals* 162 (July 1932); Charles A. Beard, "A 'Five-Year Plan' for America," in *America Faces the Future,* ed. Beard (Boston: Houghton Mifflin, 1932); George Soule, "Beard and the Concept of Planning," in *Charles A. Beard: An Appraisal* (1954; New York: Octagon Books, 1976), 64–71; Howard C. Hill and Rexford Guy Tugwell, *Our Economic Society and Its Problems: A Study of American Levels of Living and How to Improve Them* (New York: Harcourt, Brace, 1934), chaps. 28–29.

51. Chase to Tugwell, 19 September 1978, in Rexford Guy Tugwell Papers, box 5.

52. Dorothy Ross, *The Origins of American Social Science* (Cambridge: Cambridge University Press, 1991), 173, 201–204; Commons, "American Shoemakers, 1648–1895: A Sketch of Industrial Evolution," *QJE* 24 (November 1909): 39–84.

53. Commons, "The Opportunity of Management," in Commons et al., *Industrial Government* (New York: Macmillan, 1921), 266–268; Commons, "Marx To-Day: Capitalism and Socialism," *Atlantic Monthly* 136 (November 1925): 685; Joseph Dorfman, *The Economic Mind in American Civilization*, 5 vols. (New York: Viking, 1959), 4:377–395.

54. Commons, *Legal Foundations of Capitalism* (New York: Macmillan, 1924), chap. 4.

55. Calvin Bryce Hoover, *Memoirs of Capitalism, Communism, and Nazism* (Durham: Duke University Press, 1965), 78.

56. Leon Fink and Mark Perlman, "A Memoir of Selig Perlman and His Life at the University of Wisconsin," *Labor History* 32 (Fall 1991): 503–509; Leon Fink, *Progressive Intellectuals and the Dilemmas of Democratic Commitment* (Cambridge, Mass.: Harvard University Press, 1997), 69–77; interview with Mark Perlman, July 25, 2001.

57. Selig Perlman, *A Theory of the Labor Movement* (New York: Macmillan, 1928), 281, 290.

58. On Plekhanov's views of the peasantry, see his blistering critiques of Russian populism in *Sochineniia*, 24 vols., ed. D. Riazanov (Moscow: Gosizdat, 1923), vol. 10; Samuel H. Baron, *Plekhanov: The Father of Russian Marxism* (Stanford: Stanford University Press, 1966), 105–106; and Kingston-Mann, *In Search of the True West*, chap. 6.

59. Perlman, *Theory*, 53, 29; Perlman, "Bolshevism and Democracy," *Publications of the American Sociological Society* 14 (1920): 217, 219, 223. The reflections were recorded by a student of his and were based on lectures given during WWII—A. L. Riesch Owen, *Selig Perlman's Lectures on Capitalism and Socialism* (Madison: University of Wisconsin Press, 1976), 110–111, and chapter 2.

60. Hoover, *Memoirs*, 11–12, 92; William J. Barber, "The Career of Alvin H. Hansen in the 1920s and 1930s: A Study in Intellectual Transformation," *History of Political Economy* 19 (Summer 1987): 192–194.

61. Hoover, *Memoirs*, 92–93. He mentioned the problems of acquiring coffee in at least seven letters to his wife, all in Calvin Bryce Hoover Papers—Addition. On translators and guides, see the desk diaries in GARF, f. 5283, op. 8, d. 60, ll. 50, 56; GARF, f. 5283, op. 9, d. 83, ll. 23, 25; and GARF, f. 5283 s.ch., op. 1a, d. 131, l. 19.

62. Hoover, "The Fate of the New Economic Policy in the Soviet Union," *EJ* 40

(June 1930): 193; Hoover, "Some Economic and Social Consequences of Russian Communism," *EJ* 40 (September 1930): 423, 435, 425; Keynes to Hoover, 29 April 1930, Hoover Papers, box 21.

63. Hoover, *Economic Life of Soviet Russia* (New York: Macmillan, 1931), 329, 334, 331, 324; Paul Haensel, book review, *AER* 21 (June 1931): 295–297; Hindus, "The Economics of Russia," *Saturday Review of Literature* 7 (13 March 1931): 659; Lyons, "Reporting Russia: Twenty Years of Books on Soviet Russia," *Saturday Review of Literature* 17 (25 December 1937): 15.

64. Hoover in "Roundtable: The Russian Economic Situation," *AER* 21 (March 1931, supp.): 43; Hoover in Counts, *Bolshevism*, 228, 250.

65. Hoover, *Economic Life*, 67, 324; Hansen, *Economic Stabilization in an Unbalanced World* (New York: Harcourt, Brace, 1932), 333, 359.

66. Hoover, *Economic Life*, 343, 97, 110, 69; Hoover, "Religion in Soviet Russia," *South Atlantic Quarterly* 30 (April 1931): 119.

67. Rexford Guy Tugwell, "Russian Agriculture," in *Soviet Russia in the Second Decade*, 57; Karl Borders, "Local Autonomy in Russian Village Life under the Soviets," *AJS* 35 (November 1929): 419; Fischer, *Soviet Journey* (New York: Harrison Smith and Robert Haas, 1935), 132; Hoover, *Economic Life*, 85, 329; Harper, Notes on Five-Year Plan (1930), in Samuel Northrop Harper Papers, box 27; Harper, "The Soviet Five-Year Plan," *Proceedings of the Academy of Political Science of New York* 14 (June 1931): 415–416, 420.

68. Hoover, *Economic Life*, 70, 345, 343, 55, 56; Hoover, "Roundtable," 44; Hoover, "The Soviet Challenge to Capitalism," *Harper's Magazine* 161 (October 1930): 593. Although one reviewer considered the emphasis on "Asiatic characteristics" an insufficient "working hypothesis," Hoover held to them, even quoting from these remarks at length in his 1965 memoirs—A. Meyendorff review, *EJ* 41 (September 1931): 455; Hoover, *Memoirs*, 123.

69. Chamberlin, *Soviet Russia: A Living Record and History*, rev. ed. (Boston: Little, Brown, 1931), 436; Hoover book review, *PSQ* 46 (December 1931): 635; Hoover, *Economic Life*, 335; [Bernard Pares], "The Crisis of Democracy and the Slavonic World," *SEER* 9 (March 1931): 517. On Hoover's contacts with the Chamberlins, see correspondence in Hoover Papers—Addition.

70. Hoover to Harper, n. d. (spring 1931?), Hoover Papers, box 16; Hoover, "Soviet Challenge," 597–598; Hoover, *Economic Life*, 346–347.

71. I. Il'f and E. Petrov, *Zolotoi Telenok* (1931; Moscow: Poligran, 1992), 241.

72. Kelley, "The Bolshevik Regime in Russia," lecture to the National War College, 3 December 1931, in Robert F. Kelley Papers, box 2; Kelley to Phillips, 5 April 1933, SDDF, 861.5017 Living Conditions/595.

73. Hoover, *Germany Enters the Third Reich* (New York: Macmillan, 1933), chap. 9; Hoover, "Dictators Today: Adolph Hitler, Joseph Stalin, and Others,"

Encyclopedia Britannica's World To-Day 2 (September 1934): 10–11; Hoover, "Paths to Economic Change: Contrasting Tendencies in the Modern World," *AER* 25 (March 1935, supp.): 13–20.

74. Dewey, "Leningrad Gives the Clue" (1928), *LW*, 3:204 (he quickly tempered this view); see *LW*, 3:207 n. 1.

75. Counts, "A Humble Autobiography," in *Leaders in American Education,* ed. Robert J. Havighurst (Chicago: University of Chicago Press, 1971), 157; Counts interview with Warren Seyfert, 21 September 1964, George S. Counts Papers (SIU), 2.

76. Ellen Condliffe Lagemann, *An Elusive Science: The Troubling History of Education Research* (Chicago: University of Chicago Press, 2000), 66–70.

77. Counts, "Humble Autobiography," 171; Charles Duane Jay, "The Doctoral Program of George S. Counts at the University of Chicago, 1913–1916: An Intellectual History" (Ph.D. diss., Southern Illinois University, 1982), chap. 10; Counts interview with Warren Seyfert, 21 September 1964, in George S. Counts Papers (Columbia), box 1.

78. Counts, *School and Society in Chicago* (New York: Harcourt, Brace, 1928), vii, Part III.

79. Counts, "Education in Soviet Russia," in *Soviet Russia in the Second Decade,* 277, 270, 302. See Dewey's essays, later published as *Impressions of Soviet Russia and the Revolutionary World* (1928), in *LW,* vol. 3.

80. Counts letter to Charles Judd, 30 November 1929, quoted in Lawrence J. Dennis, *George S. Counts and Charles A. Beard: Collaborators for Change* (Albany: SUNY Press, 1989), 38.

81. Counts, *The American Road to Culture: A Social Interpretation of Education in the United States* (New York: John Day, 1930), ix, 7, 176, 182, v.

82. Counts, *Secondary Education and Industrialism* (Cambridge, Mass.: Harvard University Press, 1929), 3, 60.

83. On the invitation, see A. V. Lunacharskii, "Literatura i marksizm" (1928), in Lunacharskii, *O vospitanii i obrazovanii,* ed. A. M. Arsen'eva et al. (Moscow: Pedagogika, 1976), 470. On participants, see "John Dewey in Russia," *Survey* 61 (15 December 1928): 348–349.

84. Dewey, *School and Society* (1899), *MW,* vol. 1; B. L. Vul'fson, "Dzhon D'iui i sovetskaia pedagogika," *Pedagogika,* no. 9/10 (1992): 99–105; Mark Steven Johnson, "Russian Educators: The Stalinist Party-State and the Politics of Soviet Education, 1929–1939" (Ph.D. diss., Columbia University, 1995), chaps. 1–2.

85. A. P. Pinkevich, "Sovremennye burzhuaznye pedagogicheskie teorii," *Pedagogicheskaia entsiklopediia,* 3 vols. (Moscow: Rabotnik prosveshcheniia, 1927): 1:423.

86. Shatskii, "Amerikanskie pedagogiki u nas v gostiakh" (1928), in S. T. Shatskii,

Pedagogicheskie sochineniia, 4 vols. (Moscow: Izdatel'stvo pedagogicheskikh nauk, 1963), 3:214.

87. Dewey, "New Schools for a New Era" (1928), *LW,* 3:241.

88. Dewey, "The Great Experiment and the Future" (1928), *LW,* 3:247–248; Dewey, "Science and Society" (1931), *LW,* 6:60–61.

89. Dewey, "Discussion of Freedom" (1932), *LW,* 6:144; Dewey, introduction to *Humanity Uprooted,* by Maurice Hindus (1930), *LW,* 5:409; Dewey, "Why I Am Not a Communist" (1934), *LW,* 9:91–95; Robert Westbrook, *John Dewey and American Democracy* (Ithaca: Cornell University Press, 1989), chap. 12.

90. Counts, *The Soviet Challenge to America* (New York: John Day, 1931), xi, 17.

91. Ibid., 122; Counts, "The Soviet Planning System and the Five-Year Plan," in Counts et al., *Bolshevism, Fascism, and Capitalism,* 211; Counts, *A Ford Crosses Soviet Russia* (Boston: Stratford, 1930), 144, 194–195, 95.

92. Thomas Woody, *New Minds, New Men? The Emergence of the Soviet Citizen* (New York: Macmillan, 1932), 315.

93. Counts, *Ford,* 147; Huntington, *Civilization and Climate* (New Haven: Yale University Press, 1915), 287–288; Huntington, *The Geography of Europe* (New Haven: Yale University Press, 1918), 80–86. The geographer applied his ideas to Russia at greater length in Huntington, "The Geographic Background of the Revolution"; Brebner, "The Ante-Room of Time," *Soviet Russia in the Second Decade,* 4; also Pierre Jolly, "Public Utilities in France," *HBR* 9 (July 1931): 410.

94. Lawrence H. Dennis and William Edward Eaton, *George S. Counts: Educator for a New Age* (Carbondale: Southern Illinois University Press, 1980), 4–5; Counts, *Ford,* 148.

95. Counts, *Ford,* 148.

96. Counts, "Soviet Planning System," 45, 50; Counts, *Soviet Challenge,* 298; Counts, *Ford,* 139.

97. Counts, *Ford,* 50, 142–143, 184, 223; Counts, discussion in *Bolshevism, Fascism and Capitalism,* 217.

98. Counts, *Soviet Challenge,* 83, 295, 317.

99. See, for example, the review of scholarship on the Russian peasant in Ben Eklof, "Ways of Seeing: Recent Anglo-American Studies of the Russian Peasant (1861–1914)," *Jahrbücher für Geschichte osteuropas* 36:1 (1988): 57–79. A notable exception is Steven L. Hoch, *Serfdom and Social Control in Russia: Petrovskoe, A Village in Tambov* (Chicago: University of Chicago Press, 1986).

100. Chamberlin, "The Ordeal of the Russian Peasantry," *FA* 12 (April 1934): 497; Lazar Volin, "Agrarian Collectivism in the Soviet Union," *JPE* 45 (October 1937): 617; Arthur Feiler, *The Russian Experiment* (New York: Harcourt, Brace, 1930), 246. Feiler was the financial editor of *Frankfurter Allgemeine Zeitung* who fled Germany for the New School for Social Research; see Claus-

Dieter Krohn, *Intellectuals in Exile: Refugee Scholars and the New School for Social Research*, trans. Rita and Robert Kimber (Amherst: University of Massachusetts Press, 1993), 65–66. See also Ethan T. Colton, *The X Y Z of Communism* (New York: Macmillan, 1931), 163; Ellery Walter, *Russia's Decisive Year* (New York: G. P. Putnam's Sons, 1932), 266.

101. Herbert Hoover, *American Individualism* (Garden City, N.J.: Doubleday and Page, 1922), 41–47, 66; Wilfred M. McClay, *The Masterless: Self and Society in Modern America* (Chapel Hill: University of North Carolina Press, 1994), 150, 167–169.

102. Dewey, *Individualism, Old and New* (1930), *LW*, 5:45, 122, 57, 80.

103. Sherwood Eddy, *The Challenge of Russia* (New York: Farrar and Rinehart, 1931), 232–233; George Vernadsky, book review, *SEER* 10 (April 1932): 722.

104. Woody, *New Minds, New Men?*, xi, chap. 10; Hoover to Faith, 29 November 1929, in Hoover Papers—Addition; Woody, "Towards a Classless Society under the Hammer and Sickle," *Annals* 182 (November 1935): 152.

105. Harper, *Making Bolsheviks* (Chicago: University of Chicago Press, 1931), x, 155–156.

106. Counts, *Soviet Challenge*, 323, 327–328.

107. Dewey, "New Schools," 236.

108. Dewey, "A New World in the Making" (1928), *LW*, 3:221, 223.

109. Counts, *Soviet Challenge*, 210; Counts, *Ford*, 201–202.

110. Dewey, "From Absolutism to Experimentalism" (1930), *LW*, 5:156; Dewey, "Philosophy" (1930), *LW*, 5:162, 161.

111. E. A. Ross, book review, *AJS* 39 (January 1934): 562–563; Counts, *Soviet Challenge*, 288.

112. Alzada Comstock, book review, *AER* 26 (September 1936): 556; A. Abrahamson, "Social Insurance in Soviet Russia," *JPE* 37 (August 1929): 399.

113. Hoover, *Economic Life*, 337; Hoover, "The Soviet Challenge to Capitalism," *Harper's Magazine* 161 (October 1930): 598; Dewey, "Great Experiment," *LW*, 3:244.

114. Counts, "A Word to the American Reader," introduction to M. Ilin, *New Russia's Primer: The Story of the Five-Year Plan*, trans. Counts and Nucia P. Lodge (Boston: Houghton Mifflin, 1931), ix. The Book-of-the-Month Club named this as a monthly selection; see *Book-of-the-Month Club News*, April 1931. Counts, introduction to Albert P. Pinkevich, *The New Education in the Soviet Republic*, ed. Counts, trans. Nucia Perlmutter (New York: John Day, 1929), xi–xii.

115. Counts, *Dare the School Build a New Social Order?*, John Day Pamphlet no. 11 (1932): 7, 28, 30–31, 37.

116. Counts, *Soviet Challenge*, 334; Dewey, "'Surpassing America,'" (1931), *LW*, 6:266.

117. Helen Everett, "Control, Social," in *The Encyclopedia of the Social Sciences*, 15 vols., ed. E. R. A. Seligman (New York: Macmillan, 1932): 4:346.

118. Counts, "Soviet Planning System" and discussion (pp. 202–268) in Counts, *Bolshevism*.

119. Harold Kellock to H. Parker Willis, undated (1928?), AVPRF, f. 508, op. 5, por. 9, pap. 21, ll. 94–94ob; John V. A. MacMurray to Raymond Fosdick, 16 October 1931, Harper Papers, box 16; Counts to Tolokonskii, GARF, f. 5283 s.ch., op. 1a, d. 238, l. 23.

120. George Akerson to Acting Secretary of State Joseph Cotton, 17 February 1930; Robert Kelley to Counts, 21 February 1930; Counts to Kelley, 21 March 1930, all in SDDF, 861.5017 Living Conditions/122, 123, 134.

121. Counts, "Education and the Five-Year Plan of Soviet Russia," *Journal of Educational Sociology* 4 (September 1930): 29.

122. On AFT, see Marjorie Murphy, *Blackboard Unions: The AFT and the NEA, 1900–1980* (Ithaca: Cornell University Press, 1990), 162–172; Ellen Condliffe Lagemann, "Prophecy or Profession? George S. Counts and the Social Study of Education," *American Journal of Education* 100 (February 1992): 158–159.

123. George S. Counts and Nucia Lodge, *The Country of the Blind: The Soviet System of Mind Control* (Boston: Houghton Mifflin, 1949), xv; Counts, *The Challenge of Soviet Education* (New York: McGraw-Hill, 1957), vii, 286–290.

124. Gerald L. Gutek, *George S. Counts and American Civilization* (Atlanta: Mercer University Press, 1984), chaps. 4, 9; Dennis and Eaton, *George S. Counts*; Raymond Callahan, "George S. Counts: Educational Statesman," in *Leaders in American Education*.

125. Adam Ulam, Memorial Minute, 17 February 1976, in Bruce Campbell Hopper Papers, series HUG(B) H655.5; Hopper, "Soviet Economic Statecraft" (Ph.D. diss., Harvard University, 1930). On efforts at promotion, see the letters in Walter Lippmann Papers, box 78, folder 1076; also reference letter, 30 November 1959, Hamilton Fish Armstrong Papers, box 35; Armstrong to Lippmann, 25 March 1937, Armstrong Papers, box 41.

126. Hopper, book review, *APSR* 27 (April 1933): 292; Maud Russell to Mary Bentley, 20 July 1932, Maud Russell Papers, box 3 (Russell was a long-term houseguest at the Chamberlins'); Hopper to Knickerbocker, 4 January 1929, H. R. Knickerbocker Papers, Uncatalogued Correspondence; Vincent Sheean, *Personal History* (Garden City, N.J.: Doubleday Doran, 1937), 296.

127. Hopper to John Wiley, 28 July 1943, John X. Wiley Papers, box 2; Loy Henderson to Samuel Harper, 18 September 1940, Harper Papers, box 22; Hopper to Kelley, 18 July 1932, and 24 July 1932, both in SDR, Records of the Division of Eastern European Affairs, box 5; diary entry, 7 February 1934, in "Mr. Kennan's Russian Diary," George Frost Kennan Papers, box 23; Kennan memorandum of conversation, 8 January 1938, SDDF, 861.00/11747.

128. Armstrong, *Peace and Counterpeace from Wilson to Hitler: Memoirs of Hamilton Fish Armstrong* (New York: Harper and Row, 1971), 190, 411, 454.

129. Harper to Geroid Robinson, 9 October 1933, Harper Papers, box 18; see also Calvin B. Hoover, book review, *SF* 10 (December 1932): 282.

130. Hopper, book review, *APSR* 28 (February 1934): 147; Hopper, *Pan-Sovietism: The Issue before America and the World* (Boston: Houghton Mifflin, 1931), 288. Others suggesting the potential relevance of Soviet modernization strategies include Hans Kohn, "The Europeanization of the Orient," *PSQ* 52 (February 1937): 264; and Bernard Pares, "The New Crisis in Russia," *SEER* 11 (April 1933): 490.

131. Kohn, *Living in a World Revolution: My Encounters with History* (New York: Trident, 1964); Kohn, "Europeanization of the Orient," 259–260; Kohn, *Orient and Occident* (New York: John Day, 1934), v; Kohn, *The Idea of Nationalism: A Study in Its Origins and Background* (New York: Macmillan, 1944).

132. Kohn, *Nationalism in the Soviet Union* (London: George Routledge and Sons, 1933), 3–4, 6.

133. Kohn, *Nationalism*, 6–7; Kohn, *Orient*, 16, 80–81; Kohn, "The Nationality Policy of the Soviet Union," in *The Soviet Union and World-Problems*, ed. Samuel N. Harper (Chicago: University of Chicago Press, 1935), 109.

134. The biographical details are culled from Rev. Louis J. Gallagher, S. J., *Edmund A. Walsh, S. J.: A Biography* (New York: Benziger Brothers, 1962); and Seth P. Tillman, *Georgetown's School of Foreign Service: The First 75 Years* (Washington: Georgetown University, 1994), 1–8.

135. Walsh, *The Fall of the Russian Empire* (Boston: Little, Brown, 1928), 10–11 (also q.v. "peasants, dreamy idealism of" in index); Walsh, "Ten Years after the Russian Revolution" (1927?), in Edmund Aloysius Walsh Papers, box 10, folder 300; Walsh, "Some Observations of the Soviet Problem," *Annals* 132 (July 1932): 11.

136. Walsh, *Fall*, 18; Walsh, *The Last Stand: An Interpretation of the Soviet Five-Year Plan* (Boston: Little, Brown, 1931), 70, 222.

137. Walsh, *Fall*, 10–11.

138. Other contemporary writings on Russia emphasized the cheapness of human life: Will Durant, *The Tragedy of Russia: Impressions from a Brief Visit* (New York: Simon and Schuster, 1933), 47; Sherwood Eddy, *Russia Today: What Can We Learn from It?* (New York: Simon and Schuster, 1934), 14; Elisha A. Friedman, *Russia in Transition: A Business Man's Appraisal* (New York: Viking, 1932), 7; and Lyford Edwards, book review, *AJS* 33 (May 1928): 1016.

139. On the exclusion, see J. V. A. MacMurray to Roland Morris, 5 August 1931, in John van Antwerp MacMurray Papers, box 119.

140. White's book focused on Dewey and Veblen, among others—*Social Thought in America: The Revolt against Formalism* (1949; Boston: Beacon, 1957).

141. Although he examines a different cast of characters, David Caute also explains western interest in the USSR in terms of broader themes of social thought; see *The Fellow-Travelers: A Postscript to the Enlightenment* (New York: Macmillan, 1973). John Patrick Diggins intermingles incisive observations of western views with familiar political polemic in "Limping after Reality: American Intellectuals, the Six Myths of the USSR, and the Precursors of Anti-Stalinism," *Il Mito dell'URSS: La cultura occidentale e l'Unione Sovietica,* ed. Marcello Flores (Milan: Franco Angeli, 1990).

142. Hopper, *Pan-Sovietism,* 179.

9. Starving Itself Great

1. For recent estimates of the demographic impact, see E. A. Osokina, "Zhertvy goloda 1933 g.—skol'ko ikh?" *Istoriia SSSR,* no. 5 (1991): 18–26; N. A. Ivnitskii, "Golod 1932–33 godov: kto vinovat?" *Golod 1932–33 godov: sbornik statei* (Moscow: RGGU, 1995), 64–65; S. G. Wheatcroft and R. W. Davies, "Population," in *The Economic Transformation of the Soviet Union, 1913–1945,* ed. Davies, Mark Harrison, and Wheatcroft (Cambridge: Cambridge University Press, 1994), 67–69; and S. Uitkroft [Wheatcroft], "O demograficheskikh svidetel'stvakh tragediia sovetskoi derevni v 1931–1933 gg.," in *Tragediia sovetskoi derevni: kollektivizatsiia i raskulachivanie,* ed. V. Danilov, R. Manning, and L. Viola (Moscow: Rosspen, 1999–), 3: 866–887.

2. Sheila Fitzpatrick, *Stalin's Peasants: Resistance and Survival in the Russian Village after Collectivization* (Oxford: Oxford University Press, 1994); Lynne Viola, *Peasant Rebels under Stalin: Collectivization and the Culture of Peasant Resistance* (Oxford: Oxford University Press, 1996); Moshe Lewin, "The Kolkhoz and the Russian *Muzhik*" (1980), in *The Making of the Soviet System: Essays in the Social History of Interwar Russia* (New York: Pantheon, 1985).

3. Cited in Richard Pipes, *Russia under the Bolshevik Regime* (New York: Knopf, 1994), 411; Amartya Sen, *Poverty and Famines: An Essay on Entitlement and Deprivation* (Oxford: Clarendon, 1981), 1.

4. Ragnar Nurkse, *Problems of Capital Formation in Underdeveloped Countries* (Oxford: Oxford University Press, 1953), 43.

5. Questions of grain export occasionally reached the Politburo over the course of 1932–1933; see Politburo protocols of 8 January 1932, 23 October 1932, and 5 December 1933, in RGASPI, f. 17, op. 3, d. 867, pt. 24; f. 17, op. 3, d. 904, l. 10; f. 17, op. 3, d. 935, l. 25. My emphasis on economic issues has been informed especially by Stephan Merl, "War die Hungersnot von 1932–1933 eine Folge der Zwangskollektivierung der Landswirthschaft oder wurde sie bewusst im Rahmen der Nationalitätenpolitik herbeigefuhrt?" in *Ukraine: Gegenwart und Geschichte eines neuen Staates,* ed. Guido Hausmann and

Andreas Kappeler (Baden-Baden: Nomos, 1993); also I. E. Zelenin et al., "O golode 1932–33 godov i ego otsenke na Ukraine," *Otechestvennaia istoriia*, no. 6 (1994): 256–262. For contrasting arguments, see Robert Conquest, *Harvest of Sorrow: Soviet Collectivization and the Terror-Famine* (Oxford: Oxford University Press, 1986); and Mark B. Tauger, "Natural Disaster and Human Actions in the Soviet Famine of 1931–1933," Carl Beck Papers, no. 1506 (2001).

6. D'Ann Penner, "The Agrarian 'Strike' of 1932–1933," Kennan Institute for Advanced Russian Studies, Occasional Paper no. 269 (1998); Penner, "Stalin and the Ital'ianka of 1932–33 in the Don Region," *Cahiers du monde russe* 39 (1998): 27–67; and Andrea Graziosi, "The Great Soviet Peasant War: Bolsheviks and Peasants, 1917–1933," Harvard Papers in Ukrainian Studies (1996).

7. V. V. Kuibyshev, Stenogram of Grain Meeting, 11 May 1932, RGAE, f. 8040, op. 1, d. 16, l. 290.

8. E. A. Osokina, *Ierarkhiia potrebleniia: o zhizni liudei v usloviiakh stalinskogo snabzheniia, 1928–1935 gg.* (Moscow: Izdatel'stvo MGOU, 1993), 44–62; Osokina, *Za fasadom "Stalinskogo izobiliia": raspredelenie i rynok v snabzhenii naseleniia v gody industrializatsii, 1927–1941* (Moscow: Rosspen, 1998), 120.

9. N. A. Ivnitskii, *Repressivnaia politika sovetskoi vlasti v derevne (1928–1933 gg.)* (Moscow: RAN, 2000), 289.

10. Stalin to Molotov, 6 May 1933, RGASPI, f. 558, op. 1, d. 3459, ll. 2–6.

11. Podol'skii diary, 3 November 1930, AVPRF, f. 0129, op. 13, pap. 127, d. 319, ll. 6–7; Oumansky to NKID Collegium, 1 January 1933, AVPRF, f. 0129, op. 16, pap. 128a, d. 335, ll. 21–22; Joe Alex Morris, *Deadline Every Minute: The Story of the United Press* (Garden City, N.J.: Doubleday, 1957), 189.

12. The lack of evidence has not prevented insinuations of Soviet payoffs; see James E. Mace, "The American Press and the Ukrainian Famine," in *Genocide Watch*, ed. Helen Fein (New Haven: Yale University Press, 1992), 121; M. Wayne Morris, *Stalin's Famine and Roosevelt's Recognition of Russia* (Lanham, Md.: University Press of America, 1994), 94–95; and James William Crowl, *Angels in Stalin's Paradise: Western Reporters in the Soviet Union, 1917 to 1937* (Lanham, Md.: University Press of America, 1982), 142, 158.

13. Especially given the prevalence of ethnic interpretations of this famine, it is worth noting that western observers of the 1920s and 1930s did not consistently distinguish between Russian and Ukrainian "traits."

14. "The Russian Press Censorship," *Outlook* 76 (27 February 1904): 481–483; Marianna T. Choldin, *A Fence around the Empire: Russian Censorship of Western Ideas under the Tsars* (Durham: Duke University Press, 1985).

15. Melville E. Stone, *Fifty Years a Journalist* (Garden City, N.Y.: Doubleday Page, 1921), 261–278; Charles R. Crane memoirs, ed. Walter S. Rogers, Charles R. Crane Papers, reel 3, p. 74.

16. Robert W. Desmond, *Windows on the World: The Information Process in a Changing Society, 1900–1920* (Iowa City: University of Iowa Press, 1980), chap. 14.

17. Lippmann and Merz, "A Test of the News," *New Republic* 23 (4 August 1920, supp.): 25, 10–11, 3.

18. Ibid., 3, 42.

19. George Seldes, *Freedom of the Press* (Indianapolis: Bobbs-Merrill, 1935), 368–369.

20. Lippmann, *Liberty and the News* (New York: Harcourt, Brace, and Howe, 1920), 99–100, 79, 104.

21. Harrison Salisbury, *Without Fear or Favor: The* New York Times *and Its Times* (New York: Times Books, 1980), 461–462; Duranty, *I Write as I Please* (New York: Simon and Schuster, 1935), 103.

22. Duranty, *One Life, One Kopeck* (New York: Simon and Schuster, 1937), [335].

23. Reports from Samara, 6 September 1921, in *Duranty Reports Russia,* ed. Gustavus Tuckerman, Jr. (London: Victor Gollancz, 1934), 28–30. Future citations from this work will appear as *Duranty Reports Russia,* page number (dispatch date).

24. Alexander Gumberg to Walter Duranty, n.d. [early 1927], Alexander Gumberg Papers, box 3; Salisbury, *Without Fear or Favor,* 463; Robert W. Desmond, *Crisis and Conflict: World News Reporting between Two Wars, 1920–1940* (Iowa City: University of Iowa Press, 1982), 37.

25. S. J. Taylor, *Stalin's Apologist: Walter Duranty, The* New York Times*'s Man in Moscow* (Oxford: Oxford University Press, 1990), 130; Duranty to Adolph Ochs, 27 December 1924, in Adolph Ochs Papers, Duranty file; Duranty lecture (1932), quoted in Seldes, *Freedom of the Press,* 200.

26. Salisbury, *Without Fear or Favor,* 460.

27. Chamberlin, *Confessions of an Individualist* (New York: Macmillan, 1940), 15, 42.

28. Chamberlin, "My Russian Education," in *We Cover the World,* ed. Eugene Lyons (New York: Harcourt, Brace, 1937), 209.

29. Broun, "One Speaks of Rope," *Nation* 141 (16 October 1935): 441–442.

30. A. C. Freeman [William Henry Chamberlin], *Soviet Russia* 4 (21 April 1921): 368.

31. Gumberg to Chamberlin, 11 November 1923, Gumberg Papers, box 2; Erwin D. Canham to Board of Trustees, 26 August 1940, Christian Science Publishing Society (CSPS), series ME1, shelf A56045.

32. "Soviet Aims Given by Leon Trotzky," *CSM,* 28 September 1922; "Karl Radek Voices Views on Cooperation with America," *CSM,* 7 November 1922; "Lenine [*sic*] Depicted as Devoted to the Cause of the Common People," *CSM,* 21 February 1924. I have also relied on Robert H. Meyers, "William Henry Chamberlin: His Views of the Soviet Union" (Ph.D. diss., Indiana Uni-

versity, 1973), for some of Chamberlin's early writings—see pp. 134, 141, 22–40. Trilisser to Vainshtein, May 1923, AVPRF, f. 0129, op. 6, pap. 105, d. 59, l. 5.

33. Myers, "William Henry Chamberlin," 135–136; Board Minutes, 25 February 1927, 17 March 1927, CSPS, series ME1, shelf A49037.

34. Fischer essay in *The God That Failed,* ed. Richard H. Crossman (1950; New York: Columbia University Press, 2001), 197–200; Fischer, *Men and Politics: An Autobiography* (New York: Duell, Sloan and Pearce, 1940), 5–6, 240–242; Crowl, *Angels in Stalin's Paradise,* 23–25; interview with George Fischer, 17 June 1996.

35. Fischer, *Men and Politics,* 46–47, 61–62, 208; Fischer to Trotsky, 22 April 1924, AVPRF, f. 0129, op. 6, pap. 108, d. 6, ll. 69–70.

36. Fischer, "Nine Years of Bolshevism," *Nation* 123 (10 November 1926): 471–473; Fischer, "Russia's Collectivized Farms," *Nation* 131 (8 October 1930): 370.

37. Fischer, *Men and Politics,* 140; Fischer, *The Soviets in World Affairs: A History of Relations between the Soviet Union and the Rest of the World, 1917–1929,* 2 vols. (London: Jonathan Cape, 1930); Fischer, introduction to *The Soviets in World Affairs* (New York: Vintage, 1960), v–viii; also Fischer-Chicherin correspondence in Louis Fischer Papers (Yale), box 1, folders 2, 4.

38. Lyons, *Assignment in Utopia* (New York: Harcourt, Brace, 1937), 37–41, 46–49.

39. Ibid., 80. Lyons's contacts are also discussed in interviews: Henry Shapiro, 30 July 1983, in Whitman Bassow Papers, box 2, folder Shapiro, p. 10–5; and Robin Kincaid, 18 February 1985, Bassow Papers, unnumbered box, folder Kincaid, p. 1–11.

40. Lyons, introduction to *We Cover the World,* 3; James Abbe, "Men of Cablese," *New Outlook* 162 (December 1933): 28, 30.

41. Lyons, "Djugashvili: Russia's Man of Steel," *World's Work* 60 (June 1931): 77–80. The original dispatches are in Eugene Lyons Papers (Hoover), box 6, folder 21. Skvirskii to Litvinov, 11 December 1930, AVPRF, f. 0129, op. 13, pap. 126, d. 318, ll. 152–153; Whitman Bassow, *The Moscow Correspondents: Reporting on Russia from the Revolution to Glasnost* (New York: William Morrow, 1988), 74–75.

42. Milton Hindus, "Portrait of an Uncle," in Maurice Hindus, *A Traveler in Two Worlds* (Garden City, N.J.: Doubleday, 1971), 17; Hindus, *The Russian Peasant and the Revolution* (New York: H. Holt, 1920), xi, 311.

43. Robinson, "The Decentralization of Russian History," *PSQ* 36 (September 1921): 455.

44. Hindus, *Russian Peasant,* 308–323.

45. Fischer, "Humanity under Bolshevism," *Nation* 132 (27 May 1931): 587;

Fischer, *Men and Politics,* 158–159; Hindus to Oswald Garrison Villard, 8 July 1931, Oswald Garrison Villard Papers, folder 1705; interview with Eva Hindus, 14 August 2001.

46. Hindus, *Russian Peasant,* xi, 4, 89, 84; Hindus, *Broken Earth* (New York: International Publishers, 1926), 14.

47. Hindus, *Russian Peasant,* 65, 273, 277; Hindus, *Broken Earth,* 284–285, 89; Hindus, in "Social Conditions in Soviet Russia," FPA Pamphlet no. 72 (March 1931): 16–17.

48. Hindus, *Broken Earth,* 278–279, 284.

49. Michael Schudson, *Discovering the News: A Social History of American Newspapers* (New York: Basic, 1978), esp. 120, 151–155. The point is corroborated in one of the classic works of journalism history—Franklin Luther Mott, *American Journalism: A History of Newspapers in the United States through 260 Years: 1690 to 1950,* rev. ed. (New York: Macmillan, 1950), 688–689.

50. Herbert Brucker, "The Glut of Occurences" (1935), in *Interpretations of Journalism: A Book of Readings,* ed. Franklin Luther Mott and Ralph Carey (New York: F. S. Crofts, 1937), 232.

51. Robert W. Desmond, *The Press and World Affairs* (New York: D. Appleton-Century, 1937), 8–9.

52. Lippmann, "The Press and Public Opinion," *PSQ* 46 (June 1931): 161–163.

53. Hindus, "Asia's Great Wild West," *Asia* 28 (May 1928): 355; Hindus, "The Russian Peasant Reborn: The Timid but Anarchic Being Made Self-Assertively Articulate by the Revolution," *Asia* 27 (April 1927): 298–300; Hindus, "The Russian Peasant and the Soviet Government," *Annals* 126 (July 1926): 140.

54. Fischer, "Humanity under Bolshevism," *Nation* 132 (27 May 1931): 587.

55. Fischer to H. R. Knickerbocker, 29 March 1929, in H. R. Knickerbocker Papers, box 1.

56. Fischer, "Fifteen Years of the Soviets," *Nation* 135 (23 November 1932): 493; Fischer, *Soviet Journey* (New York: Harrison Smith and Robert Haas, 1935), 166, 132, 206.

57. Lyons, *Assignment in Utopia,* 491, 450; Lyons, *The Red Decade: The Stalinist Penetration of America* (1941; New Rochelle: Arlington House, 1971), 107.

58. Lyons, "Muzhiks and Machines," *World's Work* 61 (February 1932): 5; Lyons, *Assignment,* 232; Joseph Flack to Secretary, 12 January 1932, SDDF, 861.5017 Living Conditions/404.

59. Chamberlin, "The Russian Peasant Sphinx," *FA* 7 (April 1929): 477; Chamberlin, "Poor Muzhik Likes Soviet Plan," *CSM,* 25 March 1930.

60. Chamberlin, "Behind the Soviet Mask," *New Outlook* 164 (September 1934): 15; Chamberlin, "Steady Job and Food at Soviet Farm," *CSM,* 26 March 1930; Chamberlin, "Soviet Russia's Fight for Food," *Current History* 38 (August

1933): 555; Chamberlin, *The Soviet Planned Economic Order* (Boston: World Peace Foundation, 1931), 7–8; Chamberlin, "Soviets Set All Hope on 5-Year Plan," *CSM*, 21 March 1930.

61. Chamberlin, "The Soviet Russian Sphinx," *Saturday Review of Literature* 7 (18 July 1931): 973.

62. Chamberlin, *Russia's Iron Age* (Boston: Little, Brown, 1934), 13; Chamberlin, "Balance Sheet on the Five-Year Plan," *FA* 11 (April 1933): 463; Chamberlin, "Balance Sheet of the Five-Year Plan," *New Republic* 66 (25 February 1931): 44.

63. Duranty, "Russia's Ledger: Gain and Loss," *Duranty Reports Russia* 331 (1 October 1933); John Wiley to Secretary, 29 January 1930, SDDF, 861.00/11414.

64. *Duranty Reports Russia*, 178 (30 November 1930); Gorky's "On the Russian Peasantry" is translated in *The Russian Peasant, 1920 and 1984*, ed. R. E. F. Smith (London: Frank Smith, 1980), 11–28.

65. "Amerikanskaia pechat' o SSSR, noiabr' 1936 g.," AVPRF, f. 05, op. 17, pap. 134, d. 107, l. 112; "Wire Break Balks Trotsky as 6,500 Await Speech Here," *NYT*, 10 February 1937.

66. Harper, "New Books on Soviet Russia," *Publisher's Weekly* 119 (13 June 1931): 2778; Harper quoted in Kliefoth to Secretary, 12 August 1930, SDDF, 861.5017 Living Conditions/168; Fischer, "The Case of Paul Scheffer," *Nation* 135 (31 August 1932): 195–196.

67. Hopper, "All Against One," *NYHT Books*, 3 May 1931, 1; John E. Nordskog review, *SSR* 16 (September-October 1931): 87.

68. Duranty, *I Write as I Please*, 271–272.

69. *Duranty Reports Russia*, 190 (13 June 1931).

70. Ibid., 186–187 (13 June 1931), 362 (3 October 1929), 178 (18 June 1931).

71. Ibid., 228–229 (5 July 1932), 187–188 (13 June 1931), 219 (27 June 1931).

72. Samuel N. Harper, "Informal Dispatch," *New Republic* 83 (11 December 1935): 139.

73. Lyons, *Red Decade*, 31, 159; Lyons, "My Six Years in Moscow," in Overseas Press Club, *As We See Russia* (New York: E. P. Dutton, 1948), 272.

74. Chamberlin, *Russia's Iron Age* (Boston: Little, Brown, 1934), 10–11, 253, 435; Chamberlin, "Government by Terror," *Atlantic Monthly* 154 (October 1934): 420.

75. Chamberlin, *Russia's Iron Age*, 157; Chamberlin, *The World's Iron Age* (New York: Macmillan, 1940), 106–107.

76. Chamberlin, "Balance Sheet of the Five-Year Plan," 42; Chamberlin, "The Ordeal of the Russian Peasantry," *FA* 12 (April 1934): 505.

77. Chamberlin, "Peasant Progress in Soviet Russia," *Current History* 23 (October 1925): 83; Chamberlin, *Soviet Russia*, 43–44, 55–57.

78. Chamberlin, "Peasant Progress," 87; Chamberlin, *Soviet Russia*, 55, 223.

79. *Duranty Reports Russia,* 29 (17 February 1922); Duranty, "Soviet at Crisis over 5-Year Plan," *NYT,* 5 October 1930.
80. Duranty to Arthur Sulzberger, 26 September 1936, Arthur Hays Sulzberger Papers.
81. Lyons, *Moscow Carrousel* (New York: Alfred A. Knopf, 1935), 234–235.
82. For more on William Henry Chamberlin, see David C. Engerman, "William Henry Chamberlin and Russia's Revolt against Western Civilization," *Russian History/Histoire Russe* 26 (Spring 1999), 45–64.
83. John F. Roche, "Uninterpreted News of Russia Puzzles Prejudiced World, Says Duranty," *Editor and Publisher* 65 (4 June 1932), 1.
84. Quoted in Heinz-Dietrich Fischer, "The History and Development of the Pulitzer Prize for International Reporting," in *International Reporting, 1928–1985,* ed. Heinz-Dietrich Fischer (Munich: K. G. Saur, 1987), xxxiv.
85. Schudson, *Discovering the News,* 144–145, 214–215; Elmo Scott Watson, "The Return to Personal Journalism" (1931), in *Interpretations of Journalism,* 254; Morrel Heald, *Transatlantic Vistas: American Journalists in Europe* (Kent State, Ohio: Kent State University Press, 1988), chap. 6.
86. Edgar Rickard to the President, 8 June 1932, HH-PSF, box 539; Gumberg to Duranty, 22 July 1932, Gumberg Papers, box 6.
87. Hamilton Fish Armstrong, *Between Peace and Counterpeace: From Wilson to Hitler* (New York: Harper and Row, 1971), 512; dinner plans, 6 June 1932, Gumberg Papers, box 6.
88. Seldes, *Freedom of the Press,* 200–201; Ralph Barnes to Joseph Barnes (no relation), 4 June 1932, Joseph Barnes Papers, box 6; Villard to Gumberg, 7 June 1932, Gumberg Papers, box 6; Lippmann to Duranty, 6 July 1932, Walter Lippmann Papers, box 68, folder 672; Dewey mentioned in Duranty to Birchall, 19 April 1930, Edwin L. James Papers, roll 32; Robert F. Kelley to Samuel Harper, 15 March 1926, and 10 June 1928, both in Samuel Northrop Papers, boxes 11 and 13; also Kelley's marginalia on John Wiley to Kelley, 22 December 1931, SDR, Papers of the Division of Eastern Europe (hereafter EE Papers), box 5.
89. Alexander Wollcott, introduction to *Duranty Reports Russia,* v.
90. Duranty to Mrs. Ochs, 9 June 1932, Adolph Ochs Papers, Duranty file.
91. Duranty, "Europe: War or Peace?" World Affairs Pamphlet no. 7 (1935): 32.
92. The phrase first appears in Duranty, "Red Square," *NYT Magazine,* 18 September 1932.
93. Hindus to Samuel Harper, 3 February 1930, Harper Papers, box 14.
94. Podol'skii diary, 20 August 1930, AVPRF, f. 0129, op. 13, pap. 127, d. 319, l. 11.
95. Hindus to Villard, 1 February 1930, in Villard Papers, folder 1705.
96. Ronald Grigor Suny, "Maurice Hindus and *Red Bread,*" in Hindus, *Red Bread* (1931; Bloomington: Indiana University Press, 1988), xii; Peter G. Filene,

Americans and the Soviet Experiment, 1917–1933 (Cambridge, Mass.: Harvard University Press, 1967), 255.

97. Dewey, introduction to Hindus, *Humanity Uprooted* (New York: Blue Ribbon Books, 1929), xviii; Hindus to Edward Deuss, 28 October 1929, Maurice Hindus Papers, box 13; Hindus, *Red Bread* (New York: Jonathan Cape and Harrison Smith, 1931), 1, 149, 372.

98. Hindus, *The Great Offensive* (New York: Harrison Smith and Robert Haas, 1933), 189, 204, 326, 315; Berlin to Secretary, 15 September 1928, SDDF, 861.00/11284.

99. Hindus, "Has the Five-Year Plan Worked?" *Harper's Magazine* 166 (March 1933): 462; *Experiences in Russia—1931: A Diary* (Pittsburgh: Alton Press, 1932), 81.

100. Hindus, *Great Offensive*, v.

101. Bruce C. Hopper to Robert F. Kelley, July 24, 1932, in SDR, EE Papers, box 5.

102. Otto Auhagen, "Wirtschaftslage der Sowjetunion im Sommer 1932," *Osteuropa* 7 (August 1932): 644–655 (quoted at p. 645). The American "listening post" in Riga reported this article to Washington in Skinner to Secretary, 15 November 1932, SDDF, 861.6131/261. Auhagen was a former agricultural advisor at the German embassy in Moscow who left to direct the Osteuropa Institut in Breslau, under whose auspices *Osteuropa* was published; see Jutta Unser, "'Osteuropa'—Biographie einer Zeitschrift," *Osteuropa* 25 (September 1975): 562–563.

103. Schiller, "Die Krise der sozialistischen Landwirtschaft in der Sowjetunion," *Berichte über Landwirstchaft* 79. Sonderheft (1933). The Soviets viewed Schiller's and Auhagen's writings as "impudent and undisguised espionage"—Vinograd to D. G. Shtern, n.d., AVPRF, f. 05, op. 13, pap. 90, d. 14, ll. 87–87ob. Cairns's reports are reprinted in full as Andrew Cairns, *The Soviet Famine, 1932–33: An Eye-witness Account of Conditions in the Spring and Summer of 1932,* ed. Tony Kuz (Edmonton: Canadian Institute of Ukrainian Studies, 1989). German information was also available from the consulates in Kiev and Kharkov—see the reports filed in *Der ukrainischer Hunger-Holocaust: Stalins verschwiegener Völkermord 1932/33 an 7 Millionen ukrainischer Bauern im Spiegel geheimgehaltener Akten des deutschen Auswärtigen Amtes,* ed. D. Zlepko (Sonnenbühl: Helmut Wild, 1988).

104. Conversation of William Strang with Walter Duranty, 31 October 1932, in *The Foreign Office and the Famine: British Documents on Ukraine and the Great Famine of 1932–1933,* ed. Marco Carynnyk, Lubomyr Y. Luciuk, and Bohdon S. Kordan (Kingston, Ont.: Limestone Press, 1988), 204; Duranty, "Soviet in 16th Year; Calm and Hopeful," *NYT,* 13 November 1932; Duranty, "Fifteen Stern Years of Soviet Rule," *NYT Magazine,* 6 November 1932.

105. Duranty, "All Russia Suffers Shortage of Food," *NYT,* 25 November 1932;

Duranty, "Food Shortage Laid to Soviet Peasants," *NYT,* 26 November 1932; Duranty, "Soviet Not Alarmed Over Food Shortage," *NYT,* 28 November 1932; Duranty, "Soviet Industries Hurt Agriculture," *NYT,* 29 November 1932; Duranty, "Bolsheviki United on Socialist Goal," *NYT,* 30 November 1932.

106. Markel to Edwin L. James, 18 November 1932, and 22 November 1932, both in James Papers, reel 32; William Strang to Laurence Collier, 6 December 1932, *Foreign Office and the Famine,* 209–210.

107. Enclosure 1 with Walter Edge to Secretary, 10 December 1932, SDDF, 861.5017 Living Conditions/572. Upon hearing about this speech, the Soviet press attaché in Paris reported his deep disappointment to the NKID Press Office—Podol'skii to Rozenberg, November 29, 1932, AVPRF f. 0129, op. 15, pap. 128, d. 328, l. 82. A Latvian diplomat in Moscow later reported that Duranty was "no longer regarded as a friend of the Bolsheviks" by winter 1932; Felix Cole to Secretary, 8 April 1933, SDDF, 861.5017 Living Conditions/671.

108. Fischer, "Fifteen Years of the Soviets," *Nation* 135 (23 November 1932): 495; Fischer, "Stalin Faces the Peasant," *Nation* 136 (11 January 1933): 39–41.

109. Diary entry, October 4, 1932, Malcolm Muggeridge Diary. Chamberlin may have heard from German attaché Otto Schiller, whom he called, in a 1968 interview, one of his four closest friends in Moscow; see Robert H. Myers, "William Henry Chamberlin: His Views of the Soviet Union" (Ph.D. diss., Indiana University, 1973), 54–55. On speaking tour see Chamberlin, *Confessions,* 154.

110. The Royal Institute talk appeared as Chamberlin, "What Is Happening in Russia?" *International Affairs* (London) 12 (March 1933): 187–205. Soviet impressions of the talk seem slightly optimistic in comparison with the published version: "Vypiska iz dnevnika press-attashe polpredstva SSSR v Anglii Tolokonskogo," 23 November 23, 1932, AVPRF, f. 0129, op. 15, pap. 128, d. 328, ll. 11–12, and Tolokonskii to Otdel Pechati, 3 December 1932, AVPRF, f. 05, op. 12, pap. 82, d. 15, ll. 99–103. See also Chamberlin, "Impending Change in Russia," *Fortnightly Review* n.s. 139 (1 January 1933): 10.

111. Improvement—telegram 24142, in Henry Shapiro Papers, box 28, folder 4; drama—telegram 10120, Shapiro Papers, box 28, folder 7; not hopeless— telegram 15134, Shapiro Papers, box 28, folder 7; apathy—telegram 12152, Shapiro Papers, box 28, folder 7. Shapiro was Lyons's successor with the United Press syndicate in Moscow. Unfortunately, none of these telegrams is dated.

112. This narrative is reconstructed from chap. 5 of Stoneman's autobiography (dated March 1, 1967), William Stoneman Papers, box 1; Stoneman interview with Whitman Bassow, 10 November 1984, Bassow Papers, box 2. Also Lyons, *Assignment in Utopia,* 545–546; and William Stoneman to Harrison Salisbury,

16 May 1979, cited in Taylor, *Stalin's Apologist*, 202, 235. Stoneman had always taken an interest in rural food supply, ending his first tour in Russia (in 1932) with reflections on localized shortages; see Edward Brodie to Secretary, 24 February 1932, SDDF, 761.00/221.

113. Stoneman, "Russia Clamps Merciless Rule on Peasantry," *CDN* (dispatch filed 6 February 1933), found after page 16 of Stoneman's "Autobiography," box 1, Stoneman Papers. See also Stoneman, "Little Liberty Permitted Foreigner in Kuban Area," *CDN*, 28 March 1933; Stoneman, "Communists Find It Easy to Justify Peasant Exile," *CDN*, 30 March 1933; Ralph Barnes, "Soviet Terrorizes Famine Region by Night Raids for Hidden Grain," *NYHT*, February 6, 1933; Ralph Barnes to Joseph Barnes (no relation), 4 June 1932, Joseph Barnes Papers, box 6.

114. "Zapiska otdela pechati, poslannaia t. Molotovu," 25 February 1933, AVPRF, f. 05, op. 13, pap. 90, d. 13, ll. 46–47.

115. "Conversation with Comrade Podolskii, Chief Censor of Moscow Foreign Office—Tuesday, February 23rd, 1933," Stoneman Papers, box 1.

116. *Duranty Reports Russia*, 295 (29 January 1933); Duranty, "Russia's Peasant: The Hub of a Vast Drama," ibid., 265, 274 (2 February 1933), 304, 306 (27 February 1933).

117. "Russia Offers Inducements to Increase Farmer Output," *CSM*, 21 December 1932.

118. Chamberlin, "Russia Between Two Plans," *New Republic* 74 (15 February 1933): 7–8; Chamberlin, "Balance Sheet of the Five-Year Plan," 458, 466.

119. Diary entries for 16 September 1932 and 28 September 1932, Muggeridge Diary; John Bright-Holmes, introduction to *Like It Was: The Diaries of Malcolm Muggeridge* (London: Collins, 1981), 13.

120. Diary entries, 1 December 1932; 4 January 1933; and 11 January 1933, Muggeridge Diary. On his trip to the countryside, Muggeridge to Crozier (his editor at the *Manchester Guardian*), January 14, 1933, cited in Richard Ingrams, *Muggeridge—The Biography* (New York: HarperCollins, 1995), 64. The articles were published in the *Manchester Guardian:* "Famine in North Caucasus," 25 March 1933; "Hunger in the Ukraine," 27 March 1933; and "Poor Prospects for Harvest," 28 March 1933. His reports were apparently delayed and toned down (he used the word "mangled") by his editors; Ingrams, *Muggeridge*, 62–69, and David Ayerst, *The Guardian: Biography of a Newspaper* (London: Collins, 1971), 511–513.

121. *Duranty Reports Russia*, 310–312 (2 March 1933). On the political departments, see I. E. Zelenin, "Politotdely MTS—prodolzhenie politiki 'chrezvychaishchiny' (1933–1934 gg.)," *Otechestvennaia istoriia*, no. 6 (1992): 42–61.

122. "Famine in Russia—Englishman's Story—What He Saw on a Walking Tour,"

Manchester Guardian, 30 March 1933; Edgar Ansel Mowrer, "Russian Famine Now as Great as Starvation of 1921, Says Secretary to Lloyd George," *CDN,* 29 March 1933. Jones had worked with the leading British scholar of the Soviet Union, Bernard Pares; see Sir Bernard Pares, *A Wandering Student* (Syracuse: Syracuse University Press, 1948), 309–311.

123. Lyons, *Assignment,* 576.

124. Sir Esmond Ovey to Foreign Office, 5 March 1933, *Foreign Office and the Famine,* 215; Sackett to Secretary, 1 March 1933, SDDF, 861.5017 Living Conditions/595; "Zapiska otdela pechati, poslannaia t. Molotovu," 25 February 1933, AVPRF, f. 05, op. 13, pap. 90, d. 13, ll. 46–47.

125. The party is not mentioned in Stoneman's "Autobiography" (Stoneman Papers, box 1) or in Robin Kincaid's recollections (interview 18 February 1985, Bassow Papers, unnumbered box). Lyons's later recollections are quoted from Crowl, *Angels in Stalin's Paradise,* 161, citing letters from Lyons (20 June 1977) and from Armand Paul Ginsberg for Lyons (2 July 1977). Duranty biographer S. J. Taylor shares my doubts about Lyons's story; Taylor, *Stalin's Apologist,* 207, 235–236.

126. Duranty, "Russians Hungry, but Not Starving," *NYT,* 31 March 1933.

127. Fischer, *Men and Politics,* 206–209; reports on Fischer's lectures appear in "'New Deal' Needed for Entire World, Says Visiting Author," *Denver Post,* 1 April 1933, cited in Crowl, *Angels in Stalin's Paradise,* 157; "Too Much Freedom Given to Russia's Women, Says Writer," *San Francisco News,* 11 April 1933; and "New Economic Society Coming out of Russia," *Milwaukee Leader,* March 14, 1933, both in Louis Fischer Papers (Princeton), box 60; Fischer, "Russia's Last Hard Year," *Nation* 137 (9 August 1933): 154.

128. *Duranty Reports Russia,* 313 (6 April 1933); Duranty, "Soviet Peasants Are More Hopeful," *NYT,* 14 May 1933 (dateline Odessa, by mail to Paris, 26 April 1933). On the trip routing, see Duranty to Edwin James, n.d. [mid-April 1933?]; and Edwin James to Duranty, 21 April 1933, in James Papers, reel 32; Duranty, *I Write as I Please,* 61.

129. "Mr. Jones Replies" [letter to the editor], *NYT,* 13 May 1933.

130. Duranty to NYTIMES, 17 June 1933, and Edwin James to Arthur Sulzberger, 17 June 1933, both in James Papers, reel 33; Duranty to H. R. Knickerbocker, 27 June 1933, Knickerbocker Papers, Catalogued Correspondence; Duranty, "Russian Suffering Justified by Reds," *NYT,* 9 July 1933.

131. Duranty, "Russian Emigres Push Fight on Reds," *NYT,* 12 August 1933; Duranty to Edwin James, 19 August 1933, 20 August 1933, and 22 August 1933; Edwin James to Duranty, 22 August 1933, all in James Papers, reel 33. "Moscow Doubles Price of Bread" [AP], *NYT,* 21 August 1933; Duranty, "Famine Report Scorned," *NYT,* 27 August 1933.

132. Duranty to Frederick Birchall, 23 August 1933, James Papers, reel 63; "Cardi-

nal Asks Aid in Russian Famine," *NYT,* 20 August 1933; Frederick T. Birchall, "Famine in Russia Held Equal of 1921," *NYT,* 25 August 1933.

133. On Duranty's dissatisfaction, see, for instance, Duranty to Edwin James, 15 August 1933, Ochs Papers. On his editors' complaints, see, for instance, Edwin James to Arthur Hays Sulzberger, 2 August 1933, James Papers, reel 63. The NKID Press Office was well aware of these tensions; see Podol'skii diary, 31 December 1933, AVPRF, f. 0129, op. 15, pap. 128a, d. 336, l. 16.

134. Edward Coote to Sir John Simon, 12 September 1933, *Foreign Office and the Famine,* 307.

135. Duranty, "Soviet Is Winning Faith of Peasants," *NYT,* 11 September 1933; Duranty, "Abundance Found in North Caucasus," *NYT,* 14 September 1933; Duranty, "Big Soviet Crop Follows Famine," *NYT,* 16 September 1933; Duranty, "Soviet's Progress Marked in a Year," *NYT,* 21 September 1933.

136. Lyons, *Assignment,* 579–580 (ellipses in original). Anne O'Hare McCormick was a distinguished *New York Times* foreign correspondent then visiting the Lyonses. William Strang to Sir John Simon, 26 September 1933, *Foreign Office and the Famine,* 310–313.

137. Duranty to Edwin James, 28 August 1933; Edwin James to Duranty, 29 August 1933; Frederick Birchall to Edwin James, 31 August 1933, all in James Papers, reel 33. Litvinov to Iagoda, 13 September 1933, AVPRF, f. 05, op. 13, pap. 90, d. 14, l. 73.

138. Chamberlin, *Confessions,* 154–55; "Soviet Restricts Alien Reports as Food Wanes," *CSM,* 21 August 1933.

139. Chamberlin to Calvin Hoover, 25 September 1933, Calvin Hoover Papers—Addition; Chamberlin, "Diary of an Onlooker in Moscow," *CSM,* 17 August 1933.

140. William Stoneman to Samuel Harper, 12 October 1933, Harper Papers, box 18; Sir William Strang to Sir John Simon, 14 October 1933, *Foreign Office and the Famine,* 334. The Chamberlin-Strang friendship (mentioned in a 1968 interview) is reported in Myers, "William Henry Chamberlin," 54–55.

141. All *Manchester Guardian:* "Second Agrarian Revolution," 17 October 1933; "Some Cossack Villages," 18 October 1933; "Ukrainian District's Good Harvest," 19 October 1933; "New Russian Agriculture—Two Main Types," 20 October 1933; "Villages Around Kiev—Final Impressions," 21 October 1933.

142. "Russia's Ledger: Gain and Cost," *Duranty Reports Russia,* 329–341 (1 October 1933).

143. Chamberlin discussed the famine (quoted above) in Chamberlin, *Russia's Iron Age,* 76–77; Chamberlin, *Evolution of a Conservative* (Chicago: Henry Regnery, 1959), 11. Thanks to D'Ann Penner for stressing the nature of Chamberlin's later views.

144. Chamberlin, "Ordeal of the Russian Peasantry," 503, 505; Chamberlin, "Bal-

ance Sheet of the Five-Year Plan," 458, 466; Chamberlin, "As One Foreign Correspondent to Another," *CSM Magazine*, 2 May 1934; Frank Luther Mott, book review, *Journalism Quarterly* 11 (June 1934): 221. While many critics of Duranty and Fischer have cited the chapter in Chamberlin's *Russia's Iron Age* entitled "The Ordeal of the Russian Peasantry," fewer have cited his article with the same title in *Foreign Affairs*. Although the materials appear to have been written within a month of each other—and many paragraphs appear in both pieces—they differ substantially in tone. The magazine article focuses on character traits such as apathy and tenacity far more than the book does.

145. Fischer to Gumberg, 5 November 1933, Gumberg Papers, box 7, folder 2; Fischer, "Class War in Spain," *Nation* 138 (18 April 1934): 437; Fischer, "In Russia Life Grows Easier," *Nation* 138 (13 June 1934): 667, 668; Fischer, "Moscow Reports Progress," *Fortnightly Review* 135 n.s. (June 1934): 651–657.

146. Fischer, *Soviet Journey*, 174, 108, 170–172. The trip through Ukraine is described in Fischer, "Soviet Progress and Poverty," *Nation* 135 (7 December 1932): 552–555.

147. The articles appeared under the byline Thomas Walker in the *New York Evening Journal*, February 18, 19, 21, 25, and 27, 1935, as cited in Dana Dalrymple, "Soviet Famine of 1932–1934," *Soviet Studies* 14 (January 1964): 256 n. 46; Fischer, "Hearst's Russian 'Famine,'" *Nation* 140 (13 March 1935): 296–297.

148. Chamberlin, "The Ukrainian Famine" [letter to the editor], *Nation* 140 (29 May 1935): 629; Fischer, "Louis Fischer's Interpretation" [reply], ibid., 629–630; Lyons, *Red Decade*, 141. See also the correspondence between Fischer and the *Nation* editor—Kirchwey to Fischer, 14 and 22 March 1935, and June 1935, Freda Kirchwey Papers, box 10, folder 168. This last letter noted the extensive controversy about the Chamberlin-Fischer exchange and celebrated the resulting increase in newsstand sales.

149. Hindus, "Has the Five-Year Plan Worked?," 464; Hindus, *Great Offensive*, 105.

150. Milton Hindus, "Pieces of a Man's Life," in Milton Hindus Papers, box 17.

151. Neiman diary, 17 December 1936, AVPRF, f. 04, op. 16, pap. 122, d. 105, ll. 22–23.

152. Hindus, "Russia Grows Up," *Harper's Magazine* 174 (May 1937): 613; Hindus, *Green Worlds: An Informal Chronicle* (New York: Doubleday, Doran, 1938), 334–335.

153. Victor Gollancz to Hindus, 14 September 1937; Hindus to Gollancz, 29 October 1937, both in Maurice Hindus Papers, box 15.

154. Hindus, "The Triumph of Collectivization," *Soviet Russia Today* 6 (May 1937): 14–15. See the correspondence between Jessica Smith and Hindus through fall 1937, in Maurice Hindus Papers, box 13.

368   Notes to Pages 236–241

155. See the Press Office correspondence from fall 1937 in AVPRF, f. 0129, op. 20, pap. 133a, d. 392, ll. 5, 24–24ob, 32.

156. Hindus, *House without a Roof: Russia after Forty-Three Years of Revolution* (Garden City, N.J.: Doubleday, 1961), xii.

157. Duranty, *Stalin and Co.: The Politburo—The Men Who Run Russia* (New York: W. Sloan, 1949), 68–69; Taylor, *Stalin's Apologist*, 236–237. Duranty is loosely translating Stalin's speech of 11 January 1933, "O rabote v derevne," *Sochineniia*, 13 vols. (Moscow: Izdatel'stvo politicheskoi literatury, 1952), 13:233.

158. Fischer, *God That Failed*, 209.

159. Ibid., 203–204.

160. Chamberlin, *Evolution*, 11–12; Lyons, "My Six Years," 264.

161. Chamberlin, *Confessions*, chap. 7; Samuel Harper, *The Russia I Believe in: The Memoirs of Samuel N. Harper, 1902–1941*, ed. Paul V. Harper (Chicago: University of Chicago Press, 1945), 235.

162. Chamberlin, *The Russian Revolution*, 2 vols. (New York: Macmillan, 1935).

163. Chamberlin, "Farewell to Russia," *Atlantic Monthly* 154 (November 1934): 564–573; Chamberlin, "Behind the Soviet Mask," *New Outlook* 164 (September 1934): 13–16.

164. Chamberlin, *World's Iron Age*, chap. 4 (quoted p. 106).

165. See, for instance, Chamberlin, *Collectivism: A False Utopia* (New York: Macmillan, 1937), 242–245.

166. Umanskii to NKID Collegium, 1 January 1933, AVPRF, f. 0129, op. 15, pap. 128a, d. 335, ll. 21–22; Lyons, *Assignment in Utopia*, 591–599.

167. Lyons, "Russia's Second Five-Year Plan," *Literary Digest* 117 (10 February 1934): 3; Lyons to Lewis Gannett, 6 March 1935, Eugene Lyons Papers (Oregon), part 2; Lyons, "What Does Russia Prove?" *Scribner's Monthly* 100 (September 1936): 178.

168. Lyons, *Red Decade*, 15, 19.

169. Ibid., 9–19, 29, 31. On page 326, Lyons includes himself in a list of "turncoats" yet does not directly indicate his own attachment to the ideas and institutions he criticizes.

170. More recent writings on the era shed additional light on its turbulent left-wing politics. See Daniel Aaron, *Writers on the Left* (New York: Harcourt, Brace and World, 1961); Harvey Klehr, *The Heyday of American Communism: The Depression Decade* (New York: Basic, 1984); Frank A. Warren, *Liberals and Communism: The "Red Decade" Revisited* (New York: Columbia University Press, 1966); and Judy Kutulas, *The Long War: The Intellectual People's Front and Anti-Stalinism, 1930–1940* (Durham: Duke University Press, 1995).

171. Lyons, *Red Decade*, 401–402, chaps. 20, 23, 29.

172. Arendt, "The Ex-Communists," *Commonweal* 57 (20 March 1953): 595–599.

173. George H. Nash, *The Conservative Intellectual Movement in America since*

1945 (New York: Basic, 1976), 14; Dimitri von Mohrenschildt, "William Henry Chamberlin, 1897–1969," *Russian Review* 29 (Summer 1970): 1.

174. Lyons, "Everyday Life under the Soviet System," Catholic Information Society Pamphlet no. 1 (1947); Chamberlin, "Communism Means Slavery," Catholic Information Society Pamphlet no. 5 (1947). See Donald F. Crosby, *God, Church and Flag: Senator Joseph R. McCarthy and the Catholic Church, 1950–1957* (Chapel Hill: University of North Carolina Press, 1978), 19; Ellen Schrecker, *Many Are the Crimes: McCarthyism in America* (Boston: Little, Brown, 1998), chaps. 1–2.

175. Chamberlin, *Beyond Containment* (Chicago: Henry Regnery, 1953), 21–22.

176. See, for instance, his introduction to *Blueprint for World Conquest* (Washington: Human Events, 1946); as well as Chamberlin, "Communism Means Slavery."

177. Lyons, *Our Secret Allies: The People of Russia* (New York: Duell, Sloan and Pearce, 1953), 314, 373.

178. Fischer quoted in *Experiences in Russia,* 85; Knickerbocker, "Everyday Life," in *The New Russia* (London: Faber and Faber, 1931), 21; Chamberlin, "Russia between Two Plans," *New Republic* 74 (15 February 1933): 8; Hopper, *Pan-Sovietism: The Issue before America and the World* (Boston: Houghton Mifflin, 1931), 179; Brutzkus, *Economic Planning in Soviet Russia* (London: George Routledge and Sons, 1935), 226.

179. Calvin B. Hoover, *Economic Life in Soviet Russia* (New York: Macmillan, 1931), 85.

180. Chamberlin, "Some Cossack Villages," *Manchester Guardian,* 18 October 1933; Duranty, *I Write as I Please,* 288.

10. Scratch a Soviet and You'll Find a Russian

1. Lippmann, *The Stakes of Diplomacy* (New York: Henry Holt, 1915), chap. 15; Warren Frederick Ilchman, *Professional Diplomacy in the United States, 1779–1939: A Study in Administrative History* (Chicago: University of Chicago Press, 1961), 118–125.

2. Ilchman, *Professional Diplomacy,* 140–142; Robert D. Schulzinger, *The Making of the Diplomatic Mind: The Training, Outlook and Style of United States Foreign Service Officers, 1908–1931* (Middletown, Conn.: Wesleyan University Press, 1975), 59–61.

3. Robert F. Kelley, "Outline of Russian History" (21 December 1925), in Robert F. Kelley Papers, box 2, folder 10; Schulzinger, *Making of the Diplomatic Mind,* 81, 91 (quoting Bernadotte Schmitt); Ilchman, *Professional Diplomacy,* 240; Tracy Hollingsworth Lay, *The Foreign Service of the United States* (New York: Prentice-Hall, 1925), chap. 12.

4. Kennan, *Memoirs,* 2 vols. (Boston: Little, Brown, 1967), 1:14. See, for instance,

Huntington, *Civilization and Climate* (New Haven: Yale University Press, 1915). Harvard, Princeton, and Yale educated two-thirds of the FSOs in the 1920s; see Ilchman, *Professional Diplomacy*, 171.

5. Schulzinger, *Making of the Diplomatic Mind*, 83–85.

6. Loy W. Henderson, *A Question of Trust: The Origins of U.S.–Soviet Diplomatic Relations: The Memoirs of Loy W. Henderson*, ed. George W. Baer (Stanford: Hoover Institution Press, 1986), 123; [Kelley,] "The Division of Eastern European Affairs: History and Personnel," *American Foreign Service Journal* 10 (February 1933): 54–61, filed in Kelley Papers, box 1, folder 9.

7. Martin Weil, *A Pretty Good Club: The Founding Fathers of the U.S. Foreign Service* (New York: Norton, 1978), chap. 1; Ilchman, *Professional Diplomacy*, 170–171.

8. Kelley, "Autobiographical Sketch" (n.d.), in Kelley Papers, box 1, folder 9; Coolidge solicited Kelley's writing; see Coolidge to Kerner, 12 September 1924, Robert J. Kerner Papers, carton 4. Kelley's articles included "Soviet Policy on the European Border," *FA* 3 (15 September 1924): 90–98; and "Russia's New Economic Divisions," *FA* 4 (January 1924): 330–333.

9. Ilchman, *Professional Diplomacy*, 240; Frederick L. Propas, "Creating a Hard Line toward Russia: The Training of State Department Experts, 1927–1937," *Diplomatic History* 8 (Summer 1984): 209–226; conversation with George Frost Kennan, 21 February 2001; Heinrich Pohl, *Die Deutsche Auslandshochschule* (Tübingen: J. C. B. Mohr, 1913), 16–17.

10. J. V. A. MacMurray to Arthur Bliss Lane, 7 November 1936, quoted in Hugh De Santis, *The Diplomacy of Silence: The American Foreign Service, the Soviet Union, and the Cold War, 1933–1947* (Chicago: University of Chicago Press, 1979), 15–16.

11. Natalie Grant, "The Russian Section: A Window on the Soviet Union," *Diplomatic History* 2 (Winter 1978): 107–110.

12. Kelley referred to his staff as "my boys" in a 1947 letter quoted in Daniel Yergin, *Shattered Peace: The Origins of the Cold War and the National Security State* (Boston: Houghton Mifflin, 1977), 21. Johnnie von Herwath with S. Frederick Starr, *Against Two Evils* (New York: Rawson, Wade, 1981), 70–73. The close personal and professional relationships are evident in their interviews, memoirs, and letters. See, for instance, the recollections gathered in *The Soviet Union: Yesterday, Today and Tomorrow: A Colloquy of American Long-Timers in Moscow*, ed. Foy D. Kohler and Mose L. Harvey (Coral Gables, Fla.: University of Miami Center for Advanced International Studies, 1975), 157–177.

13. C. Ben Wright, "George F. Kennan: Scholar-Diplomat, 1926–1946" (Ph.D. diss., University of Wisconsin, 1972), 6; Henderson, *Question of Trust*, chap. 20.

14. Hopper to Kelley, 18 July 1932, and 24 July 1932, SDR, Papers of the Division of Eastern Europe (hereafter EE Papers), box 5; Kennan memo of conversation, 8 January 1937, SDDF, 861.00/11747. See the correspondence in the John X. Wiley Papers, box 6.

15. The Harper-Henderson correspondence is in Samuel Northrup Harper Papers, boxes 21–22; see also Henderson to Robert Rosenthal, 23 March 1976, Loy W. Henderson Papers, Special Correspondence, box 1. Kelley wrote to ask Harper's advice on numerous matters—see, for instance, the letters dated 6 June 1926 and 11 January 1927, both in Harper Papers, box 12.

16. "The Slavonic Conference in Richmond, Va.," *SEER* 3 (March 1925): 684; "List of Members," *AHR* 45 (January 1940, supp.): 43.

17. Kelley to Harper, 11 December 1929, Harper Papers, box 14.

18. All the reports are included in Skinner to Secretary, 24 March 1932, SDDF, 861.01/1742; only Felix Cole dissented from the hopes of improvement.

19. Packer, "The Five-Year Plan and Reconstruction in Russia," 25 June 1931, EE Papers, box 11, folder 24B, pp. 11–12 (hereafter cited by author and title only).

20. Kelley quoted in Packer to William R. Castle, 18 August 1932, Kelley Papers, box 3, folder 5.

21. John A. Lehrs, "Notes on a Conversation with Professor Samuel Northrup Harper," attached to Skinner to Secretary, 27 October 1930, SDDF, 861.5017 Living Conditions/550.

22. George Gordon to Secretary, 10 November 1932; Charles Kocharovsky to Herbert Hoover, 20 June 1932, both in SDDF, 861.48/2428, 2431.

23. Walter Edge to Secretary, 10 December 1932, SDDF, 861.5017 Living Conditions/572.

24. Arthur Capper to Roosevelt, 10 April 1933, FDR-OF-220; P. C. Hiebert to Cordell Hull, 27 March 1933; Kelley to Hiebert, 5 April 1933; and Hull to Senator Arthur Capper, 26 April 1933, all in SDDF, 861.48/2433.

25. Kelley to Rep. Hamilton Fish, 19 October 1929, quoted in M. Wayne Morris, *Stalin's Famine and Roosevelt's Recognition of Russia* (Lanham, Md.: University Press of America, 1994), 110.

26. E. L. Packer to Luke Myusha, 6 November 1934, EE Papers, box 28.

27. Thomas R. Maddux, *Years of Estrangement: American Relations with the Soviet Union, 1933–1941* (Tallahassee: Florida State University Press, 1980), chap. 2 (FDR quoted p. 11).

28. Kelley, "Problems Pertaining to Russian-American Relations," 27 July 1933, *FRUS: SU*, 6–11.

29. Maddux, *Years of Estrangement*, chap. 2; Robert E. Bowers, "Hull, Russian Subversion in Cuba, and Recognition," *Journal of American History* 52 (December 1966): 542–554.

30. *American Foreign Service Journal* 10 (December 1933); see also De Santis, *The Diplomacy of Silence*, 29.

31. Kennan, *Memoirs,* 1:34; Kennan, "Fair Day Adieu," in George Frost Kennan Papers, box 25, folder 2, p. 5 (hereafter cited by author and title only). The author later wrote the following explanation on this document: "All this is autobiographical material written in 1937, and never published. Should anyone else make use of it for publication, he should point out the early date of its composition, as well as the fact that it was blanketed by the *Memoirs,* published some 30 years later—G. Kennan."

32. "Mr. Kennan's Russian Diary, 1934," Kennan Papers, box 23, folder 1, entries for 15 January–2 February; Kennan, "Fair Day Adieu," 18; Charles W. Thayer, *Bears in the Caviar* (Philadelphia: J. B. Lippincott, 1951), 59–60.

33. Stalin, "Speech at the All-Union Conference of Stakhanovites" (1935), in *Works,* 13 vols. (Moscow: Foreign Language Publishing House, 1955), 6:783.

34. John A. Lehrs, "The Russian Peasant Policy, 1932–1934," in Felix Cole to Secretary of State, 15 June 1934, EE Papers, box 10.

35. Henderson to Secretary, 8 October 1935, SDDF, 861.48/2478.

36. Kennan, "Memorandum for the Minister," 19 August 1932, in Robert Skinner to Secretary, 19 August 1932, SDDF, 861.5017 Living Conditions/510; Klaus Mehnert, *Die Jugend in Sowjetrussland* (Berlin: S. Fischer, 1932), 34–39.

37. Wiley to Kelley, 7 November 1930, EE Papers, box 5.

38. George Gordon to Secretary, 15 October 1932, and Robert Skinner to Secretary, 27 October 1932, both in SDDF, 861.5017 Living Conditions/544, 550.

39. Bohlen to mother, 23 October 1934, Charles E. Bohlen Papers, box 36.

40. Henderson to Arthur Bliss Lane, 29 April 1937, quoted in H. W. Brands, *Inside the Cold War: Loy Henderson and the Rise of the American Empire, 1918–1961* (Oxford: Oxford University Press, 1991), 81.

41. Kennan, "Fair Day Adieu," 5, 20–21; Wright, "George F. Kennan," 95.

42. Chipman in Joseph Davies to Secretary, 27 October 1937, SDDF, 861.60/291.

43. Bullitt to Secretary, 2 October, 1934, FDR-PSF, box 49.

44. Kennan in Skinner to Secretary, 15 April 1933, SDDF, 861.50/810.

45. Durbrow, "Memorandum on the Difficulties in Soviet Industry," 14, enclosed in Henderson to Secretary, 2 October 1937, SDDF, 861.60/290.

46. Henderson to Harper, 13 February 1939, Harper Papers, box 21. Henderson also cited the purges as a factor in Soviet industrial woes.

47. Bohlen interview with Pete Lisagor, 2 December 1968, Bohlen Papers, box 26.

48. Alexander Kirk to Secretary, 27 October 1938, SDDF, 861.60/318; Bullitt to Secretary, 20 April 1936, in *For the President, Personal and Secret: Correspondence between Franklin D. Roosevelt and William C. Bullitt,* ed. Orville H. Bullitt (Boston: Houghton Mifflin, 1972), 155.

49. C. Louis Allen, "Digest of Two Weeks in Russia," enclosed in Roosevelt to Hull, April 1933, SDDF, 861.5017 Living Conditions/646.

50. Kennan, "Fair Day Adieu," 45.

51. Kennan, lecture to Foreign Service School, 20 May 1938 (hereafter FSS Lecture), in Kennan Papers, box 16, folder 2, p. 6; Bohlen, *Witness to History, 1929–1969* (New York: W. W. Norton, 1973), 27.

52. Kennan, FSS Lecture, 13; Kelley, "Political Structure of the Soviet Union," 30 April 1935, Kelley Papers, box 2, folder 1, p. 34; Davies [written by Chipman] to Secretary, 27 October 1937, SDDF, 861.60/291; Packer, "Five-Year Plan," 4.

53. Kelley, "The Bolshevik Regime in Russia," 16 April 1931, Kelley Papers, box 2, folder 9, p. 19.

54. Kennan memorandum, 13 February 1937, *FRUS: SU,* 369.

55. Wiley to Henderson, 29 August 1935, Wiley Papers, box 7.

56. Henderson to Secretary of State, 17 July 1936, Moscow Post Files, vol. 379, file 840.1.

57. Kennan, FSS Lecture, 4, 6–8; Kennan, "Russia and the Postwar Settlement" (summer 1942), in Kennan Papers, box 25, folder 4; Steinhardt to Secretary, 17 June 1941, *FRUS 1941,* 1:765.

58. Kennan, "Some Fundamentals of Russian-American Relations" (1938), Kennan Papers, box 16, folder 1, pp. 1, 5–6.

59. Bullitt to Secretary, 3 March 1936, *FRUS: SU,* 289–291. Kennan reports on this escapade in numerous speeches, with some variation in the details, in the late 1940s; see, for instance, Kennan, "Soviet Diplomacy," 6 October 1947, Kennan Papers, box 16, folder 38, p. 15.

60. Kennan, "Fair Day Adieu," 23; Bullitt to Secretary, 20 April 1936, FDR-PSF, box 49. See also Wiley to Bullitt, 26 November 1934, Wiley Papers, box 2.

61. Bullitt to Secretary, 20 April 1936, FDR-PSF, box 49.

62. Kennan, FSS Lecture, 8, 15; Kennan, *Memoirs,* 1:73.

63. Wiley to Bullitt, 5 March 1935, Wiley Papers, box 2; Packer, "Five-Year Plan," 4.

64. Packer, "Five-Year Plan," 4; Frederick Sackett to Secretary, 3 February 1931, SDDF, 861.5017 Living Conditions/216; while Sackett is quoting an American returning from Russia, he called the report "the most intelligent and accurate analysis yet available to me."

65. Roosevelt here is quoting from her friend Jerome Davis; Eleanor Roosevelt to FDR, April 1939, FDR-PSF, box 49.

66. Henderson to Secretary, 18 June 1937, quoted in De Santis, *Diplomacy of Silence,* 36.

67. Frederick Sackett to Secretary, 26 March 1930, SDDF, 861.5017 Living Conditions/141; Kelley lecture, 30 April 1935, Kelley Papers, box 2; Bohlen to mother, 23 October 1934, Bohlen Papers, box 36; Steinhardt to Untermeyer, 5 March 1940, quoted in Betty Crump Hanson, "American Diplomatic Reporting from the Soviet Union, 1934–1941" (Ph.D. diss., Columbia University, 1966), 303–304.

68. Bullitt to Secretary, 20 April 1936, FDR-PSF, box 49.
69. Kennan, *Memoirs*, 1:83–85.
70. Charles B. Burdick, *An American Island in Hitler's Reich: The Bad Neuheim Internment* (Menlo Park, Cal.: Markgraf, 1987), 62–63.
71. Kennan, "Russia's Middle Age," Kennan Papers, box 16, folder 4, pp. 1, 4–5, 9.
72. Kennan, notes for Bad Neuheim lectures, Kennan Papers, box 16, folder 8, pp. 3–4. (For unknown reasons, his lectures ended with the eighteenth century.)
73. Reprinted in Kennan, *Memoirs*, 1:503–531. All quotations in this paragraph come from this document.
74. Kennan, "Russia's International Position at the Close of the War with Germany" (May 1945), *FRUS 1945*, 5:853–854.
75. Kennan, "The United States and Russia" (winter/spring 1946), Kennan Papers, box 23, folder 49; the directives also appear in Kennan, *Memoirs*, 1:560–565.
76. This and subsequent citations are taken from Kennan to Secretary, 22 February 1946, *FRUS 1946*, 6:696–709.
77. The theme of pathology is illustrated in Frank Costigliola, "'Unceasing Pressure for Penetration': Gender, Pathology, and Emotion in George Kennan's Formulation of the Cold War," *Journal of American History* 83 (March 1997): 1309–1339.
78. Kennan lectures: "'Trust' as a Factor in Human Relations" (Yale, 1 October 1946), Hamilton Fish Armstrong Papers, box 38; "Russian National Objectives" (Air War College, 10 April 1947), Kennan Papers, box 16, folder 29.
79. "The Soviet Way of Thought and Its Effect on Soviet Foreign Policy" (7 January 1947), Kennan Papers, box 16, folder 20, quoted at p. 2.
80. Kennan, "The Soviet Way of Thought and Its Effect on Foreign Policy" (National War College, 24 January 1947), Kennan Papers, box 16, folder 22, quoted at pp. 6, 10–11.
81. Ibid., 29; Kennan, "Russian-American Relations" (University of Virginia, 20 February 1947), Kennan Papers, box 1, folder 25, pp. 12–14.
82. This paragraph is based on correspondence among Armstrong, his assistant Byron Dexter, and Kennan, between February and April 1947—in Armstrong Papers, box 38; also Kennan Papers, box 28, folder 8.
83. These two paragraphs are built from the following historical accounts: C. Ben Wright, "Mr. 'X' and Containment," *Slavic Review* 35 (March 1976): 1–31; David C. Mayers, *George Kennan and the Dilemmas of U.S. Foreign Policy* (Oxford: Oxford University Press, 1989), 98–99, 109–116; Lloyd C. Gardner, *Architects of Illusion: Men and Ideas in American Foreign Policy, 1941–1949* (Chicago: Quadrangle Books, 1970), chap. 10, quoted at p. 299; Kennan, *Memoirs*, 1:358 and chap. 15; Townsend Hoopes and Douglas Brinkley, *Driven Patriot:*

The Life and Times of James Forrestal (New York: Alfred A. Knopf, 1992), 266–281; and Daniel F. Harrington, "Kennan, Bohlen, and the Riga Axioms," *Diplomatic History* 2 (Fall 1978): 436.

84. Kennan, *Memoirs,* 1:358; Kennan, "Containment Then and Now" (1985), in Kennan, *At a Century's Ending: Reflections, 1982–1995* (New York: Norton, 1996), 110.

85. The following paragraphs are based on X, "The Sources of Soviet Conduct," *FA* 25 (July 1947): 566–582.

86. Kennan comments, 6 August 1953, Kennan Papers, box 24, folder 1-D-30, p. 6.

87. Kennan, *Memoirs,* 1:356; Brooks Atkinson, "America's Global Planner," *NYT Magazine,* 13 July 1947; "The Story behind Our Russian Policy," *Newsweek,* 21 July 1947, 15–17; "Soviet Conduct," *Life Magazine,* 28 July 1947, 53–54.

88. Kennan, *American Diplomacy, 1900–1950* (New York: Mentor, 1951), chap. 6; precursors to this argument are also evident in Kennan's "Prerequisites," the prologue for a never-completed book on democracy's failings. Given that the work, written in 1938, is no longer in Kennan's papers, the best account is in Wright, "George F. Kennan," 129–133.

89. This paragraph is based on Walter Lippmann, *The Cold War: A Study in U.S. Foreign Policy* (New York: Harper and Brothers, 1947), quoted at pp. 30–31; also Ronald Steel, *Walter Lippmann and the American Century* (Boston: Little, Brown, 1980), 441–449.

90. Kennan, "Formulation of Policy in the USSR" (National War College, 18 September 1947), Kennan Papers, box 16, folder 36.

91. Kennan, *Memoirs,* 1:367; some of these criticisms are addressed in John Lewis Gaddis, *Strategies of Containment: A Critical Appraisal of Postwar American National Security Policy* (Oxford: Oxford University Press, 1982), chaps. 2–3.

92. See, for example, Kennan, "Contemporary Perspective," in *Russian Foreign Policy: Essays in Historical Perspective,* ed. Ivo J. Lederer (New Haven: Yale University Press, 1962); Kennan, *Russia and the West under Lenin and Stalin* (Boston: Little, Brown, 1961), 392–394.

93. Kennan, *Russia and the United States* (Stamford, Conn.: Overbrook Press, 1960), 5–6.

94. Kennan, *Memoirs,* 1:8.

Epilogue

1. W. H. Auden, "Under Which Lyre" (1946), *Collected Poems* (New York: Vintage, 1991), 339; Carl E. Schorske, "The New Rigorism in the Human Sciences, 1940–1960," in *American Academic Culture in Transition: Fifty Years, Four Disciplines,* ed. Thomas Bender and Schorske (Princeton: Princeton

University Press, 1997); Clyde Kluckhohn, "Common Humanity and Diverse Cultures," and Daniel Lerner, "Social Science: Whence and Whither?," both in *The Human Meaning of the Social Sciences*, ed. Lerner (New York: Meridian Books, 1959); Edward A. Purcell, *The Crisis of Democratic Theory: Scientific Naturalism and the Problem of Value* (Lexington: University of Kentucky Press, 1973), chaps. 13–14.

2. Elazar Barkan, *The Retreat of Scientific Racism: Changing Concepts of Race in Britain and the United States between the World Wars* (Cambridge: Cambridge University Press, 1992); Carl N. Degler, *In Search of Human Nature: The Decline and Revival of Darwinism in American Social Thought* (Oxford: Oxford University Press, 1991), chap. 8.

3. Mead, *Soviet Attitudes toward Authority: An Interdisciplinary Approach to Problems of Soviet Character* (1951; New York: Schocken, 1966), 8.

4. On pathology, see Gabriel Almond et al., *The Appeals of Communism* (Princeton: Princeton University Press, 1954); Nathan Leites, *Study of Bolshevism* (Glencoe, Ill.: Free Press, 1953), 22, 137, 401–404; Arthur S. Barron, "Social Relations," in *American Research on Russia*, ed. Harold H. Fisher (Bloomington: Indiana University Press, 1959), 82–84; Ron Robin, *The Making of the Cold War Enemy: Culture and Politics in the Military-Intellectual Complex* (Princeton: Princeton University Press, 2001), 131–134.

5. See Alex Inkeles and Daniel J. Levinson, "National Character: The Study of Modal Personality and Sociocultural Systems," in *Handbook of Social Psychology*, 2 vols., ed. Gardner Lindzey (Reading, Mass.: Addison-Wesley, 1954), and the literature cited therein.

6. Geoffrey Gorer and John Rickman, *The People of Great Russia: A Psychological Study* (1949; New York: W. W. Norton, 1962).

7. Bell, "Ten Theories in Search of Reality: The Prediction of Soviet Behavior" (1958), in *The End of Ideology: The Exhaustion of Political Ideas in the Fifties* (1960; Cambridge, Mass.: Harvard University Press, 2000); Bell, "National Character Revisited: A Proposal for Renegotiating the Concept" (1968), in *The Winding Passage: Essays and Sociological Journeys, 1960–1980* (Cambridge, Mass.: ABT Books, 1980).

8. Schorske, "A Life of Learning," in *Recasting America: Culture and Politics in the Age of the Cold War*, ed. Lary May (Chicago: University of Chicago Press, 1989), 103; Ellen Herman, *The Romance of American Psychology: Political Culture in an Age of Experts* (Berkeley and Los Angeles: University of California Press, 1995), chap. 5.

9. Davies, *Mission to Moscow* (New York: Simon and Schuster, 1941); Kennan, *Memoirs*, 2 vols. (Boston: Little, Brown, 1967), 1:82–83; Ralph Levering, *American Opinion and the Russian Alliance, 1939–1945* (Chapel Hill: University of North Carolina Press, 1976), chap. 5.

10. Pitirim A. Sorokin, *Russia and the United States* (New York: E. P. Dutton, 1944), 48, 55–62, 208.

11. Richard Simpson, "Pitirim Sorokin and His Sociology," *SF* 32 (December 1953): 120–131; Barry V. Johnston, *Pitirim A. Sorokin: An Intellectual Biography* (Lawrence: University Press of Kansas, 1995), chap. 6.

12. Bohlen and Robinson, "The Capabilities and Intentions of the Soviet Union as Affected by American Policy" (December 1945), repr. in *Diplomatic History* 1 (Fall 1977): 394–395; Robert L. Messer, "Paths Not Taken: The United States Department of State and Alternatives to Containment, 1945–1946," *Diplomatic History* 1 (Fall 1977): 297–319.

13. Robinson, "The Ideological Combat," *FA* 27 (July 1949): 525–539.

14. Robinson, "Communism" (Army War College, 1955), Geroid Tanquary Robinson Papers, box 16; Robinson, "Factors in Soviet Intentions Abroad" (Council on Foreign Relations, 1945), Robinson Papers, box 18.

15. Robinson, "Part IV Review," in *Continuity and Change in Russian and Soviet Thought*, ed. Ernest J. Simmons (Cambridge, Mass.: Harvard University Press, 1955), 359 (emphasis in the original).

16. Bell, *End of Ideology*, 393–408.

17. Carl E. Pletsch, "The Three Worlds, or the Division of Social Scientific Labor, circa 1950–1975," *Comparative Studies in Society and History* 23 (October 1981), 565–590.

18. Barrington Moore, Jr., *Soviet Politics—The Dilemma of Power: The Role of Ideas in Social Change* (Cambridge, Mass.: Harvard University Press, 1951), 1–2.

19. Fainsod, *How Russia Is Ruled* (Cambridge, Mass.: Harvard University Press, 1953), 3–4, ix.

20. Arendt, *The Origins of Totalitarianism* (New York: Harcourt Brace, 1951); Margaret Canovan, *Hannah Arendt: A Reinterpretation of Her Political Thought* (Cambridge: Cambridge University Press, 1992), chaps. 2–3; Stephen J. Whitfield, *Into the Dark: Hannah Arendt and Totalitarianism* (Philadelphia: Temple University Press, 1989), chaps. 4–5.

21. Carl J. Friedrich, "The Unique Character of Totalitarian Society," in *Totalitarianism: Proceedings of a Conference Held at the American Academy of Arts and Sciences*, ed. Friedrich (Cambridge, Mass.: Harvard University Press, 1954), 47–60.

22. See, for instance, Abbott Gleason, *Totalitarianism: The Inner History of the Cold War* (Oxford: Oxford University Press, 1995), 127–128.

23. Kennan, "Totalitarianism in the Modern World," in *Totalitarianism*, 19.

24. Chamberlin, *Beyond Containment* (Chicago: Henry Regnery, 1953), chap. 10. He returned to Heberstein in Chamberlin, "Russia under Western Eyes," *Russian Review* 16 (January 1957): 5–6.

25. Bohlen and Robinson, "Capabilities and Intentions," 396.

26. Nils Gilman, *Mandarins of the Future: Modernization Theory and Cold War America* (Baltimore: Johns Hopkins University Press, 2003).

27. Walt Whitman, "One Thought Ever at the Fore" (1891), in *Complete Poems,* ed. Francis Murphy (London: Penguin Classics, 1975), 558, quoted in Max F. Millikan and W. W. Rostow, *A Proposal: Key to an Effective Foreign Policy* (New York: Harper and Brothers, 1958), 151.

28. See, for instance, a failed effort to get Rostow to reflect on his Jewish upbringing: Theodore Friedman to Rostow, 13 July 1961, in W. W. Rostow Papers, box 3. For more on his early years, see W. W. Rostow, *Concept and Controversy: Sixty Years of Taking Ideas to Market* (Austin: University of Texas Press, 2003), Preface, Chap. 1.

29. For more on this exhibit, see Eric J. Sandeen, *Picturing an Exhibition: The Family of Man and 1950s America* (Albuquerque: University of New Mexico Press, 1995); David A. Hollinger, "How Wide the Circle of 'We'? American Intellectuals and the Problem of Ethnos since World War II," *AHR* 98 (April 1993): 317–319.

30. Rostow, *The Stages of Economic Growth: A Non-Communist Manifesto* (Cambridge: Cambridge University Press, 1960), 65–67 (quoting Louis Hartz), 103–104.

31. Rostow, in collaboration with Alfred Levin, *The Dynamics of Soviet Society* (1952; New York: Mentor, 1954), 34–35, 133–134. On CIA funding, see Rostow, "Development: The Political Economy of the Marshallian Long Period," in *Pioneers in Development,* ed. Gerald M. Meier and Dudley Seers (Oxford: Oxford University Press, 1984), 241 n. 23.

32. Gerschenkron to Cyril Black, 13 December 1955, Alexander Gerschenkron Papers, HUG (FP) 45.10, box 2. The title was eventually changed, at Gerschenkron's insistence, to "The Transformation of Russian Society."

33. Parsons, "The Characteristics of Industrial Societies," in *The Transformation of Russian Society: Aspects of Social Change since 1861,* ed. Cyril E. Black (Cambridge, Mass.: Harvard University Press, 1960), 21.

34. Black, "The Modernization of Russian Society," in *Transformation of Russian Society,* 667–668.

35. C. E. Black, *The Dynamics of Modernization: A Study in Comparative History* (New York: Harper, 1966), 172–174.

36. Kennan, *Sketches from a Life* (New York: Pantheon, 1989), 3.

37. For examples of Kennan's wariness about industrialization, see Melvin J. Lasky, "A Conversation with George Kennan," *Encounter* 14 (March 1960): 56; Kennan, *Around the Cragged Hill: A Personal and Political Philosophy* (New York: W. W. Norton, 1993), 100–101. His most recent book suggests a nostal-

gia for agricultural life—Kennan, *An American Family: The Kennans: The First Three Centuries* (New York: W. W. Norton, 2000).

38. See, for instance, Philip E. Mosely, "The Growth of Russian Studies," in *American Research on Russia,* and the essays in *The State of Soviet Studies,* ed. Walter Z. Laqueur and Leopold Labedz (Cambridge, Mass.: MIT Press, 1965).

39. See, for instance, Kennan, "Russia and the Community of Nations" (Harvard Faculty Club, n.d.), George Frost Kennan Papers, box 17, folder 9.

40. Walter Bedell Smith, introduction to *Journey for Our Time: The Russian Journals of Marquis de Custine,* ed. and trans. Phyllis Penn Kohler (Chicago: Henry Regnery, 1951), 10.

41. A. Vucinich, book review, *ASR* 16 (August 1951): 588; Kohn, "Eternal Russia," *New Republic* 124 (21 May 1951): 19; Warren B. Walsh, "Fanfare Misplaced," *Nation* 173 (29 September 1951): 264; George Fischer, "Russian Visit—1839," *Saturday Review of Literature* 32 (14 April 1951): 56; Chamberlin, "The Land Where Time Has Stood Still," *Chicago Tribune Books,* 15 April 1951, 3.

42. Kennan, *The Marquis de Custine and His "Russia in 1839"* (Princeton: Princeton University Press, 1971), 125.

Acknowledgments

After many years of critically noting the self-indulgence of authors' acknowledgments, I am now in the unenviable position of facing the music. Thanking all those who helped me with this book is an extensive but happy endeavor. Over the decade that I have been working on one or another part of this book, I have received immeasurable help and support from friends, instructors, classmates, colleagues, and students.

Now that it nears print, I hope it is not too dangerous to admit that this book began its life as a Ph.D. dissertation, and one chapter as an M.A. thesis. My instructors and classmates at Rutgers and Berkeley heard all too much about this book's contents and my own travails with it. I am especially grateful to my thesis committees: Jim Livingston, Lloyd Gardner, Ziva Galili, Warren Kimball, and David Foglesong at Rutgers; and Diane Shaver Clemens, David Hollinger, Yuri Slezkine, and George Breslauer at Berkeley. Diane Clemens helped create a collegial and supportive environment for diplomatic history at Berkeley. David Hollinger's sage advice on matters intellectual and professional was (and is) greatly appreciated. Reggie Zelnik and Professor Nicholas Riasanovsky, while not officially on my committee, demonstrated the combination of useful advice and careful commentary upon which so many generations of students have relied. Thanks to Marjorie Murphy, my undergraduate mentor, for starting me along the path.

Reading groups and seminars at both institutions provided many opportunities to benefit from the collective wisdom of students and faculty. Thanks to all who offered their suggestions and criticisms in and around these settings, especially Peter Blitstein, Rosanne Currarino, Andrew Day, Max Friedman, Nils Gilman, Bill Littmann, D'Ann Penner, Charles Romney, Christine Skwiot, and Diana Selig. Colleagues in Moscow made my time there both more productive and more enjoyable. I am especially grateful to Viktor Kondrashin, Elena Osokina, and Nana Tsikhelashvili.

Formal presentations provided chances to correct errors and learn from the audience. This work benefited from responses to presentations at the Social History Society, the Pacific Coast Branch of the American Historical Association, the American Association for the Advancement of Slavic Studies, the Organization of American Historians, Yale's program in International Security Studies, Harvard's Charles Warren Center, and The Seminar of Johns Hopkins University's history department. Commentary from Mary Furner, Dorothy Ross, and James Kloppenberg was especially helpful.

So many scholars have read one or another section of this book that I may have shrunk the market for it. Let me thank especially those who endured the whole thing at one go. My dissertation committee slogged through 650 pages with countless suggestions and improvements and surprisingly good cheer. Readings by Bruce Kuklick and the late Hans Rogger also helped shape the course of initial revisions. David Foglesong provided an especially detailed reader's report—25 pages in length. As I have been working toward the final version, I have benefited from timely and helpful readings by Stanley Engerman, Tom Gleason, Eben Miller, Frank Ninkovich, Michael Willrich, and an anonymous reader for Harvard University Press. Other friends and colleagues have offered useful suggestions for portions of the manuscript; thanks to Michael Adas, Jane Kamensky, and David McFadden. Scholars also shared with me unpublished essays and occasionally primary sources, showing how research can be a collective endeavor; thanks to Robert Bannister, Andrew Jewett, Judy Kutulas, Charles Romney, and Joan Shelley Rubin. The editorial staff at Harvard University Press has been uniformly helpful and professional. Special thanks to Aida Donald and Jeff Kehoe for starting this project off at the Press, and to Kathleen McDermott and Christine Thorsteinsson for picking up where they left off. Thanks especially to Morton Keller for steering me to Harvard in the first place.

My debts, of course, go beyond intellectual ones. I am grateful for fellowship support from Rutgers University, the Mellon Foundation (through the Berkeley History Department), the U.S. Department of Education, and the Mabelle McLeod Lewis Memorial Fund. A semester's leave funded by the Charles Warren Center at Harvard provided the opportunity to work in and around Widener Library, one of the wonders of the American academic world. Even more important, the group of scholars assembled in Emerson Hall made for a wonderful and supportive intellectual community; I am grateful especially to Jim Campbell and Jona Hansen for their continuing conversations. The Mazer Fund at Brandeis supported the final preparation of the manuscript.

Other organizations supported research travel: the Kennan Institute for Advanced Russian Studies, the Franklin Delano Roosevelt and Herbert Hoover Presidential Libraries, the Rockefeller Archive Center, the Patrick Endowment of Berkeley's history department, and Swarthmore College's Hannah Leedom Fund. Once on the road I benefited from the extraordinary knowledge and generosity of librarians and archivists, almost uniformly helpful and kind. I am grateful to the archives listed in the Sources for permission to cite from material held in their collections, and to the American Historical Association for permission to incorporate portions of an article that first appeared in the *American Historical Review*. Special thanks to Judy Huenneke (Church History Office, First Church of Christ, Scientist), Tom Rosenbaum (Rockefeller Archive Center), and Nancy Webster (Chicago Historical Society) for their assistance.

This documentary material was rendered more meaningful by the chance to speak with individuals who knew the subjects of this book. I am grateful to George Fischer, Eva Hindus, and Mark Perlman for sharing their recollections. Elizabeth Krumpe and I have discussed her father (and other topics) in the years since our first meeting. A conversation with George Frost Kennan, brought about by the research for this book, was exciting in its own right—and also helped shape one part of my argument.

My colleagues and students at Brandeis have provided a congenial setting for continuing work on the manuscript. I am grateful to members of the history department for their ongoing support, especially the long-term perspective of David Hackett Fischer and Morton Keller, the calming advice of Paul Jankowski and Jacqueline Jones, and the wit and wisdom of Jane Kamensky and Michael Willrich. Eben Miller's research assistance has been indispensable on the home stretch.

I have saved the most important thank yous for last. Paul Sabin and Ethan Pollock have helped guide this book over or around hurdles for most of the last decade. They have read the text so often that they know it better than I. Important ideas came from our late lamented Friday breakfasts, and also from cafe meetings, bull sessions, and telephone calls. And their friendship has counted for much more.

Luckily for her but unluckily for me, Stephanie Wratten has only seen the final stretch of this long haul. While she has been spared confrontation with the text itself, her patience with, support for, and pride in its author are gratefully appreciated. So thanks.

Finally, I'd like to thank my family. One of the benefits of teaching in Boston is the chance to live near my brothers Mark and Jeff and their growing families. I'll be proud to put a copy of this book on their shelves. Special thanks go to my parents. They have not only supported my education but been a major source of it. I dedicate this book to them.

Index